Frommer's®

Rome

Here's what the critics say about Frommer's:

"Amazingly easy to use. Very portable, very complete."
—*Booklist*

♦

"The only mainstream guide to list specific prices. The Walter Cronkite of guidebooks—with all that implies."
—*Travel & Leisure*

♦

"Complete, concise, and filled with useful information."
—*New York Daily News*

♦

"Hotel information is close to encyclopedic."
—*Des Moines Sunday Register*

Other Great Guides for Your Trip:

Frommer's Italy

Frommer's Tuscany & Umbria

Frommer's Europe

Europe from $50 a Day

Italy from $50 a Day

Frommer's Driving Tours Italy

Frommer's® 99

Rome

**by Darwin Porter
and Danforth Prince**

MACMILLAN • USA

ABOUT THE AUTHORS

A native of North Carolina, **Darwin Porter** was a bureau chief for the *Miami Herald* when he was 21, and later worked in television advertising. A veteran travel writer, he wrote Frommer's first-ever guide to Italy, which launched what is today's Frommer's "Complete" series, and he has been a frequent traveler in Italy ever since. He's joined by **Danforth Prince,** formerly of the Paris bureau of the *New York Times,* who has lived and traveled in Italy extensively. This team writes a number of best-selling Frommer guides— notably to England, France, the Caribbean, and Germany.

MACMILLAN TRAVEL

A Simon & Schuster Macmillan Company
1633 Broadway
New York, NY 10019

Find us online at **www.frommers.com**

ISBN 0-02-862365-7
ISSN 1068-9338

Editor: Margot Weiss
Production Editor: Robyn Burnett
Photo Editor: Richard Fox
Design by Michele Laseau
Digital Cartography by Ortelius Design & Roberta Stockwell
Page Creation by Toi Davis, Ellen Considine & Sean Monkhouse

SPECIAL SALES

Bulk purchases (10+ copies) of Frommer's and selected Macmillan travel guides are available to corporations, organizations, mail-order catalogs, institutions, and charities at special discounts, and can be customized to suit individual needs. For more information write to Special Sales, Macmillan General Reference, 1633 Broadway, New York, NY 10019.

Manufactured in the United States of America

Contents

v

List of Maps

AN INVITATION TO THE READER

In researching this book, we discovered many wonderful places—hotels, restaurants, shops, and more. We're sure you'll find others. Please tell us about them, so we can share the information with your fellow travelers in upcoming editions. If you were disappointed with a recommendation, we'd love to know that, too. Please write to:

Frommer's Rome '99
Macmillan Travel
1633 Broadway
New York, NY 10019

AN ADDITIONAL NOTE

Please be advised that travel information is subject to change at any time—and this is especially true of prices. We therefore suggest that you write or call ahead for confirmation when making your travel plans. The authors, editors, and publisher cannot be held responsible for the experiences of readers while traveling. Your safety is important to us, however, so we encourage you to stay alert and be aware of your surroundings. Keep a close eye on cameras, purses, and wallets, all favorite targets of thieves and pickpockets.

WHAT THE SYMBOLS MEAN

✪ Frommer's Favorites

Our favorite places and experiences—outstanding for quality, value, or both.

The following abbreviations are used for credit cards:

AE	American Express	EC	Eurocard
CB	Carte Blanche	JCB	Japan Credit Bank
DC	Diners Club	MC	MasterCard
DISC	Discover	V	Visa
ER	enRoute		

The Road to Rome

Rome is a city of vivid and unforgettable images: the view of the city's silhouette from Janiculum Hill at dawn; the array of broken marble columns and ruins of temples of the Roman Forum; St. Peter's Dome against a pink and red sunset, capping a gloriously decorated basilica.

Rome is also a city of sounds, beginning, early in the morning, with the peal of church bells calling the faithful to mass. As the city awakens and comes to life, the sounds multiply and merge into a kind of *sinfonia urbana.* The streets fill with cars, taxis, and motor scooters, blaring their horns as they weave in and out of traffic; the sidewalks become overrun with bleary-eyed office workers rushing off to their desks, but not before stealing into crowded cafes for their first cappuccino of the day. The shops lining the streets open for business by raising their protective metal grilles as loudly as possible, seeming to delight in their contribution to the general din. And before long the many fruit-and-vegetable stands are abuzz with activity, as housewives, maids, widowers, cooks, and others arrive to purchase their day's supply of fresh produce, haggling over price and caviling over quality.

By 10am the tourists are on the street, battling the crowds and traffic as they wend their way from Renaissance palaces and baroque buildings to the famous ruins of antiquity. Indeed, Rome often appears to have two populations: one of Romans and one of visitors. During the summer months especially, Rome seems to become one big host for the countless sightseers who converge upon it, guidebook and camera in hand. To all of them—Americans, Europeans, Japanese—Rome extends a warm and friendly welcome, wining, dining, and entertaining them in its inimitable fashion. Of course, if you visit in August, you may see only tourists—not Romans, as the locals flee at that time. Or as one Roman woman once told us, "Even if we're too poor to go on vacation, we close the shutters and pretend we're away so neighbors won't find out we couldn't afford to leave the city."

The traffic, unfortunately, is worse than ever, restoration programs seem to drag on forever, and as the capital, Rome remains at the center of the major political scandals and corruption known as *Tangentopoli* ("bribe city"), which sends hundreds of government bureaucrats to jail each year.

But despite all this metropolitan and political horror, Romans still experience the good life. After you've done your "duty" to culture, wandered through the Colosseum, feeling awed that the Pantheon's survived the ages, after you've traipsed through St. Peter's Basilica and thrown a coin in the Trevi Fountain, you can pause in the early evening to experience the charm of Rome as evening comes. Find a cafe at summer twilight and watch the shades of pink turn to gold and copper before night finally falls. That's when another Rome comes alive, restaurants and cafes grow more animated and more fun, especially if you've found one on an antique piazza or along a narrow alley deep in Trastevere. After dinner you can stroll by the fountains, or through Piazza Navona, have a gelato (or an espresso in winter), and the night is yours.

In chapter 6 we'll take you on seemingly endless treks through ancient monuments and basilicas. But monuments are only a piece of the whole. In Rome, you'll find yourself embracing life with intensity. In other words, "When in Rome . . ."

1 Frommer's Favorite Rome Experiences

- **A Walk Through Ancient Rome:** A vast, almost unified archeological park cuts through the center of Rome—all the way from the Rome of the Caesars to Via Appia Antica. For those who want specific guidance, we have an entire chapter devoted to the most sight-filled of Roman walks. However, it's far more adventuresome to wander at will through the very streets where Julius Caesar's carriage, or (much later) that of Lucrezia Borgia, once rolled. A slice of history unfolds at every turn—an ancient fountain, a long-forgotten statue, the ruins of a temple dedicated to some long-faded cult. A narrow street suddenly opens and you'll have a vista of a triumphal arch. The Roman Forum and the Palatine Hill are the most rewarding targets for your archaeological probe, but the glory of Rome is hardly confined to these dusty fields. If you wander long enough, you'll eventually emerge onto Piazza della Rotunda—and stare in awe at one of Rome's most glorious sights, the Pantheon (described later in this list).

- **A Picnic on Isola Tiberina:** In Roman times this boat-shaped island stood across from the port of Rome, and from 293 B.C. a temple stood here dedicated to the Aesculapius, god of healing. On the ruins of this ancient temple a church was constructed in the 10th century. You can reach the island from the Jewish Ghetto by a footbridge, Ponte Fabricio, the oldest original bridge over the Tiber, dating from 62 B.C. Romans come here to sunbathe and escape the traffic and the crowds, sitting along the river's embankment. Arrive with the makings of a picnic from one of the literally hundreds of shops scattered throughout the city—and the day is yours.

- **A Sunday Bike Ride in Rome:** Weekdays are too traffic-clogged, but on a clear Sunday morning while Romans are still sleeping off Saturday night's *vino,* you can rent a bike and discover just how scenic Rome is. Start early after dawn while the streets are still cool from the night. The best places to cycle are the parks, including Villa Borghese. Within its 4-mile borders, it's a world unto itself, with museums and galleries, a riding school, an artificial lake, and a grassy amphitheater. Another choice place for Sunday biking is Villa Doria Pamphili, an extensive park lying above the Janiculum. Laid out in the mid-1600s, this is Rome's largest park, with numerous fountains and some summer houses.

- **A Sunset Stroll in the Pincio Gardens:** Above the landmark Piazza del Popolo, this terraced and lushly planted hillside is the most romantic place for a twilight walk. A dusty orange-rose glow often colors the sky, giving an aura to the park's

Impressions

Rome's just a city like anywhere else. A vastly overrated city, I'd say. It trades on belief just as Stratford trades on Shakespeare.
—Anthony Burgess, *Inside Mr. Enderby* (1963)

umbrella pines and broad avenues. The ancient Romans turned this hill into gardens, but today's look came from the design of Giuseppe Valadier in the 1800s. Everybody from King Farouk of Egypt to Mussolini found it fashionable to stroll here—even Richard Strauss or a visitor to Rome like Gandhi. Pause at the main piazza, Napoleone I, for a spectacular view of the city, stretching from the Janiculum to Monte Mario. The Egyptian-style obelisk you see was erected by Hadrian on the tomb of his great love, Antinous, a beautiful male slave who died prematurely.

- **Roma de Notte:** *La dolce vita* is still alive at night in Rome and the ancient monuments such as the Forum are bathed in a theatrical white light. Of course, don't get too carried away with the romance of the Colosseum with the moon rising behind and through its arches. Remember that this is where Henry James's Daisy Miller met her downfall. Begin your nocturnal diversions with a Roman *passeggiata* (early-evening stroll) along Via del Corso or Piazza Navona. There's plenty of action going on inside the clubs too—from Via Veneto to Piazza Navona. Clubbers flock to the colorful narrow streets of Trastevere and the Pantheon areas—even more remote Testaccio, once viewed as "Siberia." The jazz scene is especially good, and big names often pop in. All you need is a motor scooter and a young *Roman Holiday* Gregory Peck (or Audrey Hepburn, depending on your tastes) to show you around Rome by night. Open-air opera, classical music, and jazz concerts load the calendar from late June until the end of September. A little English-language publication, *Info Rome,* will keep you abreast of what's happening.

- **Hanging Out at the Pantheon:** The world's best preserved ancient monument is now a hot spot—especially at night. Find a cafe table out on the square and take in the action, which needs a young Fellini to record it on tape. The Pantheon has become a symbol of Rome itself, and we owe our thanks to Hadrian for leaving the world this monument. When you tire of people-watching and cappuccino, you can go inside to inspect the tomb of Raphael, who was buried here in 1520. (His mistress, La Fornarina, wasn't allowed to attend the services.) Nothing is more dramatic than to be in the Pantheon during a rainstorm, watching the sheets of water splatter on the colorful marble floor. It enters through the oculus on top, which provides the only light for the interior.

- **Campo de' Fiori at Mid-Morning:** In an incomparable setting of medieval houses, this is the liveliest fruit and vegetable market in Rome. At this stomping ground of everybody from aristocrats to fishmongers, the stalls peddle their wares as they've done for centuries. The market is best viewed after 9am any day but Sunday. By 1pm the stalls begin closing down. Once the major site for the medieval inns of Rome—many of which were owned by Vanozza Catanei, the 15th-century courtesan and lover of Pope Alexander VI Borgia—this square maintains some of its old bohemian atmosphere. We come here every day we're in Rome for a lively view of local life that no other place provides. Often you'll spot your favorite trattoria chef bargaining for the best and freshest produce—everything from fresh cherries to the perfect vine-ripened tomato.

- **Opening Night at the Rome Opera:** The Milanese claim that the stellar quality of their operas at La Scala diminishes the operas presented at Rome. Roman opera buffs, of course, disagree. At Rome's Teatro dell'Opera, where the season runs between December and June and programs concentrate on the classics: Bellini, Donizetti, Puccini, and Rossini. No one seems to touch the Roman's operatic soul more than Giuseppe Verdi (1813–1901), who became a national icon in his support for Italian unification. His *Aïda* used to be performed by this opera house at the Baths of Caracalla. But nowadays you're more likely to witness his *La Traviata,* which remains a perennial favorite, even though the reviewer for *The Times* of London, upon first hearing it at its debut, found it filled "with foul and hideous horrors."

- **A Tour of the Janiculum:** On the Trastevere side of the river, where Garibaldi in 1849 held off the attacking French troops, the Janiculum Hill was always strategic in Rome's defense. Today a walk in this park at the top of the hill is a much-needed retreat from the traffic-filled and often hot streets of Trastevere. Filled with monuments to Garibaldi and his brave men, the hill is no longer peppered with monasteries as it was in the Middle Ages. Today you can go for long walks, inspecting the monuments and fountains while enjoying panoramic views of Rome. The best view is from Villa Lante, a Renaissance summer residence. If you choose to visit the Janiculum, you're in good company. The poet Torquato Tasso liked to sit in the park contemplating the meaning of life before he died in 1595. The most serene part of the park is the 1883 Botanical Gardens, with their palm trees, orchids, bromeliads, and sequoias—in all, more than 7,000 plant species from all over the world.

- **Strolling Along the Tiber:** Without the Tiber, there might have been no Rome. A key player in the city's history since the founding of Rome, the river flooded the capital every winter until it was "tamed" in 1870. It is the massive *lungotevere* embankments on both sides of the Tiber that allow such memorable strolls today. You not only get to walk along the river from which Cleopatra made her grand entrance into Rome, but you'll also see the riverside life of such characteristic neighborhoods as Trastevere and the Jewish Ghetto. At some point you can cross over to visit Isola Tiburtina, the island in the middle of the Tiber, taking in panoramas of the river in both directions. You can start at Piazza della Bocca della Verità and go for some 2 or more miles or until you tire. Walks along the river are best in the early evening.

- **Following in the Footsteps of Bernini:** One of the most enjoyable ways to view Rome is to follow the trail of Giovanni Lorenzo Bernini (1598–1680), who left a greater mark on the city than even Michelangelo. Under the patronage of three different popes, Bernini "baroqued" Rome. Start at Largo di Santa Susanna, north of the Stazione Termini, at the Church of Santa Maria della Vittoria, which houses one of Bernini's most controversial sculptures, the *Ecstasy of St. Teresa* from 1646. Walk from here along Via Barberini to Piazza Barberini, in the center of which stands Bernini's second most dramatic fountain, the Fontana del Tritone. From the piazza go along Via delle Quattro Fontane, bypassing (on your left) the Palazzo Barberini designed by Bernini and others for Pope Urban VIII. At the famous crossroads of Rome, Le Quattro Fontane, take Via del Quirinale to see the facade of Sant'Andrea, one of the artist's greatest churches. Arm yourself with a good map at this point and continue west, bypassing the Pantheon to arrive eventually at Piazza Navona, which Bernini remodeled for Pope Innocent X. Bernini designed the central fountain, the Fontana dei Fiumi, his masterpiece. The figures representing the four rivers were sculpted by others to his plans. For many, this fabulous Bernini fountain, with its rocks, shells, and other natural forms, will complete their Bernini fix for the day.

- **A Day on the Appian Way:** Dating from 312 B.C., the Appian Way (Via Appia) once traversed the whole peninsula of Italy, the road on which Roman legions marched to Brindisi and their conquests in the East. One of its darkest moments was the crucifixion in 71 B.C. of the rebellious slave army of Spartacus, whose bodies lined the road from Rome to Capua. Fashionable Romans were buried here, and early Christians dug catacombs through which to flee their persecutors. Begin at the Tomb of Cecilia Metella and proceed up Via Appia Antica past a series of tombs and monuments, including everybody from Marcus Servilius and Seneca, the great moralist who committed suicide on the orders of Nero, to Pope St. Urban, who reigned from 222 to 230. The sights along Via Appia Antica are among the most evocative in Rome. You can go all the way to the Church of Domine Quo Vadis.

- **Drinking in Rome:** The grape reigns supreme, although Rome is filled with famous drinking fountains as well, bringing fresh and sweet water from the surrounding hills through a system of pipes and aqueducts (but never drink from a fountain where a sign says ACQUA NON POTABILE). While in Rome, do as the Romans do and enjoy a carafe of dry white wine from the warm climate of Lazio. In restaurants and trattorie you'll find the most popular brand, Frascati, but try some of the other wines from the Castelli Romani too, including Colli Albani, Velletri, and Marino. All these wines come from one grape: Trebbiano. Sometimes a dash of Malvasia is added for greater flavor and an aromatic bouquet. Of course, you don't have to wait until dinnertime to drink wine, but can sample it at any of the hundreds of wine bars throughout the city. At these bars you'll find all the great reds and whites of Italy. Naturally, nothing beats sipping a bitter, herb-flavored aperitif—perhaps Campari or Martini—at one of Rome's legendary cafes.

- **Gelato on a Summer Night:** Sampling Roman ice cream (gelato) at a *gelateria* is worth waiting through the long winter. Tubs of homemade ice cream—among the best in the world—await you in a dazzling array of flavors: everything from candied orange peels with chocolate to watermelon to rice. *Gelaterie* offer *semifreddi* concoctions (made with cream instead of milk), in such flavors as almond, *marengo* (a type of meringue), and *zabaglione* (eggnog). Naturally, seasonal fresh fruits are made into ice creams of blueberry, cherry, peach, or whatever. Italians often like their ice cream with espresso. *Granite* (crushed ice) flavored with sweet fruit are another cool delight on a sultry night. Tre Scalini at Piazza Navona is the most fabled spot for enjoying *divino tartufo,* a chocolate concoction with a taste to match its name.

- **A Roman Dinner on a Hidden Plaza:** If you're in Rome with that special someone, take her/him to a typical trattoria that opens onto an almost forgotten square deep in the heart of ancient Rome. And if your evening dinner extends for 3 or 4 hours, who's counting? The waiters won't rush you out the door even when you've overstayed your time at the table. This is a special experience, and Rome has dozens of these little restaurants. Two in particular come to mind: **Sant'Eustachio Archimede,** on Piazza dei Caprettari (☎ **06/6861616**), with outdoor tables placed on this tiny square with its architectural gems, including a small Renaissance palace and the Chiesa di Sant'Eustachio. Try fried zucchini flowers stuffed with cheese and anchovies or partake of one of the freshest seafood antipasti around Piazza Navona. Or sample the wares at **Vecchia Roma,** Piazza Campitella 18 (☎ **06/6864604**), with a theatrical setting on one of the loveliest squares to visit during a summer evening in Rome. Order spaghetti with double-"horned" clams or traditional pastas and seafood while enjoying an ambience that remains unspoiled in spite of the restaurant's long-lasting popularity with savvy local foodies.

- **Music in the Churches:** Classical-music lovers flock to Rome if for no other reason than to hear music in the city's churches. World-famed artists like Plácido Domingo and Luciano Pavarotti have performed in Roman venues ranging from churches to ancient ruins. Music is usually performed in concerts, not at services. By decree of Pope John Paul II, it must be sacred music—not that hip-grinding, body-slamming stuff. When church concerts are performed, programs appear not only outside the church but on various announcements posted throughout Rome. The top professionals play at the "big name" churches, but don't overlook those smaller hard-to-find churches on hidden squares. Some of the best music we've ever heard has been by up-and-coming musicians getting their start in these little-known churches. The biggest event is the RAI (national broadcasting company) concert on December 5 at St. Peter's—even the pope attends. Other favorite venues for church music include Sant'Ignazio di Loyola, on Piazza di Sant'Ignazio, and San Paolo Fuori le Mura, at Via Ostiense 186.

- **From Fountain to Fountain:** While Londoners might be on a pub crawl, Romans—especially those who live in crowded ghetto apartments without air-conditioning—are out on summer nights walking from fountain to cooling fountain. It's an artistic experience for the visitor as well, as some of Rome's greatest artists worked to create these fountains. Everybody makes at least one trip to Bernini's fountain on Piazza Navona, after stopping off at the Trevi Fountain to toss in a coin—thus ensuring their return to Rome—but there are hundreds more. Our favorite is the Fontana delle Tararughe, in tiny Piazza Mattei. It has stood there since 1581—a jewel of Renaissance sculpture showing youths helping tortoises into a basin. Despite its charm, it's still considered a "secret" fountain of Rome. Back on the main fountain-hopping trail, you'll encounter our favorite Bernini fountain at Piazza Barberini, the Fontana del Tritone, a magnificent work of art from 1642 showing the sea god blowing through a shell. If you think you can still jump into these fountains and paddle around as Anita Ekberg did in *La Dolce Vita,* forget it. That's now against the law.

- **The Campidoglio at Night:** There is no more splendid place to be at night than Piazza del Campidoglio, where Michelangelo designed both the geometric paving and the facades of the buildings. A broad flight of steps, the Cordonata, takes you up to this panoramic site, citadel of ancient Rome from which traitors to the empire were once tossed to their deaths. Home during the day to the Capitoline Museums, it takes on a different aura at night when it's dramatically lit, its measured Renaissance facades glowing like jewel boxes. The views of the brilliantly lit Forum and Palatine at night are worth the long trek up those stairs. There's no more stunning cityscape view at night than from this hill, even if the gilded temple to Jupiter is long gone the way of the empire. Few places in all of Europe are filled with as many memories of ancient glories as the Campidoglio.

- **Flea-Market Shopping:** We have never discovered an original Raphael, much less a Michelangelo, at Rome's Porta Portese flea market (which locals call *mercato delle pulci*). But we've picked up some interesting souvenirs over the years. It all began after World War II when black marketers needed an outlet for their illegal wares. Today the authentic art and antiques once sold here have given way to reproductions—but the selection remains enormous: World War II cameras, caviar from immigrant Russians, luggage (fake Gucci), spare parts, Mussolini busts, and so on. This is the largest flea market in Europe. Near Porta Sublicio in

Trastevere, the market has some 4,000 stalls, but it's estimated that only 10% of them have a license. Sunday from 5am to 2pm is the time to visit, and, yes, the pickpockets begin plying their trade early in the day.

2 Rome Today

Rome can no longer bask in its glorious past. The city today is a metropolis in transition, struggling to become a stable, viable player in the global community.

Modern Rome is a city of contradictions: A Roman Catholic state ruled by the mores and values of a staunchly religious consciousness that nevertheless is the most corrupt country in Western Europe. Italy is a land whose sons and daughters emigrated to form large populations throughout the world, especially in America, but whose citizens today in large numbers remain opposed to and prejudiced against immigrants arriving on their own shores.

"In the course of a century, we've gone from being a land of emigrants to one that takes in immigrants," said Luigi Manconi, a Milan sociologist. "We're just not equipped."

Unemployment has heightened racism and prejudice, which is primarily directed against the North African and Albanian contingents that have descended on Italy in search of jobs. Despite attempts to turn them back, these immigrants continued to arrive in droves in 1998. Some are migrant workers on farms, some are prostitutes in Rome; few are accepted into the tight-knit Italian communities.

Ironically, immigration may well be the solution to a relatively new problem, Italy's increasingly lopsided population in which there are too few young people to support the elderly. According to the *New York Times,* Italy has the lowest birth rate in the world and recently became the first nation in history with more people over 60 than under 20. Lalla Golfarelli, the head of family planning in Bologna, says: "The truth is there doesn't have to be a demographic catastrophe . . . Immigration can solve this problem. If people would just open their minds they would realize there are enough people on this earth to go around."

Prejudice is not Rome's only dirty little secret. *La politica e una cosa sporca* (politics are dirty) is an expression often heard in Rome. The charge is certainly justified. Corruption, scandal, and political chaos are parts of everyday life on the Roman landscape. The word *politician* is almost always preceded by the word *corrupt.* It's virtually assumed that anyone entering politics is doing so for personal gain.

Rome's precarious modern political system—55 governments since World War II—has been compared by many political analysts to the ill-fated First Republic.

Besides soccer (*calcio*), the family, and affairs of the heart, the national obsession of Rome as it faces the millennium is *il sorpasso,* a term that describes Italy's surpassing of its archrivals France and Britain in economic indicators. (Italy ranks sixth among world economic powers, third among European countries.) Economists disagree about whether or not il sorpasso has happened, and statistics vary widely from source to source. Italy's true economy is difficult to measure because of the vast Mafia-controlled underground economy (*economia sommersa*) that competes on a monumental scale with the official economy. Almost every Roman has some unreported income or expenditure, and people at all levels of Italian society are engaged to some degree in withholding funds from the government.

Complicating Italy's problems is the constant interference of the Mafia, whose methods continue as ruthlessly as ever. Also problematic is the unwillingness of global competitors to invest in Italian ventures because of lack of confidence in the government.

Jubilee 2000

A mood of near-Messianic fervor is building in Rome as Jubilee 2000, the Holy Year declared by the pope to celebrate the transition into a new era, approaches. As the core of world Christianity, Rome is viewed by the faithful as the centerpiece of what has been heralded as a new age: The 21st century.

Pilgrims from all over the world will journey to Rome to greet the dawn of the new millennium and witness the fading of the last. Regardless of the surprises doomsayers claim the millennium has in store for humankind, the churches of Rome are anticipating their largest congregations ever, and Rome expects upwards of 25 million visitors in the year 2000.

This upcoming tourist invasion will dwarf those of the Etruscans, Langobards, or Normans in previous centuries. Using an appropriate metaphor, the mayor of Venice, Massimo Cacciari, said "If the floods are not channeled, we all risk capsizing." Roman city authorities echoed his fears.

Already, as the end of the second millennium approaches, Rome is scrambling to prepare for the onslaught of tourists, and making some much-needed changes. Although some view the upcoming invasion with dread, zillions of trinket peddlers are eagerly awaiting the hordes. Even as you read, factories are busy turning out the souvenirs to be hawked.

A wealth of tchotchkes aside, there is other good news for those planning trips to Rome. Museums are being overhauled, hours are becoming more streamlined, and custodians even seem less grumpy as they rush you to the door warning that the museum is closing for the day. New bookshops and cafeterias, the addition of English (and other language) signs to explain what you're looking at, and better lighting are all making museums more user-friendly.

There's a long way to go, of course, and many of the city's treasures still languish in small, obscure museums or churches. But the present attention being devoted to Rome's treasures is unprecedented, and a welcome sign for upcoming visitors, thousands upon thousands of whom will be seeing Rome for the first time.

Another complicating factor is the surfeit of laws passed in Rome and their effect on the citizens. Before they get thrown out of office, politicians pass laws and more laws, adding to the horde already on the books. Italy not only has more laws on the books than any other nation of Western Europe, but also suffers from a bloated bureaucracy. Something as simple as cashing a check or paying a bill can devour half a day. To escape the brambles of red tape, Romans have become marvelous improvisers and corner-cutters. Whenever possible they bypass the sclerotic public sector and negotiate private deals *fra amici*—among friends.

Today, there are nascent signs of an economic upswing in Italy as reflected by high trade surpluses (labor costs here are below those in most European countries). But there are also anxieties, especially as the reality of the "Euro" (Europe's single currency) sets in. Many Italians fear they may face years of belt-tightening and fiscal austerity to help reduce the country's spiraling national debt. Italy signed a stability pact as part of an overall plan to reduce debt, and the government of prime minister Romano Prodi is wedded to a vigorous program of debt reduction. These measures, totaling perhaps 6.5 million U.S. dollars, are expected to be unveiled in 1999.

Nevertheless, strong forces are calling for more government spending. In particular, trade union leaders are demanding more jobs and infrastructure investment in the still-depressed south, and Prodi is moving ahead with legislation to reduce the work week from 40 to 35 hours.

Although it's a done deal—Italy entering the Euro circle—there are still dire warnings. One Catholic bishop, Don Riboldi, claimed, "This Europe of Maastricht is like the *Divine Comedy* of Dante because for a few rich people it will be paradise, for many it will be purgatory, and for the poor and unemployed it will be an inferno."

Overall, however, the pro-Europe mood remains strong. Recent polls show that 73% of Italians questioned were in favor of a single currency, the highest approval rate of any of the EU's 15 member nations.

Rome remains a city of contradictions—simultaneously strident, romantic, and sensual—and has forever altered the Western world's standards of beauty and excellence in such fields as art, religion, and government. And although today the romantic poets probably would be horrified at the traffic, pollution, overcrowding, crime, political discontent, and barely controlled chaos of modern Rome, the city endures and thrives.

In all the confusion of their city, Romans still manage to live a relatively relaxed way of life. Along with their southern cousins in Naples, they are specialists in *arte di arrangiarsi,* the ability to cope and survive with style, an art that's pursued with both passion and a sense of tragic resignation. The Romans have humanity if not humor, a 2,000-year-old sense of cynicism, and a strong feeling of belonging to a particular place. The city's attractions seem as old as time itself, and despite the frustrations of daily life, Rome will continue to lure new visitors every year—with or without a millennium celebration. For when this millennium has passed into history, the city's pleasures and temptations will endure to greet yet another. After all, Rome is "The Eternal City."

3 A Look at the Past

Many of the key events that shaped the rich and often gory tapestry of Italian history originated in Rome. Although parts of Italy (especially Sardinia and Sicily) were inhabited as early as the Bronze Age, the region around Rome was occupied relatively late. Some historians claim that the presence of active volcanoes in the region during the Bronze Age prevented prehistoric tribes from living here, but regardless of the reason, Rome has unearthed far fewer prehistoric graves and implements than neighboring Umbria and Tuscany have.

THE ETRUSCANS The arrival around 800 B.C. of the Etruscans in Umbria has never fully been understood by sociologists or historians (the many inscriptions they left behind—mostly on graves—are of little help, as the Etruscan language has not yet been completely deciphered). While the Etruscans built temples at Tarquinia and Caere (present-day Cerveteri), the few nervous Latin tribes who remained outside their sway gravitated to the strategic position of what was later known as Rome.

Dateline

- **Bronze Age** Tribes of Celts, Teutonics, and groups from the eastern Mediterranean inhabit the Italian peninsula.
- **1200 B.C.** The Etruscans migrate from the eastern Mediterranean (probably Mesopotamia) and occupy territory north and south of Rome.
- **800 B.C.** Sicily and southern Italy (especially Naples) flourish under Greek and Phoenician protection; independent of most outside domination, Rome evolves as an insignificant community of shepherds with loyalties divided among several Latin tribes.
- **753 B.C.** Rome's traditional founding date.

continues

- **660 B.C.** Etruscans occupy Rome as the capital of their empire; the city grows rapidly and a major seaport (Ostia) opens at the mouth of the Tiber.
- **510–250 B.C.** The Latin tribes, still centered in Rome, maintain a prolonged revolt against the Etruscans; alpine Gauls attack the Etruscans from the north and Greeks living in Sicily destroy the Etruscan navy.
- **250 B.C.** The Romans and their allies finally purge the Etruscans from Italy; Rome flourishes as a republic and begins the accumulation of a vast empire.
- **250–50 B.C.** Rome obliterates its chief rival, Carthage, during two Punic Wars; Carthage's defeat allows unchecked Roman expansion into Spain, North Africa, Sardinia, and Corsica.
- **44 B.C.** Julius Caesar is assassinated; his successor, Augustus, transforms Rome from a city of brick to a city of marble, and solidifies Rome's status as a dictatorship.
- **40 B.C.** Rome and its armies control the entire Mediterranean world.
- **3rd century A.D.** Rome declines under a series of incompetent and corrupt emperors.
- **4th century A.D.** Rome is fragmented politically as administrative capitals are established in such cities as Milan and Trier, Germany.
- **395** The empire splits: Constantine establishes a "New Rome" at Constantinople (Istanbul); Goths invade Rome's provinces in northern Italy.
- **410–455** Rome is sacked by barbarians—Alaric the

continues

From their base at Rome, the Latins remained free of the Etruscans until about 600 B.C., when the Etruscans were able to establish a military stronghold in Rome. Under the combined influences of the Greeks and the Mesopotamian east, Rome grew enormously. A new port was opened at Ostia, near the mouth of the Tiber. Artists from Greece carved statues of Roman gods to resemble Greek divinities. From this enforced (and not always peaceable) mixture of Latin tribes and Etruscans grew the roots of what eventually became the Republic of Rome.

THE ROMAN REPUBLIC   Gauls from the alpine regions invaded the northern Etruscan territory around 600 B.C., and the Latin tribes revolted in about 510 B.C., toppling the Etruscan-linked rulers from their power bases and establishing the southern boundary of Etruscan influence at the Tiber. Greeks from Sicily ended Etruscan sea power in 474 B.C., during the battle of Cumae off the Italian coastline just north of Naples. By 250 B.C., the Romans and their allies in Campagna had vanquished the Etruscans, wiping out their language and religion.

Tempered in the fires of military adversity, the stern Roman republic was characterized by belief in the gods, the necessity of learning from the past, strength of the family, education through books and public service, and most important, obedience. The all-powerful Senate presided as Rome defeated rival powers one after the other in a steady stream of staggering military successes.

As the population grew, the Romans gave to their Latin allies, and then to conquered peoples, partial or complete Roman citizenship, always with the obligation of military service. Colonies of citizens were established on the borders of the growing empire and were populated with soldiers/farmers and their families. Later, as seen in the history of Britain and the Continent, colonies began to thrive as semiautonomous units on their own, heavily fortified, and linked to Rome by well-maintained military roads and a well-defined hierarchy of military command.

The final obstacle to the unrivaled supremacy of Rome was the defeat, during the 3rd century B.C., of the city-state of Carthage during the two Punic Wars. An ancient Phoenician trading post on the coast of Tunisia, Carthage had grown into one of the premier naval and agricultural powers of the Mediterranean with strongly fortified positions in

Corsica, Sardinia, and Spain. Despite the impressive victories of the Carthaginian general Hannibal, Rome eventually eradicated Carthage in one of the most famous defeats in ancient history. Rome was able to immediately expand its power into North Africa, Sardinia, Corsica, and Iberia.

THE ROMAN EMPIRE   By 49 B.C., Italy ruled all of the Mediterranean world either directly or indirectly, with all political, commercial, and cultural pathways leading directly to Rome. The possible wealth and glory to be found in Rome lured many there, but drained other Italian communities of human resources. As Rome transformed itself into an administrative headquarters, imports to the city from other parts of the empire hurt local farmers and landowners. The seeds for civil discord were sown early in the empire's life, although as Rome was embellished with temples, monuments, and the easy availability of slave labor from conquered territories, many of its social problems were overlooked in favor of expansion and glory.

On the eve of the birth of Christ, Rome was a mighty empire whose generals had brought all of the Western world under the influence of Roman law, values, and civilization. Only in the eastern third of the Mediterranean did the existing cultures—notably the Greek—withstand the Roman incursions. Despite its occupation by Rome, Greece, more than any other culture, permeated Rome with new ideas, values, and concepts of art, architecture, religion, and philosophy.

Meanwhile, the ideals of democratic responsibility in the heart of the empire had begun to break down. The populace began to object violently to a government that took little interest in commerce, and seemed interested only in foreign politics. As taxes and levies increased, the poor emigrated in huge and idle numbers to Rome and the rich cities of the Po Valley. Entire generations of war captives, forced into the slave-driven economies of large Italian estates, were steeped in hatred and ignorance.

Christianity, a new and (at the time) revolutionary religion, probably gained a foothold in Rome about 10 years after Christ's crucifixion. Feared far more for its political implications than for its spiritual presuppositions, it was at first brutally suppressed before moving through increasingly tolerant stages of acceptability.

After the death of Julius Caesar, political control became entrenched in the hands of a series of

Goth, Attila the Hun, and Galseric the Vandal.

- **475** Rome falls, leaving only the primate of the Catholic church in control; the pope slowly adopts many of the responsibilities and the prestige once reserved for the Roman emperors.
- **731** Pope Gregory II renounces Rome's spiritual and political link to the authorities in Constantinople.
- **800** Charlemagne is crowned Holy Roman Emperor by Pope Leo III; Italy dissolves into a series of small warring kingdoms.
- **1065** The Holy Land falls to the Muslim Turks; the Crusades are launched.
- **1303–77** A Papal schism occurs when a rival pope is established at Avignon.
- **1377** The "antipope" is removed from Avignon, and the Roman popes emerge as sole contenders to the legacy of St. Peter.
- **Mid-1400s** Originating in Florence, the Renaissance blossoms throughout Italy; Italian artists receive multiple commissions from the ecclesiastical communities of Rome.
- **1508** Ordered by the pope, Michelangelo begins work on the ceiling of the Vatican's Sistine Chapel.
- **1527** Rome is attacked and sacked by Charles V, who—to the pope's rage—is elected Holy Roman Emperor the following year.
- **1796–97** Napoléon's military conquests of Italy arouse Italian nationalism.
- **1861** Rome is declared the capital of the newly established Kingdom of Italy; the Papal States (but not the Vatican) are absorbed into the new nation.

continues

- **1929** A concordat between the Vatican and the Italian government delineates the rights and responsibilities of both parties.
- **1935** Italian invasion of Abyssinia (Ethiopia).
- **1941** Italian invasion of Yugoslavia.
- **1943** General Patton lands in Sicily and soon controls the island.
- **1945** Mussolini killed by a mob in Milan.
- **1946** Establishment of Rome as the capital of the newly created Republic of Italy.
- **1960s** Rise of left-wing terrorist groups; flight of capital from Italy; continuing problems of the impoverished south cause an exodus from the countryside into such cities as Rome.
- **1980s** *Il Sorpasso* imbues Rome (and the rest of Italy) with dreams of an economic rebirth.
- **1994** Right-wing forces win in Italian national elections.
- **1996** Dini steps down as prime minister, as the president dissolves both houses of parliament; in general elections, the center-left coalition known as the Olive Tree sweeps both the Senate and the Chamber of Deputies; Romano Prodi becomes prime minister.
- **1997–98** Prodi survives Neo-Communist challenge and continues to press for budget cuts in an effort to "join Europe" in 1999.

all-powerful emperors, whose sweeping strengths brought Rome to new, almost giddy, heights. Augustus transformed the city from brick to marble in some of the most grandiose building projects in history, but as corruption spread, Rome endured a steady decay in the ideals and traditions upon which the empire had been founded. As the incorruptible Roman soldier of an earlier era became increasingly rare, the army became filled with barbarian mercenaries. The tax collector became the scourge of the countryside, often killing the incentive for economic development and causing many to abandon their farms altogether in favor of a life of impoverishment in the cities. For every good emperor (Augustus, Trajan, Vespasian, Hadrian, to name a few), there were three or four corrupt, debased, and possibly insane heads of state (Caligula, Nero, Domitian, Caracalla, and many more).

As the decay progressed, the Roman citizen either lived on the increasingly swollen public dole and spent his days at gladiatorial games and imperial baths, or was a disillusioned patrician at the mercy of emperors who might murder him for his property. The 3rd century saw so many emperors that it was common, as H. V. Morton tells us, to hear in the provinces of the election of an emperor together with a report of his assassination. Despite a well-intentioned series of reforms in the 4th century by Diocletian, the empire continued to weaken and decay. Although he reinforced imperial power, paradoxically at the same time he weakened Roman dominance and prestige by establishing administrative capitals of the empire at such outposts as Milan, Trier in Germany, and elsewhere.

This practice was followed by Constantine when he moved the administrative capital away from Rome altogether, an act that sounded a death knell for a city already threatened by the menace of barbarian attacks. The sole survivor of six rival emperors, Constantine recognized Christianity as the official religion of the Roman Empire, and built an entirely new, more easily defended capital on the banks of the Bosporus. Named in his honor (Constantinople, or Byzantium), it was later renamed Istanbul by the Ottoman Turks. When he moved to the new capital, Constantine and his heirs took with them the best of the artisans, politicians, and public figures of Rome. Rome, reduced to little more than a provincial capital controlling the much-threatened western half of the once-mighty empire, continued to founder and decay. As for the Christian church, although the popes of Rome were under the

Impressions

While stands the Coliseum, Rome shall stand;/When falls the Coliseum, Rome shall fall;/And when Rome falls—the world.

—Lord Byron, *Child Harold's Pilgrimage* (1812)

nominal auspices of an exarch from Constantinople, their power increased slowly but steadily as the power of the emperors declined.

THE EMPIRE FALLS   The eastern and western sections of the Roman Empire split in 395, leaving Italy without the support it had formerly received from east of the Adriatic. When the Goths moved toward Rome in the early 5th century, citizens in the provinces, who had grown to hate and fear the cruel bureaucracy set up by Diocletian and sustained by succeeding emperors, often welcomed the invaders. And then the pillage began.

Rome was sacked by Alaric in 410. After less than 40 troubled years, Attila the Hun laid siege. He was followed in 455 by Gaiseric the Vandal, who engaged in a 2-week spree of looting and destruction. The Empire of the West lasted for only another 20 years; finally, the sacking and chaos ended it in 476, and a burned-out, much humiliated Rome was left to the ministrations of the popes. Without Rome, Italy disintegrated into anarchy, with order maintained by family clans strong enough to hold power within their fortified citadels. Into the vacuum stepped the leaders of the church and a handful of ruling families, whose authority eventually became closely intertwined.

THE HOLY ROMAN EMPIRE   After the fall of the Western Empire, the pope took on more and more of the powers of the emperor, despite the lack of any political unity in Italy. Decades of mismanagement by the Roman emperors were followed by the often anarchic rule by barbarian Goths. These were followed by takeovers in different parts of the country by various strong warriors, such as the Lombards. Italy was thus divided into several spheres of control, but always with the permeating influence of the Roman popes.

In 731 Pope Gregory II renounced Rome's spiritual dependence on Constantinople. Papal Rome turned forever toward Europe, and in 800 a king of the barbarian Franks was crowned Holy Roman Emperor by Pope Leo III. The new emperor's name was Charlemagne, and he established a capital at Aachen (known today to the French as Aix-la-Chapelle). This coronation marked a major milestone whereby a Roman pope collaborated with (and later conflicted with) a temporal European power. Although Charlemagne pledged allegiance to the Catholic church, he launched northwestern Europe on a course of what would eventually become bitter political opposition to the meddling of the papacy in temporal affairs.

Meanwhile, the religious powers in Rome looked with dismay at the increasing fragmentation of Italy into war zones between Lombards, Franks, Magyars, Venetians, Saracens, and Normans. As Italy dissolved, the feudal landowners of Rome gained control of the papacy and a series of questionably religious pontiffs endured a diminishment of their powers. Eventually, even the process for determining the election of the popes fell into the hands of the increasingly Germanic Holy Roman Emperor, although this power balance would very soon shift.

During the Middle Ages Rome was a quaint, rural town. Narrow lanes with overhanging buildings filled many of what were originally built as showcases of ancient imperial power, including the Campus Martius. Great basilicas built and embellished with golden-hued mosaics, forums, mercantile exchanges, temples, and expansive theaters of the imperial era slowly disintegrated and collapsed. The decay of ancient Rome was assisted by periodic earthquakes, centuries of neglect, and the growing need for building materials. The seat of the Catholic church, it was a state almost completely controlled by priests, who had an insatiable need for new churches and convents.

By the end of the 11th century the popes shook off the controls of the Roman aristocracy, rid themselves of what they considered the excessive influence of the emperors at Aachen, and began an aggressive expansion of church influence and acquisitions. The deliberate and conscious organization of the church into a system modeled on the hierarchies of the ancient Roman Empire put the church on a collision course with the empire and the other temporal leaders of Europe, resulting in an endless series of power struggles.

THE MIDDLE AGES   The papacy soon became essentially a feudal state, and the pope became a medieval (later Renaissance) prince engaged in many of the worldly activities that brought criticism upon the church in later centuries. The fall of the Holy Land to the Turks in 1065 catapulted the papacy into the forefront of world politics, primarily because of the Crusades, most of which were judged to be military and economic disasters, and many of which the popes directly caused or encouraged. During the 12th and 13th centuries the bitter rivalries that rocked the secular and spiritual bastions of Europe took their toll on the stability of the Holy Roman Empire, which grew weaker as city-states buttressed by mercantile and trade-related prosperity grew stronger, and as France emerged as a potent nation in its own right. Each investiture of a new bishop to any influential post became a cause for endless jockeying for power among many political and ecclesiastical factions.

These conflicts achieved their most visible impasse in 1303 with the full-fledged removal of the papacy from Rome to the French city of Avignon. For more than 70 years, until 1377, viciously competing popes (one in Rome, another under the protection of the French kings in Avignon) made simultaneous claims to the legacy of St. Peter, underscoring as never before the degree to which the church was both a victim and a victimizer of European politics.

The seat of the papacy was eventually returned to Rome, where a series of popes proved every bit as fascinating as the Roman emperors they replaced. The great families—Barberini, Medici, Borgia—enhanced their status and fortunes impressively whenever one of their sons was elected pope.

THE RENAISSANCE   Rome's age of siege was not yet over. In 1527 Charles V spearheaded the worst sack in the city's history. To the horror of Pope Clement VII (a Medici), the entire city was brutally pillaged by the man who was to be crowned Holy Roman Emperor the following year.

During the years of the Renaissance, Reformation, and the Counter-Reformation, Rome underwent major physical changes. The old centers of culture reverted to pastures and fields, while great churches and palaces were built with the stones of ancient Rome. This building boom, in fact, did far more damage to the temples of the Caesars than did any barbarian or Teutonic sack. Rare marbles were stripped from the imperial baths and used as altarpieces or sent to lime kilns. So enthusiastic was the papal destruction of imperial Rome that it's a miracle anything is left.

THE MOVE TOWARD A UNITED ITALY   During the 17th, 18th, and 19th centuries the fortunes of Rome rose and fell with the general political and economic situation of the rest of Italy. Since the end of the 13th century Italy had been divided into a series of regional states, each with mercenary soldiers, its own judicial system, and an interlocking series of alliances and enmities that had created a network of intensely competitive city-states. (Some of these families had attained formidable power under such *signori* as the Esse family in Ferrara, the Medici in Florence, and the Sforza families in Milan.) Rome, headquarters of the Papal States, maintained its independence and (usually) the integrity of its borders, although at least some of the city's religious power had been quenched as increasing numbers of Europeans converted to Protestantism.

Napoléon I made a bid for power in Italy beginning in 1796, fueling his propaganda machines with what was considered a relatively easy victory. During the 1815 Congress of Vienna, which followed Napoléon's defeat, Italy was once again divided among many different factions: Austria was given Lombardy and Venetia, and the Papal States were returned to the popes. Some duchies were put back into the hands of their hereditary rulers, whereas southern Italy and Sicily went to a newly imported dynasty related to the Bourbons. One historic move, which eventually assisted in the unification of Italy, was the assignment of the former republic of Genoa to Sardinia (which at the time was governed by the House of Savoy).

By now political unrest had become a fact of Italian (and Roman) life. At least some of it was encouraged by the rapid industrialization of the north and the almost total lack of industrialization in the Italian south. Despite these barriers, in 1861 the Kingdom of Italy was proclaimed and Victor Emmanuel II of the House of Savoy, king of Sardinia, became head of the new monarchy. In 1861 the designated capital of the newly united country, following a 2,000-year-old precedent, became Rome. In a controversial move that engendered resentment many decades later, the borders of the Papal States were eradicated from the map as Rome was incorporated into the new nation of Italy. The Vatican, however, did not yield its territory to the new order, despite guarantees of nonintervention proffered by the Italian government, and relations between the pope and the political leaders of Italy remained rocky until 1929.

At that time Mussolini defined the divisions that, to the present, have separated the Italian government and the Vatican by signing a concordat that granted political and fiscal autonomy to Vatican City. It also made Roman Catholicism the official state religion of Italy, although this designation was removed through revision of the concordat in 1978. In 1984 Bruno Craxi officially annulled the concordat of 1929.

WORLD WAR II & THE AXIS   With Rome now firmly entrenched as the seat of Italian power, the history of the city was now tightly linked to that of Italy as a whole. Mussolini's support of the Fascists during the Spanish civil war helped encourage the formation of the "Axis" between Italy and Nazi Germany.

Despite its outdated military equipment, Italy added to the general horror of the era by invading Abyssinia (Ethiopia) in 1935, supposedly to protect Italian colonial interests there. In 1941 Italy invaded neighboring Yugoslavia, and in 1942 thousands of Italian troops were sent to assist Hitler in his disastrous campaign along the Russian front. In 1943 General Patton, leading American and (with General Montgomery) British troops, controlled all of Sicily within a month of their first attack.

Faced with this defeat and humiliation, Mussolini fled from Rome after being overthrown by his own cabinet. The Allies made a separate deal with Italy's king, Victor Emmanuel III. A politically divided Italy watched as battalions of fanatical German Nazis moved south to resist the Allied march northward up the Italian peninsula. The Nazis released Mussolini from his Italian jail cell to establish the short-lived Republic of Salo, headquartered on the edge of Lake Garda, hoping for a groundswell of popular opinion in favor of Italian fascism. Events quickly proved this nothing more than a futile dream.

In April 1945, with almost half a million Italians rising in a mass demonstration against him and the German war machine, and Rome almost paralyzed by public insurgencies, Mussolini was captured by Italian partisans as he fled into Switzerland. With his mistress, Claretta Petacci, and several others of his intimates, he was shot and strung up upside down from the roof of a gasoline station in Piazzale Loreto, a few blocks east of the central railway station of Milan.

MODERN ROME   Rome today serves as the capital of the Republic of Italy, which was formed in 1946 in the aftermath of World War II. In the 1950s Italy became one of the leading industrialized nations of the world, a giant in the manufacture of automobiles and office equipment, and an agricultural breadbasket of international repute.

In the 1960s Rome became the campaign ground for an increasingly powerful Socialist party. Meanwhile, as the city's wealthy grew increasingly alarmed at the growing socialization of their country, Rome and the rest of Italy suffered an unprecedented flight of capital and an increase in bankruptcies, inflation (almost 20% during most of the 1970s), and unemployment.

During the late 1970s and early 1980s Rome was rocked by the rise of terrorism instigated both by right-wing neofascists and by left-wing intellectuals from the socialist-controlled universities of the north.

In the 1990s some 6,000 businesspeople and politicians were implicated in a billion-dollar government graft scandal. Such familiar figures as Bettino Craxi, who headed the Socialist party, and Giulio Andreotti, the seven-time prime minister, were accused of corruption.

Hoping for a renewal after all this exposure of greed, Italian voters in March 1994 turned to the right wing to head their government. In overwhelming numbers, voters elected a former cruise-ship singer turned media billionaire, Silvio Berlusconi, its new leader. Berlusconi swept to an unprecedented victory in national elections, emerging as prime minister. His Forza Italia (Go, Italy) party formed an alliance with the neofascist National Alliance and the secessionist Northern League to sweep to victory. These elections were termed "the most critical" for Italy in four decades. The new government was beset with an almost hopeless array of new problems, including destabilization caused by the Mafia and its underground economies, and when the Northern League defected from the coalition in December 1994, Berlusconi resigned.

Treasury Minister Lamberto Dini, a nonpolitical international banker, replaced him. Dini signed on merely as a transitional player in Italy's topsy-turvy political game. His austerity measures enacted to balance Italy's budget, including cuts in pensions and health care, were not popular among the mostly blue-collar Italian workers or the highly influential labor unions. Pending a predicted defeat in a no-confidence vote, Dini also stepped down. His resignation in January 1996 left beleaguered Italians shouting *Basta!* (enough). This latest shuffling in Italy's political deck prompted President Oscar Scalfaro to dissolve both houses of the Italian parliament.

Once again Italians were faced with forming a new government. Elections in April 1996 proved a shocker, not only for the defeated politicians but for the victors as well. The center-left coalition known as the Olive Tree, led by Romano Prodi, swept both the Senate and the Chamber of Deputies. The Olive Tree, whose roots stem from the old Communist party, achieved victory by shifting toward the center and focusing its campaign on a strong platform protecting social benefits and supporting Italy's bid to become a solid member of the European Union. Prodi carried through on his commitment when he announced a stringent budget for 1997 in a bid to be among the first countries to enter the monetary union.

The year 1997 saw further upheavals in the Prodi government as he continued to push ahead with cuts to the country's generous social security system. In the autumn of 1997 Prodi was forced to submit his resignation when he lost critical support in Parliament from the Communist Refounding party, which balked at further pension and welfare cuts in the 1998 budget. The party eventually backed off with its demands and Prodi was returned to office, where he pledged to seek legislation for a 35-hour work week by 2001.

4 Famous Romans

Antonioni, Michelangelo (b. 1912)   One of the best-known film directors in Italian history. His films deal with the boredom, despair, and alienation of the upper-middle classes in Italy. He is best remembered for a trilogy of films: *La Notte* (1960), *L'Avventura* (1960), and *L'Eclisse* (1961).

Apuleius, Lucius (2nd century A.D.)   The works of this Roman satirist are the only extant examples of Latin-language prose fiction. His most famous work is *The Golden Ass* (also known as *Metamorphoses*).

Bernini, Giovanni Lorenzo (1598–1680)   This Renaissance sculptor and architect changed forever the architecture of Rome, designing many of its fountains (including those in Piazza Navona). Even more famous are his designs for the piazza in front of St. Peter's, and the canopy whose corkscrew columns cover the landmark's principal altar.

Caesar, Augustus (63 B.C.–A.D.14)   Designated as the favorite heir of Julius Caesar, he launched his political career as part of the triumvirate assigned to avenge the murder of his benefactor. After hunting down and destroying the conspirators and defeating the other members of the triumvirate at the battle of Actium in 31 B.C., he was elevated to the role of Rome's first emperor. During the long reign that followed, the Empire was relatively peaceful, and it flourished with the literature of such writers as Horace, Ovid, and Virgil.

Caesar, Julius (100–44 B.C.)   The most famous and multifaceted figure from the ancient world, he provided fodder for legends that outlived him by 2,000 years, and eventually helped destroy the Republican fabric of the Roman Empire. Originally a candidate for the pagan priesthood, and an acclaimed author in his own right, he subdued all of Gaul in 53 B.C., launched two major campaigns into Britain, and added regions of Iberia, the Alps, and North Africa to Roman domains. During a six-month stopover in the Roman-occupied Nile Delta, he fathered a child with Cleopatra, thereby contributing to some of the events leading to her eventual suicide and the destruction of her dynasty. In 48 B.C. he was elevated to the role of absolute dictator. His murder on the Senate steps by a group of Republican conspirators (a ringleader was his protégé, Brutus) inspired plays by such luminaries as Shakespeare centuries later.

Cellini, Benvenuto (1500–71)   The most famous goldsmith in history, and a notable sculptor (*Perseus with the Head of Medusa*) as well, he was the author of a famous *Autobiography,* which, when first published in 1728, established him as one of the greatest rakes of the Renaissance.

Fellini, Federico (1920–93)   This neorealist film director was known for his zany, visually striking, and sometimes grotesque interpretations of social and psychological dilemmas. Examples of his work include *La Strada, La Dolce Vita* (a title adopted by an entire generation of fun-loving Italians as their mode of living), *8½, Juliet of the Spirits, Satirycon,* and, of course, *Roma.*

Fermi, Enrico (1901–54)   Roman physicist, and U.S. resident after 1939, he postulated the existence of the atomic particle known as the neutrino, and produced element 93, neptunium. He was awarded the Nobel Prize for physics in 1938, and his work contributed heavily to the development of the atomic bomb.

Gregory XIII (1502–85)   Roman pope from 1572 until his death, he launched the Counter-Reformation and departed from the policies of earlier popes by maintaining an unassailable (or at least discreet) personal comportment. He also developed the calendar used today throughout the Western world.

Magnani, Anna (1908–73)   This fiery Italian actress—whom Tennessee Williams once called "my favorite"—was making films in Italy in the 1930s and 1940s, long before she won an Academy Award in 1955 for *The Rose Tattoo,* written by Williams and co-starring Burt Lancaster. Dubbed in countless languages, her films were shown around the world, including the 1960 *The Fugitive Kind* opposite Marlon Brando and the 1968 *The Secret of Santa Vittoria.*

Montessori, Maria (1870–1952)   Physician and educational theorist, she developed a method of education for young children that, within an environment of pedagogical freedom, directs the child's energies into becoming the adult he or she wants to be. In 1894 she became the first woman to receive an MD in Italy. Her most widely distributed work is *Pedagogical Anthropology.*

Moravia, Alberto (1907–90)   The most famous Italian-language author of modern times, he was born in Rome and christened Alberto Pincherle. He later adopted his parents' region of emigration—Moravia, in today's Czech Republic—as his pen name. One of the most scathing interpreters of middle-class boredom and apathy since Edward Albee, he has been judged as one of the most perceptive critics of family values and interpersonal psychologies in Europe, and an internationally acclaimed novelist and essayist.

Nero (A.D. 37–68)   During the decade that he ruled most of the known world (A.D. 58–68), he murdered both his wife and his mother, and initiated a reign of terror under which hundreds of Romans were tortured, brutalized, or executed. Although it has never been proven, he is believed to have ordered the fires in A.D. 65 that eventually destroyed most of his city. Since his suicide at the age of 31, he has been accepted as a universal symbol of how absolute power corrupts, and condemned as a persecutor of Christians and one of the greatest megalomaniacs in human history.

Sixtus V (Felice Peretti; 1520–90)   Ambitious and relentlessly hard-working, this former head of the Franciscans was one of the most influential and repressive Renaissance popes. A tireless inquisitor of heretics and Protestants, he meddled shamelessly in European politics, allying the Vatican with the fanatically religious Philip II of Spain. During his 5-year reign (1585–90) as pope, he radically

The City & Its People

Rome, according to legend, was built on seven hills. These hills are only 44 feet above sea level at the Pantheon, rising to 462 feet above sea level at Monte Mario, present site of the deluxe Cavalieri Hilton hotel.

The seven hills rise from the marshy lowlands of the Campagna and are mostly on the left bank of the Tiber. They include the Quirinale (seat of the modern Italian government), Esquiline, Viminal, Caelian, and Aventine—and all combine to form a crescent-shaped plateau of great historical fame. In its center rises the Palatine Hill, all-powerful seat of the imperial residences of ancient Rome, which looks down upon the ancient Forum and the Colosseum. To the northwest rises the Capitoline Hill. Some historians have suggested that Rome's geography—set above a periphery of marshy and swelteringly hot lowlands—contributed to the fall of the Roman Empire because of its propensity to breed malaria-inducing mosquitoes.

The modern city of Rome is composed of 22 districts, covering an area of nearly 10 square miles. The Tiber makes two distinct bends within Rome, below Ponte Cavour, one of the city's major bridges, and again at the history-rich island of Tiberina.

With bloodlines including virtually every race ever encompassed by the borders of the ancient Roman Empire, the people of Rome long ago grew accustomed to seeing foreign influences come and go. Picking their way through the architectural and cultural jumble of Rome, they are not averse to complaining (loudly) of the city's endless inconveniences, yet they are the first to appreciate the historical and architectural marvel that surrounds them. Cynical but hearty, and filled with humanity, modern Romans seem to propel themselves through the business of life with an enviable sense of style.

The crowds of pilgrims and the vast numbers of churches and convents exist side by side with fleshier and more earthbound distractions, the combination of which imbues many Romans with an overriding interest in pursuing the pleasures and distractions of the moment. This sense of theatricality can be seen in Roman driving habits; in animated conversations and gesticulations in restaurants and cafes; in the lavish displays of flowers, fountains, food, and architecture, the nation's trademark; and in the 27 centuries of building projects dedicated to the power and egos of long-dead potentates.

Despite the crowds, the pollution, the heat, and the virtual impossibility of efficiency, Romans for the most part take life with good cheer and *pazienza*. Translated as "patience," it seems to be the frequently uttered motto of modern Rome, and an appropriate philosophy for a city that has known everything from unparalleled glory to humiliation and despair. Romans know that since Rome wasn't built in a day, its charms should be savored slowly and with an appreciation for the cultures that contributed to this panoply.

reorganized church finances to make the papacy solvent after the fiscal excesses of earlier popes, and sent groups of Catholic evangelists to territories in the Philippines and South America. Best known for his lavish building programs in Rome, he altered the geography of the Eternal City by clearing away medieval debris and establishing some of the city's major roads and streets. One of the straightest of these—Via del Corso—was originally conceived as a venue for horseracing.

5 Architecture 101

The mysterious **Etruscans,** whose earliest origins probably lay somewhere in Mesopotamia, brought the first truly impressive architecture to mainland Italy. Little remains of their building, but historical writings by the Romans themselves record their powerful walls, bridges, and aqueducts, which were very similar to the Mycenaean architecture of Crete. As Rome asserted its own identity and overpowered its Etruscan masters, it borrowed heavily from their established themes.

In architecture, **ancient Rome** flourished magnificently, advancing in size and majesty far beyond the examples set by the Greeks. Part of this was because of the development of a primitive form of concrete, but even more important was the fine-tuning of the arch, which was used with a logic, rhythm, and ease never before seen. Monumental buildings were erected, each an embodiment of the strength, power, and careful organization of the empire itself. Examples include forums and baths scattered across the Mediterranean world (the greatest of which were Trajan's Forum and the Baths of Caracalla, both in Rome). Equally magnificent were the Colosseum and a building that later greatly influenced the Palladians during the Renaissance, Hadrian's Pantheon. These immense achievements were made possible by two major resources: almost limitless funds pouring in from all regions of the empire, and an unending supply of slaves captured during military campaigns.

The influence of Roman architecture was to have enormous impact on building throughout most of the world, leading in time to a neoclassic revival centuries later in Britain and America. Although unromantic, it was the use of concrete that was to have such a major influence on buildings to come. Concrete seemingly lasts forever, as evidenced by the giant concrete dome of Rome's Pantheon and the Baths of Caracalla, and makes vast buildings possible. Even in Roman times this allowed *insulae* (apartment blocks) to climb to seven floors or more, something almost unheard of before. Even though Rome didn't invent the arch or the aqueduct, or even concrete, Romans perfected these building forms.

Following in the footprints of the Romans, **early Christians** copied Roman architectural styles, although they lacked the rich marbles, slave labor, and other materials that made Rome glorious. The earliest basilicas were hastily constructed and poorly designed. Basilicas were entered at the west, with the apse in the east—the direction of Palestine. None of the basilicas remaining from this period is intact, as all were incredibly altered or changed over the centuries.

Because the Christian world was also ruled from the East, **Byzantine** architecture came into play. The roofing device of the Near East—covering a building with a dome—was adapted to the basic rectangular plan of the early Christian basilica.

The art and architecture in the centuries that followed the collapse of Rome became known as early medieval or **Romanesque.** In its many variations, it flourished between A.D. 1000 and 1200.

Roman architecture was so innovative and powerful that it continued to influence builders even beyond the Romanesque and during the **Gothic** period. The best examples of domestic Gothic architecture in Italy, however, are in Florence and Siena, not in Rome. Santa Maria Sopra Minerva (see "Near Piazza Navona & the Pantheon" in chapter 6) is the only real exception.

The **Renaissance** flowered in Italy almost 2 centuries before it reached such countries as England. In the early Renaissance, architecture in Rome was still heavily influenced by classicism, although using building techniques perfected during the Gothic period. Rome's greatest building achievement of the Renaissance is St. Peter's Basilica, until the last decade the largest church ever constructed. Its sheer massiveness overwhelms (about five times the area of a football field). Urbino-born Donato Bramante (1444–1514) was only the first in a series of architects who would create this monumental design. Regrettably, very little is left of Bramante's concept—the decorative excess of this present building was not in his original vision. Even Michelangelo was an architect of St. Peter's (from 1547 to 1564), designing and beginning construction of the massive dome.

In the early 17th century and into the 18th century, the **baroque** (meaning absurd or irregular) movement swept Europe, including Rome. This development was linked to the much-needed reforms and restructuring of the Catholic church that followed the upheavals of the Protestant Reformation. Many great Italian churches and *palazzi* were constructed during this period.

The great name from this period was Giovanni Lorenzo Bernini (1598–1680), whose chief work is the piazza in front of St. Peter's. Completion of the basilica itself was the greatest architectural accomplishment of the early baroque period. Francesco Borromini (1559–1667) was another great architect of the age. His Church of Sant'Agnese in Rome reveals his mastery, with curved indentations on its facade.

As is obvious to any visitor to Rome, the 19th and 20th centuries did not see the grand architectural achievements of the Romans or the Renaissance. The later baroque and flamboyant excesses of their more recent past were dismissed as "gay excesses" by 19th-century architects, and a revival of **neoclassicism** swept Europe in the late 1700s. Neoclassic architects of the 19th century were mainly copyists, adding little of their own creation. In the early 20th century Mussolini was more intent on producing "pompous" neoclassical buildings than in achieving break-throughs in modern architectural design. Many of the buildings constructed in Rome during his dictatorship have been called "Fascist" and uninspired architecture (visit the EUR district south of the center for an example; see chapter 6).

If Italy produced any great modern architect in the **20th century**, it was Pier Luigi Nervi, born in 1891 in Milan. He faced the same problems the Romans did: covering a vast enclosure with concrete vaulting. Nervi's innovative buildings are both poetic and practical; his daring styles and shapes are perhaps best represented by Rome's Palazzo della Sport designed for the 1960 Olympics. He went on to build a smaller sports arena in Rome, the Palazzetto, which is still called "the world's most beautiful sports arena."

6 Art Through the Ages

There's an amazing richness of Italian art, and neither enough room to display such artistic bounty, nor enough resources to maintain the art and protect it from thieves. In fact, some world-class masterpieces that would be the focal point of many museums are tucked away in obscure rooms of rarely visited galleries. Others hide in dark church corners illuminated only by coin-operated lights.

How did it all begin?

As ancient Rome continued to develop its empire, its artisans began to turn out an exact, realistic **portrait sculpture** that became its hallmark. It differed distinctly from the more idealized forms of Greek sculpture. Rome was preoccupied with sculpted images—in fact, sculptors made "bodies" en masse and later fitted a par-ticular head on the sculpture upon the demand of a Roman citizen. Most Roman painting that survives is in the form of **murals in the fresco technique,** and most of these were uncovered when Pompeii and Herculaneum, on the Bay of Naples, were excavated. Rome's greatest artistic expression was in architecture, not in art such as painting.

The aesthetic concepts of the Roman Empire eventually evolved into **early Christian and Byzantine art.** More concerned with moral and spiritual values than with the physical beauty of the human form or the celebration of political grandeur, early Christian artists turned to the supernatural and spiritual world for their inspiration. Basilicas and churches were lavishly decorated with mosaics and colored marble, whereas paintings depicted the earthly suffering (and heavenly rewards) of martyrs and saints. Supported by monasteries or churches, art was almost wholly concerned with ecclesiastical subjects, frequently with the intention of educating the often illiterate worshippers who studied it. Biblical parables were carved in stone or painted into frescoes, often useful teaching aids for a church eager to spread its messages.

Early in the 1300s, Tuscan artists such as Cimabue and Giotto blazed new trails and brought emotional realism into their work in what was later seen as a complete break from Byzantine gloom and rigidity, and an early harbinger of the Renaissance. However, artists in Rome continued to retain reminders of ancient Rome in their work.

The Italian **Renaissance** was born in Florence during the 15th century and almost immediately spread to Rome. Brunelleschi designed a dome for Florence's cathedral that has been hailed ever since as "a miracle of design." Keenly competitive with Florence, ecclesiastical planners in Rome hired Urbino-born Donato Bramante to work on a design for an amplified version of St. Peter's Basilica, the most significant and imposing building of the High Renaissance. Its interior required massive amounts of sculpture and decoration. To fill the void, artists, including Michelangelo, flooded into Rome from throughout Italy.

Perhaps it was in painting, however, that the Renaissance excelled. The artistic giant Raffaello (Raphael) Santi was commissioned to fresco the apartments of Pope Julius II in Rome. Simultaneously, Michelangelo painted the ceiling frescoes of the Sistine Chapel, an assignment that took 4 backbreaking years to complete. Italy—with infinite input from the patrons and artists in Rome—remained Europe's artistic leader for nearly 200 years.

The transitional period between the Renaissance and the baroque came to be called **"mannerism."** Although Venice's Tintoretto remains the most famous artist of this group, out of this period emerged such other (Rome-based) artists as Giulio Romano, Perin del Vaga, Rosso Fiorentino, and Parmigianino. Although little remains of their work (Rome was sacked and many artworks destroyed or carried away in 1527 during the siege of the city by Charles V), their restless and sometimes contorted style soon spread from Rome throughout the rest of Italy.

In the early 17th century and into the 18th century, the **baroque** (meaning absurd or irregular) age altered forever the architectural skyline of Rome (see "Architecture 101," earlier in this chapter). Simultaneously, great artists emerged, including Bernini, renowned both as a sculptor and painter; Carracci, who decorated the Roman palace of Cardinal Farnese; and Caravaggio, one of the baroque masters of earthy realism and dramatic tension.

Shortly thereafter the even more flamboyant **rococo** grew out of the baroque style. The baroque age also represented the high point of **trompe l'oeil** (illusionistic painting) whereby ceilings and walls were painted with disturbingly realistic landscapes that fool the eye with architecturally sophisticated perspectives and angles. Drop in on the second floor of Trastevere's Villa Farnesina for an excellent example (see Walking Tour 4, "Trastevere," in chapter 7).

During the 17th, 18th, and 19th centuries the great light had gone out of art in Italy. Rome in particular, capitalizing on the vast ruins that lay scattered within its boundaries, became a magnet for the **neoclassical** craze sweeping through France, Britain, and Germany. Thousands of foreign and Italian artists descended upon Rome to feed off its 2,000 years of artistic treasures. The era's return to the aesthetic ideals of ancient Greece and Rome helped to fuel the growing sense of pan-Italian nationalism. By the 19th century the beacon of artistic creativity was picked up by France, whose artists ushered in a wide array of different artistic traditions (including impressionism) whose tenets were for the most part ignored in Italy.

The **20th century** witnessed the creative apexes of several major Italian artists whose works once again captured the imagination of the world. De Chirico and Modigliani (the latter's greatest contribution lay in a new concept of portraiture) were only two among many. Today the works of many of Italy's successful futurist and metaphysical painters can be seen in Rome's Galleria Nazionale d'Arte Moderna. Sadly, although many of the works contained therein are world-class art of international stature, they tend to be overlooked in a city whose artworks encompass two millennia of treasures.

7 Literature: The Classics & Beyond

The passion for empire building spilled over into the development of forms of Roman literature that would affect every literary development in the Western world for the next 2,000 years.

The first true Latin poet was Livius Andronicus (c. 284–2044 B.C.), a Greek slave who translated Homer's *Odyssey* into Latin, but abandoned the poetic rhythms of ancient Greek in favor of Latin's Saturnian rhythm. Quintus Ennius (239–169 B.C.) was the father of Roman epic literature, his *Annales* permeated with a sense of the divine mission of Rome to civilize the world. Quintus's bitter rival was M. Porcius Cato the Censor (234–149 B.C.), who passionately rejected Rome's dependence on Hellenistic models in favor of a distinctly Latin literary form.

Part of the appeal of Latin literature was the comedies performed in front of vast audiences. The Latin cadences and rhythms of Plautus (254–184 B.C.) were wholly original, and C. Lucilius (c. 180–102 B.C.) is credited as the first satirist, developing a deliberately casual, sometimes lacerating, method of revealing the shortcomings and foibles of individuals and groups of people (statesmen, poets, gourmands, etc.).

Latin prose and oratory reached their perfect form with the cadences of Marcus Tullius Cicero (106–43 B.C.). A successful and popular general and politician, he is credited with the development of the terms and principles of oratory, which are still used by debating societies everywhere. His speeches and letters are triumphs of diplomacy, and his public policies are credited with binding Rome together during some of its most wrenching civil wars.

Poetry also flourished. The works of Catullus (84–54 B.C.), primarily concerned with the immediacy and strength of his own emotions, presented romantic passion in startlingly vivid ways. Banned by some of the English Victorians, Catullus's works continue to shock anyone who bothers to translate them.

One of the Roman republic's most respected historians was Livy, whose saga of early Rome is more or less the accepted version. Julius Caesar himself (perhaps the most pivotal—and biased—eyewitness to the events he recorded) wrote accounts of his military exploits in Gaul and his transformation of the Roman republic into a dictatorship. Military and political genius combine with literary savvy in his *De Bello Gallica* (Gallic Wars) and *De Bello Civili* (Civil War).

Ancient Roman literature reached its most evocative peak during the Golden Age of Augustus (42 B.C.–A.D. 17). Virgil's (70–19 B.C.) *The Aeneid*, a 12-volume Roman creation myth linking Rome to the demolished city of Troy, has been judged equal to the epics of Homer.

Horace (Quintus Horatius Flaccus; 63–8 B.C.) became a master of satire, as well as the epic "Roman Odes," whose grandeur of style competes with Virgil. Frequently used as an educational text for princes and kings during the Renaissance 1,500 years later, Horace's works often reveal the anxiety he felt about the centralization of unlimited power in Rome after the end of the Republic. Many centuries later some of the themes of Horace were embraced during the Enlightenment of 17th-century Europe, and were even used as ideological buttresses for the tenets that led to the French Revolution.

Ovid (43 B.C.–A.D. 17), master of the elegy, had an ability to write prose that reflected the traumas and priorities of his own life and emotional involvements. Avoiding references to politics (the growing power of the emperors was becoming increasingly repressive), the elegy grew into a superb form of lyric verse focused on such tenets as love, wit, beauty, pleasure, and amusement. Important works that are read thousands of years later for their charm and mastery of Latin include *Metamorphoses* and *The Art of Love*.

Between A.D. 17 and 170 Roman literature was stifled by a growing fear of such autocrats as Tiberius, Claudius, Nero, and Caligula. An exception is the work of the great Stoic writer, Lucius Annaeus Seneca (4 B.C.?–A.D. 65), whose work commented directly, and sometimes satirically, on events of his time, advocating self-sufficiency, moderation, and emotional control.

For several hundred years after the collapse of the Roman Empire very little was written of any enduring merit in Rome. The exceptions include Christian Latin-language writings from such apologists and theologians as St. Jerome (A.D. 340–420) and St. Augustine (354–430), whose works helped bridge the gap to the beginning of the Middle Ages.

From this time onward literature in Rome parallels the development of Italian literature in general. Medieval Italian literature was represented by religious poetry, secular lyric poetry, and sonnets. Although associated with Florence, and not Rome, Dante Alighieri (1265–1321) broke the monotony of a thousand-year literary silence with the difficult-to-translate *terza rima* of *The Divine Comedy*. Called the first masterpiece in Italian—to the detriment of Rome, the Tuscan dialect in which he wrote gradually became accepted as the purest form of Italian—it places Dante, rivaled only by medieval Italian-language poets Petrarch and Boccaccio, in firm control as the founder of both the Italian language and Italian literature.

Rome, however, continued to pulsate with its own distinctive dialect and preoccupations. The imbroglios of the city's power politics during the 1400s and 1500s, and the mores of its ruling aristocracy, were recorded in *The Courtier*, by Baldassare Castiglione (1478–1529), still read as a source of insight into customs, habits, and ambitions during the Renaissance.

Between 1600 and around 1850, as the reins of international power and creativity shifted from Italy, literature took a second tier to such other art forms as music, opera, and architecture. The publication of Alessandro Manzoni's (1785–1873) romantic epic *I Promessi Sposi* (The Betrothed) in 1827 signaled the birth of the modern Italian novel.

During the 19th century Rome's literary voice found its most provocative spokesperson in Giuseppe Gioacchino Belli (1792–1863), who wrote more than 2,000 satirical sonnets (*I Sonetti Romaneschi*, published 1886–96) in Roman dialect rather than academic Italian. A statue in his honor decorates Piazza Belli in Trastevere.

In modern times, Alberto Moravia has won an international following. Born in Rome of a well-to-do family, Moravia (the pseudonym of Alberto Pincherle) initiated the neorealism movement in the Italian novel, winning fame for *Two Women* and *The Empty Canvas*. His novels describe in painful detail the apparent emptiness of life in an era of mass conformity.

8 The Romans: From Myth to Language

ON STAGE   Rome is one of the world's leading cultural centers. It's a city of music, with concerts performed in venues that range from medieval churches and Renaissance *palazzi* to parks and cloisters to *piazze* and local auditoriums. Even more popular with Romans is opera, which continues as a growth industry among new legions of the young every year.

In theater, Pirandello and Goldoni remain perennial favorites, although Roman audiences are also quite familiar with the works of Shakespeare, particularly those plays using Italy as a background, such as *Romeo and Juliet*.

The RAI—Radio Televisione Italiana, the state network—dazzles Roman audiences with a symphony orchestra and chorus rated among the finest on earth. The Rome orchestra most often performs its regular season at the Foro Italico. Annually a special concert is staged for the pope, either at St. Peter's or within the precincts of the Vatican.

There is no national theater; instead, different theater companies perform in repertory in Rome. Of course, you need to have a good understanding of Italian to appreciate these programs. Outstanding Roman theater companies include Teatro di Roma, Teatro di Genoa, and Centro Teatrale Bresciano.

MYTH   Although modern visitors know Rome as the headquarters of Catholicism, the city also developed one of the world's most influential bodies of mythology.

During the days when Rome was little more than a cluster of sheepherder's villages, a body of gods whose characters remained basically unchanged throughout the course of Roman history were worshipped. To this panoply, however, were added and assimilated the deities of other conquered territories (especially Greece) until the roster of Roman gods bristled with imports from around the Mediterranean. In its corrupted (later) version, the list grew impossibly unwieldy as more-or-less demented emperors forced their own deification and worship upon the Roman masses. After the Christianizing of Europe, the original and ancient gods retained their astrological significance and provided poetic fodder for endless literary and lyrical comparisons.

A brief understanding of each of the major gods' functions will enhance insights during explorations of the city's museums and excavations.

Apollo was the representative of music, the sun, prophecy, healing, the arts, and philosophy. He was the brother of **Diana** (symbol of chastity and goddess of the hunt, the moon, wild animals, and later, of commerce) and the son of **Jupiter** (king of the gods and god of lightning), by a lesser female deity named Leto. **Cupid** was the god of falling in love.

Juno, the wife of Jupiter, was attributed with vague but awesome powers and a very human sense of outrage and jealousy. Her main job seemed to be wreaking vengeance against the hundreds of nymphs seduced by Jupiter, and punishment of the thousands of children he supposedly fathered.

Mars, the dignified but bloodthirsty god of war, was reputed to be the father of **Romulus,** cofounder of Rome.

Mercury, symbol of such Geminis (twins) as Romulus and Remus, was one of the most diverse and morally ambiguous of the gods. He served as the guide to the dead as they approached the underworld, and as the patron of eloquence, travel, negotiation, diplomacy, good sense, prudence, and (to a very limited extent) thieving.

Neptune, god of the sea, was assigned almost no moral attributes, but represents solely the watery domains of the earth.

Minerva was the goddess of wisdom, arts and crafts, and (occasionally) of war. A goddess whose allure was cerebral and whose discipline was severe, she wears a helmet and breastplate emblazoned with the head of **Medusa** (the snake-haired monster whose gaze could turn men into stone). During the Renaissance she became a symbol much associated, oddly enough, with the wisdom and righteousness of the Christian popes.

Venus, whose mythological power grew as the empire expanded, was the goddess of gardens and every conceivable variety of love. She was reportedly the mother of **Aeneas,** mythical ancestor of the ancient Romans. Both creative and destructive, Venus's appeal and duality are as primeval as the earth itself.

Ceres, goddess of the earth and of the harvest, mourned for half of every year (during winter) when her daughter, **Proserpine,** abandoned her to live in the house of **Pluto,** god of death and the underworld.

Vulcan was the half-lame god of metallurgy, volcanoes, and furnaces, whose activities at his celestial forge crafted superweapons for an array of military heroes beloved by the ancient Romans.

Finally, **Bacchus,** the god of wine, undisciplined revelry, drunkenness, and absence of morality, gained importance in Rome as the city grew decadent and declined.

RELIGION   Rome is the world's greatest ecclesiastical center. Few regions on earth have been as religiously prolific—or had such a profound influence on Christianity—as Italy.

Even before the Christianizing of the Roman Empire, the ancient Romans artfully (and sometimes haphazardly) mingled their allegiance to the deities of ancient Greece with whatever religious fad happened to be imported at the moment. After its zenith, ancient Rome resembled a theological hodgepodge of dozens of religious and mystical cults, which found fertile soil amid a crumbling empire. Eastern (especially Egyptian) cults became particularly popular, and dozens of emperors showed no aversion to defining themselves as gods and enforcing worship by their subjects.

In A.D. 313 the emperor Constantine, a Christian convert himself, signed the Edict of Milan, stopping the hitherto merciless persecution of Christians. Since then, Italy has adhered, in the main, to Catholicism.

Today the huge majority (99%) of Italians describe themselves as Roman Catholic, although their form of allegiance to Catholicism varies widely according to individual conscience. Despite the fact that only about one-third of the country attends mass with any regularity, and only about 10% claim to receive the sacrament at Easter, the country is innately—to its very core—favored by the Catholic tradition. That does not always mean that the populace follows the dictates of the Vatican. An example of this is that, despite the pressure by the Holy See against voting in favor of Communist party members (in 1949 the Vatican threatened to excommunicate—ipso facto—any Italian who voted for Communist or

Communist-inspired candidates), the Communist platform in Italy used to receive up to 33% of the popular vote in certain elections.

Modern Italy's adherence to Catholicism is legally stressed by a law enacted in 1848 by the Kingdom of Sardinia (later reaffirmed by the Lateran Treaty) which states: "The Catholic apostolic and Roman religion is the sole religion of the [Italian] State." The same treaties, however, give freedom of worship to other religions, but identify Rome as "the center of the Catholic world and a place of pilgrimage," and confer onto the State of Italy the responsibility of safeguarding the security of the pope and his emissaries, and of respecting church property and church law in the treatment of certain matters, such as requests for divorces or annulments.

Significantly, throughout history Italy has produced more upper-echelon leaders to staff the Vatican than any other country in the world. Only recently, with the election of a Polish-born pope (John Paul II), has a pattern of almost complete domination of the papacy by Italian prelates been altered. Because of the sometimes inconvenient juxtaposition of the Vatican inside the administrative capital of Italy, the Lateran Treaty of February 11, 1929, which was confirmed by Article 7 of the constitution of the Italian republic, recognizes the Vatican City State as an independent and sovereign state and established and defined its relationship to the Italian State. That treaty, originally signed by Mussolini, lasted until 1984.

FOLKLORE   The most formal manifestation of folk rituals in all of Rome is the Commedia dell'Arte. Although it greatly influenced theatrical styles of France in the 17th century, it is unique to Italy. The plots almost always develop and resolve an imbroglio in which the beautiful wife of an older curmudgeon dallies with a handsome swain, against the advice of her maid and much to the amusement of the husband's valet.

Italy, even before the Christian era, was a richly religious land ripe with legends and myths. Modern Italy blends superstition, ancient myths and fables, and Christian symbolism in richly folkloric ways. Throughout Rome, rites of passage—births, first communions, marriages, and deaths—are linked to endless rounds of family celebrations, feasts, and gatherings. Faithful Romans might genuflect when in front of a church, when entering a church, when viewing an object of religious veneration (a relic of a saint, for example), or when hearing a statement that might tempt the Devil to meddle in someone's personal affairs.

LANGUAGE   Italian, of course, is the official language of Rome, but it's spoken with a particular dialect that delights everyone born in the city. Although the purest form of Italian is said to be spoken in Tuscany (a legacy of medieval author Dante Alighieri, who composed *The Divine Comedy* in the Tuscan dialect), Romans have always maintained a fierce pride in the particular stresses, intonations, and vocabulary of their own native speech patterns.

Regardless of the dialect, Italian is more directly derived from Latin than any of the other Romance languages. Many older Italians had at least a rudimentary grasp of ecclesiastical (church) Latin because of the role of Latin in the Catholic mass. Today, however, as the vernacular Italian has replaced the use of Latin in most church services, the ancient tongue can be read and understood only by a diminishing number of academics and priests.

Linguists consider Italian the most "musical" and mellifluous language in the West, and the Italian language easily lends itself to librettos and operas. The language is a phonetic one; this means that you pronounce a word the way it's written, unlike many other languages, including English. It has been said that if an Italian sentence sounds "off key," it's because the grammar is incorrect.

The Italian alphabet is not as extensive as the English alphabet in that it doesn't normally use such letters as *j, k, w, x,* and *y.*

Even as late as World War II, many Italian soldiers couldn't understand each other, as some men spoke only in their local dialects. But with the coming of television, more and more Italians speak the language with similarity.

9   Rome at the Table

MEALS & DINING CUSTOMS   You'll find restaurants of international renown here and an infinite number of *trattorie* and *rosticcerie* that offer good meals at moderate prices. The main meals are from noon to 3pm and 8 to 11pm, but you can get food at other hours at the more informal trattorie and rosticcerie. Many restaurants throughout Rome offer fixed-price meals that include two courses, a dessert, a house wine, and service. For more details, see chapter 5.

THE CUISINE   Many visitors from North America erroneously think of Italian cuisine as one-dimensional. Of course, everybody's heard of minestrone, spaghetti, chicken cacciatore, and spumoni ice cream. But chefs hardly confine themselves to such a limited repertoire.

Throughout your Roman holiday you'll encounter such savory treats as *zuppa di pesce* (a soup or stew of various fish, cooked in white wine and herbs, *cannelloni* (tube-shaped pasta baked with any number of stuffings), *riso col gamberi* (rice with shrimp, peas, and mushrooms, flavored with white wine and garlic), *scampi alla griglia* (grilled prawns, one of the best-tasting, albeit expensive, dishes in the city), *quaglie con risotto e tartufi* (quail with rice and truffles), *lepre alla cacciatore* (hare flavored with tomato sauce and herbs), *zabaglione* (a cream made with sugar, egg yolks, and marsala), *gnocchi alla romana* (potato-flour dumplings with a sauce made with meat and covered with grated cheese), *stracciatella* (chicken broth with eggs and grated cheese), *abbacchio* (baby spring lamb, often roasted over an open fire), *saltimbocca alla romana* (literally "jump-in-your-mouth"—thin slices of veal with cheese, ham, and sage), *fritta alla romana* (a mixed fry that's likely to include everything from brains to artichokes), *carciofi alla romana* (tender artichokes cooked with mint and garlic, and flavored with white wine), *fettuccine all'uovo* (egg noodles served with butter and cheese), *zuppa di cozze o vongole* (a hearty bowl of mussels or clams cooked in broth), *fritta di scampi e calamaretti* (baby squid and prawns fastfried), *fragoline* (wild strawberries, in this case from the Alban Hills), and *finocchio* (or fennel, a celerylike raw vegetable, the flavor of anisette, often eaten as a dessert and in salads).

Incidentally, except in the south, Italians do not use as much garlic in their food as most foreigners seem to believe. Most northern Italian dishes are butter based. Virgin olive oil is preferred in the south. Spaghetti and meatballs is not an Italian dish, although certain restaurants throughout the country have taken to serving it "for homesick Americans."

Rome also has many specialty restaurants that represent every major region of the country. The dishes they serve carry such designations as *alla genovese* (Genoa), *alla milanese* (Milan), *alla napolitana* (Naples), *alla fiorentina* (Florence), and *alla bolognese* (Bologne).

WINES & OTHER DRINKS   Italy is the largest wine-producing country in the world; as far back as 800 B.C. the Etruscans were vintners. It's said that more soil is used in Italy for the cultivation of grapes than for growing food. Many Italian farmers produce wine just for their own consumption or for their relatives in a big city. It wasn't until 1965, however, that laws were enacted to guarantee regular consistency in winemaking. Wines regulated by the government are labeled "DOC" (*Denominazione di Origine Controllata*). If you see "DOCG" on a label (the "G" means *garantita*), that means even better quality control.

Lazio (Rome's region) is a major wine-producing region of Italy. Many of the local wines come from the Castelli Romani, the hill towns around Rome. Horace and Juvenal sang the praises of Latium wines even in imperial times. These wines, experts agree, are best drunk when young, and they are most often white, mellow, and dry (or else demi-sec). There are seven different types, including **Falerno** (yellowish straw in color) and **Cecubo** (often served with roast meat). Try also **Colli Albani** (straw-yellow with amber tints and served with both fish and meat). The golden-yellow wines of **Frascati** are famous, produced both in a demi-sec and a sweet variety, the latter served with dessert.

Romans drink other libations as well. Their most famous drink is **Campari,** bright red in color and herb flavored, with a quinine bitterness to it. It's customary to serve it with ice cubes and soda.

Beer is also made in Italy and, in general, is lighter than German beer. If you order beer in a Roman bar or restaurant, chances are it will be imported unless you specify otherwise, for which you'll be charged accordingly. Some famous names in European beer making now operate plants in Italy, where the brew has been "adjusted" to Italian taste.

High-proof **grappa** is made from the "leftovers" after the grapes have been pressed. Many Romans drink this before or after dinner (some put it into their coffee). To an untrained foreign palate, it often appears rough and harsh; some say it's an acquired taste.

Italy has many **brandies** (according to an agreement with France, it is not supposed to use the word *cognac* in labeling them). A popular one is Vecchia Romagna.

Other popular drinks include several **liqueurs.** Try herb-flavored Strega, or perhaps an almond-flavored Amaretto. One of the best known is Maraschino, taking its name from a type of cherry used in its preparation. Galliano is also herb flavored, and Sambuca (anisette) is made of aniseed and is often served with a "fly" (coffee bean) in it. On a hot day a true Roman orders a vermouth, Cinzano, with a twist of lemon, ice cubes, and a squirt of soda water.

10 Recommended Books, Films & Recordings

BOOKS

GENERAL & HISTORY   Luigi Barzini's *The Italians* (Macmillan, 1964) should almost be required reading for anyone contemplating a trip to Rome. Critics have hailed it as the liveliest analysis yet of the Italian character.

Giuliano Procacci surveys the spectrum in his *History of the Italian People* (Harper & Row, 1973), which provides an encompassing look at how Italy became a nation.

One of the best books on the long history of the papacy—detailing its excesses, triumphs, defeats, and most vivid characters—is Michael Walsh's *An Illustrated History of the Popes: Saint Peter to John Paul II* (St. Martin's Press, 1980).

The roots of modern Italy are explored in Christopher Hibbert's *Garibaldi and His Enemies: The Clash of Arms and Personalities in the Making of Italy* (Penguin, 1989).

In the 20th century the most fascinating period in Italian history was the rise and fall of Fascism, as detailed in countless works. One of the best biographies of Il Duce is Denis M. Smith's *Mussolini: A Biography* (Random House, 1983). Eugen Weber writes of *Varieties of Fascism: Doctrines of Revolution in the Twentieth Century*

(Krieger, 1982). Stein Larsen edited *Who Were the Fascists? Social Roots of European Fascism* (Oxford University Press, 1981). With the rise of neofascists within the Italian government, this book is being read with even more interest in the 1990s.

One subject that's always engrossing is the Mafia, which is detailed in Pino Arlacchi's *Mafia Business: The Mafia Ethic and the Spirit of Capitalism* (Routledge, Chapman & Hall, 1987).

William Murray's *The Last Italian: Portrait of a People* (Prentice Hall, 1991) is his second volume of essays on his favorite subject—Italy, its people and civilization. The *New York Times* called it "a lover's keen, observant diary of his affair."

Once Upon a Time in Italy: The Vita Italiana of an American Journalist, by Jack Casserly (Roberts Rinehart, 1995), is the entertaining and affectionate memoir of a former bureau chief in Rome from 1957 to 1964. He captures the spirit of Italia *sparita* (bygone Italy) with such celebrity cameos as those of Maria Callas and the American expatriate singer, Bricktop.

ART & ARCHITECTURE   T. W. Potter provides one of the best accounts of the art and architecture of Rome in *Roman Italy* (University of California Press, 1987), which is also illustrated. Another good book on the same subject is *Roman Art and Architecture,* by Mortimer Wheeler (World of Art Series, Thames & Hudson, 1990).

The Sistine Chapel: A Glorious Restoration, by Michael Hirst et al. (Abrams, 1994), uses nearly 300 color photographs to illustrate the lengthy and painstaking restoration of Michelangelo's 16th-century frescoes in the Vatican.

FICTION & BIOGRAPHY   John Hersey's Pulitzer Prize–winning *A Bell for Adano* (Knopf, 1944) is a frequently reprinted classic. It's a well-written and disturbing story of the American invasion of Italy.

Giorgio Bassani, born in 1916, provides the bourgeois milieu of a Jewish community under Mussolini in *The Garden of the Finzi-Contini* (Harcourt Brace Jovanovich, 1977).

The novels of Alberto Moravia, born in 1907, are classified as neorealism. Moravia is one of the best-known Italian writers read in English. Notable works include *Roman Tales* (Farrar, Straus, and Cudahy, 1957), *The Woman of Rome* (Penguin, 1957; also available in the Playboy paperback series), and *The Conformist* (Greenwood Press, 1975).

First published in 1959, when it caused a scandal, Pier Paolo Pasolini's *A Violent Life* (Pantheon, 1991) is a novel written by the controversial filmmaker. Once viewed with disdain, it's now a classic of postwar Italian fiction.

I, Claudius (Vintage, 1989) and *Claudius the God* (Vintage, 1989) both by Robert Graves, top the list of historically accurate yet wildly entertaining books on ancient Rome. Borrowing from the histories of Tacitus and Suetonius, the series begins at the end of the Emperor Augustus's reign and ends with the death of Claudius in the first century A.D. In 1998 the Modern Library placed *I, Claudius* at number 14 on its list of the 100-finest English language novels published this century.

Colleen McCullough's "Masters of Rome" series immerses the reader in the eventful world of the Roman republic. Rich, fascinating, and historically detailed, this series brings to vivid life such greats as Gaius Marius (*The First Man in Rome,* Avon, 1991), Lucius Cornelius Sulla (*The Grass Crown,* Avon, 1992), and Julius Caesar (*Fortune's Favorites,* Avon, 1994, and *Caesar's Women,* Avon, 1997.)

Irving Stone's *The Agony and the Ecstasy* (Doubleday, 1961), which was filmed with Charlton Heston playing Michelangelo, is the easiest to read and the most pop version of the life of this great artist.

Star Tracks

In the 1976 BBC production of *I, Claudius* a pre-*Star Trek* Patrick Stewart plays Sejanus, a much fiercer commander than Jean-Luc Picard, and John Hurt shows up as Caligula, everyone's favorite baddie.

FILMS

Italian films have never regained the glory they enjoyed in the postwar era. Roberto Rossellini's *Rome, Open City* (1946) influenced Hollywood's films noirs of the late 1940s and Vittorio De Sica's *Bicycle Thief* (1948) achieved world renown.

The late Federico Fellini burst into Italian cinema with his highly individual style, beginning with *La Strada* (1954) and going on to such classics as *Juliet of the Spirits* (1965), *Amarcord* (1974), *Roma* (1972), and *The City of Women* (1980). *La Dolce Vita* (1961) helped to define an era.

Marxist, homosexual, and practicing Catholic, Pier Paolo Pasolini was the most controversial of Roman filmmakers until his mysterious murder in 1975. Explicit sex scenes in *Decameron* (1971) made it a world box-office hit.

Bernardo Bertolucci, once an assistant to Pasolini, achieved fame with such films as *The Conformist* (1970), based on the novel by Moravia. His *1900* is an epic that spans 20th-century Italian history and politics.

Michelangelo Antonioni swept across the screens of the world with his films of psychological anguish, including *La Notte* (1961), *L'Avventura* (1964), and *The Red Desert* (1964).

Mediterraneo, directed by Gabriele Salvatores, is a whimsical comedy that won an Oscar for best foreign-language film in 1991. It tells the story of eight Italian soldiers stranded on a Greek island in World War II.

Giuseppe Tornatore, who achieved such fame with *Cinema Paradiso,* which won the Academy Award for best foreign-language film of 1989, directed one of three vignettes in the 1992 film *Especially on Sunday.* The Taviani brothers, Paolo and Vittorio, both directors, created a stir in 1994 with the release of their film *Fiorile.*

Caro Diario (1994), starring and directed by Nanni Moretti, is a three-part traipse through modern-day Italy. Moretti, a cult figure in Italy, began to make an impression in America with this film. The actor-director is noted for his prickly personality, quirky sense of humor, and deadpan tone.

The Flight of the Innocent (1995) is one of the finest films to come out of Italy in recent times—and one that quickly gained an international audience. The director, Carlo Carlei, takes us inside the world of a 10-year-old boy fleeing for his life. It's one of the best depictions ever of a child alone who must improvise and cope with a world he doesn't understand.

Bernardo Bertolucci's 1996 film, *Stealing Beauty,* stars Jeremy Irons and Liv Tyler. Against a gorgeously lush Tuscan backdrop, Tyler's innocence and beauty re-inspire a jaded and deathly-ill Irons.

Although directors more than stars have dominated Italian cinema, three actors have emerged to gain worldwide fame: Marcello Mastroianni, Fellini's favorite male actor and star of such hits as *La Dolce Vita* (1961) and *8½* (1963); Sophia Loren, whose best film is considered *Two Women* (1961); and Anna Magnani, who not only starred in Italian films, but made many American films as well, including *The Rose Tattoo* (1955), with Burt Lancaster, and *The Fugitive Kind* (1960), with Marlon Brando.

RECORDINGS

MEDIEVAL & RENAISSANCE MUSIC   An excellent collection of the late Renaissance's sonatas, canzonettas, and madrigals, played on original Renaissance instruments, is entitled *Music from the Time of Guido Reni.* (Guido Reni, born 1575 and died 1642, was a Renaissance painter whose philandering and political intrigues created waves of public discord. He was eventually exiled from Rome in 1622.) This particular collection of works by this artist's musical contemporaries was recorded by the Aurora Ensemble (Tactus TAC 56012001).

ORCHESTRAL & OPERATIC WORKS   The best way for most novices to begin an appreciation of opera is to hear an assemblage of great moments of opera. A good example contains works by the most evocative and dramatic singer who ever hit a high "C" on the operatic stage, Maria Callas. *La Voce: Historic Recordings of the Great Diva* (Suite SUI 5002) brings together "La Callas's" spectacular arias from *Lucia di Lammermoor, La Traviata, Norma,* and *The Barber of Seville.*

Recordings of complete and unedited operas are even more rewarding. Excellent examples include the following: Bellini's *Norma,* featuring the divine and legendary Maria Callas, accompanied by the orchestra and the chorus of Milan's La Scala, is one of the world's great operatic events; Tullio Serafin conducts (Angel Records 3517C/ANG 35148-35150). Giuseppe Verdi's genius can be appreciated through *Nabucco,* performed with Plácido Domingo by the Rydl Choir and Orchestra of the Dutch National Opera, conducted by Giuseppe Sinopoli (Deutsche Gramophone DDD 410 512-2-GH2). Also insightful for the vocal techniques of Verdi, his *Complete Songs* is recorded by Renata Scotto (soprano) and Paolo Washington (bass), accompanied by Vincenzo Scalera (piano) (Nuova Era NUO 6855). Rossini's great opera *Il Barbiere di Siviglia* and Puccini's *Tosca,* were both recorded in their complete versions by the Turin Opera Orchestra and Chorus, and conducted by Bruno Campanella (Nuova Era NUO 6760 and Foyer FOY 2023, respectively).

And no compendium of Italian opera would be complete without including the immortal tenor Luciano Pavarotti, whose interpretations of Verdi's idealistic heroes have become almost definitive. His *La Traviata* is particularly memorable and passionate. A classic, this version is available on a two-cassette collection from C.I.M.E. (PTP-5123-4).

Planning a Trip to Rome

2

This chapter is devoted to the where, when, and how of the advance trip-planning issues required to get you on the road.

After deciding where to go, most people have two fundamental questions: What will it cost? and How do I get there? This chapter will answer both these questions and also resolve other important issues, such as when to go, what pretrip preparations are needed, where to obtain more information about Rome, and much more.

1 Visitor Information & Entry Requirements

VISITOR INFORMATION

Before you go, you can contact the **Italian National Tourist Office** at 630 Fifth Ave., Suite 1565, New York, NY 10111 (☎ **212/ 245-4822;** fax 212/586-9249); 401 N. Michigan Ave., Chicago, IL 60611 (☎ **312/644-0990;** fax 312/644-3109); or 12400 Wilshire Blvd., Suite 550, Los Angeles, CA 90025 (☎ **310/820-0098;** fax 310/820-6357). In **Canada,** contact the Italian National Tourist Office at 1 place Ville-Marie, Suite 1914, Montréal, QB H3B 3M9 (☎ **514/866-7667;** fax 514/392-1429); and in **England** at 1 Princes St., London W1R 8AY (☎ **0171/408-1254;** fax 0171/493-6695).

ROME

Although **Yahoo (www.yahoo.com/Recreation/Travel)**, **Excite (www.excite.com/Subject/Regional)**, **Lycos (www.lycos.com)**, **Infoseek (www.infoseek.com)**, and the other major Internet indexing sites all have travel subcategories, one of the best hotlists for travel and destination-specific information in general is Excite's **city.net (www.city.net/countries/italy/rome)**.

The best Rome site, no holds barred, is run by **Travelocity (www.travelocity.com)**. From the homepage, click on the "Destinations & Interests" button, then navigate your way to "Rome and Environs." It has hundreds of listings—full-fledged write-ups in most cases—for everything from sights, hotels, and restaurants to shopping, nightlife, tour companies, and an excellent festivals and events calendar.

Another great site, complete with pictures, is **Roma 2000** (**www.roma2000.it**). It's very graphics-heavy, and the English translation reads a bit like stereo instructions, but it has a wealth of information on sightseeing, including some walking tours. It also lists dozens of hotels, restaurants, and shops, but mostly gives just the addresses and phone numbers. For information on the **Vatican** check out (**www.vatican.com**) where in 1998the pope made his first live Internet appearance. **In Italy** (**www.lainet.com/~initaly**) not only contains solid information on Italy and Rome presented in a very personal and friendly way, but it also has one of the best sets of links to other Italy-related sites on the Net. If you want still more, try the **Webfoot Guides** (**www.webfoot.com**), which has links to information on Italy and the Vatican. And for an unrelentingly religious site with a wonderful armchair photo tour of the Vatican and its art treasures, head to **Christus Rex** (**www. christusrex.org**).

ENTRY REQUIREMENTS

DOCUMENTS   U.S., Canadian, Australian, New Zealand, and Irish citizens, South African citizens, and British subjects, with a valid passport do not need a visa to enter Italy if they don't expect to stay more than 90 days and don't plan to work there. Those who, after entering Italy, find that they'd like to stay more than 90 days can apply for a permit for an additional stay of 90 days, which as a rule is granted immediately. Check with your nearest Italian consulate. If you plan to drive while abroad, it may prove helpful (although not strictly necessary) to obtain an International Driver's Permit to accompany your state or territorial driver's license. You can get an application from your local AAA office.

CUSTOMS   Most items designed for personal use can be brought to Rome duty-free. This includes clothing (new and used), books, camping and household equipment, fishing tackle, a sporting gun and 200 cartridges, a pair of skis, two tennis racquets, a tape recorder, a baby carriage, two ordinary hand cameras with 10 rolls of film, one video camera with 10 blank tapes, a portable radio set (subject to a small license fee), and 400 cigarettes (two cartons) or a quantity of cigars or pipe tobacco not exceeding 500 grams (1.1 lb.). There are strict limits on importing alcoholic beverages. However, limits are much more liberal for alcohol bought tax-paid in other countries of the European Union.

Returning U.S. citizens who have been away for 48 hours or more are allowed to bring back, once every 30 days, $400 worth of merchandise duty-free. You'll be charged a flat rate of 10% duty on the next $1,000 worth of purchases. On gifts, the duty-free limit is $100. For more specific guidance, write to the **U.S. Customs Service,** P.O. Box 7407, Washington, DC 20044 (☎ **202/927-6724**), requesting the free pamphlet *Know Before You Go.* You can download the pamphlet from the Internet at **www.customs.ustreas.gov/travel/kbygo.htm**. If you make purchases in Italy, it's important to keep your receipts and keep them handy when you leave.

For EU citizens: On January 1, 1993, the borders between European countries were relaxed as the European markets united. When you're traveling within the EU, this will have a big impact on what you can buy and take home with you for personal use.

If you buy your goods in a duty-free shop, then the old rules still apply—you're allowed to take home 200 cigarettes and 2 liters of table wine, plus 1 liter of spirits or 2 liters of fortified wine. But if you buy your wine, spirits, or cigarettes in an ordinary shop in Italy, you can take home almost as much as you like. (U.K. Customs and Excise does not set theoretical limits.) If you're returning home from

The Italian Lira, the U.S. Dollar & the U.K. Pound

At this writing, $1 U.S. = approximately 1,720L (or 100L = 6¢), and this was the rate of exchange used to calculate the dollar values given throughout this book. The rate fluctuates from day to day, depending on a complicated series of economic and political factors, and might not be the same when you travel to Italy.

Likewise, the ratio of the British pound to the lira fluctuates constantly. At press time, £1 = approximately 2,960L (or 100L = 3.4p), an exchange rate reflected in the table below.

Lire	U.S.$	U.K.£	Lire	U.S.$	U.K.£
50	0.03	0.02	20,000	11.60	6.80
100	0.06	0.03	25,000	14.50	8.50
300	0.17	0.10	30,000	17.40	10.20
500	0.29	0.17	35,000	20.30	11.90
700	0.41	0.24	40,000	23.20	13.60
1,000	0.58	0.34	45,000	26.10	15.30
1,500	0.87	0.51	50,000	29.00	17.00
2,000	1.16	0.68	100,000	58.00	34.00
3,000	1.74	1.02	125,000	72.50	42.50
4,000	2.32	1.36	150,000	87.00	51.00
5,000	2.90	1.70	200,000	116.00	68.00
7,500	4.35	2.55	250,000	145.00	85.00
10,000	5.80	3.40	500,000	290.00	170.00
15,000	8.70	5.10	1,000,000	580.00	340.00

a non-EU country, the allowances are the standard ones from duty-free shops. You must declare any goods in excess of these allowances. British Customs tends to be strict and complicated in its requirements. For details, get in touch with **Her Majesty's Customs and Excise Office,** Dorset House, Stamford Street, London, SE1 9PY (☎ **0171/202-4510**).

2 Money

There are no restrictions as to how much foreign currency you can bring into Italy, although visitors should declare the amount brought in; this proves to the Italian Customs Office that the currency came from outside the country and therefore the same amount or less can be taken out. Italian currency taken into or out of Italy may not exceed 200,000 lire in denominations of 50,000 lire or lower.

The basic unit of Italian currency is the **lira** (plural: **lire**), abbreviated in this book as **L.** Because of fluctuations in relative values of world currencies, we suggest that you contact any bank for the latest official exchange rate before going to Italy.

Coins are issued in denominations of 10, 20, 50, 100, 200, and 500 lire; there are two different versions of both the 50- and 100-lire pieces (the new ones are much smaller). Bills come in denominations of 1,000, 5,000, 10,000, 50,000, 100,000, and 500,000 lire.

TRAVELER'S CHECKS   Before leaving home, purchasing traveler's checks can give you an extra measure of security. In the event of theft, if the traveler's checks are properly documented, their value will be refunded. Most large banks sell traveler's checks, charging fees that average between 1% and 2% of the value of the checks you buy, although some out-of-the-way banks, in rare instances, charge as much as 7%. If your bank wants more than a 2% commission, it sometimes pays to call the traveler's check issuers directly for the address of outlets where this commission charge will be less.

Issuers sometimes have agreements with groups to sell checks commission-free. For example, the American Automobile Association (AAA) clubs sell their members American Express traveler's checks in several currencies without a commission charge.

American Express (☎ 800/221-7282 in the U.S. and Canada) is one of the largest and most immediately recognized issuers of traveler's checks, and for holders of certain types of American Express charge cards, no commission is charged. For questions or problems that arise outside the U.S. or Canada, contact any of the company's many regional representatives.

There's also **Citicorp** (☎ 800/645-6556 in the U.S. and Canada, or 813/623-1709, collect, from anywhere else) and **Thomas Cook** (☎ 800/223-7373 in the U.S. and Canada, or 609/987-7300, collect, from other parts of the world), which issues MasterCard traveler's checks. **Interpayment Services** (☎ 800/732-1322 in the U.S. and Canada, or 212/858-8500 and 44-1733/318-949, Collect, from other parts of the world) sells Visa checks which are issued by a consortium of member banks and the Thomas Cook organization.

Each of these agencies will refund your money if the checks are lost or stolen, provided you produce sufficient documentation. When purchasing checks, ask about refund hot lines; American Express and Bank of America have the greatest number of offices around the world.

CURRENCY EXCHANGE   For the best exchange rate, go to a bank, *not* to hotels or shops. Currency and traveler's checks (for which you'll receive a better rate than cash) can be changed at the airport and some travel agencies, such as American Express and Thomas Cook. Note the rates—it can pay to shop around.

ATM NETWORKS   ATM machines are becoming more and more common in Italy. If your bank card has been programmed with a PIN, it's likely that you can use your card at ATMs abroad to withdraw money from your account or as a cash advance on your credit card—just look for ATM machines that display your network's (PLUS, Cirrus, etc.) symbol. You might want to check with your home bank to see whether your PIN code must be reprogrammed for usage in Italy. It's also a good idea to determine the frequency limits for withdrawals and cash advances on your credit card. American Express holders have access to the ATM machines of Banco Popolare di Milano; the transaction fee is 2% with a minimum charge of $2.50 and a maximum of $20. ATMs give a better exchange rate than banks, but some ATMs exact a service charge on every transaction. For Cirrus locations abroad call ☎ 800/424-7787, or check out MasterCard's World Wide Web site (**www.mastercard.com**). For PLUS usage abroad, call **800/843-7587,** or contact your local bank or visit Visa's Web site (**www.visa.com**).

MONEYGRAM   If you find yourself out of money, a new wire service provided by American Express can help you tap willing friends and family for emergency funds. Through **MoneyGram,** 7501 W. Mansfield, Lakewood, CO 80235 (☎ 800/926-9400), money can be sent around the world in less than 10 minutes. Senders should call AMEX to learn the address of the closest outlet that handles

What Things Cost in Rome	U.S. $
Taxi from airport to city center	42.00
Taxi from central rail station to Piazza di Spagna	6.80
Subway or public bus (to any destination)	0.95
Local telephone call	0.15
Double room at the Hassler (very expensive)	403.10
Double room at Hotel Columbus (moderate)	214.60
Double room at Hotel Corot (inexpensive)	92.80
Continental breakfast (cappuccino and croissant, standing, at most cafes and bars)	3.75
Lunch for one at Ristorante da Pancrazio (moderate)	26.10
Dinner for one, without wine, at Relais Le Jardin (expensive)	58.00
Dinner for one, without wine, at Girarrosto Toscano (moderate)	30.00
Dinner for one, without wine, at Otello alla Concordi (inexpensive)	18.00
Pint of beer	3.30
Glass of wine	3.80
Coca-Cola	1.50–2.40
Cup of coffee	1.30
Roll of color film, 36 exposures	7.00
Admission to the Vatican museums and Sistine Chapel	9.00
Movie ticket	7.50

MoneyGrams. Cash, credit card (Visa, MasterCard, or Discover only, *not* the American Express card), or the occasional personal check (with ID) are acceptable forms of payment. AMEX's fee for the service is $20 for the first $200 with a sliding scale for larger sums. The service includes a short telex message and a 3-minute phone call from the sender to the recipient. The claimant must present a photo ID at the outlet where the money is received.

3 When to Go

CLIMATE

The most pleasant times to be in Rome, weatherwise, are spring and fall. In the height of summer it can get quite hot and humid. The temperatures can stay in the 90s for days, but nights are most often comfortably cooler. The high temperatures begin in May and often last until October. Rome experiences its lowest average temperatures in December, 47°F; its highest in July, 82°F.

Rome's Average Daytime Temperature & Rainfall

	Jan	Feb	Mar	Apr	May	June	July	Aug	Sept	Oct	Nov	Dec
Temp (°F)	49	52	57	62	70	77	82	78	73	68	56	47
Rain (in.)	3.6	3.2	2.9	2.2	1.4	0.7	0.2	0.7	3.0	4.0	3.9	2.8

HOLIDAYS

Offices and shops are closed on the following days: January 1 (New Year's Day), Easter Monday, April 25 (Liberation Day), May 1 (Labor Day), August 15 (Assumption of the Virgin), November 1 (All Saints' Day), December 8 (Feast of the Immaculate Conception), December 25 (Christmas), and December 26 (Santo Stefano).

ROME CALENDAR OF EVENTS

For more information about these and other events, contact the Rome tourist office, **Ente Provinciale per il Turismo,** Via Parigi 11, Roma 00185 (☎ **06/48899253**). Dates may vary from year to year.

January
- **Carnival, in Piazza Navona.** This marks the last day of the children's market and lasts until dawn of the following day. On or around January 5.
- **Festa di Sant'Agnese,** at Sant'Agnese Fuori le Mura. In this ancient ceremony, two lambs are blessed and shorn. The wool is then used later for palliums. On or around January 17.

March
- **Festa di Santa Francesca Romana,** at Piazzale del Colosseo, near the Church of Santa Francesca Romana in the Roman Forum. It's a blessing of cars. On or around March 9.
- **Festa di San Giuseppe,** in the Trionfale Quarter, north of the Vatican. The heavily decorated statue of the saint is brought out at a fair with food stalls, concerts, and sporting events. On or around March 19.

April
- **Festa della Primavera.** The Spanish Steps are decked out with banks of flowers, and later orchestral and choral concerts are presented in Trinità dei Monti. Dates vary.
- **Holy Week.** The most notable procession is led by the pope, passing the Colosseum and the Roman Forum up to Palatine Hill. A torchlit parade caps the observance. Sometimes at the end of March, but often in April.
- **Easter Sunday,** from the balcony of St. Peter's Basilica. The pope gives his blessing, and it's broadcast around the world.

May
- **International Horse Show** (Concorso Ippico Internazionale di Piazza di Siena), at Piazza di Siena in the Villa Borghese. May 1–10, but dates vary.

June
- **Son et Lumière.** The Roman Forum and Tivoli are dramatically lit at night. Early June to the end of September.
- **Festa di San Pietro,** in St. Peter's Basilica. The most significant Roman religious festival is observed with solemn rites. Usually around June 29.

July
- ✪ **La Festa Di Noiantri.** Trastevere, the most colorful quarter of Old Rome, becomes a gigantic outdoor restaurant in mid-July as tons of food and drink are consumed at tables lining the streets. Merrymakers and musicians provide the entertainment. After reaching the quarter, find the first empty table and try to get a waiter. But guard your valuables. Mid-July.

August
- **Festa della Catene,** in the Church of San Pietro in Vincoli. The relics of St. Peter's captivity go on display. August 1.
- **Ferragosto.** Beginning on August 15, most city residents not directly involved with the tourist trade take a two-week vacation (many restaurants are closed as well). This is a good time *not* to be in Rome.

September
- **Sagra dell'Uva,** in the Basilica of Maxentius in the Roman Forum. During the harvest festival, musicians in ancient costumes entertain, and grapes are sold at reduced prices. Usually early September, but dates vary.

December
- **Papal Blessing** "Urbi et Orbi" (to the city and to the world), from the balcony of St. Peter's Basilica. It's broadcast around the world. December 25 at noon.

4 Calendar of Events for Rome's Jubilee 2000

Below you'll find a calendar of events for Rome's year-long celebration of the Millennium—Jubilee 2000. Although this was the most up-to-date version available at press time, we recommend you obtain the *most recent information possible* before making any concrete plans. For more information contact **Ente Provinciale per il Turismo,** Via Parigi 11, Roma 00185 (☎ **06/48899253**) or check the Jubilee Web site (**www.roma2000.com**). For information on the Vatican, with subdivisions concerning their own participation in the jubilee, contact (**www.vatican.com**).

December
- **Friday, December 24, 1999.** Midnight Mass celebrating the Birth of Christ: St. Peter's Basilica.
- **Saturday, December 25, 1999.** Celebrations and masses commemorating the Birth of Christ: Basilica di San Giovanni in Laterano, Basilica di Santa Maria Maggiore, and St. Peter's Basilica. Papal High Mass in St. Peter's Basilica invoking the blessings of Heaven and Earth for the Holy Land. Official opening of the Jubilee festivities in local churches throughout Rome.
- **Friday, December 31, 1999.** Invocation of hopes and prayers for the passage into the new millennium: St. Peter's Basilica.
- ✪ **December 31, 1999** at midnight. The "greatest street party in the history of the world," is predicted on this night of nights. Bars, restaurants, clubs, taverns, whatever, plan to stay open until the sun rises on a new millennium. There are those who predict that "The Eternal City" will be the finest venue on earth to herald the arrival of a new age.

January
- **Saturday, January 1, 2000.** Worldwide prayers for peace, with high masses commemorating the Virgin Mary: St. Peter's Basilica.
- **Sunday, January 2, 2000.** Masses commemorating the second Sunday after the birth of Christ. Jubilee and celebration of all the world's children: St. Peter's Basilica.
- **Thursday, January 6, 2000.** Celebration of Epiphany, with ordination of priests: St. Peter's Basilica.
- **Sunday, January 9, 2000.** Festival of the Baptism of Christ, with emphasis on the celebration of the sacrament of baptism for children from around the world: Parish churches throughout Rome.

- **Tuesday, January 18, 2000.** Ecumenical inauguration of the Week of Prayer for the Unity of Christians Worldwide: Basilica di San Paolo Fuori le Mura (St. Paul Outside the Walls).
- **Tuesday, January 25, 2000.** Festival of the conversion of St. Paul the Apostle; an ecumenical celebration marking the conclusion of the Week of Prayer for the Unity of Christians Worldwide: Basilica di San Paolo Fuori le Mura.
- **Friday, January 28, 2000.** Memorial service for St. Efrem, as part of a holy liturgy in the Syrian Coptic tradition: Church of Santa Cecilia in Trastevere.

February

- **Wednesday, February 2, 2000.** Festival of the Presentation of Christ, and a celebration of the Holy Life of Monastic and Conventual vows: St. Peter's Basilica.
- **Wednesday, February 9, 2000.** Syrian Maronite Mass celebrating the memory of San Marone: Basilica di Santa Maria Maggiore.
- **Friday, February 11, 2000.** Commemoration of the life of Santa Maria of Lourdes, welcoming the infirm: St. Peter's Basilica.
- **Friday, February 18, 2000.** Memorial mass for Fra Angelico (Beato Giovanni), with a celebration of the talents of artists worldwide: Basilica di Santa Maria Sopra Minerva.
- **Tuesday, February 22, 2000.** Mass celebrating the authority of the Roman Curia: St. Peter's Basilica.
- **Friday–Sunday, February 25–27, 2000.** Convocation of the representatives of the Ecumenical Council of Vatican II (by invitation only): The Vatican.

March

- **Sunday, March 5, 2000.** Beatification and canonization of various candidates for sainthood: St. Peter's Basilica.
- **Wednesday, March 8, 2000.** Penitential procession culminating with Holy Absolution from sins: From the Basilica di Santa Sabina to the Circo Massimo.
- **Thursday, March 9, 2000.** Celebration of the Holy Eucharist: Basilica di San Paolo Fuori le Mura.
- **Friday, March 10, 2000.** Observation of the Stations of the Cross, emphasizing the act of penitence: Basilica di San Giovanni in Laterano.
- **Saturday, March 11, 2000.** Prayers of the Rosary: Basilica di Santa Maria Maggiore.
- **Sunday, March 12, 2000.** First Sunday of Lent; ecclesiastical scrutiny of those who are about to receive the catechism: Basilica di San Giovanni in Laterano.
- **Thursday, March 16, 2000.** Adoration of the Holy Eucharist: Basilica di San Paolo Fuori le Mura.
- **Friday, March 17, 2000.** The Way of the Cross and a Celebration of Penance: Basilica di San Giovanni in Laterano.
- **Saturday, March 18, 2000.** Prayers of the Rosary: Basilica di Santa Maria Maggiore.
- **Sunday, March 19, 2000.** Second Sunday of Lent; ecclesiastical scrutiny of those who are about to receive the catechism: Basilica di San Giovanni in Laterano.
- **Monday, March 20, 2000.** Celebration of Joseph, husband of the Blessed Virgin, and acknowledgment of artisans worldwide: Parish churches throughout Rome.
- **Thursday, March 23, 2000.** Holy Eucharist: Basilica di San Paolo Fuori le Mura.

- **Friday, March 24, 2000.** The Way of the Cross and a Celebration of Penance: Basilica di San Giovanni in Laterano.
- **Saturday, March 25, 2000.** Celebration of the Annunciation of Our Lord to the Virgin Mary: Basilica of the Annunciation/Basilica di Santa Maria Maggiore.
- **Sunday, March 26, 2000.** Third Sunday of Lent; ecclesiastical scrutiny of those who are about to receive the catechism: Basilica di San Giovanni in Laterano.
- **Thursday, March 30, 2000.** Holy Eucharist: Basilica di San Paolo Fuori le Mura.
- **Friday, March 31, 2000.** The Way of the Cross and a Celebration of Penance: Basilica di San Giovanni in Laterano.

April

- **Saturday, April 1, 2000.** Prayers of the Rosary: Basilica di Santa Maria Maggiore.
- **Sunday, April 2, 2000.** Fourth Sunday of Lent; ecclesiastical scrutiny of those who are about to receive the catechism: Basilica di San Giovanni in Laterano.
- **Thursday, April 6, 2000.** Holy Eucharist: Basilica di San Paolo Fuori le Mura.
- **Friday, April 7, 2000.** The Way of the Cross and a Celebration of Penance: Basilica di San Giovanni in Laterano.
- **Saturday, April 8, 2000.** Prayers of the Rosary: Basilica di Santa Maria Maggiore.
- **Sunday, April 9, 2000.** Fifth Sunday of Lent: Basilica di San Giovanni in Laterano.
- **Monday, April 10, 2000.** Jubilee celebrating the homeless and refugees of war: Parish churches throughout Rome.
- **Thursday, April 13, 2000.** Holy Eucharist: Basilica di San Paolo Fuori le Mura.
- **Friday, April 14, 2000.** The Way of the Cross and a Celebration of Penance: Basilica di San Giovanni in Laterano.
- **Saturday, April 15, 2000.** Prayers of the Rosary, and celebration marking the beginning of Holy Week: Basilica di Santa Maria Maggiore.
- **Sunday, April 16, 2000.** Celebration of Palm Sunday, Our Lord's entrance into Jerusalem, and His Passion: St. Peter's Square.
- **Friday, April 21, 2000.** Celebration of the Passion of Our Lord: Saint Peter's Basilica.
- **Sunday, April 23, 2000.** Easter Sunday; celebration of the Resurrection of Our Lord, Papal blessing of the masses: St. Peter's Basilica/St. Peter's Square.
- **Sunday, April 30, 2000.** Mass celebrating recently baptized adult converts to Catholicism: Basilica di San Pancrazio.

May

- **Monday, May 1, 2000.** Mass celebrating the patron saint of laborers, San Giuseppe Lavoratore; Jubilee celebration of all laborers: Parish churches throughout Rome.
- **Saturday, May 6, 2000.** Prayers of the Rosary: Basilica di Santa Maria Maggiore.
- **Sunday, May 7, 2000.** Third Sunday after Easter; ecumenical commemoration of recent Christian martyrs: The Colosseum.
- **Saturday, May 13, 2000.** Prayers of the Rosary: Basilica di Santa Maria Maggiore.
- **Sunday, May 14, 2000.** Fourth Sunday of Easter; worldwide day of prayer for guidance in the Holy Ordinations: St. Peter's Basilica.

- **Thursday, May 18, 2000.** Worldwide Jubilee celebration in honor of the clergy: St. Peter's Square.
- **Saturday, May 20, 2000.** Prayers of the Rosary: Basilica di Santa Maria Maggiore.
- **Thursday, May 25, 2000.** Jubilee celebrating the sciences: Parish churches throughout Rome.
- **Friday, May 26, 2000.** Divine Liturgy in the Alexandrine-Ethiopian Coptic tradition: Basilica di Santa Maria degli Angeli.
- **Saturday, May 27, 2000.** Prayers of the Rosary: Basilica di Santa Maria Maggiore.
- **Sunday, May 28, 2000.** Sixth Sunday after Easter. Jubilee celebration in honor of the Diocese of Rome: Parish churches throughout Rome.
- **Wednesday, May 31, 2000.** Vigil Mass celebrating the eve of the Assumption of Our Lord: St. Peter's Basilica.

June

- **Thursday, June 1, 2000.** Mass celebrating the Assumption of Our Lord: St. Peter's Basilica.
- **Sunday, June 4, 2000.** Seventh Sunday after Easter; day of communication regarding social ills, worldwide jubilee celebrating writers and journalists: Parish churches throughout Rome.
- **Saturday, June 10, 2000.** Mass celebrating the eve of Pentecost: St. Peter's Square.
- **Sunday, June 11, 2000.** Pentecost Sunday; worldwide day of prayer for the peaceful reconciliation of religions worldwide: St. Peter's Basilica.
- **Sunday, June 18, 2000.** Mass of the Holy Trinity; opening ceremonies of the Congress for the Celebration of the International Eucharist (by invitation only): Basilica di San Giovanni in Laterano.
- **Thursday, June 22, 2000.** Mass celebrating the Holy Body and Blood of Christ, with a eucharistic procession: Basilica di San Giovanni in Laterano.
- **Sunday, June 25, 2000.** Closing ceremonies of the Congress for the Celebration of the International Eucharist (by invitation only): The Vatican.
- **Thursday, June 29, 2000.** Mass celebrating the Apostles Peter and Paul, and the evangelistic outreach of St. Paul to the early Christian church: St. Peter's Basilica.

July

- **Sunday, July 2, 2000.** Masses celebrating the halfway point of the Jubilee year 2000: Parish churches throughout Rome.
- **Sunday, July 9, 2000.** Jubilee Masses in honor of the incarcerated worldwide: Parish churches throughout Rome.
- **Sunday, July 16, 2000.** Jubilee Masses: Parish churches throughout Rome.
- **Sunday, July 23, 2000.** Jubilee Masses: Parish churches throughout Rome.
- **Sunday, July 30, 2000.** Jubilee Masses: Parish churches throughout Rome.

August

- **Saturday, August 5, 2000.** Prayer vigil for the eve of the Transfiguration of Our Lord: Basilica di Santa Maria Maggiore.
- **Sunday, August 6, 2000.** Festival of the Transfiguration of Our Lord: Basilica di San Paolo Fuori le Mura.
- **Monday, August 14, 2000.** Prayer vigil celebrating the eve of the Assumption of the Virgin Mary: Parish churches throughout Rome.

- **Tuesday, August 15, 2000.** Festival of the Assumption of the Virgin Mary, with an emphasis on the well-being of the world's children: Parish churches throughout Rome.
- **Sunday, August 27, 2000.** Jubilee Masses: Parish churches throughout Rome.

September

- **Sunday, September 3, 2000.** Beatification/Canonization Mass: St. Peter's Basilica.
- **Friday, September 8, 2000.** Festival of the Birth of the Blessed Virgin: Parish churches throughout Rome.
- **Sunday, September 10, 2000.** Jubilee Masses celebrating the accomplishments of academics and scholars worldwide: Parish churches throughout Rome.
- **Thursday, September 14, 2000.** Festival of the Elevation of the Holy Cross from the Basilica of Santa Croce in Jerusalem through Heaven to the Basilica di San Giovanni in Laterano; mass and the religious procession are conducted in the Armenian Orthodox rite: Basilica di San Giovanni in Laterano.
- **Friday, September 15, 2000.** Opening of the International Congress for the Study of the Attributes of the Virgin Mary: The Vatican (by invitation only).
- **Sunday, September 17, 2000.** Masses: Parish churches throughout Rome.
- **Sunday, September 24, 2000.** Masses: Parish churches throughout Rome.

October

- **Sunday, October 1, 2000.** Festival of Pokrov, invoking the protection of Mary. Masses conducted in accordance with the Byzantine rite: Basilica di Santa Maria Sopra Minerva.
- **Tuesday, October 3, 2000.** Day of Hebrew-Christian dialogues and discussions: The Vatican and parish churches throughout Rome.
- **Saturday, October 7, 2000.** Memorial Mass for the memory of the Blessed Virgin of the Rosary. Torchlit procession celebrating the meaning of the rosary: To be announced.
- **Sunday, October 8, 2000.** High Mass invoking the protection of the Blessed Virgin during the Millennium: St. Peter's Basilica.
- **Sunday, October 15, 2000.** Holy Mass emphasizing the importance of the sacrament of marriage within the context of the family: St. Peter's Square.
- **Friday–Sunday, October 20–22, 2000.** International Conference on Missionary Work: The Vatican (by invitation only).
- **Saturday, October 21, 2000.** Prayers of the Rosary: Basilica di Santa Maria Maggiore.
- **Sunday, October 22, 2000.** International Celebration of Missionary Work Worldwide, Holy Mass: St. Peter's Basilica, and parish churches throughout Rome.
- **Saturday, October 28, 2000.** Prayers of the Rosary: Basilica di Santa Maria Maggiore.
- **Sunday, October 29, 2000.** Jubilee Mass celebrating professional and amateur athletes worldwide: Rome's Olympic Stadium.
- **Tuesday, October 31, 2000.** Vigil for the eve of All Saints' Day: St. Peter's Basilica.

November

- **Wednesday, November 1, 2000.** Mass in honor of the assembly of saints (All Saints' Day): St. Peter's Basilica and parish churches throughout Rome.

- **Thursday, November 2, 2000.** Commemoration mass for the deceased faithful: Parish churches throughout Rome.
- **Saturday, November 4, 2000.** Celebratory mass honoring St. Ambrose: To be announced.
- **Sunday, November 5, 2000.** Jubilee Mass honoring persons holding civic duties and responsibilities: Parish churches throughout Rome.
- **Sunday, November 12, 2000.** Jubilee Mass celebrating farmers and agricultural workers; Day of thanks for the Creation of Heaven and Earth: Parish churches throughout Rome.
- **Sunday, November 19, 2000.** Jubilee Mass celebrating soldiers and police officers: St. Peter's Basilica.
- **Tuesday, November 21, 2000.** Festival of the Presentation of the Blessed Virgin, with liturgical masses conducted according to the rites of Antioch: Basilica di Santa Maria in Trastevere.
- **Friday, November 24, 2000.** Opening of the Worldwide Congress of the Apostolic Laity: The Vatican (by invitation only).
- **Sunday, November 26, 2000.** High Mass celebration of Our Lord Jesus Christ, King of the Universe; and conclusion of the Worldwide Congress of the Apostolic Laity: St. Peter's Basilica.

December, 2000
- **Saturday, December 2, 2000.** Celebration of the Eve of the first Sunday of Advent: St. Peter's Basilica.
- **Sunday, December 3, 2000.** Masses celebrating the first Sunday of Advent: Basilica di San Paolo Fuori le Mura.
- **Friday, December 8, 2000.** Mass celebrating the Immaculate Conception of the Blessed Virgin, conducted with contributions from the Greek Orthodox tradition: Basilica di Santa Maria Maggiore.
- **Sunday, December 10, 2000.** Mass celebrating the second Sunday of Advent: Basilica di San Giovanni in Laterano.
- **Saturday, December 16, 2000.** Religious celebration conducted in the tradition of the Mozarabic rite: Basilica di Santa Maria Maggiore.
- **Sunday, December 17, 2000.** Third Sunday of Advent, with Jubilee masses celebrating the world of entertainment, TV, and cinema: Basilica di San Paolo Fuori le Mura.
- **Sunday, December 24, 2000.** Night mass celebrating the eve of the Birth of Our Lord: St. Peter's Basilica.
- **Monday, December 25, 2000.** Papal benedictions invoking Heaven and Earth: St. Peter's Basilica.
- **Sunday, December 31, 2000.** Vigil of preparation for the passage of the new millennium: St. Peter's Basilica.

January
- **Monday, January 1, 2001.** World Day of Peace, with masses celebrating the Virgin Mary: St. Peter's Basilica.
- **Thursday, January 5, 2001.** Vigil masses celebrating the eve of the Epiphany of Our Lord, and official closure of the Jubilee of the year 2000: Basilicas of San Giovanni in Laterano, Santa Maria Maggiore, and San Paolo Fuori le Mura.
- **Friday, January 6, 2001.** Mass celebrating the Epiphany of Our Lord: St. Peter's Basilica.

5 Health & Insurance

STAYING HEALTHY You'll encounter few health problems while visiting in Rome. The tap water is generally safe to drink, the milk is pasteurized, and health services are good. Occasionally the change in diet may cause some minor diarrhea.

Carry all your vital medication in your carry-on luggage and take enough prescribed medicines to last you during your stay. Bring along copies of your prescriptions written in the generic—not brand-name—form. If you need a doctor, your hotel can recommend one or you can contact your embassy or consulate. You can also obtain a list of English-speaking doctors before you leave from the **International Association for Medical Assistance to Travelers (IAMAT)** in the United States at 417 Center St., Lewiston, NY 14092 (☎ **716/754-4883**), or in Canada at 40 Regal Rd., Guelph, ON N1K 1B5 (☎ **519/836-0102**).

If you suffer from a chronic illness or special medical condition, talk to your doctor before taking the trip. For conditions such as epilepsy, diabetes, or a heart condition, wear Medic Alert's identification bracelet or necklace, which will immediately alert any doctor to your condition, and provide Medic Alert's 24-hour hot line phone number so that foreign doctors can obtain medical information on you. The initial membership costs $35, then $15 annually. Contact the **Medic Alert Foundation,** 2323 Colorado Ave., Turlock, CA 95382 (☎ **800/825-3785**).

INSURANCE Insurance needs for the traveler fall into three categories: (1) health and accident, (2) trip cancellation, and (3) lost luggage. Before purchasing any additional insurance, check your home-owner's, automobile, and medical insurance policies as well as the insurance provided by credit- and charge-card companies and auto and travel clubs. You may have adequate off-premises theft coverage, or your card company may even provide cancellation coverage if the ticket is paid for with its card.

Note that to submit any claim you must always have thorough documentation, including all receipts, police reports, medical records, and such. Medicare only covers U.S. citizens traveling to Mexico and Canada.

If you're prepaying your vacation or are taking a charter or any other flight that has cancellation penalties, look into cancellation insurance.

The following companies will provide further information:

Travel Guard International, 1145 Clark St., Stevens Point, WI 54481 (☎ **800/826-1300**), offers comprehensive policies, including a $44 7-day policy that covers basically everything: emergency assistance, accidental death, trip cancellation and interruption, medical coverage abroad, and lost luggage. This company is the only one to offer "cancel-for-any-reason coverage."

At **Travel Insured International, Inc.,** P.O. Box 280568, East Hartford, CT 06128-0568 (☎ **800/243-3174** in the U.S., or 203/528-7663 outside the U.S.), accident and illness coverage starts at $10; $500 worth of coverage for lost, damaged, or delayed baggage costs $20; and trip cancellation goes for $6 for $100 worth of coverage (written approval is necessary for cancellation coverage above $10,000).

Travelex Insurance Services, P.O. Box 9408, Garden City, NY 11530 (☎ **800/228-9792**), offers travel insurance packages that feature travel assistance services, trip cancellation, trip interruption, flight and baggage delays, accident medical, sickness, 24-hour accidental death and dismemberment, and medical evacuation coverage. Packages are priced at $67 per person.

HealthCare Abroad (MEDEX), ℅ Wallach & Co., 107 W. Federal St. (P.O. Box 480), Middleburg, VA 22118-0480 (☎ **800/237-6615** or 540/687-3166), offers a $3-a-day package, including accident and sickness coverage to the tune of $100,000. Medical evacuation is also included, along with $25,000 accidental death and dismemberment compensation. Trip cancellation can be written into this policy at a nominal cost.

Access America, 6600 W. Broad St., Richmond, VA 23230 (☎ **800/ 284-8300**), has a 24-hour emergency hot line for advice and help on medical, legal, and travel problems. The company also offers comprehensive travel insurance packages, including medical expenses, on-the-spot hospital payments, medical transportation, baggage insurance, trip cancellation/interruption insurance, and collision insurance for car rentals.

Insurance for British Travelers   Most big travel agents offer their own insurance and will probably try to sell you their package when you book a holiday. Think before you sign. Britain's Consumers' Association recommends that you insist on seeing the policy and reading the fine print before buying travel insurance.

You should also shop around for better deals. You might contact **Columbus Travel Insurance Ltd.** (☎ **0171/375-0011** in London) or, for students, **Campus Travel** (☎ **0171/730-3402** in London). Columbus Travel will sell travel insurance only to people who have been official residents of Britain for at least a year. If you're unsure about who provides what kind of insurance and the best deal, contact the **Association of British Insurers,** 51 Gresham St., London EC2V 7HQ (☎ **0171/600-3333**).

6 Tips for Travelers with Special Needs

FOR PEOPLE WITH DISABILITIES   If you're flying around Europe, the airlines and ground staff will help you on and off planes and reserve seats for you with sufficient legroom, but *it's essential to arrange for this assistance in advance by contacting your airline.*

Recent laws in Italy have compelled railway stations, airports, hotels, and most restaurants to follow a stricter set of regulations about wheelchair accessibility to rest rooms, ticket counters, and the like. Even museums and other sightseeing attractions have conformed to the regulations, which mimic many of the regulations presently in effect in the United States. **Alitalia,** as the most visible airline in Italy, has made special efforts to make its planes, public areas, rest rooms, and access ramps as wheelchair-friendly as possible.

Before you go, there are several agencies that can provide advance-planning information. One is the **Travel Information Service of Philadelphia's Industrial Rehab Program** (☎ **215/456-9600,** or 215/456-9602 for TTY), which provides information to telephone callers only.

You may want to consider joining a tour for visitors with disabilities. For the names and addresses of operators offering such tours—as well as other miscellaneous travel information—contact the **Society for the Advancement of Travel for the Handicapped,** 347 Fifth Ave., Suite 610, New York, NY 10016 (☎ **212/ 447-7284**). Annual membership dues are $45, or $30 for senior citizens and students.

You can also obtain a copy of *Air Transportation of Handicapped Persons,* published by the U.S. Department of Transportation. It's free if you write to **Free Advisory Circular No. AC12032,** Distribution Unit, U.S. Department of Transportation, Publications Division, M-4332, Washington, DC 20590.

Another good organization is **Flying Wheels Travel,** 143 W. Bridge (P.O. Box 382), Owatona, MN 55060 (☎ **800/525-6790**), which offers various escorted tours, cruises, and private tours all over the world for persons with disabilities.

For a $25 annual fee, **Mobility International USA,** P.O. Box 10767, Eugene, OR 97440 (☎ **541/343-1284** voice and TDD; fax 541/343-6182), provides members with information on various destinations and also offers discounts on videos, publications, and programs it sponsors.

For the blind or visually impaired, the best information source is the **American Foundation for the Blind,** 15 W. 16th St., New York, NY 10011 (☎ **800/ 232-5463** in the U.S., or 212/502-7600). It offers information on travel and various requirements for the transport and border formalities for seeing-eye dogs. It also issues identification cards to those who are legally blind.

Tips for British Travelers with Disabilities   The **Royal Association for Disability and Rehabilitation (RADAR),** Unit 12, City Forum, 250 City Rd., London ECIV 8AF (☎ **0171/250-3222**), publishes three holiday "fact packs," which sell for £2 each or £5 for the set of all three. The first one provides general information, including planning and booking a holiday, insurance, finances, and useful organization and holiday providers. The second outlines transport and equipment, transportation available when going abroad, and equipment for rent. The third deals with specialized accommodations.

Another good resource is **Holiday Care Service,** Imperial Building, 2nd Floor, Victoria Road, Horley, Surrey RH6 7PZ (☎ **01293/774-535;** fax 01293/ 784-647), a national charity that advises on accessible accommodations for the elderly and persons with disabilities. Annual membership costs £30. Once a member, one can receive a newsletter and access to a free reservation service offering discounted rates for hotels throughout the world.

FOR GAYS & LESBIANS   Since 1861 Italy has had liberal legislation regarding gay rights, but that doesn't mean that this Catholic country has always looked favorably on homosexuality. Homosexuality is much more accepted in the north than in the south, especially in Sicily, although Taormina has long been a gay Mecca. However, all major towns and cities have an active gay life, especially Florence, Rome, and Milan, which considers itself the "gay capital" of Italy and is the headquarters of ARCI Gay, the country's leading gay organization with branches throughout Italy. Capri is the gay resort of Italy, rivaled only by the gay beaches of Venice.

In the year 2000, Rome will serve as the site for the first ever World Pride. This historic event will take place from June 28 to July 9, and honor gays, lesbians, bisexuals, and transgender peoples from throughout the world and focus on international gay civil rights. A host of art exhibit, gay and lesbian performances, and cultural and political events will take place throughout the 12-day period, culminating in a mass demonstration in downtown Rome on Saturday, July 8.

Men can order **Spartacus,** the international gay guide, for $33 from Giovanni's Room, 1145 Pine St., Philadelphia, PA 19107 (☎ **215/923-2960**) and other gay and lesbian bookstores around the country. Both lesbians and gay men also might want to pick up a copy of **Gay Travel A to Z** ($16).

Our World, 1104 N. Nova Rd., Suite 251, Daytona Beach, FL 32117 (☎ **904/441-5367;** fax 904/441-5604), is a magazine devoted to options and bargains for gay and lesbian travel worldwide. It costs $35 for 10 issues. **Out and About,** 8 W. 19th St., Suite 401, New York, NY 10011 (☎ **800/929-2268;** fax 800/929-2215), has been hailed for its "straight" reporting about gay travel. It profiles the best gay and gay-friendly hotels, gyms, clubs, and other places, with coverage of destinations throughout the world. Its cost is $49 a year for 10 information-packed issues. It aims for the more upscale gay traveler, and has been praised by everybody from *Travel & Leisure* to the *New York Times*. Both of these publications are also available at most gay and lesbian bookstores. The **International Gay Travel Association (IGTA),** 4331 N. Federal, Suite 304, Fort Lauderdale, FL 33308 (☎ **800/448-8550** for voicemail, or 954/776-2626), encourages gay and lesbian travel worldwide. With around 1,200 member travel agencies, it specializes in networking travelers with the appropriate gay-friendly service organization or tour specialist. It offers a quarterly newsletter, marketing mailings, and a membership directory that's updated four times a year.

FOR SENIORS   Many senior discounts are available, but note that some may require membership in a particular association.

For information before you go, write for a free booklet called "101 Tips for the Mature Traveler," available from **Grand Circle Travel,** 347 Congress St., Suite 3A, Boston, MA 02210 (☎ **800/221-2610,** or 617/350-6206).

SAGA International Holidays, 222 Berkeley St., Boston, MA 02116 (☎ **800/343-0273** in the U.S.; fax 617/375-5951), runs all-inclusive tours for seniors, preferably for those 50 and over.

In the United States, the best organization to belong to is the **American Association of Retired Persons (AARP),** 601 E St. NW, Washington, DC 20049 (☎ **202/434-AARP**). Members are offered discounts on car rentals, hotels, and airfares.

Information is also available from the **National Council of Senior Citizens,** 8403 Colesville Road, Suite 1200, Silver Spring, MD 20910 (☎ **301/578-8800**), which charges $13 per person or per couple, for which you receive a bimonthly magazine, part of which is devoted to travel tips. Reduced discounts on hotel and auto rentals are also offered.

Mature Outlook, P.O. Box 9390, Des Moines, IA 50306-9519 (☎ **800/ 336-6330;** fax 515/252-7855), is a travel organization for people over 50. Members are offered discounts at ITC-member hotels and a bimonthly magazine. The $15 to $20 annual membership fee entitles members to coupons for discounts at Sears, Roebuck & Co. Savings are also offered on selected auto rentals and restaurants.

Tips for British Seniors   Wasteels, Victoria Station, opposite Platform 2, London SW1V 1JZ (☎ **0171/834-6744**), currently provides an over-60s **Rail Europe Senior Card** that offers discounts ranging from 25% to 40% off regular second-class fares. Keep in mind, however, that discounts depend on the time of day and year and even the type of train. Its price is £5 to any British person with government-issued proof of his or her age. To qualify, British residents must present a valid British Senior Citizen rail card, which you can get for £16, along with proof of age and British residency, at any BritRail office.

FOR SINGLES   Unfortunately for the 85 million single Americans, the travel industry is far more geared toward couples, and singles often wind up paying the penalty. It pays to travel with someone, and one company that resolves this problem is **Travel Companion Exchange,** which matches single travelers with like-minded companions. It's headed by Jens Jurgen, who charges $99 for a 6-month listing in his well-publicized records. People seeking travel companions fill out forms stating their preferences and needs and receive a minilisting of potential travel partners. A bimonthly newsletter averaging 46 large pages also gives numerous money-saving travel tips of special interest to solo travelers. A sample copy is available for $5.

For an application and more information, contact Jens Jurgen, Travel Companion, P.O. Box P-833, Amityville, NY 11701 (☎ **516/454-0880**).

Another agency to check is **Grand Circle Travel,** 347 Congress St., Suite 3A, Boston, MA 02210 (☎ **800/221-2610** in the U.S., or 617/350-7500; fax 617/350-3206), which offers escorted tours and cruises for retired people, including singles.

Since single supplements on tours can be rather hefty, some tour companies will arrange for you to share a room with another single traveler of the same gender. One such company that offers a "guaranteed-share plan" is **Globus/Cosmos** (☎ **800/221-0090**). Book through your travel agent or call directly.

Tips for British Singles   Single people sometimes feel comfortable traveling with groups composed mostly of other singles. One tour operator whose groups are usually at least 50% unattached persons is **Explore World-wide Ltd.,** 1 Frederick St., Aldershot, Hampshire GU11 1LQ (☎ **01252/344-161**). Groups rarely include more than 20 participants, and children under 14 are not allowed.

FOR FAMILIES   *Family Travel Times* is published 10 times a year by **TWYCH, Travel with Your Children,** and includes a weekly call-in service for subscribers. Subscriptions cost $40 a year and can be ordered by writing to TWYCH, 40 Fifth Ave., New York, NY 10011 (☎ **212/477-5524;** fax 212/477-5173). An information packet, including a sample newsletter, is available for $2.

Families Welcome!, 4711 Hope Valley Rd., Suite 4B, Durham, NC 27705 (☎ **800/326-0724** in the U.S., or 919/489-2555), a travel company specializing in worry-free vacations for families, offers "City Kids" packages to Rome, featuring accommodations in family-friendly hotels or apartments. Some hotels include a second room for children free or at a reduced rate during certain time periods. Packages can include car rentals, train and ferry passes, and special air prices, and are individually designed for each family. A welcome kit is distributed, containing "insider's information" for families traveling in Rome—reliable baby-sitters, where to buy diapers, restaurants that are good to visit with children, and similar advice.

Tips for British Families   The best deals for families are often package tours put together by some of the giants of the British travel industry. Foremost among these is **Thomsons Tour Operators**. Through its subsidiary, **Skytours** (☎ **0171/387-9321**), it offers dozens of air/land packages to Italy where a designated number of airline seats are reserved for the free use of children under 18 who accompany their parents. To qualify, parents must book airfare and hotel accommodations lasting two weeks or more, and book as far in advance as possible. Savings for families with children can be substantial.

FOR STUDENTS   **Council Travel Service (CTS)** (a subsidiary of the Council on International Educational Exchange) is America's largest student, youth, and budget travel group, with more than 60 offices worldwide. The main office is at 205 E. 42nd St., New York, NY 10017 (☎ **800/226-8624** in the U.S. to find your local branch, or 212/822-2700; **www.ciee.org/travel/index**). Council Travel can issue International Student Identity Cards (ISIC), available to all bona fide students for $19, which entitle holders to generous travel and other discounts. These cards also provide holders with a basic health and life insurance plan and a 24-hour help line. If you're no longer a student but are still under 25, you can get a GO 25 card, which will get you the insurance and some of the discounts as well (but not student admission prices in museums). CTS also sells Eurail and YHA (Youth Hostel Association) passes and can book hostel or hotel accommodations. The CTS in the United Kingdom is at 28A Poland St. (Oxford Circus), London W1V 3DB

(☎ **0171/437-7767**). CTS's Italy office is in Rome, near the train station, at Via Genova 16, 00184 Roma (☎ **06/46791**). In Canada, **Travel CUTS,** 187 College St., Toronto, Ont. M5T 1P7 (☎ **416/798-2887**), offers similar services.

The **International Youth Hostel Federation (IYHF)** was designed to provide bare-bones overnight accommodations for serious budget-conscious travelers. For information, contact **Hostelling International/American Youth Hostels (HI-AYH),** 733 15th St. NW, Suite 840, Washington, DC 20005 (☎ **202/ 783-6161**). Membership costs $25 annually; it's $10 for children 17 and under, and $15 for seniors 54 and over.

Tips for British Students   The British equivalent of Council Travel is **Campus Travel,** 52 Grosvenor Gardens, London SW1W 0AG (☎ **0171/730-3402**), which provides a wealth of information and offers for the student traveler, ranging from route planning to flight insurance, including railcards. It also sells the International Student Identity Card (ISIC) for £5. See the description under Council Travel, above, for details.

Youth hostels are the place to stay if you're a student. You'll need an International Youth Hostels Association card, which you can purchase from the youth hostel store at **Covent Garden,** 14 Southampton St., London WC23 7HY (☎ **0171/ 836-1036**), or from **Campus Travel** (☎ **0171/730-3402**). More information on membership is available from the **Youth Hostels Association of England and Wales (YHA),** 8 St. Stephen's Hill, St. Albans, Hertfordshire AL1 2DY (☎ **01727/855-215**).

The Youth Hostel Association puts together *The Hostelling International Budget Guide,* listing every youth hostel in 31 European countries. It costs £6.99 at the Southampton Street store in London (see above). Add 61p postage for delivery within the United Kingdom.

7 Getting There

BY PLANE

"All roads lead to Rome" in ways the emperors never dreamed of. But of all the ways to reach Rome, especially from overseas, the airplane is the best . . . and the cheapest.

If you're already in Europe, you'll have an easy time booking a flight to Rome. Alitalia flies to all the major capitals of Europe, while each of the national carriers of the various countries (such as Air France, British Airways, and Lufthansa) flies to Rome and/or Milan. However, for Americans and Canadians, it's sometimes expensive to book these flights once you're in Europe; it's cheaper to have Rome or Milan written into your ticket when you first book your flight to Europe from North America.

THE MAJOR AIRLINES

Specific upheavals that shook the airline industry during the early 1990s have subsided a bit as of this writing. Despite the relative calm, the industry may still undergo some changes during the life of this edition. For last-minute conditions, including a list of the carriers that fly to Rome, check with a travel agent or the individual airlines. Here's a rundown on the current status:

From North America   American Airlines (☎ **800/433-7300** in the U.S.; **www.americanair.com**) was among the first North America–based carriers to fly into Italy. From Chicago's O'Hare Airport, American flies nonstop every evening to Milan, where there are frequent connections into Rome. Flights from all parts of American's vast network fly regularly into Chicago.

TWA (☎ **800/221-2000** in the U.S.; **www.twa.com**) offers daily nonstop flights from New York's JFK to both Rome and Milan. Because of the frequency of flights, it's often convenient and cost-effective to fly into Rome and depart from Milan, or vice versa, depending on your travel plans.

Delta (☎ **800/241-4141** in the U.S.; **www.delta-air.com**) flies from New York's JFK to both Milan and Rome. Flights depart every evening for both destinations, with fine links to the rest of Delta's network of domestic and international destinations. In midwinter, service might be reduced to six flights a week.

United Airlines (☎ **800/538-2929; www.ual.com**) has service to Milan only from Dulles Airport in Washington, DC.

US Airways (☎ **800/428-4322; www.usairways.com**) offers one flight daily to Rome out of Philadelphia (you can connect through Philly from most major U.S. cities).

Continental (☎ **800/231-0856; www.flycontinental.com**) flies twice daily to Rome from its hub in Newark, NJ.

For anyone interested in combining a trip to Italy with a stopover in, say, Britain or Germany along the way, there are sometimes attractive deals offered by **British Airways** (☎ **800/AIRWAYS** in the U.S.; **www.british-airways.com**) and **Lufthansa** (☎ **800/645-3880** in the U.S.; **www.lufthansa-usa.com**).

Canadian Airlines International (☎ **800/426-7000** in the U.S.; **www.cdnair.ca/**) flies daily from Toronto to Rome. Two of the flights are nonstop, whereas others touch down en route in either Montréal or Milan.

One well-known Italian specialist, **Alitalia** (☎ **800/223-5730** in the U.S.; **www.alitalia.it/english/index.html**), flies nonstop to both Rome and Milan from several American cities, including New York's JFK, Boston, Chicago, Los Angeles, and Miami.

Be aware that Alitalia's (and most other airlines') cheapest tickets are nonrefundable. Alitalia's sole exception to this rule is in the event of your hospitalization or the death of someone in your immediate family. Fares are higher for weekend (Friday to Sunday) travel.

From Great Britain   Both British Airways (☎ **0181/897-4000** in London) and **Alitalia** (☎ **0181/745-8200** in London) have frequent flights from London's Heathrow Airport to Rome, Milan, Venice, Pisa (the gateway to Florence), and Naples. Flying time from London to these cities is anywhere from 2 to 3 hours. British Airways also has one direct flight a day from Manchester to Rome.

REGULAR FARES

Most of the major airlines that fly to Rome charge approximately the same fare, but if a price war should break out over the Atlantic (and these are almost always brewing over the most popular routes), fares could change overnight.

The key to getting a budget ticket is "advance booking." The number of seats allocated to low-cost "advance-purchase" fares is severely limited (sometimes to less than 25% of the capacity of a particular plane), so you have to make your reservations early to book a low-cost seat.

CyberDeals for Net Surfers

It's possible to get some great deals on airfare, hotels, and car rentals via the Internet. So go grab your mouse and start surfing—you could save a bundle on your trip. The Web sites highlighted below are worth checking out, especially since all services are free (but don't forget that time is money when you're online).

Microsoft Expedia (www.expedia.com)   The best part of this multipurpose travel site is the "Fare Tracker": You fill out a form on the screen indicating that you're interested in cheap flights to Rome from your hometown, and, once a week, they'll e-mail you the best airfare deals. The site's "Travel Agent" will steer you to bargains on hotels and car rentals, and you can book everything, including flights, right online.

Preview Travel (www.reservations.com and www.vacations.com)   Another useful travel site, reservations.com has a "Best Fare Finder," which will search the Apollo computer reservations system for the three lowest fares for any route on any days of the year. Say you want to go from Chicago to Rome and back between December 6 and 13: Just fill out the form on the screen with times, dates, and destinations, and within minutes, Preview will show you the best deals. If you find an airfare you like, you can book your ticket right online—you can even reserve hotels and car rentals on this site. If you're in the preplanning stage, head to Preview's vacations.com site, where you can check out the latest package deals for destinations around the world by clicking on "Hot Deals."

Travelocity (www.travelocity.com)   This is one of the best travel sites out there. In addition to its "Personal Fare Watcher," which notifies you via e-mail of the lowest airfares for up to five different destinations, Travelocity will track, in minutes, the three lowest fares for any routes on any dates. You can book a flight right then and there, and if you need a rental car or hotel, Travelocity will find you the best deal via the SABRE computer reservations system (a huge database used by travel agents worldwide). Click on "Last Minute Deals" for the latest travel bargains.

Trip.Com (www.thetrip.com)   This site is really geared toward the business traveler, but vacationers-to-be can also use Trip.Com's valuable fare-finding engine, which will e-mail you every week with the best city-to-city airfare deals on your selected route or routes.

Priceline (www.priceline.com)   This buying service lets you name the price you want to pay for your flight and then tries to find a major airline willing to release seats on flights at your price. The more "reasonable" your offer (in other

A large number of discounts are also available for passengers who can travel either midweek or midwinter in either direction. High season on most airlines' routes to Rome usually stretches from June 1 until September 15 (this could vary), and it's both the most expensive and most crowded time to travel.

All the major carriers offer an **APEX (advance-purchase excursion)** ticket, which is generally their cheapest transatlantic option. Usually such a ticket must be purchased between 14 and 21 days in advance and a stopover in Italy must last at least 7 days but not more than 30 days. Changing the date of departure from North America within 21 days of departure will sometimes entail a penalty of around $150 with some APEX tickets, whereas with others no changes of any kind are permitted.

words, the more you're willing to pay) the more likely it is that Priceline will be able to find you a ticket. This service is available only to those flying from the U.S. or Puerto Rico.

Discount Tickets (www.discount-tickets.com)   Operated by the **ETN (European Travel Network)**, this site offers discounts on airfares, accommodations, car rentals, and tours. It deals in flights between the U.S. and other countries.

E-Savers Programs   Several major airlines offer a free e-mail service known as **E-Savers,** via which they'll send you their best bargain airfares on a weekly basis. Here's how it works: Once a week (usually Wednesday), subscribers receive a list of discounted flights to and from various destinations, both international and domestic. Now here's the catch: These fares are available only if you leave the very next Saturday (or sometimes Friday night) and return the following Monday or Tuesday. It's really a service for the spontaneously inclined and travelers looking for a quick getaway, but the fares are cheap, so it's worth taking a look. If you have a preference for certain airlines (in other words, the ones you fly most frequently), sign up with them first. Another caveat: You'll get frequent-flier miles if you purchase one of these fares, but you can't use miles to buy the ticket.

You can sign up for e-savers at the Web site addresses at the beginning of the "Getting There" section. Or check out another good Web site, **Epicurious Travel (travel.epicurious.com)**, which allows you to sign up for all these airline e-mail lists at once. If you'd like to receive e-mail that *only* concerns flights leaving from your hometown, sign on with **Smarter living (www.smarterliving.com)**, a free service that compiles weekend special fares from 19 airlines in about 30 North American cities.

Other sites maintained by travel services and agencies offer basically the same service as the airline sites, but on a wider scale. **Travel (www.travel.com)** allows you to search travel destinations to decide on that perfect vacation and has links to travel agencies all over the world and in all 50 states.

Moment's Notice (www.moments-notice.com) is a bargain hunter's dream. Many of the deals, which are updated each morning, are snapped up by the end of the day. A drawback is that many of these vacations require you to drop everything and go almost immediately.

Hotel Reservations Network (www.180096hotel.com) offers budget reservations at prestigious hotels all over the world, with many accommodations up to 65% off. Bookings can be made online.

A more flexible (but more expensive) option is the regular economy fare. This offers the same seating and the same services offered to passengers using an excursion ticket, but doesn't require the 7-day minimum stay that the APEX ticket does. One of the most attractive benefits of a regular economy-class ticket is the absolute freedom granted to a passenger (if space is available) regarding last-minute changes in flight dates.

OTHER GOOD-VALUE CHOICES

Alitalia clusters the price of tickets to its destinations in Italy into four different zones, each centered around a major city—Milan, Rome, Naples, and Palermo. If you intend to fly from North America to local airports at, say, Genoa, Venice, Rimini, or any of the towns of Sardinia or Sicily, you can add on a connecting flight from the main airport of that region to a secondary airport within the same region without any additional charge. (Alitalia calls these "common-rated" fares, meaning that it costs no more to fly to Venice from New York than it would have cost to fly to Milan from New York). Considering the distance between Milan and Venice, or the distance from Rome to Pisa or Florence, and the extra expense you'd have encountered on the train or highway, it's an attractive offer.

And for students, or anyone aged 12 to 24, special extensions are granted on the length of time they can stay abroad. Alitalia's youth fare permits a stay abroad for up to 1 year. The round-trip high-season fare from New York to Rome is currently $1,008. With the year-long validity of the return half of the ticket, a North American student could, say, complete two full semesters at the University of Bologna and still fly home at a substantial savings over equivalent fares on some other airlines.

CONSOLIDATORS   Tickets at consolidators (sometimes called "bucket shops") are frequently—but not always—up to 35% less than the full fare. Terms of payment can vary—anywhere from 45 days prior to departure to last-minute sales offered in a final attempt by an airline to fill an empty aircraft.

Since dealing with unknown consolidators might be a little risky, it's wise to call the Better Business Bureau in your area to see whether complaints have been filed against the company from which you plan to purchase a ticket. You can often locate consolidators by ads in small boxes at the bottom of the page in your newspaper's Sunday travel section, but here are a few listings to get you started:

In New York, try **TFI Tours International,** 34 W. 32nd St., 12th Floor, New York, NY 10001 (☎ **800/745-8000** in the U.S. outside New York State, or 212/736-1140 in New York State). This tour company offers services to 177 cities worldwide, including Rome.

For the Midwest, explore the possibilities of **Travel Avenue,** 10 S. Riverside Plaza, Suite 1404, Chicago, IL 60606 (☎ **800/333-3335** in the U.S.). Its tickets are often cheaper than at most consolidators, and it charges the customer only a $25 fee on international tickets, rather than taking the usual 10% commission from an airline. Travel Avenue rebates most of that commission back to the customers—hence, the lower fares.

Another possibility is **TMI (Travel Management International),** 3617 Dupont Ave. South, Minneapolis, MN 55409 (☎ **800/245-3672** in the U.S.), which offers a wide variety of discounts, including youth fares, student fares, and access to other kinds of air-related discounts as well.

One of the biggest U.S. consolidators is **Travac,** 989 Ave. of the Americas, New York, NY 10018 (☎ **800/TRAV-800** in the U.S., or 212/563-3303), which offers discounted seats from the United States to most cities in Europe, including Rome, on airlines such as TWA, United, and Delta. Another branch office is at 2601 E. Jefferson St., Orlando, FL 32803 (☎ **407/896-0014**).

UniTravel, 1137 Administration Dr., Suite 120, St. Louis, MO 63146 (☎ **800/325-2222** in the U.S.), offers tickets to Rome and elsewhere in Europe at prices that may or may not be lower than the regular fare, but it can provide discounts if you decide (or need) to get to Europe on short notice.

Another option, suitable only for clients with supremely flexible travel plans, is **Airhitch,** 2641 Broadway, 3rd Floor, New York, NY 10025 (☎ **800/864-2000**). You provide any 5 consecutive days in which you're available to fly and Airhitch agrees to find you a flight within those 5 days from a particular region in the

United States (the Northeast, Southeast, Midwest, West Coast, or Northwest). It will attempt to fly you to and from the city of your choice, but makes no guarantees. One-way fares range from $169 to $269.

One final name for our list is **1-800-FLY-4-LESS.** Even if you're unable to buy tickets 3 weeks in advance, you can still use this service to obtain low discounted fares. 1-800-FLY-4-LESS specializes in finding only the lowest fares.

CHARTER FLIGHTS   There's no way to predict whether a proposed flight to Rome will cost less on a charter or less through a bucket shop. You'll have to investigate at the time of your trip.

Some charter companies have proved unreliable in the past. Among the reliable charter-flight operators is **Council Charter,** 205 E. 42nd St., New York, NY 10017 (☎ **800/COUNCIL** in the U.S., or 212/822-2900). This company, run by the Council on International Educational Exchange, can arrange charter seats on regularly scheduled aircraft to most major European cities.

One of the biggest New York charter operators is **Travac,** (see the "Consolidators" section, above, for contact information).

TRAVEL CLUBS   Another possibility for low-cost air travel is the travel club, which supplies an unsold inventory of tickets, offering discounts in the usual range of 20% to 60%.

After you pay an annual fee, you're given a hot line number to call to find out what discounts are available. Many of these discounts become available several days in advance of actual departure, sometimes as long as a week and sometimes as much as a month. Of course, you're limited to what's available, so you have to be fairly flexible.

Some of the best clubs are:

Moment's Notice, 7301 New Utrecht Ave., New York, NY 11228 (☎ **212/486-0500; www.moments-notice.com**), charges $25 per year for membership, which allows spur-of-the-moment participation in dozens of tours. Each is geared to impulse purchases and last-minute getaways, and each offers air and land packages that sometimes represent a substantial savings over what you'd have paid through more conventional channels. Although membership is required for participation in the tours, anyone can call the company's hot line (☎ **212/873-0908**) to learn what options are available. Most of the company's best-valued tours depart from New Jersey's Newark airport.

Travelers Advantage, 3033 S. Parker Rd., Suite 900, Aurora, CO 80014 (☎ **800/548-1116** in the U.S.), offers members, for $49, a catalog (issued four times a year), maps, discounts at select hotels, and a limited guarantee that equivalent packages will not be undersold by any other travel organization. It also offers a 5% rebate on the value of all airline tickets, tours, hotels, and car rentals purchased through the company. (To collect this rebate, you must fill out some forms and photocopy your receipts and itineraries.)

Encore Travel Club, 4501 Forbes Blvd., Lanham, MD 20706 (☎ **800/638-8976** in the U.S.), charges $60 a year for membership in a club that offers 50% discounts at more than 4,000 well-recognized hotels, sometimes during off-peak periods. It also offers substantial discounts on airfares, cruises, and car rentals through its volume-purchase plans. Membership includes a travel package outlining the company's many services and use of a toll-free phone number for advice and information.

A Note for British Travelers   A regular fare from the U.K. to Rome is extremely high, so savvy Brits usually call a travel agent for a "deal"—either a charter flight or some special air travel promotion. If one is not possible for you, then an APEX ticket might be the way to keep costs trimmed. These tickets must be reserved in advance, but they offer a discount without the usual booking restrictions. You might also ask the airlines about a **"Eurobudget ticket,"** which has restrictions or length-of-stay requirements.

British newspapers are always full of classified advertisements touting "slashed" fares to Rome. One good source is *Time Out* magazine. London's *Evening Standard* has a daily travel section, and the Sunday editions of almost any newspaper will run many ads. Recommended companies include **Trailfinders** (☎ **0171/937-5400**), which offers access to tickets on such carriers as SAS, British Airways, and KLM.

In London, there are many **bucket shops** around Victoria and Earl's Court that offer low fares. Make sure that the company you deal with is a member of the IATA, ABTA, or ATOL. These umbrella organizations will help you out if anything goes wrong.

CEEFAX, a British television information service included on many home and hotel TVs, runs details of package holidays and flights to Europe, including Rome. Just switch to your CEEFAX channel and you'll find a menu of listings that includes travel information.

BY TRAIN

If you plan to travel heavily on the European and/or British railroads, you'll do well to secure the latest copy of the ***Thomas Cook European Timetable of Railroads.*** This comprehensive, 500+-page timetable documents all of Europe's mainline passenger rail services with detail and accuracy. It's available exclusively in North America from **Forsyth Travel Library,** 226 Westchester Ave., White Plains, NY 10604 (☎ **800/FORSYTH**), at a cost of $28 plus $5 postage (priority airmail in the U.S.; U.S. $5 for shipments to Canada).

Train from the U.K.   Many different rail passes are available in the U.K. for travel in Europe. Stop in at the **International Rail Centre,** Victoria Station, London SW1V 1JY (☎ **0171/834-2345** or 0990/848-848 in the U.K.), or **Wasteels,** 121 Wilton Rd., London SW1V 1JZ (☎ **0171/834-6744**). They can help you find the best option for the trip you're planning. Some of the most popular passes, such as the Eurail Youth Pass, are only for travelers under 26 years of age, entitling them to unlimited second-class travel in 26 European countries.

EURAILPASS   Many travelers to Europe take advantage of one of its greatest travel bargains, the **Eurailpass,** which permits unlimited first-class rail travel in any country in Western Europe except the British Isles, and also includes Hungary in Eastern Europe. Oddly, it does *not* include travel on the rail lines of Sardinia, which are organized independently of the rail lines of the rest of Italy. Passes are for periods as short as 15 days or as long as 3 months.

Here's how it works: The pass is sold only in North America. Adults can purchase a pass for unlimited first-class travel lasting 15 days for $538, 21 days for $698, 1 month for $864, 2 months for $1,224, or 3 months for $1,512. Children under 4 travel free providing they don't occupy a seat (otherwise, they're charged half fare); children under 12 travel for half fare. If you're under 26, you can purchase a **Eurail Youthpass,** which entitles you to unlimited second-class travel for 15 days for $376, 1 month for $605, or 2 months for $857.

Travel agents in all towns, and railway agents in such major cities as New York, Montréal, and Los Angeles, sell all these tickets. A Eurailpass is available at the North American offices of CIT Travel Service, the French National Railroads, the German Federal Railroads, and the Swiss Federal Railways.

The **Eurail Saverpass** is a money-saving ticket for groups (three or more people traveling together between April and September; two or more people between October and March). The price of a Saverpass, valid all over Europe, good for first class only, is $458 per person for 15 days, $594 per person for 21 days, and $734 per person for 1 month. Even more freedom is offered by the **Saver Flexipass,** which is similar to the Eurail Saverpass, except that you are not confined to consecutive-day travel. For travel over any 10 days in 2 months, the fare is $540; for any 15 days in 2 months, the fare is $710.

The **Eurail Flexipass** allows passengers to visit Europe with more flexibility. For adults, it's valid in first class and provides a number of individual travel days that can be used over a much longer period of time. That makes it possible to stay in one city and yet not lose a single day of travel. There are two passes: 10 days of travel within 2 months for $634, and 15 days of travel within 2 months for $836. For those under age 26, the **Youth Flexipass,** which operates the same way but in second class, offers 10 days within 2 months for $444 and 15 days within 2 months for $585.

Bonuses with any of the passes include discounted Eurostar fares, free or discounted fares on selected ferries, lake steamers, boats, and buses.

Travel agents or national rail offices of European countries can provide further details. General brochures are available by contacting **Rail Europe,** 500 Mamaroneck Ave., Suite 314, Harrison, NY 10528 (☎ **800/4-EURAIL**).

BY CAR

If you're already on the Continent, particularly in a neighboring country such as France or Austria, you may want to drive to Rome. However, arrange this in advance with your car-rental company.

It's also possible to drive from London to Rome, a distance of 1,124 miles via Calais/Boulogne/Dunkirk or 1,085 miles via Oostende/Zeebrugge, not counting Channel crossings. You can cross over from England to France using either one of the ferries or the Chunnel. Once you arrive on the northern coast of France by whatever mode of transport you selected, you still face a 24-hour drive to Rome. Most drivers play it safe and budget a leisurely 3 days for the journey.

Most of the roads from Western Europe leading into Italy are toll free, with some notable exceptions. If you use the Swiss superhighway network, you'll have to purchase a special tax sticker at the frontier. You'll also pay to go through the St. Gotthard Tunnel into Italy. Crossings from France are through the Mont Blanc Tunnel, for which you'll pay, or you can leave the French Riviera at Menton (France) and drive directly into Italy along the Italian Riviera heading toward San Remo.

If you don't want to drive such distances, ask a travel agent to book you on a Motorail arrangement where the train carries your car. This service, however, is good only to Milan, as there are no car-and-sleeper expresses running the 390 or so miles south to Rome.

ORGANIZED TOURS

Although a sampling of the best-rated tour companies follows, you should consult a good travel agent for advice.

Of the many different operators eager for a share of your business, one that meets with consistent approval from participants is **Perillo Tours,** 577 Chestnut Ridge Rd., Woodcliff Lake, NJ 07675-9888 (☎ **800/431-1515** in the U.S. or 201/307-1234; **www.perillotours.com**), family operated for three generations. Since it was established in 1945, it has sent more than a million travelers to Italy.

Perillo tours cost much less than you would spend if you arranged a comparable trip yourself. Accommodations are in first-class hotels, and guides tend to be well qualified, well informed, and sensitive to the needs of tour participants.

Perillo operates hundreds of departures year round. Between April and October, nine different itineraries, ranging from 8 to 15 days each, cover broadly different regions of the peninsula. Between November and April, the "Off-Season Italy" tour covers three of Italy's premier cities during a season when they're likely to be less crowded with tourists.

Another contender for the package-tour business in Italy is **Italiatour,** a company of the Alitalia Group (☎ **800/845-3365** or 212/765-2183; **www. italiatour.com**), which offers a wide variety of tours through all parts of the peninsula. It specializes in tours for independent travelers who ride from one destination to another by train or rental car. In most cases the company sells prereserved hotel accommodations, which usually cost less than what you'd pay if you had made the reservations yourself. Because of the company's close link with Alitalia, the prices quoted for air passage are sometimes among the most reasonable on the retail market.

Trafalgar Tours, 11 E. 26th St., New York, NY 10010 (☎ **800/854-0103; www.trafalgartours.com**), is one of Europe's largest tour operators. It offers cost-conscious packages with lodgings in unpretentious hotels. The 14-day "Best of Italy" tour begins and ends in Rome, with five stops including Sorrento, Venice, and Florence. Some meals and twin-bed accommodations in first-class hotels are part of the package. The 12-day "Bellissimo" tour also begins and ends in Rome and includes the Isle of Capri, Assisi, Venice, and Montecatini. Check with your travel agent for more information on these tours. Trafalgar only takes calls from agents.

One of Trafalgar's leading competitors, known for offering roughly equivalent, cost-conscious tours, is **Globus/Cosmos Tours,** 5301 S. Federal Circle, Littleton, CO 80123-2980 (☎ **800/221-0090; www.globusandcosmos.com**). Globus offers first-class escorted coach tours of various regions of Italy, lasting from 8 to 16 days. Cosmos, a budget branch of Globus, sells escorted tours of about the same length. Tours must be booked through a travel agent, but you can call the 800 number for brochures. Other competitors are **Insight International Tours,** 745 Atlantic Ave., #720, Boston, MA 02111 (☎ **800/582-8380**), which books superior first-class, fully escorted motorcoach tours lasting from 1 week to a 36-day grand tour of Italy, and **Tauck Tours,** P.O. Box 5027, Westport, CT 06881 (☎ **800/468-2825**).

Finally, **Abercrombie & Kent,** 1520 Kensington Rd., Oak Brook, IL 60523 (☎ **800/323-7308; www.abercrombiekent.com**) and Sloane Square House, Holbein Place, London SW1W 8NS (☎ **0171/730-9600**), offers a medley of luxurious premium packages. Your overnight stays will be in meticulously restored castles and exquisite Italian villas, most of which are four- and five-star accommodations. Several trips are offered, including tours of the Lake Garda region and the southern territory of Calabria.

Getting to Know Rome

3

This chapter will provide what you need to know to settle into Rome, from arriving at the airport and the basic city layout to driving rules and how to use the buses. There's a quick breakdown of neighborhoods to help you figure out where you'll want to base yourself, and that will help organize and orient all the hotels, restaurants, and sights in the following chapters. We'll round it off with a list of "Fast Facts"—everything from embassies and English-speaking doctors to how to tip people and make a phone call.

1 Orientation

ARRIVING

BY PLANE Chances are that you'll arrive in Italy at Rome's **Leonardo da Vinci International Airport** (☎ **06/65951,** or 06/65953640 for information), popularly known as Fiumicino, 18½ miles from the center of the capital. (If you're flying by charter, you might arrive at Ciampino Airport; see below.)

After leaving Passport Control, two information desks—one for Rome, one for Italy—come into view. Call ☎ **06/65956074** for information. At the Rome desk you can pick up a general (not a detailed) map and some pamphlets Monday to Saturday from 8:30am to 7pm. This desk will also make hotel reservations for you in the price range of your choice. A *cambio* (currency exchange) operates daily from 7:30am to 11pm. Luggage storage, in the main arrivals building and open daily, costs 5,000L ($2.90) per bag.

To get into the city, follow the signs marked TRENI for the shuttle service directly to the main rail station, Stazione Termini (arriving on Track 22). It runs between 7am and 10pm for 15,000L ($9) one-way. A local train, costing 8,000L ($4.65), runs every hour between the airport and Tiburtina Station, from which you can go the rest of the way to Termini by subway Linea B, costing another 1,000L (60¢).

Should you arrive on a charter flight at **Ciampino** (☎ **06/794941**), take a **Cotral** bus, departing every 30 minutes or so, which will deliver you to the Anagnina stop of Metropolitana (subway) Linea A. Take Linea A to Stazione Termini where your final connections can be made. Trip time is about 45 minutes, and the cost is 2,000L ($1.15).

Rome Orientation

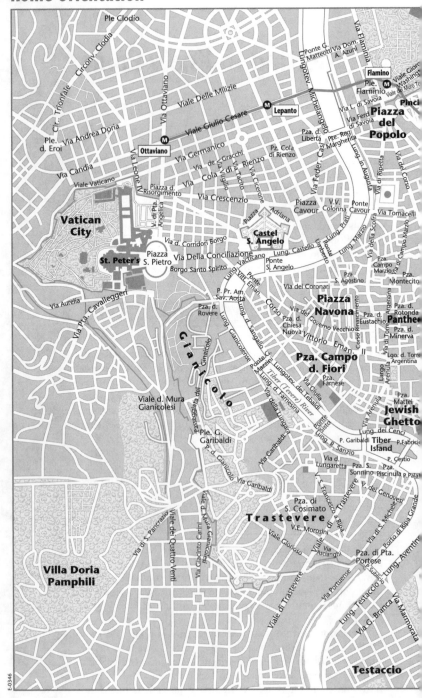

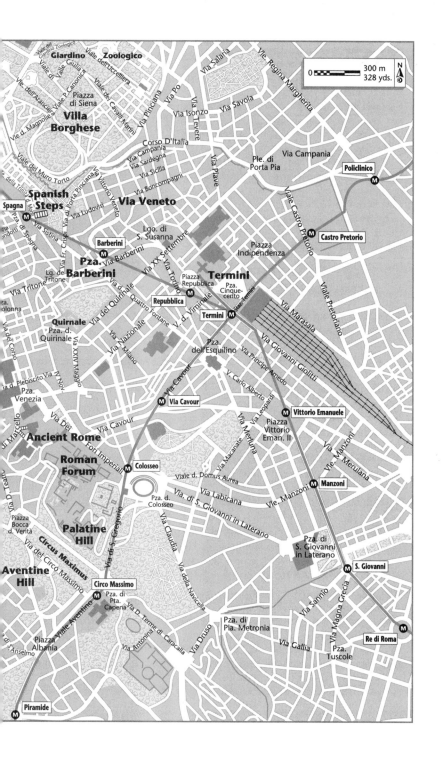

A Few Train Station Warnings

In Stazione Termini, you'll almost certainly be approached by touts claiming to work for a tourist organization. They really work for individual hotels (not always the most recommendable) and will say almost anything to sell you a room. Unless you know something about Rome's layout and are savvy, it's best to ignore them.

Be aware of all your belongings at all times and be sure to keep your wallet and purse away from professionally experienced fingers. Never *ever* leave your bags unattended for even a second, and while making phone calls or waiting in line, make sure your attention doesn't wander from any bags you've set by your side or on the ground. Be aware if someone asks *you* for directions or information—it's meant to distract you and easily will.

Ignore the taxi drivers soliciting passengers right outside the terminal; they can charge unaware travelers as much as triple the normal amount. Instead, line up in the taxi queue in Piazza dei Cinquecento.

Taxis from Fiumicino are quite expensive—70,000L ($41) and up—and therefore not recommended for the trip from the airport. If you arrive at Ciampino, you're closer to the city, only about a half-hour ride, but the fare still averages 70,000L ($41) into the heart of Rome. Call ☎ **06/6645,** 06/3570, or 06/4994 for information.

BY TRAIN   Trains arrive in the center of old Rome at the **Stazione Termini,** Piazza dei Cinquecento (☎ **1478/880-881**), the train and subway transportation hub for all of Rome, surrounded by many, especially cheaper, hotels.

If you're taking the Metropolitana (Rome's subway network), follow the illuminated red M signs. To catch a bus, go straight through the outer hall of the Termini and enter the sprawling bus lot of Piazza dei Cinquecento. You'll also find taxis here (see "Getting Around," later in this chapter, for details on public transportation).

The Termini is filled with services. At a branch of the Banca Nazionale delle Communicazioni (between Tracks 8–11 and Tracks 12–15) you can exchange money. Informazioni Ferroviarie (in the outer hall) dispenses information on rail travel to other parts of Italy. There's also a tourist information booth here, along with baggage services, barbershops, gift shops, restaurants, and bars.

BY BUS   Arrivals are at the **Stazione Termini** (see "By Train," above). Information on buses is dispensed at a booth operated by ATAC (the city bus company) at Piazza dei Cinquecento, which is open daily from 7:30am to 7:30pm. For information, call ☎ **06/46591**.

BY CAR   From the north, the main access route is **A1 (Autostrada del Sole),** cutting through Milan and Florence, or you can take the coastal route, SSI Aurelia, from Genoa. If you're driving north from Naples, you take the southern lap of the **Autostrada del Sole, A2.** All these autostrade join with the **Grande Raccordo Anulare,** a ring road that encircles Rome, channeling traffic into the congested city. Long before you reach this ring road, you should study a map carefully to see which part of Rome you plan to enter and mark your route accordingly. Route markings along the ring road tend to be confusing.

VISITOR INFORMATION

Information that concerns the region of **lazio** (*Latium* in English) which includes Rome and some of the cities that surround it, is available at three well-defined locations maintained by the **Azienda Provinciale di Turismo (APT).** These locations include a kiosk in the city's main railway station, **Stazione Termini** (☎ **06/4871270**), whose facilities are shared by those operated by the Comune di Roma (see below), and a kiosk in the **Fiumicino Airport** (☎ **06/65956074**). The organization's administrative headquarters and an information kiosk are maintained at Via Parigi 5 (☎ **06/48899255**). Each of these kiosks is open Monday to Friday from 8:15am to 7:15pm, and Saturday from 8:15am to 2pm.

More helpful, and more intensely focused on facilities in Rome itself, are the tourist offices maintained by the **Commune di Roma** (City of Rome) in a half-dozen sites throughout central Rome. Identified by red-and-orange or yellow-and-black signs saying COMMUNE DI ROMA—PUNTI DI INFORMAZIONE TURISTICA, all but one are staffed daily from 9am to 6pm. The exception is the largest of the group—the one in the Stazione Termini—which is open daily from 8am to 9pm. Here are their addresses and telephone numbers: in the **Stazione Termini** (☎ **06/68809707**); in **Piazza Pia,** near the Castelo Sant'Angelo (☎ **06/68809707**); in **Piazza San Giovanni in Laterano** (☎ **06/77203535**); on the **Largo Carlo Goldoni** (☎ **06/68136061**), near the intersection of Via del Corso and Via Condotti; on **Via Nazionale** (☎ **06/47824525**), near the Palazzo delle Esposizioni; on **Largo Corrado Ricci**, near the corner of the Via Cavour and the Colosseum (☎ **06/69924307**); and in **Trastevere,** on the Piazza Sonnino (☎ **06/58333457**).

CITY LAYOUT

The drive in to the city is rather uneventful until you pass through the remarkably intact **Great Aurelian Wall,** started in A.D. 271 to calm Rome's barbarian jitters. Suddenly, ruins of imperial baths loom on one side and great monuments can be seen in the middle of blocks. Inside the walls you'll find a city designed for a population that walked to get where it was going. Parts of Rome actually look and feel more like an oversized village than the former imperial capital of the Western world.

The Termini faces a huge piazza, **Piazza dei Cinquecento,** named after 500 Italians who died heroically in a 19th-century battle in Africa.

The bulk of ancient, Renaissance, and baroque Rome (as well as the train station) is on the east side of the **Tiber River (Fiume Tevere),** which meanders through town between 19th-century stone embankments. However, several important monuments are on the other side: **St. Peter's Basilica** and the **Vatican;** the **Castel Sant'Angelo** (formerly the tomb of the emperor Hadrian), and the colorful **Trastevere** neighborhood.

The various quarters of the city are linked by large boulevards (large at least in some places) that have mostly been laid out since the late 19th century. Starting from the **Victor Emmanuel monument,** a highly controversial pile of snow-white Brescian marble, there's a street running practically due north to **Piazza del Popolo** and the city wall. This is **Via del Corso,** one of the main streets of Rome—noisy, congested, always crowded with buses and shoppers, called simply "Il Corso." To its left (west) lie the Pantheon, Piazza Navona, Campo de' Fiori, and the Tiber River. To its right (east) you'll find the Spanish Steps, Trevi Fountain, Borghese Gardens, and Via Veneto. Back at the Vittorio Emanuele monument, the major artery going west (and ultimately across the Tiber to St. Peter's) is **Corso Vittorio Emanuele.** Behind you to your right, heading toward the Colosseum, is **Via dei Fori Imperiali,** laid out in the 1930s by Mussolini to show off the ruins of imperial forums he had excavated that line it on either side. Yet another central conduit is **Via Nazionale,** running from **Piazza Venezia** (just in front of the Vittorio Emmanuel monument) east to **Piazza della Repubblica** (near the Termini). The final lap of Via Nazionale is called Via Quattro Novembre.

FINDING AN ADDRESS Finding an address in Rome can be a problem because of the narrow streets of old Rome and the little, sometimes hidden *piazze* (squares). Numbers usually run consecutively, with odd numbers on one side of the street and even numbers on the other. However, in the old districts the numbers will sometimes run consecutively up one side of the street to the end, then back in the opposite direction on the other side. Therefore, no. 50 could be opposite no. 308.

STREET MAPS Arm yourself with a detailed street map—such as the one included with this guide—rather than the general overview handed out free at tourist offices. You'll need a detailed map even to find such attractions as the Trevi Fountain. Another good choice are **Falk maps,** available at most newsstands. The best selections of maps are sold in bookstores (see "Shopping A to Z" in chapter 8).

TRAFFIC For the 2½ millennia before the modern wide boulevards were built, the citizens had to make their way through narrow byways and curves that defeated all but the best senses of direction. These streets—among the most charming aspects of the city—still exist in large numbers, mostly unspoiled by the advances of modern construction. However, this tangled street plan has one troublesome element: automobiles. The traffic in Rome is awful! When the claustrophobic street plans of the Dark Ages open unexpectedly onto a vast piazza, every driver accelerates full throttle for the distant horizon, while pedestrians flatten themselves against marble fountains for protection or stride with firm jaws right into the thick of the howling traffic.

NEIGHBORHOODS IN BRIEF

Here are the main districts of interest, spiraling roughly out from the ancient center, through the heart of old Rome, and on to some of the more interesting outlying residential areas. This section will give you some idea of where you want to stay and where the major attractions are.

Around Stazione Termini The main train station adjoins Piazza della Repubblica, and for many, this will be your introduction to Rome. Much of the area is seedy and filled with gas fumes from all the buses and cars, but it has been improving. If you stay here, you may not get a lot of atmosphere, but you'll have a lot of affordable options and a very convenient location, near the city's transportation hub and not too far from ancient Rome. There's a lot to see here, including the **Basilica di Santa Maria Maggiore** and the **Baths of Diocletian**. There are some high-class hotels sprinkled in the area, including the **Grand,** but many are long past their heyday.

The neighborhoods on either side of Stazione Termini have improved greatly recently and some streets are now attractive. The best-looking area is ahead and to your right as you exit the station on the Via Marsala side. Most budget hotels here occupy a floor or more of a palazzo, and the entries are often drab, though upstairs they're often charming or at least clean and livable. In the area to the left of the station, as you exit, the streets are wider, the traffic is heavier, and the noise level is higher. This area off Via Giolitti is being redeveloped, and now most streets are in good condition. There are a few that still need improvement, and caution at night is a given.

Via Veneto & Piazza Barberini In the 1950s and early 1960s this was the haunt of the *dolce vita* set, as the likes of King Farouk and Swedish actress Anita Ekberg paraded up and down Via Vittorio Veneto to the delight of the *paparazzi*. The street is still there, still the site of luxury hotels and elegant cafes and restaurants, although it no longer has the allure it did in its heyday. Rome city authorities would like to restore this legendary street to some of its former glory by banning vehicular traffic on the top half of the street.

To the south Via Veneto comes to an end at **Piazza Barberini,** dominated by the 1642 **Triton Fountain,** a baroque celebration with four dolphins holding up an open scallop shell in which sits a triton blowing into a conch. Overlooking the square is **Palazzo Barberini** or Barberini Palace, which can be entered at 13 Via delle Quattro Fontane. In 1623 when Cardinal Maffeo Barberini became Pope Urban VIII, he ordered Carlo Maderno to construct a palace here for his family. The structure was later completed by Bernini and Borromini.

Ancient Rome   Most visitors explore this area first, taking in the **Colosseum, Palatine Hill,** the **Roman Forum,** the **Imperial Forums,** and the **Circus Maximus.** The area forms part of the *centro storico* (historic district)—along with **Campo de' Fiori** and **Piazza Navona** and the **Pantheon,** described below. Because of its narrow streets, airy piazzas, antique atmosphere, and great location, visitors enjoy staying here instead of in the less attractive, duller, and rather seedier districts like the section around the train station (although that neighborhood has improved recently). If you base yourself here, you can walk to the monuments and avoid the hassle of Rome's inadequate public transportation. But room prices are often 30% to 50% higher than those in other less desirable areas. So if you want atmosphere, you've got to pay for it.

Campo de' Fiori & the Jewish Ghetto   South of Corso Vittorio Emanuele, centered around **Piazza Farnese** and the market square of **Campo de' Fiori,** many buildings in this district were constructed in Renaissance times as private homes. Walk on **Via Giulia**—the most fashionable street in Rome in the 16th century—with its antiques stores, interesting hotels, and modern art galleries.

West of Via Arenula lies one of the city's most intriguing districts, the old **Jewish Ghetto,** which has far more opportunities for dining than for lodgings. The Jews, about 8,000 at the time, were ordered here by Pope Paul IV in 1556, and the walls were not torn down until 1849. This is another of the most desirable places to base yourself in Rome, close to many attractions, although we think Ancient and Medieval Rome have a lot more atmosphere. Nevertheless, hoteliers still sock it to you on prices.

Piazza Navona & the Pantheon   One of the most desirable areas of Rome, this district is a maze of narrow streets and alleys from the Middle Ages and is filled with churches and palaces built during the Renaissance and baroque eras, often with rare marbles and other materials stripped from ancient Rome. The only way to explore it is on foot. Its heart is **Piazza Navona,** built over the emperor Domitian's stadium, and bustling with sidewalk cafes, *palazzi* (palaces), street artists, musicians, and pickpockets. There are several hotels in the area and plenty of trattorie. Rivaling it—in general activity, the cafe scene, and nightlife—is the area around the **Pantheon,** which remains from ancient Roman times surrounded by a district built much later. (This "pagan" temple was turned into a church and rescued, whereas the buildings that once surrounded it are long gone.) If you'd like to anchor in Medieval Rome, you face the same 30% to 50% increase in hotel prices you do in Ancient Rome.

Piazza di Spagna & Piazza del Popolo   At press time undergoing a major facelift, **Piazza del Popolo** was laid out by Guiseppe Valadier and is one of Rome's largest squares. It's characterized by an obelisk brought from Heliopolis in lower

Egypt during the reign of Augustus. At the end of the square is the **Porta del Popolo,** the gateway in the 3rd-century Aurelian wall. In the mid-16th century this was one of the major gateways into the old city. If you enter the piazza along Via del Corso from the south, you'll see twin churches, **Santa Maria del Miracoli** and **Santa Maria di Montesanto,** flanking the street. But the square's major church is **Santa Maria del Popolo** (1442–47), one of the best examples of a Renaissance church in Rome.

Ever since the 17th century, the **Spanish Steps** (former site of the Spanish ambassador's residence) have been a meeting place for visitors. Keats lived in a house opening onto the steps, and some of Rome's most upscale shopping streets fan out from it, including **Via Condotti.** The elegant **Hassler,** one of Rome's grandest hotels, lies at the top of the steps. If you want to sleep in the hippest part of town, you must be willing to part with a lot of extra lire. This area charges some of the capital's highest prices, not only for hotels but also for restaurants, designer silk suits, and leather loafers.

Around Vatican City   Across the Tiber, **Vatican City** is a small city-state, yet its influence extends around the world. The **Vatican Museums** and **St. Peter's** take up most of the land area, and popes have lived here for 6 centuries. Although the neighborhood contains some good hotels (and several bad ones), it's somewhat removed from the more happening scene of Ancient or Renaissance Rome, and getting to and from it can be time-consuming. Also, the area is rather dull at night and contains few of Rome's finer restaurants. Vatican City and its surrounding area is best for exploring during the day.

Trastevere   The most authentic district of Rome—it has been called the last of the capital's old *rioni* (neighborhoods)— lies across the Tiber. **Trastevere** is a place where you can see how real Romans live. Its people are of mixed ancestry, including Jewish, Roman, and Greek, and speak their own dialect. The area centers around the ancient Churches of **Santa Cecilia** and **Santa Maria.** Home to many young expatriates, the district became a gathering place for hedonists and bohemians after World War II. There are those who speak of it as a "city within a city"—or at least a village within a city. It's said that the language is rougher and the cuisine spicier, (Trastevere doesn't have the glamorous hotels of central Rome, but it does have some of the last remaining authentic Roman dining). Trastevere used to be a bastion of the budget traveler, but foreigners from virtually anywhere have been buying real estate en masse here, so change is in the air.

Testaccio   In A.D. 55 Nero ordered that Rome's thousands of broken amphoras and terra-cotta roof tiles be stacked in a designated pile to the east of the Tiber, just west of Pyramide and today's Ostiense Railway Station. Over the centuries the mound rose to 200 feet, then compacted to form the centerpiece for one of the city's most unusual neighborhoods, **Testaccio.** Eventually, houses were built on the terracotta mound and caves dug into its mass to store wine and foodstuffs.

The Appian Way   **Via Appia Antica** is a 2,300-year-old road that has witnessed much of the history of the ancient world. By 190 B.C. it extended from Rome to Brindisi on the southeastern coast, and its most famous sights today are the **catacombs,** the graveyards of patrician families (despite what it says in *Quo Vadis?,* they were not used as a place for Christians to hide out while fleeing persecution). This is one of the most history-rich areas of Rome to explore—but don't go there seeking a hotel. There are several restaurants, however.

Prati   This little-known district is a 19th-century middle-class suburb north of the Vatican. Its low-cost *pensioni* (boarding houses) have been discovered by budget travelers, but it's not conveniently located for much of the sightseeing you to do. The **Trionfale flower-and-food market** itself is worth the trip. The area also abounds in less expensive shopping streets than those found in central Rome, and street crime isn't much of a problem.

Parioli   Rome's most elegant residential section is framed by the green spaces of **Villa Borghese** to the south and **Villa Glori** and **Villa Ada** to the north. It's a setting for some of the city's finest restaurants, hotels, and nightclubs. It's not the most central, however, and staying here can be a hassle if you're dependent on public transportation. Parioli lies adjacent to the Prati but across the Tiber to the east, and, like Prati, is one of Rome's safer districts.

Monte Mario   A northwestern precinct of Rome, **Monte Mario** is the site of the deluxe **Cavalieri Hilton,** where you can have a drink and take in the view of Rome. If you plan to spend a lot of time shopping and sightseeing in the heart of Rome, it's a difficult and often expensive commute. The area lies north of Prati, away from the hustle and bustle (and in summer, the heat) of central Rome. Take bus no. 913 from the Spanish Steps to the district's heart, Piazzale Maresciallo Giardino.

EUR   Originally built under the Fascist regime in hopes of hosting a World's Fair, this cold micro-city of white granite—Mussolini was trying to invoke the look and glory of ancient Rome—was rehabilitated after World War II as both a government administrative headquarters and a rather deluxe apartment suburb. Today it's of interest mainly as an architectural oddity, and for its Museum of Roman Civilization, which houses a scale model of what ancient Rome looked like at the height of its imperial power.

2 Getting Around

BY PUBLIC TRANSPORTATION

SUBWAY   The **Metropolitana,** or **Metro** for short, is the fastest means of transportation in Rome. It has two underground lines: **Line A** (Linea A) runs between Via Ottaviano, near St. Peter's, and Anagnina, stopping at Piazzale Flaminio (near Piazza del Popolo), Piazza di Spagna, Piazza Vittorio Emanuele, and Piazza San Giovanni in Laterano. **Line B** (Linea B) connects the Rebibbia district with Via Laurentina, stopping at Via Cavour, Stazione Termini, the Colosseum, Circus Maximus, the Pyramid, St. Paul's Outside the Walls, and EUR. A big red letter **M** indicates the entrance to the subway.

Tickets are 1,500L (85¢), and are available from vending machines at all stations. These machines accept 50-, 100-, and 200-lire coins, and some of them take 1,000L notes. Some stations have managers, but they don't make change. Booklets of tickets (*carnet*) are available at tobacco shops (*tabacchi*) and in some terminals. You can also purchase a tourist pass good for either a day or a week (see "By Bus & Tram," below).

Building an underground system for Rome has not been easy, since every time workers start digging, they discover an old temple or other archeological treasure and heavy earth-moving has to cease for a while.

BY BUS AND TRAM   Roman buses are operated by **Azienda Tramvie e Autobus del Commune di Roma (ATAC),** Via Volturno 65 (☎ **06/46954444** for information).

For only 1,500L (85¢) you can ride to most parts of Rome on quite good bus service. The ticket is valid for 1 hour and 15 minutes, and you can get on many buses during that time period using the same ticket. At the Stazione Termini you can purchase a special **tourist bus pass,** costing 6,000L ($3.50) for 1 day or 24,000L ($14) for a week. This allows you to ride on the ATAC network without bothering to purchase individual tickets. The tourist pass is also valid on the subway—but never ride the trains when the Romans are going to or from work or you'll be mashed flatter than fettuccine. On the first bus you board, you place your ticket in a small machine that prints the day and hour you boarded. And you do the same on the last bus you take during the validity period of the ticket.

Buses and trams stop at areas marked FERMATA. At most of these, a yellow sign will display the bus numbers that stop there, and then lists of all the stops along each bus's route in order, so you can easily search out your destination. In general they're in service from 6am to midnight daily. After that and until dawn, you can ride on special night buses (they have an "N" in front of their bus number), which only run on main routes. It's best to take a taxi in the wee hours—if you can find one.

At the bus information booth at Piazza dei Cinquecento, in front of the Stazione Termini, you can purchase a directory complete with maps summarizing the particular routes. Ask there about where to purchase bus tickets, or buy them in a *tabacchi* or at a bus terminal. You must have your ticket before boarding the bus, as there are no ticket-issuing machines on the vehicles.

BY TAXI

If your wallet is accustomed to hopping a cab in New York or London, then do so in Rome. If not, take less expensive means of transport. Avoid paying your fare with large bills—invariably, taxi drivers claim they don't have change, hoping for a bigger tip (only give about 15%). Don't count on hailing a taxi on the street or even getting one at a stand. If you're going out, have your hotel call one. At a restaurant, ask the waiter or cashier to dial for you. If you want to phone for yourself, try one of these numbers: ☎ **06/6645,** 06/3570, or 06/4994.

The meter begins at 4,500L ($2.60) for the first 3 kilometers, then adds 200L (10¢) per kilometer. Every suitcase is 2,000L ($1.15) extra, and on Sunday a 2,000L ($1.15) supplement is assessed, plus another 5,000L ($2.90) supplement from 10pm to 6am.

BY CAR

RENTING A CAR Renting a car is easy. All drivers in Rome must have nerves of steel, a sense of humor, a valid driver's license, and a valid passport, and in most cases they must be between the ages of 21 and 70. In all cases, payment and paperwork are simple if you present valid credit or charge cards with your completed rental contract. If that isn't possible, a substantial cash deposit will probably be required in advance. Insurance on all vehicles is compulsory in Italy. A *carta verde* ("green card") is valid for 15, 30, or 45 days and should be issued to cover your car before your trip to Italy. Beyond 45 days you must have a regular Italian insurance policy.

You'll find a bewildering assortment of car-rental kiosks at the airports and railway stations of Rome, and agencies are also located downtown. **Hertz** has its main office near the parking lot of the Villa Borghese, Via Vittorio Veneto 156 (☎ **06/3216831**). The **Budget** headquarters are at Via Ludovisi 60 (☎ **06/4820966**) and **Avis** is at Via Sardegna 38A (☎ **06/41999** or 06/42824728). **Maggiore,** an Italian company, has an office at Via di Tor Cervara (☎ **06/229351**).

Kemwel Holiday Autos (☎ **800/678-0678; www.kemwel.com**) and **Auto Europe** (☎ **800/223-5555; www.autoeurope.com**) are 2 agencies that serve as European car-rental agency brokers for American travelers.

Two Bus Warnings

Any map of the Roman bus system will likely be outdated before it's printed. Many buses listed on the "latest" map no longer exist; others are enjoying a much-needed rest, and new buses suddenly appear without warning. There's also talk of completely renumbering the whole system soon, so be aware that the route numbers listed here may have changed by the time you travel.

Watch out for pickpockets on Rome's overcrowded buses, particularly on bus no. 64 (aka. the "Pickpocket Express" or the "Wallet Eater"), a favorite of visitors because of its route through the historic districts.

When your itinerary is set, you can procure a car rental in Rome prior to departure through either of these agencies, paying the entire rental fee before leaving the United States. If your itinerary should change, these agencies will allow a full refund; because neither company maintains offices in Italy, however, all refunds are made after your return home.

DRIVING & PARKING All roads may lead to Rome if you're driving, but don't count on much driving once you get here. Since reception desks of most Roman hotels have at least one English-speaking person, it's wise to call ahead to find out the best route into Rome from wherever you're starting out.

Find out whether the hotel has a garage. If not, you're usually allowed to park your car in front of the hotel long enough to unload your luggage. Someone at the hotel—a doorman, if there is one—will direct you to the nearest garage or place to park.

To the neophyte, Roman driving will appear like the chariot race in *Ben Hur.* Those used to driving in Boston will have no problems, however. When the light turns green, go forth with caution. Many Roman drivers are still going through the light even though it has turned red. Roman drivers in traffic gridlock move bravely on, fighting for every inch of the road until they can free themselves from the tangled mess. To complicate matters, many zones, such as that around Piazza di Spagna, are traffic-free, and other traffic-free zones are being tried out in various parts of the city.

It's virtually impossible—an act of sheer madness, really—to drive around in Rome. But if you plan to take many excursions from the city—for example, into the hill towns—you'll find a car a most reliable and convenient means of transport.

In other words, try to get your car into Rome as safely as possible, park it, and proceed on foot or by public transportation from then on.

BY BICYCLE, MOTOR SCOOTER & MOTORCYCLE

Bichi & Bachi, Via dei Viminale 5 (☎ **06/48288443**), maintains an inventory of about 50 motor scooters and motorcycles that you can rent as a means of zipping through the city's dense traffic. (We recommend this only if you're an experienced urbanite who's familiar with the mechanics of hysterical city driving in the Italian style.) Open daily from 8am to 7pm, the charge is between 40,000L and 80,000L ($24 to $47) per day including the cost of insurance, depending on the model you select. Metro: Termini or Repubblica. Another agency that provides mopeds is **Happy Rent,** conveniently located at Via Farimi 3 (☎ **06/4818185**), 300 yards from the Termini. Most mopeds cost 20,000L ($12) for 1 hour or 60,000L ($35) for the entire day. Happy Rent also offers several guided moped tours of Rome and the surrounding area. It's open Monday to Saturday from 9am to 7pm.

You'll find many places to rent bikes throughout Rome. Ask at your hotel for the nearest rental location, or go to **I Bike Rome,** Via Vittorio Veneto 156 (☎ **06/3225240**), which rents bicycles from the underground parking garage at the Villa Borghese. Most bikes cost 4,000L ($2.30) per hour or 10,000L ($6) per day. Mountain bikes rent for 7,000L ($4.05) per hour or 18,000L ($11) per day. It's open daily from 9am to 7pm.

Bike riders are permitted anywhere in the city, including pedestrian-only zones and traffic-free areas such as St. Peter's Square, where you can ride within the arcaded confines of what's been called the world's most magnificent oval. Also appealing is a 30km (18.5-mile) bike lane beside the Tiber that extends from central Rome north, to the industrial suburb of Castel Jubileo.

ON FOOT

Although Rome is a large city, interesting sites are often clustered together—particularly along the ancient narrow cobbled streets of Old Rome. Much of the inner core of Rome is traffic-free—so you'll need to walk whether you like it or not. However, in many parts of the city it's hazardous and uncomfortable because of the crowds, heavy traffic, and very narrow sidewalks. Sometimes sidewalks don't exist at all, and it becomes a sort of free-for-all with pedestrians competing for space against vehicular traffic (the traffic always seems to win). *Caution:* When walking, always be on guard for speeding traffic.

FAST FACTS: Rome

American Express   The offices of American Express are at Piazza di Spagna 38 (☎ **06/67641**). The travel service and tour desk are open Monday to Friday from 9am to 5:30pm and on Saturday from 9am to 12:30pm (May to October the tour desk is also open on Saturday afternoon from 2 to 2:30pm). The financial and mail services are open Monday to Friday from 9am to 5pm and on Saturday from 9am to noon.

Bookstores   See "Shopping A to Z" in chapter 8.

Business Hours   In general, banks are open Monday to Friday from 8:30am to 1:30pm and again from 3 to 4pm. A U.S. bank in Rome is **Citibank,** Via Bruxelles 61 (☎ **06/478171**). Shopping hours are governed by the *riposo* (siesta). Most stores are open year round Monday to Saturday from 9am to 1pm and then from 3:30 or 4pm to 7:30 or 8pm. Most shops are closed Sunday.

Car Rentals   See "Getting Around," earlier in this chapter.

Climate   See "When to Go" in chapter 2.

Crime   See "Safety," below.

Currency Exchange   This is possible at all major rail and airline terminals in Rome, including the Stazione Termini, where the *cambio* (exchange booth) beside the rail information booth is open daily from 8am to 8pm. At some *cambi* you'll have to pay commissions, often 1.5%. Banks, likewise, often charge commissions. Many so-called moneychangers will approach you on the street, but often they're pushing counterfeit lire. To be on the safe side, we recommend that money be exchanged only at banks, hotels, or currency exchange booths.

Dentist   To secure a dentist who speaks English, call the **U.S. Embassy** in Rome (☎ **06/46741**). You may have to call around in order to get an appointment. There's also the 24-hour **G. Eastman Dental Hospital,** Viale Regina Elena 287 (☎ **06/844831**).

Doctor   Call the U.S. Embassy (see "Dentist," above), which will provide a list of doctors who speak English. All big hospitals in Rome have a 24-hour first-aid service (go to the emergency room). You'll find English-speaking doctors at the privately run **Salvator Mundi International Hospital,** Viale delle Mura Gianicolense 67 (☎ **06/588961**). For medical assistance, the **International Medical Center** is on 24-hour duty at Via Giovanni Amendola 7 (☎ **06/4882371**). You could also contact the **Rome American Hospital,** Via Emilio Longoni 69 (☎ **06/22551**), with English-speaking doctors on duty 24 hours a day. A more personalized medical service is provided by **MEDI-CALL,** Studio Medico, Via Salaria 300, Palazzina C, interno 5 (☎ **06/8840113**). Staffed by a small core of administrators who are available 24 hours a day, it can arrange for qualified doctors to make house calls, to your hotel or wherever, anywhere in Rome. In most cases, the doctor will be a general practitioner who's well versed in either prescribing an appropriate medication or, if the problem is more serious, referring a patient to a qualified specialist. Fees begin at around $100 per visit, but can go higher if a specialist or specialized treatments are necessary. Frankly, paying this organization's fee, and waiting for a doctor to arrive at your hotel room, is usually a lot more convenient than waiting in the emergency of any hospital. For information via Internet, contact **www.olgiata.com/medi-call**.

Drugstores   A reliable pharmacy is the **Farmacia Internazionale,** Piazza Barberini 49 (☎ **06/6794680**), open day and night. Most pharmacies are open from 8:30am to 1pm and then from 4 to 7:30pm. In general, pharmacies follow a rotation system so that several are always open on Sunday (the rotation schedule is posted outside each).

Electricity   It's generally 220 volts, 50 Hz A.C., but you might find 125-volt outlets, with different plugs and sockets for each. Pick up a transformer either before leaving home or in any appliance shop in Rome if you plan to use electrical appliances. Check the exact local current at your hotel. You'll also need an adapter plug.

Embassies/Consulates   The Embassy of the **United States** is at Via Vittorio Veneto 119A (☎ **06/46741**), open Monday to Friday 8:30am to 12:30pm and 2 to 4:30pm. The consular and passport services are also at Via Vittorio Veneto 119A (same phone); for **Canada,** it's at Via Zara 30 (☎ **06/445981**), open Monday to Friday from 10am to 12:30pm. For the **United Kingdom,** consular offices are at Via XX Settembre 80A (☎ **06/4825441**), open Monday to Friday from 9:15am to 1:30pm. For **Australia,** the embassy is at Via Alessandria 215 (☎ **06/852721**), open Monday to Thursday from 8:30am to noon and 2 to 4pm, and on Friday from 8:30am to 1:15pm. The Australia Consulate is around the corner in the same building at Corso Trieste 25 (☎ **06/852721**). For **New Zealand,** the consular office is at Via Zara 28 (☎ **06/4402928**), and it's open Monday to Friday from 8:30am to 12:45pm and 1:45 to 5pm. The Embassy of **Ireland** in Rome is at Piazza di Campitelli 3 (☎ **06/6979121;** fax 06/679-2354). For consular queries, dial ☎ **06/69791211.** Open Monday to Friday from 9:30am to 12:30pm and 2 to 4pm. The Embassy for **South Africa** is at Via Tenaro 14 (☎ **06/8419794**), open Monday to Friday from 9:30am to 4pm. In case of emergency, embassies have a 24-hour referral service.

Emergencies   The police "hot line" number is ☎ **21-21-21.** Usually, however, dial ☎ **112** for the police, to report a fire, or to summon an ambulance. For the state police with an English interpreter, dial ☎ **113.** If your car breaks down, dial ☎ **116;** the Automobile Club of Italy (ACI) will come to your aid.

Eyeglasses   Try **Vasari,** Piazza della Repubblica 61 (☎ **06/4882240**), adjacent to the Grand Hotel, a very large shop with lots of choices. They serve wearers of contact lenses and conventional eyeglasses.

Hospitals   See "Doctors," above.

Hot Lines   Dial ☎ **113,** which is a general SOS, to report any kind of danger, such as rape. You can also dial ☎ **112,** the police emergency number. For an ambulance call ☎ **5100.** And for personal crises call **Samaritans,** Via San Giovanni in Laterano 250 (☎ **06/70454444**). From October to May, hours are from 1 to 10pm daily; from June to September, hours are from 4 to 10pm daily.

Information   See "Visitor Information," earlier in this chapter.

Legal Aid   The consulate of your country is the place to turn. Although consular officials cannot interfere in the Italian legal process, they can inform you of your rights and provide a list of attorneys. You'll have to pay for the attorney out of pocket—there's no free legal assistance. If you're arrested for a drug offense, about all the consulate will do is notify a lawyer and perhaps inform your family.

Liquor Laws   Wine with meals has been a normal part of Italian family life for hundreds of years. There is no legal drinking age for buying or ordering alcohol, and alcohol is sold day and night throughout the year.

Lost Property   Usually lost property is gone forever. But you might try checking at **Ogetti Rinvenuti,** Via Nicolò Bettoni 1 (☎ **06/5816040**), open Monday to Friday from 9am to 1pm and Tuesday to Thursday from 2:30 to 6pm. A branch at the Stazione Termini off Track 1 (☎ **06/47306682**) is open from 7am to 11pm daily.

Luggage Storage/Lockers   These are available at the Stazione Termini along Tracks 1 and 22 daily from 5am to 1am. The charge is 5,000L ($2.90) per piece of luggage per 12-hour period.

Mail   Mailboxes in Italy are red and are attached to walls. The left slot is only for letters intended for the city; the right slot is for all other destinations.

The main post office of Rome is at Piazza San Silvestro 19, 00186 Roma (☎ **06/6771**), between Via del Corso and Piazza di Spagna. It's open Monday to Friday from 9am to 6pm and on Saturday from 9am to 2pm. To claim mail addressed to you in care of this central office, with *fermo posta* written after the name and address of the post office, simply present your passport as identification. Stamps (*francobolli*) can be purchased at *tabacchi* (tobacconists).

Vatican City mailboxes are blue, and you can buy Vatican stamps at the Vatican City Post Office, adjacent to the information office in St. Peter's Square. It's open Monday to Friday from 8:30am to 7pm and on Saturday from 8:30am to 6pm. Letters mailed at Vatican City reach North America far more quickly than does mail sent from within Rome for the same cost. With both the Vatican and the Italian mail, letters and postcards to the U.S. cost about 1,300L (75¢).

Newspapers/Magazines   You can get the *International Herald Tribune* and *USA Today* at most newsstands, and the *New York Times* at many, as well as *Time* and *Newsweek* magazines. The expatriate magazine (in English) *Wanted in Rome* comes out monthly and lists current events and shows. If you want to try your hand at reading Italian, the Thursday edition of the newspaper *La Repubblica* contains *TrovaRoma,* a magazine supplement full of cultural and entertainment listings.

Police   The police "hot line" number is ☎ **21-21-21.** Usually, however, dial ☎ **112** for the police, to report a fire, or to summon an ambulance. ☎ **113** is reserved for general SOS calls and for English-speaking members of the state police.

Radio/TV   Major radio and television broadcasts are on RAI, the Italian state radio and TV network. Occasionally during the tourist season it will broadcast special programs in English; look in the radio and TV guide sections of local newspapers. Vatican Radio also carries foreign-language religious news programs, often in English. Shortwave transistor radios pick up broadcasts from the BBC (Britain), Voice of America (United States), and CBC (Canada). More expensive hotels often have TVs in the bedrooms with the CNN news network.

Rest Rooms   All airport and railway stations, of course, have rest rooms, often with attendants, who expect to be tipped (200L to 500L [10¢ to 30¢] is fine.) Bars, nightclubs, restaurants, cafes, and all hotels have facilities as well. Public toilets are also found near many of the major sights. Usually they are designated as WC (water closet), *donne* (women), or *uomini* (men). The most confusing designation is *signori* (gentlemen) and *signore* (ladies), so watch those final *i's* and *e's!*

Safety   Pickpocketing is the most common problem. Men should keep their wallets in their front pockets or inside jacket pockets. Purse-snatching is also commonplace, with young men on Vespas who will ride past you and grab your purse. To avoid trouble, women should stay away from the curb, and keep their purse on the wall side of their body and the strap over both shoulders across their chest. In general, don't lay anything valuable on tables or chairs where it can be grabbed up easily. Children are a particular menace. You'll often virtually have to fight them off, if they completely surround you. They'll often approach you with pieces of cardboard hiding their stealing hands.

Taxes   As a member of the European Union, Italy imposes a tax on most goods and services. It's a "value-added tax," called IVA in Italy. The tax affecting most visitors is at hotels, ranging from 9% in first- and second-class hotels and *pensioni* to 13% in deluxe hotels. The value-added tax is not the same for all items—for example, it's 12% on clothing but 19% on most luxury goods. Tax rebates may be given on large purchases (see "The Shopping Scene" in chapter 8).

Telephone/Fax/Telegrams   If your hotel doesn't have a **fax,** try a *tabacchi* (tobacconist) or photocopy shop. You can send **telegrams** from all post offices during the day and from the telegraph office at the central post office in San Silvestro, off Via della Mercede, at night. Through ITALCABLE, you can dictate both internal and foreign telegrams over the phone (dial ☎ **186**).

A **public telephone** is always near at hand in Italy, especially if you're near a bar. Local calls cost 200L. You can use 100-, 200-, or 500-lire coins. Most phones, especially in the cities, accept a multiple-use phone card called a *carta telefonica,* which can be purchased at all *tabacchi* and bars in increments of 5,000L or 10,000L. Break off the corner, insert the card into the slot, and then dial. A digital display will keep track of how many lire you use up during your call. The card is good until it runs out of lire, so don't forget to take it with you when you hang up.

Thanks to ITALCABLE, **international calls** to the United States and Canada can be dialed directly. Dial 00 (the international access code from Italy), then the country code (1 for the United States and Canada), the area code, and the

Know Your Codes

The **country code** for Italy is **39**. The **city code** for Rome is **6**. People calling from abroad must dial the country code (39), then a 0 in front of the city area code. For example, someone calling Rome from New York should dial ☎ 011-39-06 and then the local number. Note: even telephone calls made within a city must be preceded by that city's area code. If you're in Rome and calling another Roman number, you must dial 06 before the local number.

---

number. Calls dialed directly are billed on the basis of the call's duration only. A reduced rate is applied from 11pm to 8am Monday to Saturday and all day Sunday.

If you wish to make a **collect call** from a pay phone, simply deposit 200L (don't worry—you'll get it back when you're done) and dial ☎ **170** for an English-speaking ITALCABLE operator. For **calling-card calls,** drop in the refundable 200L, then dial the number for your card's company to be connected with an operator in the States: ☎ **172-1011** for **AT&T,** ☎ **172-1022** for **MCI,** and ☎ **172-1877** for **Sprint**. You can also call ☎ **06/1721001** for Canada, ☎ **06/1721061** for Australia, and ☎ **06/1720044** for the United Kingdom.

If you make a long-distance call from a public telephone, there is no surcharge. However, hotels have been known to double or triple the cost of the call, so be duly warned.

Time   Rome is 6 hours ahead of eastern time in the United States. Daylight saving time goes into effect in Italy each year from May 22 to September 24.

Tipping   This custom is practiced with a flair in Italy—many people depend on tips for their livelihoods. In hotels, the service charge of 15% or 18% is already added to a bill. In addition, it's customary to tip the chambermaid 2,000L ($1.15) per day; the doorman (for calling a cab), 1,000L (60¢); and the bellhop or porter, 2,000L ($1.15) per bag. A concierge expects 3,000L ($1.75) per day, as well as tips for extra services performed, which could include help with long-distance calls, newspapers, or stamps.

In restaurants, 15% is added to your bill to cover most charges. An additional tip for good service is almost always expected. It's customary in certain fashionable restaurants to leave an additional 10%, which, combined with the assessed service charge, is a very large tip indeed. The sommelier expects 10% of the cost of the wine. Checkroom attendants now expect 1,500L (85¢). Romans still hand washroom attendants 200L to 300L (10¢ to 15¢), more in deluxe and first-class establishments. Restaurants are required by law to give receipts.

In cafes and bars, tip 15% of the bill, and give a theater usher 1,500L (85¢). Taxi drivers expect at least 15% of the fare.

Transit Information   Call the following numbers: ☎ **06/65951** for Leonardo da Vinci International Airport, ☎ **06/794941** for Ciampino Airport, ☎ **06/46591** for bus information, and ☎ **1478/880-881** for rail information.

Water   Rome is famed for its drinking water, which is generally safe, even from its outdoor fountains. If it isn't, there's a sign reading ACQUA NON POTABILE. Romans traditionally order bottled mineral water in restaurants to accompany the wine with their meals.

Accommodations 4

The good news is that Roman hoteliers are sprucing up for the Jubilee 2000 visitors. The bad news is that some of this "sprucing" (read: renovating) might be going on when you visit in 1999.

Our selections are divided into four major categories: "Very Expensive," "Expensive," "Moderate," and "Inexpensive." Rome's poshest hotels, while no bargain, are among the most luxurious in Europe. The bulk of this chapter, however, concerns moderately priced hotels, where you'll find rooms with a private bath. The final group is "Inexpensive" hotels; each hotel has been judged clean and cheerful and offers more in services and facilities than you might expect from the price. In the less expensive categories, you'll find a few *pensiones,* the Rome equivalent of a boarding house.

HOTELS   Italy controls the prices of its hotels, designating a minimum and a maximum rate. The difference between the two may depend on the season, the location of the room, or even its size. Hotels are classified by stars indicating their category of comfort: five stars for deluxe, four for first class, three for second class, two for third class, and one for fourth class. Most former *pensiones* are now rated as one- or two-star hotels. The distinction between a pensione hotel (where some degree of board was once required along with the room) and a regular hotel is no longer officially made, although many smaller, family-run establishments still call themselves *pensiones.* Government ratings don't depend on sensitivity of decoration or frescoed ceilings, but rather on facilities, such as elevators and the like. Many of the finest hostelries in Rome have a lower rating because they serve only breakfast.

The concierge of your hotel, incidentally, is usually a reliable dispenser of information.

BED & BREAKFASTS   In Rome, these establishments are commonplace, and they offer the best accommodation value. Finding a suitable one, however, may be tricky. Often B&Bs are family homes or apartments, so don't count on hotel services, or even private baths. Sometimes, however, B&Bs are in beautiful private homes, lovely guesthouses, or restored mansions. Prices range from $35 to $65 or more per person nightly, including breakfast. Sometimes you can arrange to order an evening meal. Tourist offices generally keep a list of this type of accommodation.

PARKING   It's rare for hotels to have private garages; many were constructed before the advent of the automobile. Others built after the automobile couldn't find enough room in overcongested Rome for garage space. Hotel reception desks will advise you about nearby garages. Fees range from 5,000L to 60,000L ($2.90 to $35) per night. Of course, the higher price would be for garage space in the heart of Rome where your car would be under a roof, guarded and protected by a night-watchman. The lower price would be for an open-air unguarded place somewhere on the outskirts of Rome.

RESERVATIONS   It's always a good idea to make reservations before you go, and this can be done through a travel agent or by writing, e-mailing, or faxing the hotel directly (some establishments require deposits, and this takes a great deal of time, especially considering how slow the Italian mails are). Some of the more expensive hotels have toll-free 800 numbers in North America. It's invariably easy to obtain an expensive room at any time of the year, but low-cost accommodations are generally heavily booked.

In case you haven't made reservations, however, you're bound to find some place that can put you up for the first night. Our advice, in that event, is to time your arrival for shortly before 9am and head straight for your first choice of hotel. If there's any space to be had, you'll be assured of getting first dibs. *If you're planning to be in Rome for the Jubilee 2000 celebration, reservations months in advance are advised.*

TAXES   All Italian hotels impose an IVA (Imposta sul Valore Aggiunto), or value-added tax. This tax is in effect throughout the European Union countries. It replaces some 20 other taxes and is an effort to streamline the tax structure.

What that means for you is an increase in the price you'll pay for a hotel room. Deluxe hotels will slap you with a whopping tax of 13%, whereas first-class, second-class, and other hotels will impose 9%. Most hotels will quote you a rate inclusive of this tax. However, other establishments prefer to add it on when you go to pay the bill. To avoid unpleasant surprises, ask to be quoted an all-inclusive rate—that is, with service, even a continental breakfast (which is often obligatory)—when you check in.

THE PRICE CATEGORIES   In hotels rated **"Very Expensive,"** you can spend 550,000L ($319) and up for a double room. Hotels judged **"Expensive"** charge 350,000L to 550,000L ($203 to $319) for a double room; those in the **"Moderate"** category ask 260,000L to 350,000L ($151 to $203) for a double. Anything from 80,000L ($46) all the way up to 260,000L ($151) is judged **"Inexpensive,"** at least by the inflated Roman standards of hotel pricing.

1 Best Bets

- **Best Historic Hotel:** The truly grand **Le Grand Hotel** (☎ **800/325-3589** in the U.S.) was inaugurated by its creator, César Ritz, in 1894, with the great chef, Escoffier, presiding over a lavish banquet. Its roster of guests has been topped by some of the greatest names in European history, including royalty, naturally, but also such New World moguls as Henry Ford and J. P. Morgan. The diarist, Anaïs Nin, met her old friend (then nemesis) Gore Vidal here, trying to win his permission to print passages in her diary that virtually libeled him. He granted it!
- **Best for Business Travelers:** On the west side of the Tiber about 6 short blocks northeast of the Vatican, **Hotel Atlante Star** (☎ **06/6873233**) operates in conjunction with its sibling, the **Atlante Garden,** a block away. Together they share a conference room and a well-run business center. Many young executives check

Food for Thought

Hotels in Rome today are divided on the question of whether breakfast is included in the room price. Usually the more expensive establishments charge extra for this meal, which most often consists of cappuccino (coffee with milk) and *cornetti* (croissants), with fresh butter and jam. First-class and deluxe establishments serve what is known as either an English breakfast or an American breakfast—meaning ham and eggs—but this must nearly always be ordered from the à la carte menu. Many smaller hotels and *pensiones* serve only continental breakfast. If you're really watching your lire, check the information carefully for exactly what's included and what's extra.

into either hotel (depending on their expense account) and find a willing, helpful staff composed mainly of multilingual European interns eager to help visitors with their problems in the Eternal City. All the latest business equipment is available, and the reception desk is excellent at receiving messages.

- **Best for a Romantic Getaway:** A private villa in the exclusive Parioli residential area, the **Hotel Lord Byron** (☎ 06/3220404) is an elite retreat and one of the most fashionable ones in Rome. It still maintains its clublike ambience, and everybody is oh, so very discreet here—regardless of the party you check in with! You get personal attention in a subdued opulence, and the staff definitely respects that DO NOT DISTURB sign on the door. You don't even have to leave the romantic premises for dinner, as the Relais Le Jardin is among the finest—some say the very best—restaurants in Rome.
- **Best Trendy Hotel:** Hemingway and Ingrid Bergman don't hang out here anymore, but the **Hotel Eden** (☎ 800/225-5843 in the U.S.) remains glamorous. After a $20-million renovation by Forte, it's better than ever. Fellini, a former guest, isn't around to record the scene today, but the rich and famous (and often infamous) of the world parade through its fin-de-siècle grandeur. Everything looks as if it's waiting for photographers from *Architectural Digest* to arrive.
- **Best Lobby for Pretending You're Rich:** In the "Hollywood on the Tiber" heyday of the 1950s, you might have encountered Elizabeth Taylor in the lobby, accompanied by her husband of the moment—usually Richard Burton or Eddie Fisher. They're gone now, but the grandeur of the lobby in the **Excelsior** (☎ 800/325-3589 in the U.S.) retains its memories. The city's most opulent hotel is just the place to meet someone you're trying to impress (even if you're not a guest). Its sprawling lounges are formal, with all those elegant touches such as glittering chandeliers, lots of marble, and high ceilings.
- **Best for Families:** Near the Stazione Termini (in one of the safer areas), the **Hotel Venezia** (☎ 06/4457101) is blessed with rooms often large enough to accommodate families. Some have balconies for surveying the action on the street below. The housekeeping is superb, and the management caring. Extra beds for children can be brought into the room.
- **Best Moderately Priced Hotel:** On an ancient street in the old quarter of Rome, the **Albergo Cesàri** (☎ 06/6792386) lies between the Trevi Fountain and the Pantheon. Since 1787, it has welcomed everybody from Garibaldi to Stendhal. Recently renovated in 1998, the hotel is better than ever. Some rooms are triples and quads; all have furnishings that are solidly comfortable, though not grand.
- **Best Friendly Pensione:** You can't get much simpler than the **Pensione Papà Germano** (☎ 06/486919). It's a favorite budget choice, and warm and welcoming to boot. A high-turnover clientele of European and American

students check in here—often with backpacks—as the address is passed around by word of mouth. The energetic family owners may not speak the Queen's English, but they are receptive to your needs and happy to share their home.

- **Best Service:** Both management and staff at the **Hotel de la Ville Inter-Continental Roma** (☎ **800/327-0200** in the U.S. and Canada) prove highly professional and exceedingly hospitable. The staff is particularly adept at taking messages, giving you helpful hints about what to see and do in Rome, and fulfilling any special room service requests. However, it is the general attentiveness to the needs of a guest, an alertness about how to solve problems, and a sensitivity to good manners and a friendly helpfulness that makes this place so exceptional. Room service is available 24 hours daily.

- **Best Location:** Right at the top of the Spanish Steps, directly across the small piazza from the deluxe Hassler, is the **Scalinata di Spagna** (☎ **06/6793006**). Could there be any more desirable location in all of Rome? The interior is like an old inn—the public rooms are small with bright print slipcovers, old clocks, and low ceilings. You can soak up the atmosphere inside or head for the roof garden with its sweeping view of the dome of St. Peter's across the Tiber. When you step out your door, the heart of Rome is at your feet, including the best shopping streets, at the bottom of the Spanish Steps.

- **Best Views:** From its perch on top of Monte Mario, set on 15 acres of landscaped grounds, the deluxe **Cavalieri Hilton** (☎ **800/445-8667** in the U.S. and Canada) opens onto panoramic views of the Eternal City that are almost unequaled in the capital. The skyline of Rome is especially evocative at either dawn or sunset. Of course, views are available from all the bedrooms, but many guests, even Romans themselves, drive up here for a drink at night just to take in the lights of the city. It's memorable, and you'll want to linger.

- **Best View from Your Window:** You can't beat the view at the **Albergo del Sole al Pantheon** (☎ **06/6780441**). From your bedroom window you can gaze out at the Pantheon, one of the architectural gems of the ancient world. The present-day Albergo is one of the oldest hotels in the world—the first records of it as a hostelry appeared in 1467—and one can certainly see how the view led the original builders to chose this particular site. Seemingly everybody from Frederick III of the Hapsburg dynasty to Simone de Beauvoir and Jean-Paul Sartre, has taken in the scene over the centuries.

- **Best Elegant Hotel:** Of course, it's not as elegant or as grand as the Excelsior, Eden, or Hassler, but the **Hotel d'Inghilterra** (☎ **06/69981**) has its own unique brand of subdued opulence. Two blocks west of the Spanish Steps, its public rooms feature black-and-white checkerboard marble floors and its upholstered lounges are filled with antiques. The fifth floor has some of the loveliest terraces in Rome, and the romantic restaurant below has trompe l'oeil clouds that give the impression of a courtyard terrace open to the sky.

- **Best in a Roman Neighborhood:** You can't get more Roman than the **Teatro di Pompeo** (☎ **06/68300170**). The hotel is actually built on top of the ruins of the Theater of Pompey, where Caesar met his fate. It's on a quiet piazzetta near the Palazzo Farnese and Campo de' Fiori, whose open-air market makes this one of Rome's most colorful neighborhoods. Shopping and nightlife abound in this fascinating section of Renaissance Rome, and restaurants and pizzerie keep the area lively at all hours.

- **Best Value:** A three-star establishment, the **Hotel delle Muse** (☎ **06/8088333**) lies half a mile north of the Villa Borghese. It's run by the efficient, English-speaking Giorgio Lazar. The furnishings are modern and come in a wide range

Keeping Your Cool

Nearly all hotels are heated in the cooler months, but not all are air-conditioned in summer, which can be vitally important during July and August. The deluxe and first-class ones are, but after that it's a toss-up. Be sure to check the listing carefully before you book a stay during the dog days of summer!

of splashy colors. In summer Mr. Lazar operates a garden restaurant serving a reasonably priced fixed-price menu, and the bar is open 24 hours a day. This is one of Rome's best bargains, and you should consider checking in before he wises up and raises his rates.

2 Near the Termini

VERY EXPENSIVE

✪ **Le Grand Hotel.** Via Vittorio Emanuele Orlando 3, 00185 Roma. ☎ **800/325-3589** in the U.S. and Canada, or 06/47091. Fax 06/4747307. 170 units. A/C MINIBAR TV TEL. 610,000L–670,000L ($354–$389) double; from 1,000,000L ($580) suite. Continental breakfast 56,000L ($34). AE, DC, MC, V. Parking 50,000L–60,000L ($29–$35). Metro: Repubblica.

When César Ritz founded the Grand in 1894, it struck a note of elegance the hotel has tried to maintain ever since. The service is first-rate. The location, near the rail station, isn't the most charming, but it's certainly convenient and only a few minutes from Via Veneto. The Grand looks like a large late-Renaissance palace, its facade covered with carved loggias, lintels, quoins, and cornices. Inside, the floors are marble, with Oriental rugs, and the walls a riot of baroque plasterwork and crystal chandeliers. Louis XVI furniture, antique clocks, and wall sconces complete the picture.

The spacious, soundproof guest rooms are conservatively decorated with matching curtains and carpets and come with a dressing room and fully tiled bath. Each room is unique: Most are traditional and the rest modern; some are less grand than you might expect from the impressive lobby.

Dining: Le Grand Bar is an elegant meeting place where tea is served every afternoon, sometimes accompanied by a harpist or pianist. You can enjoy quick meals at the Salad Bar or try Le Restaurant, the more formal dining room. Dietetic and kosher foods can be arranged with advance notice.

Amenities: 24-hour room service, baby-sitting, laundry/valet.

EXPENSIVE

Hotel Massimo d'Azeglio. Via Cavour 18, 00184 Roma. ☎ **800/223-9832** in the U.S., or 06/4870270. Fax 06/4827386. www.italyhotelcom/home/roma/azeglio/azeglio.html. E-mail: massimo.d'azeglio@italyhotelcom. 200 units. A/C MINIBAR TV TEL. 430,000L ($249) double. Rates include breakfast. DC, MC, V. Parking 35,000L–45,000L ($20–$26). Metro: Termini.

This up-to-date hotel near the train station and opera was opened as a small restaurant by one of the founders of an Italian hotel dynasty more than a century ago. In World War II, it was a refuge for the king of Serbia and also a favorite with Italian generals. Today this centrally located hotel is the flagship of the Bettoja chain. Run by Angelo Bettoja and his charming wife, it offers comfortable accommodations, plus a well-trained staff. The hotel boasts one of the area's most elegant neoclassical facades.

Dining: For many decades the hotel restaurant, Massimo d'Azeglio, was a neighborhood fixture. It's no longer *the* place to go around here, but if you're too tired to venture out, it's still a safe bet for good food with market-fresh ingredients. There's also a bar.

Amenities: Concierge, room service, dry cleaning/laundry, baby-sitting, car-rental desk.

Hotel Mediterraneo. Via Cavour 15, 00184 Roma. ☎ **800/223-9832** in the U.S., or 06/4884051. Fax 06/4744105. www.italyhotelcom/home/roma/mediterraneo/mediterianeo. html. E-mail: mediterraneo@venere.it. 271 units. A/C MINIBAR TV TEL. 480,000L ($278) double; 575,000L–1,140,000L ($334–$661) suite. Rates include breakfast. AE, DC, MC, V. Parking 35,000L ($20). Metro: Stazione Termini.

Hotel Mediterraneo sports vivid Italian art deco styling. Its height, coupled with its position on one of Rome's hills, provides panoramic views from the most expensive rooms on the highest floors (some of which have lovely terraces) and from its roof garden and bar (open May to October), which is especially charming at night.

Mario Loreti, one of Mussolini's favorite architects, was the genius who planned for an interior sheathing of gray marble, the richly allegorical murals of inlaid wood, and the art deco friezes ringing the ceilings of the enormous public rooms. The lobby is also decorated with antique busts of Roman emperors.

Our only quibble with this otherwise award-winning hotel are the few jarring notes—like the 1960s-style orange elevators and the furniture (rustic and slightly battered if still solid and dependable). However, these are just slight imperfections in an otherwise marvelous and historically evocative setting.

Dining/Diversions: Although completely unheralded, the hotel restaurant serves excellent Roman and Italian cuisine, including tenderloin of beef with a green peppercorn and cognac sauce and roast baked breast of duck with muscadet grapes.

Amenities: Car-rental desk, concierge, room service, dry cleaning/laundry, baby-sitting.

Mecenate Palace Hotel. Via Carlo Alberto 3. 00185 Roma. ☎ **06/44702024.** Fax 06/4461354. www.venere.it/home/roma/mecenate/mecenate.html. E-mail: mecenate@venere.it. 62 units. A/C MINIBAR TV TEL. 500,000L ($290) double; 1,000,000L ($580) suite. Rates include continental breakfast. AE, DC, MC, V. Parking 40,000L (23). Metro: Termini.

One of Rome's newest four-star hotels opened on the site of what was once a private villa built in the Liberty (art nouveau) style around 1900. It rises five stories above a neighborhood near the main rail station. The pastel-colored rooms, where traces of the original detailing mix with contemporary furnishings, overlook such monuments as Santa Maria Maggiore. Each contains a safe-deposit box and multilanguage satellite TV.

Dining: The hotel offers a bar and a rather formal restaurant serving lunch and dinner Monday to Saturday, plus a roof garden with sweeping views over Roman rooftops.

Amenities: Concierge, room service, dry cleaning/laundry, twice-daily maid service, baby-sitting, secretarial services.

San Giorgio. Via Giovanni Amendola 61, 00185 Roma. ☎ **800/223-9832** in the U.S., or 06/4827341. Fax 06/4883191. www.italyhotelcom/home/roma/sangiorgio/sangiorgio.html. E-mail: san.giorgio@italyhotelcom. 191 units. A/C MINIBAR TV TEL. 370,000L ($215) double; from 500,000L ($290) suite. Rates include breakfast. AE, DC, MC, V. Parking 35,000L–45,000L ($21–$27). Metro: Termini.

Dining Near Via Veneto & Termini

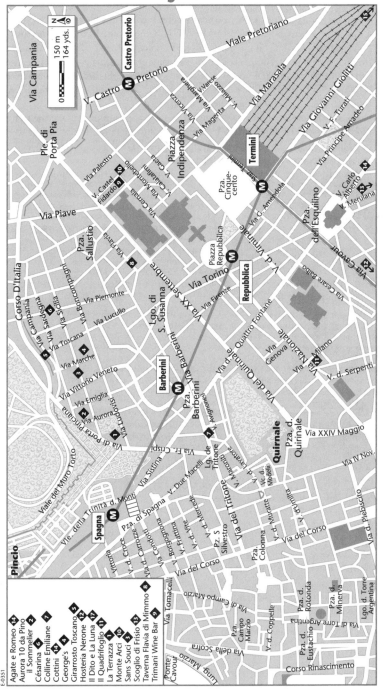

Agate e Romeo 14
Aurora 10 da Pino
   il Sommelier 2
Césarina 6
Colline Emiliane 1
Cottini 4
George's 3
Girarrosto Toscano 5
Hosteria Nerone 12
Il Dito e La Luna 11
Il Quadrifoglio 7
La Terrazza 10
Monte Arci 3
Sans Souci 1
Scoglio di Frisio 13
Taverna Flavia di Mimmo 8
Trimani Wine Bar 9

E-0351

A four-star hotel built in 1940, the San Giorgio is constantly being improved by its founders, the Bettoja family (it was the first air-conditioned hotel in Rome, and is now also soundproof). It's a more inspired choice than the Nord Nuova Roma (below). The hotel is ideal for families, as many of its corner rooms can be converted into larger quarters. Behind wood-veneer doors, the bedrooms are neither glamorous nor dowdy, but clean, well maintained and functionally furnished. All units, except some on the upper-floor, are spacious.

Dining/Diversions: Breakfast is served in a light and airy room, and the staff is most attentive. The hotel doesn't have a restaurant of its own, but sends clients to its siblings (both described above), Massimo d'Azeglio or the nearby Hotel Mediterraneo with its summer-only roof garden and cafe.

Amenities: Car-rental desk, concierge, room service, dry cleaning/laundry, baby-sitting.

MODERATE

Nord Nuova Roma. Via Giovanni Amendola 3, 00185 Roma. ☎ **800/223-9832** in the U.S., or 06/4885441. Fax 06/4817163. www.venere.it/roma/bettoja. E-mail: bettoja@uni.net. 159 units. A/C MINIBAR TV TEL. 300,000L ($174) double. Rates include breakfast. AE, DC, MC, V. Parking 35,000L–45,000L ($20–$26). Metro: Termini.

Although rather plain, this is the best bargain in the Bettoja chain, and a good choice for families. It has garage parking for 100 cars and a small, intimate bar; the standard rooms are well maintained and modern. You can arrange a savory lunch or dinner at the nearby Massimo d'Azeglio Restaurant.

INEXPENSIVE

Aberdeen Hotel. Via Firenze 48, 00184 Roma. ☎ **06/4823920.** Fax 06/4821092. 26 units. A/C MINIBAR TV TEL. 260,000L ($151) double. Rates include buffet breakfast. AE, DC, MC, V. Parking 30,000L–40,000L ($17–$23). Metro: Termini.

This completely renovated hotel is near the opera house, central to both landmarks and the train station. It's in a quiet and fairly safe area of Rome—in front of the Ministry of Defense. The rooms are furnished with rather anonymous modern styling and include conveniences like hair dryers. The breakfast buffet is the only meal served, but many inexpensive trattorie are nearby.

Fiamma. Via Gaeta 61, 00185 Roma. ☎ **06/4818436.** Fax 06/86800124. 79 units. TV TEL. 150,000L–280,000L ($87–$162) double. Rates include breakfast. AE, DC, MC, V. Parking 10,000L ($6). Metro: Termini.

The Fiamma, on the far side of the Baths of Diocletian, is in a renovated building, with five floors of shuttered windows and a ground floor faced with marble and plate-glass windows. It's an enduring favorite, although critics claim it's long past its heyday. The lobby is long and bright, filled to the brim with a varied collection of furnishings, including overstuffed chairs and blue enamel railings. On the same floor is an austere breakfast room made of marble. Some of the comfortably furnished bedrooms are air-conditioned.

Hotel Columbia. Via del Viminale 15, 00184 Roma. ☎ **06/4744289.** Fax 06/4740209. E-mail: columbia@flashnet.it. 45 units. A/C MINIBAR TV TEL. 211,000L–240,000L ($122–$139) double. Rates include breakfast. AE, DC, MC, V. Metro:Repubblica.

Near the train station, this is one of the neighborhood's newest hotels, a three-star choice with a hardworking multilingual staff. It's a very well-done radical renovation (1997) of a hotel built around 1900. The interior contains Murano chandeliers and simple, conservatively modern furniture. The guest rooms are compact and cozy and can hold their own with some of the best of the three-star hotels nearby. There's an appealing roof garden, with a bar and a view over surrounding rooftops. Under the same management, on the opposite side of the rail station, is the Columbia's sibling, **Hotel Venezia** (see below), which sometimes accommodates the Columbia's overflow.

Hotel Italia. Via Venezia 18, 00184 Roma. ☎ **06/4828355.** Fax 06/4745550. www.dinf. com/hitalia/Hotelitalia.ht. E-mail: hitalia@pronet.it. 31 units. TV TEL. 110,000L–170,000L ($64–$99) double. Rates include breakfast. Parking in public lot nearby 25,000L ($15) per night. Metro: Repubblica.

This turn-of-the-century building and its eight-room annex across the street has functioned as a hotel for at least 20 years, but has never been as well managed as it is now under the stewardship of the Valentini family. Both buildings employ a night porter/security guard, and both funnel their overnight guests toward a breakfast buffet that's one of the most appealing in the neighborhood—it even includes pizza. Bedrooms are well maintained, conservatively decorated with comfortable yet uncomplicated furniture, and often have parquet floors. Eleven rooms are equipped with air conditioning. Only one (room no. 6) doesn't have direct access to its bathroom, although a full bathroom that's reserved for the exclusive use of room no. 6 lies just across the hallway. All other rooms in the hotel have direct access to a private bathroom.

Hotel Pavia. Via Gaeta 83, 00185 Roma. ☎ **06/483801.** Fax 06/4819090. 25 units. A/C MINIBAR TV TEL. 170,000L–225,000L ($99–$131) double. Rates include breakfast. AE, DC, MC, V. Parking 15,000L–20,000L ($9–$12). Metro: Termini.

The Pavia, in a much-renovated 100-year-old villa, is a popular choice on this quiet street near the gardens of the Baths of Diocletian. You'll pass through a wisteria-covered passage that leads to the recently modernized reception area and the tasteful public rooms, where the staff is attentive and friendly. The front rooms tend to be noisy, but that's the curse of all Termini hotels. Nevertheless, the rooms are comfortable and fairly attractive. It's a true haven in an area where you can't always be sure of quality.

Hotel Ranieri. Via XX Settembre 43, 00187 Roma. ☎ **06/4814467.** Fax 06/4818834. www.italyhotelcom/roma/ranieri. E-mail: hotelranieri@venere.it. 47 units. A/C MINIBAR TV TEL. 200,000L–280,000L ($116–$162) double. Rates include breakfast. Weekend discounts available Dec–Feb; daily discount rates in Aug. AE, MC, V. Parking 28,000L–35,000L ($16–$20). Metro: Repubblica.

The Ranieri is a winning three-star hotel in an old but restored building. The guest rooms received a substantial renovation in 1995, complete with new furniture, carpets, wall coverings, and even new bathrooms. The location is good—from here you can easily stroll to the opera, Piazza della Repubblica, and Via Vittorio Veneto. The public rooms, the lounge, and the dining room are attractively decorated, in part with contemporary art. You can arrange for a home-cooked meal in the dining room.

✪ **Hotel Venezia.** Via Varese 18 (near Via Marghera), 00185 Roma. ☎ **06/4457101.** Fax 06/4957687. E-mail: venezia@flashnet.it. 61 units. A/C MINIBAR TV TEL. 248,000L ($149) double; 336,000L ($202) triple. Rates include breakfast. AE, DC, MC, V. Metro: Termini.

Just when you decide the whole city is full of overpriced hotels, the Venezia will restore your faith in affordable rooms. The location is good—3 blocks from the rail station, in a relatively quiet, part-business, part-residential area dotted with a few old villas and palms. The Venezia is a good-looking and cheerful choice

---

ⓘ Family-Friendly Hotels

Cavalieri Hilton (*see p. 99*)   This hotel is like a resort at Monte Mario, with a swimming pool, gardens, and plenty of grounds for children to run and play. It's only 15 minutes from the center of Rome, which you can reach by the hotel shuttle bus.

San Giorgio (*see p. 80*)   Near the train station, this family-owned hotel is ideal for parents traveling with children. Many of its corner rooms can be converted into larger quarters by opening doors.

Hotel Venezia (*see p. 83*)   At this good, moderately priced family hotel near the Stazione Termini, the rooms have been renovated and most are large enough for extra beds for children.

---

with charming public rooms. In some cases, the guest rooms are furnished in 17th-century style, although some are beginning to look worn (the last renovation was in 1991). All units are spacious and boast Murano chandeliers and conveniences like hair dryers; some have balconies for surveying the street action. The house-keeping is superb—the management really cares and the helpful staff speaks English.

Medici. Via Flavia 96, 00187 Roma. ☎ **06/4827319.** Fax 06/4740767. 68 units. MINIBAR TV TEL. 200,000L ($116) double. Rates include breakfast. AE, DC, MC, V. Air-conditioning 20,000L ($12) extra. Parking 28,000L–35,000L ($16.25–$20.30). Metro: Repubblica.

The Medici, built in 1906, is a substantial hotel with easy access to the shops along Via XX Settembre and the train station. Many of its better rooms overlook an inner patio garden, with Roman columns holding up greenery and climbing ivy. The lounge, with its white, coved ceiling, has many nooks connected by wide white arches. The furnishings in the public areas and the generous-sized rooms are traditional, with lots of antiques. Only a few rooms are air-conditioned.

✪ Pensione Papà Germano. Via Calatafimi 14A, 00185 Roma. ☎ **06/486919.** 16 units, 6 with bathroom. TEL. 65,000L ($38) double without bathroom, 85,000L ($49) double with bathroom; 75,000L ($44) triple without bathroom; 100,000L ($58) triple with bathroom. 10% discount Nov–Mar. AE, MC, V. Metro: Termini.

This is about as basic as anything in this book, but it's clean and decent. This 1892 building has undergone some recent renovations yet retains its modest ambience. Chances are that your fellow travelers will arrive, backpack in tow, directly from the train station 4 blocks south. Located on a block-long street immediately east of the Baths of Diocletian, this *pensione* has clean accommodations with plain furniture, hair dryers, well-maintained showers, and a high-turnover crowd of European and North American students. The energetic English-speaking owner, Gino Germano, offers advice on sightseeing. No breakfast is served, but dozens of cafes nearby open early.

3 Near Via Veneto & Piazza Barberini

VERY EXPENSIVE

✪ Excelsior. Via Vittorio Veneto 125, 00187 Roma. ☎ **800/325-3589** in the U.S. and Canada, or 06/47081. Fax 06/4826205. 365 units. A/C MINIBAR TV TEL. 671,000L–737,000L ($389–$427) double; 1,265,000L–2,035,000L ($734–$1,180) suite. Breakfast 35,000L ($21). AE, MC, V. Metro: Barberini.

If money is no object, here's a top contender. The Excelsior (Ess-*shell*-see-or) is far livelier and better than its sibling, the Grand. It has a lot more style, with guests like Arab princesses and international financiers. This limestone palace's baroque corner tower, which looks right over the U.S. Embassy, is a landmark in Rome. You enter a string of cavernous reception rooms with thick rugs, marble floors, gilded garlands decorating the walls, and Empire furniture. Everything looks just a little bit dowdy today, but the Excelsior endures, seemingly as eternal as Rome itself. In no small part that's because of the exceedingly hospitable staff.

The guest rooms come in two varieties: new (the result of a major renovation) and traditional. The older ones are a bit worn; the newer rooms have more imaginative color schemes and plush carpeting. They're spacious and elegantly furnished, often with antiques and silk curtains. Most of the rooms are unique, and many have sumptuous Hollywood-style marble bathrooms with separate tub and shower, sinks, and bidet.

Dining: The Excelsior Bar, open daily from 10:30am to 1am, is the most famous on Via Vittorio Veneto, and La Cupola is known for its national and regional cuisine, with spa cuisine and kosher food prepared on request.

Amenities: Room service, baby-sitting, laundry/valet, beauty salon, barbershop.

✪ **Hotel Eden.** Via Ludovisi 49, 00187 Roma. ☎ **800/225-5843** in the U.S., or 06/478121. Fax 06/4821584. www.forte-hotels.com. 112 units. A/C MINIBAR TV TEL. 810,000L–950,000L ($470–$551) double; from 2,100,000L ($1,218) suite. Breakfast 54,000L ($32). AE, DC, MC, V. Parking 50,000L ($29). Bus: 119.

For several generations after it opened in 1889, this ornate hotel, near the top of the Spanish Steps, reigned over one of the world's most stylish shopping neighborhoods. Hemingway, Callas, Ingrid Bergman, Fellini all checked in during its heyday. Purchased in 1989 by Trusthouse Forte, it reopened in 1994 after 2 years (and $20 million) of renovations that enhanced its grandeur and added the amenities its five-star status calls for. The hotel's hilltop position guarantees a panoramic view over the city from most rooms. You expect a lovely room at these prices, and that's what you get, including a marble-sheathed bathroom, draperies worthy of *Architectural Digest,* and decor that harks back to the late 19th century. Understated elegance is the rule.

Dining/Diversions: There are a piano bar and a glamorous restaurant, La Terrazza (see chapter 5, "Dining,").

Amenities: Concierge, 24-hour room service, dry cleaning/laundry, newspaper delivery on request, secretarial service (prior notification necessary), valet parking, gym and health club.

EXPENSIVE

Victoria Roma. Via Campania 41, 00187 Roma. ☎ **06/473931.** Fax 06/4871890. 108 units. A/C MINIBAR TV TEL. 400,000L ($232) double. Rates include breakfast. AE, DC, MC, V. Parking 30,000L–40,000 lire ($17–$23). Metro: Barberini. Bus: 52, 53, 490, 495, or 910.

Its chic *la dolce vita* glory days have passed, but this hotel still keeps abreast of changing times. The location overlooking the Borghese Gardens remains one of its most desirable assets; you can sit in the roof garden drinking your *aperativo* amidst palm trees and potted plants, and imagine you're in a country villa. The lounges and living rooms retain a country-house decor, with soft touches that include high-backed chairs, large oil paintings, bowls of freshly cut flowers, provincial tables, and Oriental rugs. The Swiss owner, Alberto H. Wirth, has set unusual restrictions—no groups—and over the years has attracted a fine clientele which includes diplomats, executives, and artists.

Dining/Diversions: The recently refurbished guest rooms are well furnished and maintained. Meals can be taken à la carte in the elegant grill room, which serves the best of Italian and French cuisine.

Amenities: Concierge, dry cleaning/laundry, room service, massage, twice-daily maid service, car-rental and tour desk. Plentiful shopping is a short walk from the hotel.

MODERATE

Hotel Alexandra. Via Vittorio Veneto 18, 00187 Roma. ☎ **06/4881943.** Fax 06/4871804. www.venere.it/roma/alexandra. E-mail: alexandra@venere.it. 45 units. A/C MINIBAR TV TEL. 350,000L ($203) double; 430,000L ($249) triple; 470,000L ($273) suite. Rates include buffet breakfast. AE, DC, MC, V. Parking 35,000L ($20). Metro: Barberini.

This is one of your few chances to stay on Via Veneto without going broke (although it's not exactly cheap). Set behind the dignified stone facade of what was a 19th-century mansion, this hotel offers immaculate rooms filled with antique furniture and modern conveniences. Rooms facing the front are exposed to the roaring traffic and animated street life of Via Veneto; those in back are quieter but have less of a view. Breakfast is the only meal served, although a staff member can carry drinks to you in the reception area. The breakfast room is especially appealing: Inspired by an Italian garden, it was designed by noted architect Paolo Portoghesi.

Hotel Oxford. Via Boncompagni 89, 00187 Roma. ☎ **06/42828952.** Fax 06/42815349. www.italyhotelcom/roma/oxford/oxford.html. E-mail: oxford@star.flashnet.it. 59 units. A/C MINIBAR TV TEL. 290,000L ($168) double; 340,000L ($197) triple; 390,000L ($226) suite. Rates include buffet breakfast. 20% reduction Jan–Mar 15, Aug, and Nov–Dec. AE, DC, MC, V. Parking 35,000L–45,000L ($20–$26). Bus: 56 or 58.

The Oxford is a decent, although not spectacular, choice adjacent to the Borghese Gardens. Recently renovated, it's now centrally heated and fully carpeted throughout. There's a pleasant lounge and Tony's bar (serving snacks), plus a dining room offering good Italian cuisine. The guest rooms contain simple modern furnishings; they're a bit sterile and functional but well maintained.

La Residenza. Via Emilia 22–24, 00187 Roma. ☎ **06/4880789.** Fax 06/485721. www.italyhotelcom/roma/la_residenza. E-mail: hotella.residenza@italyhotelcom. 29 units. A/C MINIBAR TV TEL. 295,000L–305,000L ($171–$177) double; 335,000L–355,000L ($194–$206) suite. Rates include buffet breakfast. AE, MC, V. Parking (limited) 10,000L ($6). Metro: Barberini.

La Residenza, in a superb but noisy location, successfully combines the intimacy of a generously sized town house with the elegant appointments of a four-star hotel. It's a bit old-fashioned and homelike but still a favorite among international travelers. The converted villa has an ivy-covered courtyard and a labyrinthine series of upholstered public rooms with Empire divans, oil portraits, and cushioned rattan chairs. A series of terraces is scattered strategically throughout.

4 Near Ancient Rome

EXPENSIVE

Hotel Forum. Via di Tor de Conti 25–30, 00184 Roma. ☎ **06/6792446.** Fax 06/6786479. www.hotelforum.com. 86 units. A/C TV TEL. 390,000L–520,000L ($226–$302) double; 550,000L ($319) triple; 630,000L ($365) suite. Rates include breakfast. AE, DC, MC, V. Parking 40,000L ($23). Bus: 27, 81, 85, 87, or 186.

At the peak of the *dolce vita* in the 1950s, this former convent was converted into a hotel. Built around a medieval bell tower off the Fori Imperiali, Hotel Forum offers an elegance that recalls the drama of Old Rome, and accommodations that range from tasteful to opulent. The guest rooms, which look out on the sights of the ancient city, are well appointed with antiques, mirrors, marquetry, and Oriental rugs.

Accommodations Near The Spanish Steps & Ancient Rome

Casa Kolbe **17**
Colosseum Hotel **15**
Grand Hotel Plaza **3**
The Hassler **6**
Hotel Condotti **4**
Hotel de la Ville
    Inter-Continental
    Roma **7**
Hotel Duca d'Alba **14**
Hotel d'Inghliterra **12**
Hotel Forum **13**
Hotel Madrid **10**
Hotel Margutta **1**
Hotel Nerva **16**
Hotel Piazza
    di Spagna **11**
Hotel Scalinata
    di Spagna **5**
Hotel Trinità
    dei Monti **8**
Pensione Fiorella **2**
Pensionne Lydia
    Venier **9**

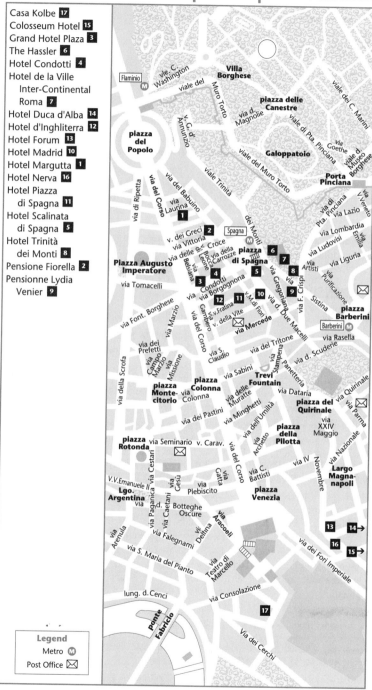

ning/Diversions: The hotel's lounges are conservatively conceived as a country estate, with paneled walls and furnishings that combine Italian and French provincial styles. Dining is an event in the roof-garden restaurant. Reserve well in advance.

Amenities: Twice-daily maid service, baby-sitting, concierge, dry cleaning/laundry, 24-hour room service, in-room massage, secretarial and business services, conference rooms, car-rental and tour desk.

MODERATE

Hotel Nerva. Via Tor di Conti 3–5. 00184 Roma. ☎ **06/6781835.** Fax 06/69922204. 19 units. AC MINIBAR TV TEL. 200,000L–340,000L ($116–$197). Rates include breakfast. AE, DC, MC, V. Metro: Colosseo.

Some of its walls and foundations date from the 1500s, others from a century later, but thankfully the modern amenities are just that—dating only to 1997. The site, on a terrace above and a few steps from the Roman Forum, will appeal to anyone fascinated by archaeology and literature. The welcome from the Cirulli brothers is warm and accommodating. The decor is accented with wood panels and terra-cotta tiles; some rooms even have the original ceiling beams. Otherwise, the furniture is serviceable, contemporary, and comfortable.

INEXPENSIVE

Casa Kolbe. Via San Teodoro 44. ☎ **06/6794974.** 65 units. TEL. 130,000L ($75) double. Breakfast 7,000L ($4.20). AE, DC, MC, V. Metro: Circo Massimo.

This three-story hotel often caters to tour groups from North America and Germany, who arrive en masse by bus. The rooms, painted in old-fashioned tones of deep red and brown, are deliberately very simple. They're well scrubbed, even if some are a bit battered from frequent use. Many overlook a small garden, and the hotel's location, underneath the Palatine, is convenient to the archaeological treasures of Old Rome. The hotel dining room, open only to guests, serves set menus for 25,000L ($15).

Colosseum Hotel. Via Sforza 10, 00184 Roma. ☎ **06/4827228.** Fax 06/4827285. www.venere.it/home/roma/colosseum/colosseum.html. E-mail: colosseum@venere.it. 47 units. A/C TV TEL. 180,000L–215,000L ($104–$125) double. Rates include breakfast. AE, DC, MC, V. Parking 30,000L ($17). Metro: Cavour.

Two short blocks southwest of Santa Maria Maggiore, this hotel offers affordable and comfortable (but small) rooms. Someone with flair and lots of lire designed the public areas and upper hallways, which have a hint of baronial grandeur. The drawing room, with its long refectory table, white walls, red tiles, and provincial armchairs, invites lingering. The guest rooms are furnished with well-chosen antique reproductions (beds of heavy carved wood, dark-paneled wardrobes, leatherwood chairs), and all have stark white walls and sometimes old-fashioned plumbing.

Hotel Duca d'Alba. Via Leonina 14, 00184 Roma. ☎ **06/484471.** Fax 06/4884840. www.venere.it/home/duca_dalba/duca_dalba.html. E-mail: duca.d'alba@venere.it. 27 units, 11 with shower only, 16 with bathroom. A/C MINIBAR TV TEL. 190,000L ($110) double with shower only, 270,000L ($157) double with bathroom. Rates include breakfast. AE, DC, MC, V. Parking 40,000L ($23). Metro: Cavour.

A bargain near the Roman Forum and the Colosseum, this hotel lies in the Suburra neighborhood, which was once pretty seedy but is being gentrified. Although completely renovated, the hotel still retains an old-fashioned air (it was built in the 19th century). The rooms are tasteful, even a bit decorated, with soothing colors, light wood pieces, personal safes, and hair dryers. The most desirable roon four with private balconies.

5 Near Campo de' Fiori

MODERATE

✪ **Teatro di Pompeo.** Largo del Pallaro 8, 00186 Roma. ☎ **06/68300170**. Fax 06/68805531. 12 units. A/C TV TEL. 300,000L ($174) double. Rates include breakfast. AE, DC, MC, V. Parking 30,000L ($17). Bus: 46, 62, or 64.

Built on top of the ruins of the Theater of Pompey, from about A.D. 55, this small charmer lies near the spot where Julius Caesar met his end on the Ides of March. Intimate and refined, it's on a quiet piazzetta near the Palazzo Farnese and Campo de' Fiori. The rooms are decorated in an old-fashioned Italian style with hand-painted tiles, and the beamed ceilings date from the days of Michelangelo. Reserve as early as possible.

INEXPENSIVE

✪ **Albergo Campo de' Fiori.** Via del Biscione 6, 00186 Roma. ☎ **06/68806865.** Fax 06/6876003. 27 units, 9 with bathroom, 4 with shower only; 1 honeymoon suite. 140,000L ($81) double without bathroom, 200,000L ($116) double with bathroom. Rates include breakfast. MC, V. Bus: 46, 62, or 64 from Stazione Termini to Museo di Roma; then arm yourself with a good map for the walk.

Lying in the historic center of Rome in a market area that has existed since the 1500s, this cozy, narrow, six-story hotel offers rustic rooms—many quite tiny and sparsely adorned, but others with a lot of character. The best (restored) rooms are on the first floor, but the most lavish is the honeymoon retreat on the sixth floor with a canopied king-sized bed.

6 Near Piazza Navona & the Pantheon

VERY EXPENSIVE

Albergo Nazionale. Piazza Montecitorio 131, 00186 Roma. ☎ **06/695001.** Fax 06/6786677. 102 units. A/C MINIBAR TV TEL. 480,000L–650,000L ($278–$377) double; 900,000L ($522) suite. Rates include breakfast. AE, DC, MC, V. Parking 40,000L ($23). Bus: 52, 53, 58, 85, or 95.

Albergo Nazionale faces one of Rome's most historic squares, Piazza Colonna, with its Column of Marcus Aurelius, the Palazzo di Montecitorio, and the Palazzo Chigi. Because it's next to the parliament buildings, the Albergo is often frequented by government officials and diplomatic staff. The lobbies are wood-paneled, and there are many antiques throughout the hotel. The guest rooms are high-ceilinged, comfortably proportioned, and individually decorated in a style inspired by the late 19th century, each with a different color scheme of brown, yellow, green, or bordeaux. Rooms are either carpeted or floored with marble, and some offer interesting views over the ancient bronze-sheathed column in the square outside.

Dining/Diversions: The hotel restaurant serves adequate Italian fare, and a complementary breakfast each morning. There are many nooks conducive to conversation in the public lounges.

Amenities: Twice-daily maid service, room service, laundry/dry cleaning, concierge, baby-sitting, secretarial services.

Hotel Raphael. Largo Febo 2, 00186 Roma. ☎ **06/682831.** Fax 06/6878993. www. raphaelhotelcom. E-mail: info@raphaelhotelcom. 73 units. A/C MINIBAR TV TEL.

Staying in J. Paul Getty's Former Villa

La Posta Vecchia, in Palo Laziale, just south of Ladispoli (☎ 06/9949501; fax 06/9949507), lies 22 miles northwest of Rome and about 14 miles up the coast from Leonardo da Vinci airport. Set on foundations of villas possibly built by Tiberius, this palatial villa was owned between 1960 and 1976 by one of the world's richest men, J. Paul Getty. In 1654 it was a guest house for the nearby Castello Oldescalchi. Set behind iron gates, the stucco-sided building stands amid formal gardens in an 8-acre park.

The villa contains many antiques collected by Getty, as well as many carefully disguised steel doors, escape routes, and security devices installed to protect him from intruders. Following the tragic kidnapping of his son in the early 1970s, Getty declared that the building's access to the sea was an unacceptable security risk. The house was sold and became a private home until 1990, when it was transformed into an exceptionally elegant hotel. Guests stay in 14 sumptuously decorated suites, which range in price from 704,000L to 2,354,000L ($409 to $1,366) a night. With discretion and politeness, staff members serve international cuisine at dinner and lunch in a richly formal dining room. The villa is closed from November 7 to March 15.

Extensive renovations initiated during Getty's ownership revealed hundreds of ancient Roman artifacts, many of which are on display in a mini-museum. There's an indoor pool, plus a staff (some of whom used to work for Getty) adept at maintaining the illusion that clients have arrived as friends of the long-departed billionaire.

495,000L–595,000L ($287–$345) double; 660,000L–760,000L ($383–$441) suite. Breakfast 31,000L ($19). AE, DC, MC, V. Parking 40,000L ($23). Bus: 70, 81, 87, or 115.

Adjacent to Piazza Navona, this hotel is within easy walking distance of many attractions and boasts a rooftop garden terrace with a panoramic view of the ancient city. The charming ivy-covered facade invites you to enter the lobby, which is decorated with antiques that might rival those in local museums. Some of the suites have private terraces, and all the well-appointed guest rooms have direct-dial phones and satellite TV. Some are quite small, however.

Dining: The elegant restaurant/bar, Café Picasso, serves a French/Italian hybrid cuisine.

Amenities: Room service, fitness room, baby-sitting, laundry, currency exchange.

EXPENSIVE

✪ **Albergo del Sole al Pantheon.** Piazza della Rotonda 63, 00186 Roma. ☎ 06/6780441. Fax 06/69940689. E-mail: hotsole@flashnet.it. 30 units. A/C MINIBAR TV TEL. 500,000L ($290) double; 600,000L–700,000L ($348–$406) suite. Rates include breakfast. AE, DC, MC, V. Parking 35,000L ($20). Bus: 119.

You're obviously paying for the million-dollar view and the location, but you may find it's worth it to be across from the Pantheon, one of antiquity's greatest surviving architectural relics. (Okay, so you're above a McDonald's, but one look at the Pantheon at sunrise and you'll forget about burgers.) This is one of the oldest hotels in the world; the first records of it as a hostelry appear in 1467. The hotel is amazingly eccentric in its layout and built on various levels—be prepared to walk up and down a lot of three- or four-step staircases. The guest rooms vary greatly in decor, none of it award-winning and much hit or miss. Windows are double glazed but,

Accommodations Near Campo de' Fiori & Piazza Navona

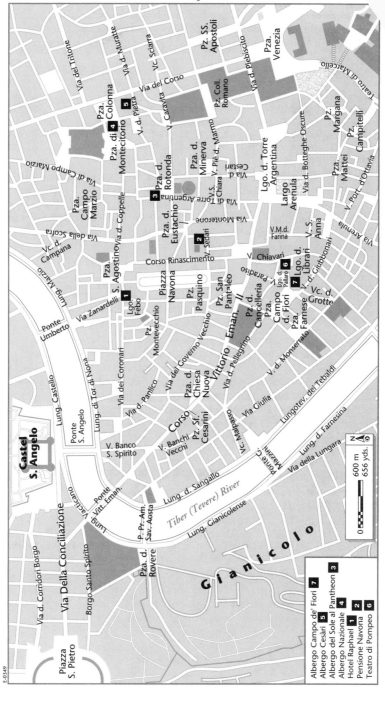

Albergo Campo de' Fiori 7
Albergo Cesàri 5
Albergo del Sole al Pantheon 4
Hotel Raphael 1
Pensione Navona 2
Teatro di Pompeo 6
Albergo del Sole al Pantheon 3

pening onto Piazza della Rotonda tend to be noisy at all hours. The ommodations overlook the courtyard but are sans view.

uning: Breakfast is the only meal served, but there are dozens of trattorie in the neighborhood.

Amenities: Only laundry/dry cleaning, baby-sitting (not always available).

MODERATE

✪ **Albergo Cesàri.** Via di Pietra 89A, 00186 Roma. ☎ **06/6792386.** Fax 06/6790882. www.venere.it/home/roma/cesari/cesari.html. E-mail: cesari@venere.it. 50 units. A/C TV TEL. 230,000L–300,000L ($133–$174) double; 270,000L–340,000L ($157–$197) triple; 390,000L ($226) quad. Rates include breakfast. AE, DC, MC, V. Parking 45,000L ($26). Bus: 492 from Stazione Termini.

The Cesàri, on an ancient street in the old quarter, has occupied its desirable location between the Trevi Fountain and the Pantheon since 1787. Its well-preserved exterior harmonizes with the Temple of Neptune and many little antiques shops nearby. The rooms have mostly functional modern pieces, but there are a few traditional trappings as well to maintain character. In 1998, all guest rooms and the breakfast room were completely renovated.

INEXPENSIVE

Pensione Navona. Via dei Sediari 8, 00186 Roma. ☎ **06/6864203.** Fax 06/68803802. 30 units, 22 with bathroom. 130,000L ($75) double without bathroom, 140,000L ($81) double with bathroom; 210,000L ($122) triple with bathroom. Rates include breakfast. No credit cards. Bus: 70, 81, 87, or 115.

The *pensione* is on a small street that radiates out from Piazza Navona's southeastern tip. The rooms aren't as glamorous as the exterior, but the Navona offers decent accommodations, many of which have been renovated and some of which open to views of the quiet central courtyard. Run by an Australian-born family of Italian descent, the place boasts tiled bathrooms, ceilings high enough to help relieve the midsummer heat, and an array of architectural oddities (the legacy of the continual construction this palace has undergone since 1360). By request, you can get an air-conditioned room for 40,000L ($23) extra per night (only in the doubles with bathrooms).

7 Near Piazza di Spagna & Piazza del Popolo

VERY EXPENSIVE

The Hassler. Piazza Trinità dei Monti 6, 00187 Roma. ☎ **800/223-6800** in the U.S., or 06/699340. Fax 06/6789991. E-mail: hasselroma@maclink.it. 100 units. A/C MINIBAR TV TEL. 695,000L–1,030,000L ($403–$597) double; from 2,250,000L ($1,305) suite. Breakfast 55,000L ($33). AE, DC, MC, V. Parking 40,000L ($23) in nearby garage. Metro: Spagna.

The Hassler, the only deluxe hotel in this old part of Rome, uses the Spanish Steps as its grand entrance. The original 1885 Hassler was rebuilt in 1944. Its crown has become a bit tarnished, but trading on a mystique of long tradition and a one-of-kind-location, it still gets away with charging astronomical rates. The lounges and the guest rooms, with their "Italian Park Avenue" trappings, strike a faded if still glamorous 1930s note.

The rooms, some of which are small, have a personalized look—Oriental rugs, tasteful draperies at the French windows, brocade furnishings, comfortable beds, and (the nicest touch of all) bowls of fresh flowers. Some have balconies with views of the city. Despite all this, you can get better rooms elsewhere in Rome for this kind of money.

Dining: The Hassler Roof Restaurant is a favorite with visitors and Romans alike for its fine cuisine and view. Its Sunday brunch is a popular rendezvous time. The Hassler Bar is ideal, if a little formal, for cocktails; in the evening it has piano music.

Amenities: Room service, telex and fax, limousine, in-room massages, laundry, nearby fitness center, tennis court (summer), free bicycles available.

✪ **Hotel d'Inghliterra.** Via Bocca di Leone 14, 00187 Roma. ☎ **06/69981.** Fax 06/6992243. www.charminghotels.it/inghliterra. E-mail: hir@charminghotelit. 98 units. A/C MINIBAR TV TEL. 660,000L ($383) double; 825,000L ($479) triple; 1,133,000L ($657) suite. Rates include breakfast. AE, DC, MC, V. Parking 40,000L ($23). Metro: Piazza di Spagna.

The Inghliterra holds onto its traditions and heritage, even though it has been renovated. If you're willing to spend a king's ransom, Rome's most fashionable small hotel is up there with the Hassler and Inter-Continental. It has hosted big names from Ernest Hemingway and Franz Liszt to Alec Guinness. The rooms have mostly old pieces (gilt and lots of marble, mahogany chests, and glittery mirrors) as well as modern conveniences. Some, however, are just too small. The preferred rooms are higher up, opening onto a tile terrace, with a balustrade and a railing covered with flowering vines and plants.

Dining: The Roman Garden serves excellent Roman dishes. The English-style bar with its paneled walls, tip-top tables, and old lamps is a favorite gathering spot in the evening. The Roman Garden Lounge offers light lunches and snacks.

Amenities: Concierge, room service, dry cleaning/laundry, baby-sitting, car-rental desk, secretarial services, gym.

✪ **Hotel de la Ville Inter-Continental Roma.** Via Sistina 67–69, 00187 Roma. ☎ **800/327-0200** in the U.S. and Canada, or 06/67331. Fax 06/6784213. www. interconti.com. E-mail: rome@interconti.com. 215 units. A/C MINIBAR TV TEL. 560,000L–730,000L ($325–$423) double; from 990,000L ($574) suite. Rates include continental breakfast. AE, DC, MC, V. Parking 35,000L ($20). Metro: Spagna or Barberini.

We prefer this place to the overpriced glory of the Hassler next door. The hotel looks deluxe (it's officially rated first class) from the minute you walk through the revolving door, where a smartly uniformed doorman greets you. Once inside this palace, built in the 19th century on the site of the ancient Gardens of Lucullus, you'll find Oriental rugs, marble tables, brocade furniture, and an English-speaking staff. There are endless corridors leading to what at first seems a maze of ornamental lounges. Some of the public rooms have a sort of 1930s elegance, others are strictly baroque, and in the middle of it all is an open courtyard.

The guest rooms and public areas have been renovated in a beautifully classic and yet up-to-date way. The higher rooms with balconies have wonderful views of Rome, and you're free to use the roof terrace with the same view.

Dining/Diversions: La Piazzetta de la Ville Restaurant, on the second floor overlooking the garden, serves an Italian and international cuisine. The hotel also has an American bar with a pianist during cocktail hours.

Amenities: 24-hour room service, baby-sitting, laundry/valet.

EXPENSIVE

Grand Hotel Plaza. Via del Corso 126, 00186 Roma. ☎ **06/69921111.** Fax 06/69941575. A/C MINIBAR TV TEL. 520,000L–580,000L ($302–$336) double; 800,000L–1,000,000L ($464–$580) suite. AE, DC, MC, V. Parking 40,000L ($23). Bus: 81, 90, 90b, or 119.

Empress Carlotta of Mexico received Pope Pius IX here in 1866; in 1933 Pietro Mascagni composed his *Nerone* in one of its guest rooms; and Vincent Price stayed here while making "all those bad movies." When you see the very grand decor, you'll understand why. Partially renovated in 1993, this hotel's public rooms are vintage 19th century and contain stained-glass skylights, massive crystal chandeliers, potted palms, inlaid marble floors, and a life-size stone lion guarding the entrance to the ornate stairway. If you're interested in living amid the theatrical grandeur that the lobby hints at, you'll want to rent one of the suites where the furnishings mimic the gilded-age splendor of the public rooms on a smaller scale. Otherwise guest rooms are contemporary and streamlined, with efficient but comfortable furniture and monochromatic color schemes of blue, green, or off-white.

Dining: The hotel does not have a restaurant; its bar does serve light sandwiches and snacks, however, and a pasta dish may be available from time to time.

Amenities: Concierge, 24-hour room service, baby-sitting, laundry/dry cleaning, conference rooms.

✪ Hotel Scalinata di Spagna. Piazza Trinità dei Monti 17, 00187 Roma. ☎ **06/ 6793006.** Fax 06/69940598. www.italyhotelcom/home/roma/scalinata/scalinata.html. 16 units. A/C MINIBAR TV TEL. 450,000L ($261) double; 500,000L ($290) triple; 700,000L ($406) suite. Rates include breakfast. AE, MC, V. Parking 40,000L ($23). Metro: Spagna.

This hotel near the Spanish Steps has always been one of Rome's top choices. Think of it as an intimate inn or boutique hotel rather than a full-service hotel. It's at the top of the steps, across from the Hassler, in a delightful little building—only two floors are visible from the outside—nestled between much larger structures, with four relief columns across the facade and window boxes with bright blossoms. The recently redecorated interior is like an old inn's—the public rooms are small with bright print slipcovers, old clocks, and low ceilings.

The decorations vary radically from one guest room to the next. Some have low beamed ceilings and ancient-looking wood furniture; others have loftier ceilings and more run-of-the-mill furniture. Everything is spotless and pleasing to the eye.

Dining: Breakfast is the only meal served, but you'll enjoy it on one of the most panoramic terraces in all Rome.

Amenities: Concierge, dry cleaning/laundry, baby-sitting.

MODERATE

Hotel Condotti. Via Mario de' Fiori 37, 00187 Roma. ☎ **06/6794661.** Fax 06/6790484. 16 units. A/C MINIBAR TV TEL. 230,000L–320,000L ($133–$186) double; 290,000L– 350,000L ($168–$203) minisuite. Rates include breakfast. AE, DC, MC, V. Metro: Spagna.

Small, choice, and terrific for shoppers intent on being near the toniest boutiques, this hotel is chic, intimate, and comfortable. It's small scale (no bar, no restaurant, although breakfast is served). The mostly English-speaking staff is cooperative and hardworking. The modern, mainly blue-and-white rooms may not have much historic charm, but they're comfortable and soothing.

Hotel Madrid. Via Mario de' Fiori 94–95, 00187 Roma. ☎ **06/6991511.** Fax 06/6791653. 33 units. A/C MINIBAR TV TEL. 285,000L ($165) double; 390,000L ($226) suite for four. Rates include breakfast. AE, DC, MC, V. Parking 30,000L–40,000L ($17–$23). Metro: Spagna.

Despite modern intrusions into the well-maintained and comfortable, if rather minimalist, bedrooms, the interior of the Hotel Madrid manages to evoke fin-de-siècle Roma. Guests often take their breakfast amid ivy and blossoming plants on the roof terrace with a panoramic view of rooftops and the distant dome of St. Peter's. Some of the doubles are large, equipped with small scatter rugs, veneer armoires, and shuttered windows. Others are quite small, so make sure you know what you're getting before you check in. Overall, this hotel offers a good standard of service. Look for an ocher building with a shuttered facade on a narrow street practically in the heart of the boutique area centering around Via Frattina, near the Spanish Steps.

Hotel Piazza di Spagna. Via Mario de' Fiori 61, 00187 Roma. ☎ **06/6796412.** Fax 06/6790654. 16 units. A/C MINIBAR TV TEL. 270,000L–330,000L ($157–$191) double. Rates include breakfast. AE, MC, V. Metro: Spagna. Bus: 590.

Set about a block from the downhill side of the Spanish Steps, this hotel was just an unknown run-down *pensione* until new owners took it over in the 1990s and substantially upgraded it. It's small but classic, with an inviting atmosphere. The rooms have a functional streamlined decor; some even have Jacuzzis.

Hotel Trinità dei Monti. Via Sistina 91, 00187 Roma. ☎ **06/6797206.** Fax 06/6990111. 23 units. MINIBAR TV TEL. 220,000L–290,000L ($128–$168) double. Rates include breakfast. AE, MC, V. Parking 30,000L ($17). Metro: Barberini or Spagna.

This well-maintained, friendly hotel sits conveniently between two of the most-visited piazzas in Rome (Barberini and di Spagna), The rooms come in subdued colors and are comfortable if not flashy. They're outfitted with elaborate herring-bone-patterned parquet floors and big windows that flood the interior with sunlight. The hotel's social center is a simple coffee bar near the reception desk. Don't expect anything terribly fancy, but the welcome is warm and the location ultraconvenient.

INEXPENSIVE

Hotel Margutta. Via Laurina 34, 00187 Roma. ☎ **06/3223674.** Fax 06/3200395. 21 units. 165,000L ($96) double; 220,000L ($128) triple. Rates include breakfast. AE, DC, MC, V. Metro: Flaminio.

The Margutta, on a cobblestone street near Piazza del Popolo, offers attractively decorated rooms, a helpful staff, and a simple breakfast room. The best guest rooms are the three on the top floor, offering a great view. Two of these three (nos. 50 and 51) share a terrace, and the larger room has a private terrace. (There's usually a 20% to 35% supplement for these.) Drawbacks? No air-conditioning, no room phones.

Pensione Fiorella. Via del Babuino 196, 00187 Roma. ☎ **06/3610597.** 7 units, none with bathroom. 110,000L ($64) double. Rates include breakfast. No credit cards. Metro: Flaminio.

A few steps from Piazza del Popolo is this utterly basic but comfortable *pensione*. Antonio Albano and his family are one of the best reasons to stay here—they speak little English, but their humor and warm welcome make renting one of their very clean rooms a lot like visiting a lighthearted Italian relative. Logistical drawbacks: The doors of the Fiorella shut at 1am, and reservations can be made only a day before you check in.

Pensione Lydia Venier. Via Sistina 42, 00187 Roma. ☎ **06/6791744.** Fax 06/6797263. 28 units, 17 with shower only, 10 with bathroom. TV TEL. 180,000L ($104) double without bathroom, 220,000L ($128) double with shower only, 240,000L ($139) double with bathroom. Rates include breakfast. AE, DC, MC, V. Metro: Barberini or Spagna.

This respectable *pensione* is on one of the upper floors of a gracefully proportioned apartment building on a street jutting out from the top of the Spanish Steps. The rooms are utterly simple, with understated furnishings—a dignified combination of slightly battered modern and antique and an occasional reminder of an earlier era (like a ceiling fresco). The service here is wonderful, and the staff go out of their way to be helpful, especially to those who don't speak Italian.

8 Near Vatican City

EXPENSIVE

✪ **Hotel Atlante Star.** Via Vitelleschi 34, 00193 Roma. ☎ **06/6873233.** Fax 06/6872300. www.atlantehotels.com. E-mail: atlante.star@atlantehotels.com. 65 units. A/C MINIBAR TV TEL. 540,000L ($313) double; from 600,000L ($348) suite. Rates include breakfast. AE, DC, MC, V. Parking 40,000L ($23). Metro: Ottaviano. Tram: 19 or 30.

The Atlante Star is a first-class hotel near the Vatican, with striking views of St. Peter's. The tastefully renovated lobby is covered with dark marble, chrome trim, and exposed wood; the upper floors give the impression of being inside a luxurious ocean liner. This stems partly from the lavish use of curved and lacquered surfaces, walls upholstered in printed fabrics, modern bathrooms, and wall-to-wall carpeting. Even the door handles are deco. The rooms are small but posh, with all the modern comforts. There's also a royal suite with a Jacuzzi. If there's no room at this inn, the owner will try to accommodate you in his less expensive **Atlante Garden** nearby.

Dining: Les Etoiles is an elegant roof-garden choice at night, with a 360° view of Rome and an illuminated St. Peter's in the background. The flavorful cuisine is inspired in part by Venice.

Amenities: 24-hour room service, laundry/valet, baby-sitting, express checkout, foreign-currency exchange, secretarial services in English, translation services.

✪ **Hotel Atlante Garden.** Via Crescenzio 78, 00193 Roma. ☎ **06/6872361.** Fax 06/6872315. www.atlantehotels.com. E-mail: atlante.garden@atlantehotels.com. 60 units. A/C MINIBAR TV TEL. 420,000L ($244) double. Rates include breakfast. AE, DC, MC, V. Parking 40,000L ($23). Metro: Ottaviano. Bus: 23, 32, 49, 51, or 492. Tram: 19 or 30.

Atlante Garden stands on a tree-lined street near the Vatican. Although not as attractive or well appointed as its sibling, the Atlante Star (above), this hotel is much cheaper. The entrance takes you through a garden tunnel lined with potted palms, which eventually leads into a series of handsomely decorated public rooms. More classical in its decor than the Atlante Star, the Garden offers freshly papered and painted 19th-century–style bedrooms that contain tastefully conservative furniture and all the modern accessories. The renovated baths are tiled, and each is equipped with a Jacuzzi.

Dining: The hotel restaurant serves an authentic nouvelle Italian cuisine, with main courses ranging from 14,000L to 15,000L ($8 to $9), and fixed-price meals starting at 100,000L ($58).

Amenities: Baby-sitting, laundry/dry cleaning, room service, concierge, car-rental desk, Jacuzzi.

Hotel Columbus. Via della Conciliazione 33, 00193 Roma. ☎ **06/6865435.** Fax 06/6864874. 92 units. MINIBAR TV TEL. 370,000L ($215) double. Rates include buffet breakfast. AE, DC, MC, V. Free parking. Bus: 62.

The building looks much as it must have centuries ago—a severe time-stained facade, small windows, and heavy wooden doors leading from the street to the colonnades and arches of the inner courtyard. The cobbled entranceway leads to a reception hall with castlelike furniture, then on to a series of baronial public rooms. Note the main salon with its walk-in fireplace, oil portraits, battle scenes, and Oriental rugs.

The guest rooms are considerably simpler than the tiled and tapestried salons, done in soft beiges and furnished with comfortable modern pieces. All the accommodations are spacious, but a few are enormous and still have such original details

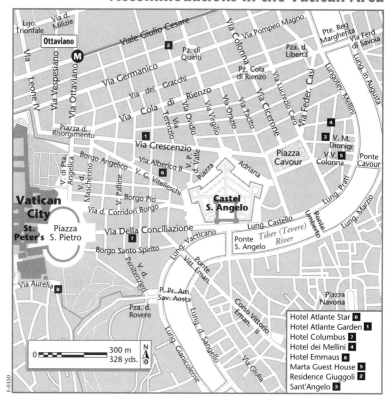

Hotel Atlante Star **6**
Hotel Atlante Garden **1**
Hotel Columbus **7**
Hotel dei Mellini **4**
Hotel Emmaus **8**
Marta Guest House **5**
Residence Giuggoli **2**
Sant'Angelo **3**

as decorated wood ceilings and frescoed walls. However, only some are air-conditioned.

Dining: Many guests like La Veranda so much they prefer to dine here at night instead of roaming the streets looking for a trattoria. Standard Italian cuisine is served: time-tested recipes made with fresh ingredients rather than anything too innovative.

Amenities: Concierge, room service, dry cleaning/laundry, car-rental desk.

Hotel dei Mellini. Via Muzio Clementi 81. 00193 Roma. ☎ **06/324771.** Fax 06/32477801. www.benere.it/roma/dei-mellini. E-mail: dei.mellini/net.it. 80 units. A/C MINIBAR TV TEL. 410,000L ($238) double; 500,000L–600,000L ($290–$348) suite. Rates include breakfast. AE, DC, MC, V. Parking 35,000L ($20). Metro: Lepanto or Flaminio.

This hotel consists of two interconnected buildings, one with four floors and one with six; the top is graced with a terrace overlooking the baroque cupolas of at least three churches. A small staff, headed by the highly capable Roberto Altezza, maintains comfortable, carefully decorated guest rooms whose decor includes art deco touches, Italian marble, heavy draperies, and mahogany furniture. One of its best drawing points is a quiet neighborhood that doesn't have a lot of traffic.

Dining: Other than a simple platter of food that the staff might rustle up on short notice, breakfast is the only meal served. The breakfast room is extremely pleasant, adjoining a small green courtyard. There's also a hospitable American bar.

Amenities: Concierge, room service, dry cleaning/laundry, courtesy car, car-rental desk, nearby gym.

INEXPENSIVE

Hotel Emmaus. Via delle Fornaci 23, 00165 Roma. ☎ **06/6380370.** Fax 06/635658. 26 units. MINIBAR TV. 150,000L–180,000L ($87–$104) double. Rates include breakfast. AE, DC, MC, V. Metro: Ottaviano. Bus: 65.

Relatively low prices and a location a short walk west of the Vatican make it likely that you will share this hotel with Catholic pilgrims from all over the world. Unpretentious and basic but comfortable accommodations occupy an older building that was last renovated and upgraded in 1992. There's an elevator and a breakfast area.

Marta Guest House. Via Marianna Dionigi 17. 00193 Roma. ☎ **06/3240428.** Fax 06/3230184. 9 units, 1 with bathroom. 95,000L ($55) double without bathroom, 130,000L ($75) double with bathroom. AE, DC, MC, V. Bus: 492 to Piazza Cavour.

Named after one of its owners, Marta Balbi, this is a friendly and well-scrubbed but simple *pensione* with a good location near Piazza Cavour, not far from the Spanish Steps. It fills the entire second floor of a 10-story apartment house built around 1900. Take an elevator upstairs to the unassuming reception area, where a staff member will lead you to one of the airy and high-ceilinged but utterly plain and unassuming rooms. No breakfast is served, but the neighborhood is filled with cafes where you can get your morning cappuccino.

Residence Giuggioli. Via Germanico 198, 00192 Roma. ☎ **06/3242113.** 5 units, 1 with bathroom. 110,000L ($64) double without bathroom, 130,000L ($75) double with bathroom. No credit cards. Parking 25,000L–40,000L ($15–$23) in nearby garage. Metro: Ottaviano.

This guest house occupies most of the second floor of a five-story apartment house from the 1870s, with accommodations in high-ceilinged rooms that were originally much grander than they are today but whose noble proportions are still obvious. Three of the five rooms have balconies overlooking the street; the one with the private bathroom is no. 6. Residence Giuggioli is always popular and crowded, partly because the owner is so convivial and partly because the rooms are larger than one might expect and have a scattering of antiques and reproductions.

If this place is full, walk a few flights to the similar **Pensione Lady** (☎ **06/3242112**), whose seven rooms go for about the same rates.

Sant'Angelo. Via Mariana Dionigi 16, 00193 Roma. ☎ **06/3220758.** Fax 06/3204451. 25 units. AC TV TEL. 150,000L–220,000L ($87–$128) double; 210,000L–250,000L ($122–$145) triple. Rates include continental breakfast. AE, DC, MC, V. Parking 35,000L ($20). Metro: Cavour.

Right off Piazza Cavour (northeast of the Castel Sant'Angelo) and a 10-minute walk from St. Peter's, this hotel is in a relatively untouristy area. Maintained and operated by several members of the Torre family, it occupies the second and third floors of an imposing 200-year-old building whose other floors house offices and private apartments. The rooms are simple, modern, and clean, with wooden furniture and views of either the street or of a rather bleak but quiet courtyard.

9 In Prati

EXPENSIVE

Giulio Cesare. Via degli Scipioni 287, 00192 Roma. ☎ **06/3210751.** Fax 06/3211736. 86 units. A/C MINIBAR TV TEL. 450,000L ($261) double. Rates include breakfast. AE, DC, MC, V. Free parking. Bus: 280.

The tasteful Giulio Cesare, an elegant villa that was the former house of Countess Paterno Solari, lies in a sedate part of Rome across the Tiber from Piazza del Popolo.

The guest salon, where the countess once entertained diplomats from all over the globe, is mostly furnished with antiques and Oriental carpets. Tapestries, Persian rugs, mirrors, ornate gilt pieces, and crystal chandeliers grace the public rooms; and guests gather for drinks in a smaller salon with fruitwood paneling and 18th-century furniture. The carpeted guest rooms look like part of a lovely private home; some contain needlepoint-covered chairs. Other facilities include a garden where breakfast is served, a snack bar, and a piano bar.

10 In Monte Mario

VERY EXPENSIVE

✪ **Cavalieri Hilton.** Via Cadlolo 101, 00136 Roma. ☎ **800/445-8667** in the U.S. and Canada, or 06/35091. Fax 06/35092241. 393 units. A/C MINIBAR TV TEL. 625,000L–825,000L ($375–$495) double; from 1,350,000L ($810) suite. AE, CB, DC, DISC, MC, V. Parking 5,000L–35,000L ($2.90–$21). Free shuttle bus to/from city center.

The Cavalieri Hilton combines all the advantages of a resort hotel with the convenience of being a 15-minute drive from the city center. Overlooking Rome and the Alban Hills from atop Monte Mario, it's set among 15 acres of trees, flowering shrubs, and stonework. Its facilities are amazingly complete. The entrance leads into a lavish red-and-gold lobby, whose sculpture and winding staircases are usually flooded with sunlight from the massive windows.

The guest rooms and suites, many with panoramic views, are contemporary and stylish. Soft furnishings in pastels are paired with Italian furniture in warm-toned woods. Each unit has a keyless electronic lock, individually controlled heating and air-conditioning, a color TV with in-house movies, a radio, and a bedside control for all the gadgets, as well as a spacious balcony. The bathrooms, sheathed in Italian marble, come with large mirrors, a hair dryer, international electric sockets, a vanity mirror, piped-in music, and a phone. There are facilities for the disabled.

Dining/Diversions: The stellar La Pergola restaurant boasts one of the best views in Rome; its light Mediterranean menu emphasizes seafood like tagliolini with tiger prawns in pesto. In summer, Il Giardino dell'Uliveto, with a pool veranda, is an ideal choice.

Amenities: Concierge, room service, laundry/valet, tennis courts, jogging paths, indoor arcade of shops, outdoor pool. The hotel's health and fitness center could be the setting for a film on late Empire decadence, with its triple-arched Turkish bath, marble, and mosaics; there's a 55-foot indoor pool and a state-of-the-art weight room.

11 In Parioli

VERY EXPENSIVE

✪ **Hotel Lord Byron.** Via G. de Notaris 5, 00197 Roma. ☎ **06/3220404.** Fax 06/3220405. www.italyhotelcom/roma/lord-byron. E-mail: lord.byron@italyhotel.com. 37 units. A/C MINIBAR TV TEL. 470,000L–620,000L ($273–$360) double; from 800,000L ($464) suite. Rates include buffet breakfast. AE, DC, MC, V. Metro: Flaminio. Bus: 26 or 52.

Lots of sophisticated travelers with hefty wallets are forgetting about the old landmarks (the Grand and Excelsior) and choosing to check into this chic boutique hotel. The Lord Byron exemplifies modern Rome—an art deco villa set on a residential hilltop in Parioli, an area of embassies and exclusive town houses at the edge of the Villa Borghese. From the curving entrance steps off the staffed parking lot in front, you'll notice striking design touches. Flowers are everywhere, the lighting is discreet, and everything is on an intimate scale—it seems more like a private home than a hotel. Each of the guest rooms is unique, but most have lots of mirrors, upholstered walls, a spacious bathroom with gray marble accessories, a big dressing room/closet, and all the amenities. Check into room no. 503, 602, or 603 for the most panoramic views.

Dining: Relais Le Jardin is one of Rome's best restaurants (see chapter 5, "Dining").

Amenities: Concierge, 24-hour room service, laundry/valet.

MODERATE

Hotel degli Aranci. Via Barnaba Oriani 9–11, 00197 Roma. ☎ **06/8085250.** Fax 06/8070202. 57 units. A/C MINIBAR TV TEL. 300,000L ($174) double; 350,000L ($203) suite. Rates include breakfast. AE, DC, MC, V. Free parking. Bus: 3 or 53.

This former villa is on a tree-lined street, surrounded by similar villas now used, in part, as consulates and diplomats' homes. Most of the accommodations have tall windows opening onto city views and are filled with provincial furnishings or English-style reproductions. The public rooms have memorabilia of ancient Rome scattered about, such as medallions of soldiers in profile, old engravings of ruins, and classical vases. A marble-topped bar in an alcove off the sitting room adds a relaxed touch. From the glass-walled breakfast room at the rear, you can see the tops of orange trees.

INEXPENSIVE

✪ **Hotel delle Muse.** Via Tommaso Salvini 18, 00197 Roma. ☎ **06/8088333.** Fax 06/8085749. E-mail: hmuse@flashnet.it. 61 units. TV TEL. 160,000L–200,000L ($93–$116) double; 220,000L–260,000L ($128–$151) triple. Rates include buffet breakfast. AE, CB, DC, DISC, MC, V. Parking 30,000L ($17). Bus: 4. Tram: 19.

This three-star hotel, half a mile north of the Villa Borghese, is a winning but undiscovered choice. It's run by the efficient English-speaking Giorgio Lazar. Most rooms have been renovated but remain rather spartan and minimalist. In summer, Sr. Lazar operates a restaurant in the garden. A bar is open 24 hours a day in case you get thirsty at 5am. There's also a TV room, a writing room, and a dining room.

Dining 5

Rome is one of the world's greatest cities for dining. From elegant, deluxe spots with lavish trappings to little trattorie opening onto hidden piazzas deep in the heart of Old Rome, the city abounds in good restaurants in all price ranges.

The better-known restaurants have menus printed in English. Even some of the lesser-known establishments have at least one person on the staff who speaks English a bit to help you get through the menu.

Most Italian restaurants are either called a *trattoria* or a *ristorante*. In theory there's a difference, but in reality it's difficult to discern. Traditionally trattorie are smaller and less formal, but sometimes in a kind of reverse snobbism the management will call an elegant place a trattoria. A ristorante is supposed to be more substantial, but often the opposite is true.

It's difficult to compile a list of the best restaurants in a city such as Rome. Everybody—locals, expatriates, even those who have chalked up only one visit—has favorites. What follows is not a list of all the best restaurants of Rome, but simply a personal running commentary on a number of our favorites. For the most part, we've chosen not to review every deluxe spot known to all big spenders. Rather, we've tried to seek out equally fine (or better) restaurants patronized by some of the finest palates in Rome—but not necessarily by the fattest wallets.

Rome's cooking is not subtle, but its kitchen rivals anything the chefs of Florence or Venice can turn out. A feature of Roman restaurants is skill at borrowing—and sometimes improving upon—the cuisine of other regions. Throughout the capital you'll come across Neapolitan (*alla neapolitana*), Bolognese (*alla bolognese*), Florentine (*alla fiorentina*), and even Sicilian (*alla siciliana*) specialties. One of the oldest sections of the city, Trastevere, is a gold mine of colorful streets and restaurants with a time-tested cuisine.

Roman meals customarily include at least three separate courses: pasta, a main course (usually a meat dish with vegetables or salad), and dessert. Meats, while tasty, are definitely secondary to the pasta dishes, which are much more generous and filling. The wine is so excellent (especially the white Frascati wine from the nearby Castelli Romani) and moderate in price that you may want to do as the Romans do and have it with both lunch and dinner.

A Dining Note

In rock-bottom restaurants you may be charged a *pane e coperto* ("bread and cover charge") of from 1,000L to 3,000L (60¢ to $1.75) per person. Also note that a *servizio* (tip) of 10% to 15% will often be added to your bill or included in the price, although patrons often leave an extra 1,000L to 3,000L (60¢ to $1.75) as a token.

Meal hours are rather confining in Italy. If you don't take continental breakfast at your hotel, you can have coffee and a pastry at any **bar** (really a café, although there will be liquor bottles behind the counter) or a ***tavola calda*** ("hot table"). These are stand-up snack bar–type arrangements, open all day long and found all over the city. Restaurants generally serve lunch between 1 and 3pm and dinner between about 8 and 10:30pm; at all other times, restaurants are closed. Dinner, by the way, is taken late in Rome, so while the restaurant may open at 7:30, even if you get there at 8pm, you'll often be the only one in the place. Romans think in terms of "dinner" in the afternoon (*pranzo*) and "supper" in the evening (*cena*). In Rome, as in much of the rest of Europe, a heavier meal is typically eaten at midday and a lighter one in the evening.

We recommend that you leave a few hours free for dinner and go to a restaurant in a different part of town each night. It's a great way to get a real "taste" of Rome.

PRICES   For our purposes, restaurants rated **"Very Expensive"** usually charge more than 130,000L ($75) for a three-course meal for one; **"Expensive,"** 80,000L to 130,000L ($46 to $75); and **"Moderate,"** 50,000L to 80,000L ($29 to $46). Any restaurant charging less than 50,000L ($29) is rated **"Inexpensive,"** at least in Rome. These prices are computed on the basis of a three-course meal (not the most expensive items on the menu), including a carafe of the house wine, service, and taxes.

A FINAL CAVEAT   Most Roman restaurants are closed at least one day a week—usually Sunday or Monday, but that varies. Also, beware of the month of August, when most Romans go on holiday. Scores of restaurants close down, displaying only a lonely CHIUSO PER FERIE (closed for vacation) sign. It's always best to call a restaurant before you head there.

1 Best Bets

- **Best Romantic Dinner:** If you're getting ready to propose, a great place to pop the question is **Relais Le Jardin** (☎ 06/3613041), a stunner of a place which also just happens to serve the best Italian cuisine in town. The decor is as romantic as the atmosphere—all white lattice and bold Italian colors highlighted by masses of fresh flowers. The setting is in the Relais & Châteaux–member hostelry the Lord Byron, an art deco villa set on a residential hilltop in Parioli, an area of embassies and exclusive town houses at the edge of the Villa Borghese.
- **Best Business Lunch:** The location of **George's** (☎ 06/42084575) on Via Marche, right off Via Veneto, is most central (not far from the heartbeat Piazza Barberini), and the discreet staff and clubby atmosphere are just perfect for doing business—and for dining well. Here, one of the most professional and best-trained staffs in Rome will serve you in elegantly decorated dining rooms. If the weather is fair, you may want to request a table in the lovely garden. Making those deals go down even easier is one of Rome's finest wine cellars.

- **Best for a Celebration:** Romans have been flocking to **Checchino dal 1887** (☎ **06/5743816**) since the early 19th century for fun and hearty food. With a bountiful array of wine and foodstuff, every night seems like a party. The location is Monte Testaccio, which was once a pile of broken amphoras and terracotta roof tiles collected back in Nero's day. The tables are packed nightly, and the place is a local legend. You'll have fun while still enjoying some of the best cuisine in town.

- **Best Decor:** By night chic Romans and savvy foreign visitors alike show up at **El Toulà** (The Hayloft)(☎ **06/6873498**), an elegant establishment set near the fabled Caffè Greco and some of the most fashionable boutiques in Rome. It's no bargain, but once you see the sumptuous setting and, more important, enjoy the cuisine, you'll think it's worth the price. Haute cuisine is served in a subdued, tasteful setting of antiques, paintings, ever-so-discreet lighting, and oh-to-die-for flower arrangements.

- **Best View:** The stars really do come out at night at **Les Etoiles** (The Stars) (☎ **06/6893434**), which has been labeled "the most beautiful rooftop in Italy." This restaurant is a virtual garden in the sky, with a 360° view of Roman landmarks, including the floodlit dome of St. Peter's. Try for a table alfresco in summer, but even in winter the same incredible view can be seen through picture windows. Fortunately, the food—delicately prepared Mediterranean cuisine using the freshest of ingredients—is the best in the area around the Vatican.

- **Best Wine List:** The food is only secondary at the **Trimani Wine Bar** (☎ **06/4469630**), but the wine list is fabulous, a deluxe tour through the vineyards of Italy. One of the best "tasting centers" in Rome for both French and Italian vintages, this elegant wine bar offers a dazzling array of wines at reasonable prices. The Trimani family has had a prestigious name in the wine business since 1821, and visitors to their wine bar will experience a palate-pleasing tour of the oenological bounty of their land— simply sit down at one of their tables and let the pouring begin.

- **Best Value:** For less than $20, at the **Ristorante del Pallaro** (☎ **06/68801488**) you'll be served one of the finest fixed-price menus in Rome, each dish lovingly prepared by the chef-owner, Paola Fazi, who urges her diners to *Mangia! Mangia!* The moment you're seated at the table the dishes start to arrive: First a selection of antipasto, then the homemade, succulent pastas of the day which in turn are followed by such meat courses as tender roast veal. Everything's included—even a carafe of the house wine.

- **Best for Kids:** After their tour of the Vatican or St. Peter's, many savvy Roman families head for the **Ristorante Il Matriciano** (☎ **06/3212327**), a long-established and widely respected family dining room. It's not fancy, but the price is right, and in summer you can opt for a sidewalk table. Let your kids feast on good, reasonably priced, homemade fare that includes such crowd pleasers as ricotta-stuffed ravioli. At the next table you're likely to see some priests from the Vatican dining. It's a safe, wholesome environment, and the food is really tasty.

- **Best Continental Cuisine:** The city's finest restaurant is now **La Terrazza** (☎ **06/478121**), edging out a position long held by Sans Souci. In the restored Hotel Eden, former stamping ground of Hemingway, Ingrid Bergman, and Fellini, you can dine on continental cuisine that is both bold and innovative. The seasonal menu offers the most polished, sophisticated cuisine in Rome, as reflected by such dishes as a "symphony" of seafood or a warm salad of grilled vegetables.

- **Best Italian Cuisine:** Italian food as you've (almost) never had it before is served at the **Relais Le Jardin** (☎ 06/3613041), a refined citadel of haute cuisine. In a luxurious setting you can feast on some of the best traditional fare—prepared with a light, innovative touch—of such regions as Lazio and Abruzzi. The most demanding Roman palates wine and dine here and enjoy the freshest of seasonal produce, beginning with the bright zucchini blossoms of spring.

- **Best Emilia Romagna Cuisine:** The area around Bologna has long been celebrated for serving the finest cuisine in Italy, and the little **Trattoria Colline Emiliane** (☎ 06/4817538) does much to maintain that stellar reputation among Romans. The pastas here are among the best in Rome, especially the handmade tortellini alla panna (cream sauce) with truffles. You can order less expensive pastas as well, all of them good. Their prosciutto comes from a small town near Parma, and is reputedly the best in the world.

- **Best Neapolitan Cuisine:** It's so cornball "O Sole Mio" that you'll think you've been sent to a tourist trap. But the food that emerges from the Neapolitan kitchen at **Scoglio di Frisio** (☎ 06/4872765) is the best of its kind in the city. You get not only the crunchy, oozy, and excellent Neapolitan pizzas here, but an array of foodstuff ranging from chicken cacciatore to veal scaloppine that's perfectly prepared. Near the Stazione Termini, the trattoria has been a longtime favorite of visitors to Rome in spite of its somewhat sleazy location.

- **Best Roman Cuisine:** The tempting selection of antipasto is enough of a treat to lure you to **Al Ceppo** (The Log) (☎ 06/8419696). Try such appetizers as stuffed yellow or red peppers or finely minced cold spinach blended with ricotta. Only 2 blocks from the Villa Borghese, this is a dining address jealously guarded by Romans, who often take their friends from out of town here. They feast on the succulent lamb chops—charcoal-grilled to perfection—or other grilled meats such as quail, liver, and bacon. These Roman dishes and flavors have proven a powerful culinary allure over the years.

- **Best Tuscan Cuisine:** For the most delicious and tenderest bistecca alla fiorentina (beefsteak Florentine style) in Rome, head for **Girarrosto Toscano,** off Via Veneto (☎ 06/4823835). The chefs grill the meats to perfection, using only virgin olive oil, salt, and pepper for seasoning. You get an array of other dishes as well, including one of the best selections of antipasto in town, everything from vine-ripened melon with prosciutto to a delectable Tuscan salami. Oysters and fresh fish from the Adriatic are also served.

- **Best Fruits of the Sea:** For not only the best but the most beautiful seafood restaurant in Rome, go to **Alberto Ciarla** (☎ 06/5818668). This place was among the first to create new and innovative preparations of seafood, which Romans traditionally have either fried or put into soups. Overcooked seafood is definitely not on the agenda; some Romans even tried raw fish for the first time here. Although this restaurant doesn't enjoy the fame it did when it opened, it's just as good as ever. Fish dishes are perfectly seasoned but designed to bring out the natural flavor of the sea—and not "drown" the "sea fruits."

- **Best Pizzeria:** If you try a pie at **Da Vittorio** (☎ 06/5800353), deep in the heart of Trastevere, you'll probably agree with Vittorio's claim that he makes the best pizzas in Rome. The pizza Vittorio—with fresh basil, fresh tomato, parmesan, and mozzarella—is our favorite. This is a popular, fun place, with outdoor tables in fair weather. The youthful crowd of diners fairly bursts with exuberance (not to mention pizza).

- **Best Nuova Cucina:** Near the Vittorio Emanuele monument, the well-decorated **Agata e Romeo** (☎ 06/4466115) prepares one of Rome's most inventive new-style cuisines. If you'd like a sampling of the best tastings of the day, you can order one of the fixed-price menus, available with or without wine. The menu reflects the agrarian bounty of Italy, with ample culinary rewards for meat eaters, fish fanciers, and vegetarians.

- **Best Newcomer:** Although it's been around since 1995, more and more discriminating Romans are discovering **Il Sanpietrino** (☎ **06/68806471**), the culinary shrine of Chef Marco Cardio. He prepares one of the city's finest traditional, yet contemporary cuisines, based on market-fresh ingredients which he interprets in a creative and inventive style. His medley of fish antipasto is reason enough to show up here for dinner.

- **Best in the Jewish Ghetto:** For centuries Romans have flocked to the Jewish Ghetto to sample at least one dish: the Jerusalem artichoke. No one prepares them better than **Piperno** (☎ **06/68806629**), which serves savory (though non-Kosher) Roman food. Of course, you can order more than these deep-fried artichokes here. A full array of delights includes everything from stuffed squash blossoms to succulent pastas.

- **Best Wild Game:** The best selection of unusual meat specialties in Rome is served at **Da Mario** (☎ **06/6783818**), although you can order other excellently prepared dishes as well if your dining partner isn't game. You could begin with pappardelle, which comes with a game sauce known as *caccia,* or the roast quail with polenta (a better version of which you'd have to go to Lombardy (Milan) to find). The best wild game dishes are served in autumn; but unusual, delectable offerings from both field and stream are always available.

- **Best Restaurant for Desserts:** It's a bit of an exaggeration to say that people fly to Rome just to sample the dessert specialty—a tartufo—at **Tre Scalini** (☎ **06/6879148**), but that would be reason enough to buy an airplane ticket. The dessert is fabled, consisting of a grated bitter chocolate–covered chocolate ice cream ball swathed in whipped cream. It's named for its resemblance to the knobby truffle. There are other desserts as well, and on almost any night you'll find cone seekers (those not dining upstairs) often 3 feet deep at the ice-cream counter outside. If you can take your mind off the tartufo, you'll have a ringside seat at Rome's most beautiful square, Piazza Navona, facing Bernini's Fontana dei Fiumi.

- **Best Restaurant for a 4-Hour Lunch:** On the historic Appian Way, only a short walk from the catacombs of St. Sebastian, the family-run **Hostaria l'Archeologia** (☎ **06/7880494**), which looks like an 18th-century village tavern, is a place for lingering. If the day is sunny, you can sit late into the afternoon enjoying the wines of Lazio after a robust and satisfying Roman-style meal. Opt for the garden out back and find a table shaded from the sun by the spreading wisteria—and you may end up lingering until the waiters start closing down the joint. The wines emerge from a cellar that used to be a Roman tomb. You never know what might happen after a long meal here; we once took travel guru and founder of this travel series, Arthur Frommer, here for lunch, and before it was over he'd proposed that we write a guide to Italy.

- **Best Late-Night Pastry Shop:** Right on Piazza del Popolo, where young men and women drive up in their Maseratis and Porsches, the **Café Rosati** (☎ **06/3225859**) gets active as the night wears on. Although you can order whisky, many come for the delectable Italian pastries. A sidewalk table makes an ideal spot to enjoy an ice cream dish.

- **Best Outdoor Restaurant:** In Trastevere, Piazza Santa Maria comes alive at night. It's almost a scene straight from Fellini's *Roma*. If you reserve a sidewalk table at **Sabatini** (☎ **06/5812026**), you'll have a view of all the action, including the floodlit golden mosaics of the church on the piazza, Santa Maria in Trastevere. At the next table you're likely to see—well, just about anybody (on our most recent visit, Roman Polanski). In addition to the view, you get some of the best grilled fish and Florentine steaks here.

- **Best Restaurant for People-Watching:** Join the fashionable young actors, models, and artists from nearby Via Margutta who descend at night on Piazza del Popolo, which is said to be haunted by the memories of Nero. The square still retains its fashion whereas Via Veneto long ago faded with the memories of *la dolce vita*. Young men with their silk shirts unbuttoned (the better to show off what they view as their Davidesque chests), alight from sports cars to go on the prowl. At **Dal Bolognese** (☎ 06/3611426), you not only can take in this fascinating scene, but you can also enjoy fine Bolognese cuisine as delectable and enticing as the spectacle unfolding before you. Sometimes, however, the scene is so lively it's hard to concentrate on the food.

- **Best Cafe for People-Watching:** In the 1950s during the heyday of *la dolce vita*, **Caffè de Paris** (☎ 06/4885284) was a gathering place for the *bella gente* (beautiful people) of that era, many of whom hid behind night-owl sunglasses. The sunglasses are still around, although the big names like Fellini have long gone. However, this remains the best cafe in Rome if you'd like to see a passing parade from the mainstream of world tourism. Opt for a sidewalk table to fully check out this see-and-be-seen scene—all fashions, all persuasions, and all types stroll by, inspecting you as you inspect them.

- **Best for a Cappuccino with a View:** Surely the most desirable cafe in Rome is **Di Rienzo** (☎ 06/6869097), but only because of its location. It stands directly on Piazza della Rotonda fronting the Pantheon, one of the greatest of all monuments to come down from ancient Rome. On a summer night there's no better place to be than "the living room" of Rome (as the square before you has been dubbed) as you sit and slowly sip your cappuccino.

- **Best Tavola Calda:** One of the best *tavola caldas* ("hot tables") in Rome is **Cottini** (☎ 06/4740768), convenient for those staying in hotels around the Stazione Termini. The food is artfully displayed, and the selection is bountiful—not only freshly made salads but hot pastas and just-prepared main courses. Portions are very generous, and you can fill up fast on the cornucopia of agrarian Latium's bounty. Tempting desserts such as a melt-in-your-mouth chocolate cake are prepared at the in-house bakery.

- **Best Open-Air Food Market:** Between Corso Vittorio Emanuele II and the Tiber, is **Campo de' Fiori,** seemingly everybody's favorite market in Rome—and that's been true for centuries. The luscious produce of Lazio is on display here right in the heart of the old city. In spite of its name "field of flowers" (the English translation), this is not a flower market. The name is derived from Flora, lover of Pompey, the great Roman general. If you wish, you can purchase vegetables already chopped and ready to be dropped into the minestrone pot. Romans are particular about their food: You'll see some people inspecting cherries or other items one by one by one.

- **Best Picnic Fare:** When the weather is cool and the day is sunny, the countryside of Lazio beckons. It's time for an alfresco meal, and there's no better place to purchase the makings of a picnic than the **Campo de' Fiori** open-air market, where stall after stall sells everything from open baskets of fresh broccoli to legumes. There are also several excellent delicatessen shops on the square. Visit one of the shops selling freshly baked Roman bread, pick up a bottle of wine and a companion—and the day is yours.

- **Best Ristorante:** With one dining room decorated in the style of an 18th-century tavern and another occupying Pompey's ancient theater, the **Ristorante da Pancrazio** (☎ **06/6861246**) is not only architecturally amusing, but serves good Roman food. It's a national monument, in fact. Here you sample one of the widest selections of Roman dishes, including the kitchen's fabled mixed fish fry. There's also a savory risotto made with a medley of "fruits of the sea."
- **Best Trattoria:** In the heart of the old Jewish Ghetto, a short walk from Michelangelo's Campodoglio, is **Vecchia Roma** (☎ **06/6864604**), a landmark trattoria that's been feeding savvy Roman foodies for years. Even movie stars have been slipped this address as a place where they can enjoy good food and the "paparazzi will never find you." The antipasto selection is prepared fresh daily and is one of the finest in the area. The pasta and risotto dishes are succulent, and the meats—especially the lamb roasted in Roman ovens to crispy perfection—are from excellent cuts.
- **Best Osteria:** Near Campo de' Fiori, the **Hostaria Grappolo d'Oro** (☎ **06/6864118**) was put on the tourist map by a *New Yorker* article that praised its cuisine. Although the article drew the international world to this previously unheralded spot, the owner admits to never having read it. One reviewer wrote that this neighborhood place, often frequented by Romans who live nearby, is pure "gastronomic ecstasy." We wouldn't go that far, but it's certainly good, everything washed down with the house white wine.
- **Best Restaurant to See a Movie Star:** Although Elizabeth Taylor is long gone and no one talks about "Hollywood on the Tiber" anymore, glitz and glamour—whatever's left of it—still reign at **Sans Souci** (☎ **06/4821814**), Rome's most fashionable and flashiest dining room. You'll rarely find a Roman here, but those on the hipster international circuit show up. If you had to invite Madonna to dinner during a visit to Rome, this is where you'd take her.

2 Restaurants by Cuisine

ABRUZZESE
Abruzzi (Near Ancient Rome, *I*)
Ristorante al Cardello (Near Ancient Rome, *I*)
Ristorante Edy (Near Piazza di Spagna & Piazza de Popolo, *I*)

BOLOGNESE
Dal Bolognese (Near Piazza di Spagna & Piazza del Popolo, *M*)

CALABRESE
Le Maschere (Near Campo de' Fiori & the Jewish Ghetto, *I*)

CONTINENTAL
Trimani Wine Bar (Near the Termini, *M*)

EMILIA-ROMAGNOLA
Césarina (Near Via Veneto & Piazza Barberini, *M*)

Colline Emiliane (Near Via Veneto & Piazza Barberini, *M*)

ENGLISH
Babington's Tea Rooms (Near Piazza di Spagna & Piazza del Popolo, *M*)

FLORENTINE
Da Mario (Near Piazza di Spagna & Piazza del Popolo, *I*)

FRENCH
L'Eau Vive (Near Piazza Navona & the Pantheon, *I*)
Sans Souci (Near Via Veneto & Piazza Barberini, *VE*)

INTERNATIONAL
Alfredo alla Scrofa (Near Piazza Navona & the Pantheon, *M*)
George's (Near Via Veneto & Piazza Barberini, *E*)

Key to Abbreviations: *VE* = Very Expensive; *E* = Expensive; *M* = Moderate; *I* = Inexpensive.

La Terrazza (Near Via Veneto &
Piazza Barberini, *VE*)

L'Eau Vive (Near Piazza Navona &
the Pantheon, *I*)

Les Etoiles (Near Vatican City, *E*)

Ristorante Giardinaccio (Near Vatican City, *I*)

Ristorante Ranieri (Near Piazza di
Spagna & Piazza del Popolo, *M*)

Taverna Flavia di Mimmo (Near the
Termini, *M*)

ITALIAN

Alvaro al Circo Massimo (Near
Ancient Rome, *E*)

Aurora 10 da Pino il Sommelier
(Near Via Veneto & Piazza Barberini, *M*)

Cottini (Near the Termini, *I*)

Hostaria l'Archeologia (On the
Appian Way, *I*)

Hostaria Nerone (Near Ancient
Rome, *I*)

Il Convivio (Near Piazza Navona &
The Pantheon, *E*)

Il Dito e La Luna (Near the
Termini, *I*)

La Majella (Near Campo de' Fiori &
the Jewish Ghetto, *I*)

La Terrazza (Near Via Veneto &
Piazza Barberini, *VE*)

Montevecchio (Near Piazza Navona
& the Pantheon, *M*)

Passetto (Near Piazza Navona & the
Pantheon, *E.*)

Quirino (Near Piazza Navona & the
Pantheon, *I*)

Relais Le Jardin (In Parioli, *VE*)

Ristorante Giardinaccio (Near Vatican City, *I*)

Ristorante Ranieri (Near Piazza di
Spagna & Piazza del Popolo, *M*)

Sans Souci (Near Via Veneto &
Piazza Barberini, *VE*)

Vecchia Roma (Near Campo de' Fiori
& the Jewish Ghetto, *M*)

JEWISH

Da Giggetto (Near Campo di Fiori &
the Jewish Ghetto, *I*)

MEDITERRANEAN

Babington's Tea Rooms (Near Piazza
di Spagna & Piazza del Popolo,
M)

Les Etoiles (Near Vatican City, *E*)

MOLISIAN

Ristorante Giardinaccio (Near Vatican City, *I*)

NEAPOLITAN

Il Quadrifoglio (Near the Termini,
M)

Scoglio di Frisio (Near the
Termini, *M*)

PASTA

Da Vittorio (In Trastevere, *I*)

PIZZA

Da Vittorio (In Trastevere, *I*)

Scoglio di Frisio (Near the
Termini, *M*)

ROMAN

Abruzzi (Near Ancient Rome, *I*)

Agata e Romeo (Near Piazza
Venezia, *E*)

Al Ceppo (In Parioli, *M*)

Alfredo alla Scrofa (Near Piazza
Navona & the Pantheon, *M*)

Césarina (Near Via Veneto & Piazza
Barberini, *M*)

Checchino dal 1887 (In Testaccio,
M)

Cottini (Near the Termini, *I*)

Da Giggetto (Near Campo de' Fiori &
the Jewish Ghetto, *I*)

Da Mario (Near Piazza di Spagna &
Piazza del Popolo, *I*)

El Toulà (Near Piazza di Spagna &
Piazza del Popolo, *E*)

Enoteca Corsi (Near Piazza di Spagna
& Piazza del Popolo, *I*)

Hostaria dei Bastioni (Near Vatican
City, *I*)

Hostaria Grappolo d'Oro (Near
Campo de' Fiori & the Jewish
Ghetto, *I*)

Hostaria l'Archeologia (On the
Appian Way, *I*)

Hostaria Nerone (Near Ancient Rome *I*)

Il Convivio (Near Piazza Navona & the Pantheon, *E*)

Il Miraggio (Near Piazza Navona & the Pantheon, *I*)

Il Sanpietrino (Near Campo di Fiori & the Jewish Ghetto, *M*)

Il Ristorante 34 (Near Piazza di Spagna & Piazza del Popolo, *M*)

La Cisterna (In Trastevere, *M*)

Monte Arci (Near the Termini, *I*)

Montevecchio (Near Piazza Navona & the Pantheon, *M*)

Osteria dell'Angelo (Near Vatican City, *I*)

Otello alla Concordia (Near Piazza di Spagna & Piazza del Popolo, *I*)

Passetto (Near Piazza Navona & the Pantheon, *E*)

Piperno (Near Campo di Fiori & the Jewish Ghetto, *E*)

Quirino (Near Piazza Navona & the Pantheon, *I*)

Ristorante al Cardello (Near Ancient Rome *I*)

Ristorante Edy (Near Piazza di Spagna & Piazza de Popolo, *I*)

Ristorante da Pancrazio (Near Campo de' Fiori & the Jewish Ghetto, *M*)

Ristorante del Pallaro (Near Campo de' Fiori & the Jewish Ghetto, *I*)

Ristorante Il Matriciano (Near Vatican City, *M*)

Ristorante Pierdonati (Near Vatican City, *M*)

Sabatini (In Trastevere, *VE*)

Taverna Flavia di Mimmo (Near the Termini, *M*)

Tre Scalini (Near Piazza Navona & the Pantheon, *M*)

Vecchia Roma (Near Campo di Fiori & the Jewish Ghetto, *M*)

SARDINIAN

Il Drappo (Near Campo de' Fiori & the Jewish Ghetto, *VE*)

Il Miraggio (Near Piazza Navona & the Pantheon, *I*)

Monte Arci (Near the Termini, *I*)

SEAFOOD

Alberto Ciarla (In Trastevere, *E*)

La Rosetta (Near Piazza Navona & the Pantheon, *VE*)

Sabatini (In Trastevere, *VE*)

SICILIAN

Il Dito e la Luna (Near the Termini, *I*)

Quirino (Near Piazza Navona & the Pantheon, *I*)

TUSCAN

Girarrosto Toscano (Near Via Veneto & Piazza Barberini, *M*)

Ristorante Nino (Near Piazza di Spagna & Piazza del Popolo, *E*)

VENETIAN

El Toulà (Near Piazza di Spagna & Piazza del Popolo, *E*)

3 Near the Termini

MODERATE

Il Quadrifoglio. 19 Via del Boschetto. ☎ **06/4826096**. Reservations recommended. Main courses 20,000L–25,000L ($12–$15). AE, DC, MC, V. Mon–Sat 7pm–midnight. Metro: Cavour. NEAPOLITAN.

In a grandiose palace, this likable, well-managed restaurant lets you sample the flavors of Naples and southern Italy. You'll find a tempting selection of antipasto, featuring anchovies, peppers, capers, onions, and breaded and fried eggplant, all garnished with regional herbs and olive oil. Pastas are made daily, usually with tomato- or oil-based sauces, always with herbs and usually aged crumbling cheeses, and perhaps garnished with squid or octopus. Try a rice dish (one of the best is sartù di riso, studded with vegetables, herbs, and meats), followed by grilled octopus or a simple but savory granatine (meatballs, usually of veal, bound together with mozzarella). Dessert anyone? A longtime favorite is torta caprese, with hazelnuts and chocolate.

◯ **Scoglio di Frisio.** Via Merulana 256. ☎ **06/4872765.** Reservations recommended. Main courses 18,000L–32,000L ($10–$19). AE, DC, MC, V. Mon–Fri 12:30–3pm and 7:30–11pm, Sat–Sun 7:30–11pm. Metro: Manzoni. Bus: 714 or 16 from Termini. NEAPOLITAN/PIZZA.

Scoglio di Frisio is the choice *suprême* to introduce yourself to the Neapolitan kitchen. Get up close and personal with a genuine plate-sized Neapolitan pizza (crunchy, oozy, and excellent) with clams and mussels. Or you could start with a medley of stuffed vegetables and antipasto before moving on to chicken cacciatore or veal scaloppine. Scoglio di Frisio also makes for an inexpensive night of slightly hokey but still charming entertainment, as cornball "O Sole Mio" renditions and other Neapolitan songs spring forth from a guitar, mandolin, and strolling tenor (Mario Lanza incarnate). The nautical decor (in honor of the top-notch fish dishes) is complete with a high-ceilinged grotto of fishers' nets, crustaceans, and a miniature three-masted schooner.

Taverna Flavia di Mimmo. Via Flavia 9. ☎ **06/4745214.** Reservations recommended. Main courses 16,000L–30,000 lire ($9–$17). AE, DC, MC, V. Mon–Fri 12:30–3pm and 7:30–11pm, Sat 7:30–11pm. Metro: Repubblica. ROMAN/INTERNATIONAL.

Taverna Flavia di Mimmo, just a block from Via XX Settembre, is a robustly Roman restaurant where movie people used to meet and eat during the heyday of *la dolce vita*. The restaurant still serves the food that once delighted the late Frank Sinatra and the "Hollywood on the Tiber" crowd of the 1950s. As a chic rendezvous, however, its day is long past. Specialties include a risotto with scampi and spaghetti al champagne. A different regional dish is featured daily, which might be Roman-style tripe prepared in such a savory manner that it tastes far better than you might expect. Exceptional dishes include osso bucco with peas, a seafood salad, and fondue with truffles.

◯ **Trimani Wine Bar.** Via Cernaia 37b. ☎ **06/4469630.** Salads and platters 10,000L–35,000L ($6–$20); glass of wine (depending on vintage) 5,000L–12,000L ($2.90–$7). AE, DC, MC, V. Mon–Sat 11:30am–3pm and 5:30pm–midnight. Closed several weeks in Aug. Metro: Repubblica or Castro Pretorio. CONTINENTAL.

Opened as a tasting center for French and Italian wines, spumantis, and liqueurs, this elegant wine bar has a lovely decor (stylish but informal) and comfortable seating. More than 30 wines are available by the glass, and to accompany them you can choose from a bistro-style menu, with light dishes like salade niçoise, vegetarian pastas, herb-laden bean soups (fagiole), quiche, Hungarian goulash, and platters of French and Italian cheeses and pâtés. Trimani also maintains a well-stocked shop about 40 yards from its wine bar, at Via Goito 20 (☎ **06/4469661**), where an astonishing array of Italian wines is for sale.

INEXPENSIVE

◯ **Cottini.** Via Merulana 286–287. ☎ **06/4740768.** Reservations not accepted. Main courses 7,500L ($4.35) each at lunch, 7,500L–16,000L ($4.35–$9) at dinner. AE, DC, MC, V. Daily 7am–midnight. Metro: Termini. ROMAN.

Large, bustling, and confident of its role as one of the most popular tavola caldas in this congested neighborhood, this establishment feeds hundreds of hungry office workers and shopkeepers. The venue is self-service, not unlike an American cafeteria, with the noteworthy difference that the food represents the bounty of agrarian Italy (and is rather lacking on the tuna casserole front). Separate areas are devoted to hot pastas—most priced at 4,500L ($2.60) per heaping portion—meats, and to

Dining Near Via Veneto & Termini

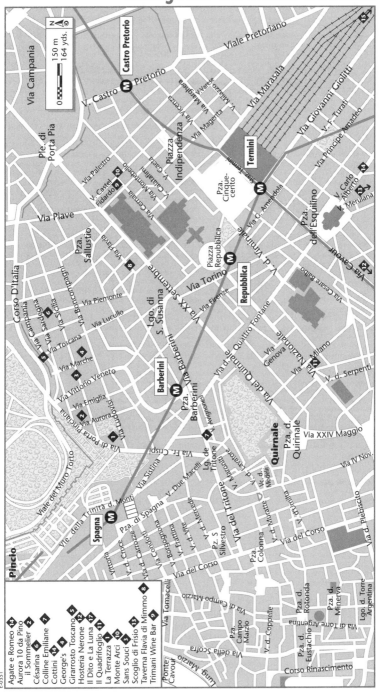

Agate e Romeo 14
Aurora 10 da Pino 2
il Sommelier 1
Césarina 6
Colline Emiliane 4
Cottini 3
George's 5
Girarrosto Toscano 5
Hosteria Nerone 12
Il Dito e La Luna 17
Il Quadrifoglio 7
La Terrazza 11
Monte Arci 10
Sans Souci 3
Scoglio di Frisio 13
Taverna Flavia di Mimmo 8
Trimani Wine Bar 9

E-0351

a lesser extent, fish. High turnover ensures a relatively fresh, if not particularly stylish, array of mass-produced, pan-Italian cuisine. The place becomes more like a pub in the evening when the venue is considerably more relaxed. Alcohol is served.

Il Dito e La Luna. Via dei Sabelli 47–51, San Lorenzo. ☎ **06/4940726.** Reservations recommended. Main courses 18,000L–22,000L ($10–$13). No credit cards. Mon–Sat 8pm–midnight. Metro: Termini. SICILIAN/ITALIAN.

This charming small-scale restaurant has a menu that's equally divided between traditional Sicilian and more creative and up-to-date recipes prepared with gusto and flair. Il Dito e La Luna is an unpretentious bistro, with counters and service areas accented with the fruits of a bountiful harvest. The menu includes fresh orange-infused anchovies served on orange segments, a creamy flan of mild onions and mountain cheese, and seafood couscous loaded with shellfish. Pastas like square-cut spaghetti (tonnarelli) prepared with mussels, bacon, tomatoes, and exotic mushrooms are delicious. Even those not particularly enamored of fish might like the baccalà mantecato (baked and pulverized salt cod) with lentils.

Monte Arci. Via Castelfidardo 33. ☎ **06/4941220.** Reservations recommended. Main courses 15,000L–20,000L ($9–$12). AE, V. Mon–Fri 12:30–3pm and 7–11:30pm, Sat 7–11:30pm. Bus: 36, 75, 310, or 492. ROMAN/SARDINIAN.

Monte Arci, on a cobblestone street near Piazza Indipendenza and not far from the Termini, is set behind a sienna-colored facade. The restaurant features low-cost Roman and Sardinian specialties (you'll spend even less for pizza). Typical dishes include nialoreddus (a regional form of gnocchetti); pasta with clams, lobster, or the musky-earthy notes of porcini mushrooms; green and white spaghetti with bacon, spinach, cream, and cheese; saltimbocca; and lamb sausage flavored with herbs and pecorino cheese. Much of this food is just like mamma would make, with all the strengths and weaknesses that that implies.

4   Near Via Veneto & Piazza Barberini

VERY EXPENSIVE

✪ **Sans Souci.** Via Sicilia 20. ☎ **06/4821814.** Reservations required. Main courses 40,000L–70,000L ($23–$41). AE, DC, MC, V. Tues–Sun 8pm–1am. Closed Aug 10–30. Metro: Barberini. FRENCH/ITALIAN.

Not long ago, Sans Souci was getting a little tired but now has bounced back, and Michelin has restored its coveted star. If you want to splurge on a big night out, this is a great place for glitz and old-time glamour. As you step into the dimly lit lounge, the maître d' will present you with the menu, which you can peruse while sipping a drink amid tapestries and glittering mirrors. The menu is ever-changing, although the classics never disappear. A great beginning is the goose-liver terrine with truffles, one of the chef's signature dishes. The fish soup is, according to one Rome restaurant critic, "a legend to experience." The soufflés are also popular (including artichoke, asparagus, and spinach), or perhaps you'll choose ravioli filled with truffles, homemade foie gras, or Normandy lamb. If you decide to have one of the special dessert soufflés (prepared for two in flavors such as chocolate and Grand Marnier) make sure to place your order in advance as they take a long time to make.

✪ **La Terrazza.** In the Hotel Eden, Via Ludovisi 49. ☎ **06/478121.** Reservations recommended. Main courses 42,000L–72,000L ($24–$42); fixed-price menu 120,000L ($70). AE, DC, MC, V. Daily 12:30–2:30pm and 7:30–10:30pm. Metro: Barberini. ITALIAN/INTERNATIONAL.

🏛 Family-Friendly Restaurants

Césarina (*see p. 114*)   A long time family favorite, this restaurant with a cuisine from the Emiliana-Romagna region serves the most kid-pleasing pastas in town, each handmade and presented with a different sauce. You can request a selection of three kinds of pasta on one plate so finicky young diners can try a little taste of each.

Otello alla Concordia (*see p. 126*)   This place is as good as any to introduce your child to the hearty Roman cuisine. If your child doesn't like the spaghetti with clams, then maybe the eggplant parmigiana will tempt. Families can dine in an arbor-covered courtyard.

Planet Hollywood, Via del Tritone 118 (☎ **06/42828012**).   If the kids abso lutely insist they can't take another day without a burger or a taco, then head to Rome's Planet Hollywood. Behind its stately neoclassical facade, you'll find all the usual suspects on the menu, as well as a souvenir stand if you want to bring some Americana back to America with you.

McDonald's, Piazza della Republica 40 (☎ **06/4815510**).   It's just like the ones at home—if you ignore the 18th-century crystal chandelier and the architectural gem housing it. Sure you can eat here any time, but when your kids start com-plaining of spaghetti burnout, this might just be the answer. There's another loca-tion at Piazza di Spagna, 46–47 (☎ **06/69922400**).

Tre Scalini (*see p. 122*)   All families visit Piazza Navona at some point, and this is the best choice if you'd like a dining table overlooking the square. Perhaps a jug-gler or a fire eater will come by to entertain the crowds. The cooking is Roman, the menu wide enough to accommodate most preferences—including children's. Even if your child doesn't like the main course, how could anyone pass up the tartufo (ice cream with a coating of bittersweet chocolate, cherries, and whipped cream) for dessert?

This restaurant serves the city's finest cuisine (a distinction shared with Relais Le Jardin) and offers a sweeping view over St. Peter's from the fifth floor of the Eden. The service manages to be formal and flawless, yet not at all intimidating. Chef Enrico Derfligher, the wizard behind about a dozen top-notch Italian restaurants around Europe, prepares a menu that varies with the seasons and is among the most polished in Rome. Selections might include a warm salad of grilled vegetables lightly toasted with greens in balsamic vinegar, red tortelli (whose pink coloring comes from tomato mousse) stuffed with mascarpone cheese and drizzled with lemon, or grilled tagliata of beef with eggplant and tomatoes. On our last visit, we shared a superb "symphony" of seafood—artfully arranged and prepared only for two or more, it includes perfectly seasoned Mediterranean sea bass, turbot, gilthead, and prawns.

EXPENSIVE

✪ **George's.** Via Marche 7. ☎ **06/42084575.** Reservations required. Main courses 36,000L–46,000 lire ($21–$27). AE, DC, MC, V. Mon–Sat 12:30–3pm and 7:30pm–midnight. Metro: Barberini. INTERNATIONAL.

George's has been a favorite of ours seemingly forever. Right off Via Veneto, in a dignified 18th-century building, it's run by Michele Pavia, maître d'hôtel for a quarter of a century before becoming George's owner. Many guests drop in for a before-dinner drink, enjoying the music in the piano bar and the relaxed, clublike atmosphere. Meals are served in an elegantly decorated raised dining room with a tented ceiling. The kitchen has an uncompromising dedication to quality, as reflected by such dishes as smoked trout with horseradish sauce, grilled scampi with bacon and sliced tomatoes, orange-scented duckling, and all kinds of veal and steak dishes. From June to October, in good weather the action shifts to the garden, suitably undisturbed because it's in the garden of a papal villa.

MODERATE

Aurora 10 da Pino il Sommelier. Via Aurora 10. ☎ **06/4742779.** Reservations recommended. Main courses 20,000L–30,000L ($12–$17). AE, DC, MC, V. Tues–Sun noon–3pm and 7–11:15pm. Metro: Barberini. ITALIAN.

Skip those tourist traps along Via Veneto and walk another block or two—you'll be glad you did, for much better food and lovely service await. The wait staff is very welcoming to foreigners, (although you'll also dine with regulars from the chic neighborhood). The place is noted for its awesome array of more than 250 wines, representing every province. Dishes may include linguine with lobster, a Sicilian-style fish fry, swordfish in herb sauce, beef filet with porcini mushrooms, risotto with asparagus, and beef stew flambé. The savory, first-rate cooking makes use of top-quality ingredients; several dishes are prepared tableside with a flourish.

Césarina. Via Piemonte 109. ☎ **06/4880828.** Reservations recommended. Main courses 17,000L–45,000L ($10–$26). AE, DC, MC, V. Mon–Sat 12:30–3pm and 7:30–11pm. Metro: Barberini. EMILIANA-ROMAGNOLA/ROMAN.

Specializing in the dishes of Rome and the region around Bologna, this former hole-in-the-wall has grown since matriarch Césarina Masi opened it around 1960 (many Rome veterans fondly remember Ms. Masi's strict supervision of her kitchen and the way she'd lecture regulars who didn't finish their tagliatelle). Although Césarina died in the mid-1980s, her traditions live on. The tactful, polite staff roll an excellent bollito misto (an array of well-seasoned boiled meats) from table to table on a trolley and often follow with misto Césarina—four kinds of handmade pasta, each served with a different sauce. Equally appealing is the saltimbocca and the cotoletta alla bolognese, a veal cutlet baked with ham and cheese. A dessert specialty is semifreddo Césarina with hot chocolate. The food is excellent and the selection of fresh antipasto very appealing.

☺ Colline Emiliane. Via Avignonesi 22 (right off Piazza Barberini). ☎ **06/4817538.** Reservations highly recommended. Main courses 16,000L–25,000L ($9–$15). MC, V. Sat–Thurs 12:45–2:45pm and 7:45–10:45pm. Closed Aug. Metro: Barberini. EMILIANA-ROMAGNOLA.

Colline Emiliane is a small place serving the *classica cucina bolognese*. It's family-run—the owner is the cook and his wife makes the pasta (about the best you'll encounter in Rome). The house specialty is an inspired tortellini alla panna (with cream sauce and truffles), but the less expensive pastas, such as maccheroni al funghetto and tagliatelle alla bolognese, are excellent as well. As an appetizer, we suggest culatello di Zibello, a delicacy from a small town near Parma known for having the finest prosciutto in the world. Main choices include braciola di maiale (boneless rolled pork cutlets that have been stuffed with ham and cheese, breaded, and sautéed) and giambonnetto (roast veal Emilian-style with roast potatoes).

☺ Girarrosto Toscano. Via Campania 29. ☎ **06/4823835.** Reservations required. Main courses 22,000L–55,000L ($13–$32). AE, DC, MC, V. Thurs–Tues 12:30–2:30pm and 7:30–11pm. Bus: 95, 116. Metro: Barberini, then a long stroll. TUSCAN.

Girarrosto Toscano, facing the walls of the Borghese Gardens, draws large crowds, so you may have to wait to sample some of Rome's finest Tuscan fare. Under a cellar's vaulted ceilings, you can begin your meal with any of an enormous selection of antipasto—from succulent little meatballs and melon with prosciutto to frittate (omelets) or an especially delicious Tuscan salami. You're then given a choice of pasta, such as fettuccine in cream sauce. Although expensive, bistecca alla fiorentina (grilled steak seasoned with oil, salt, and pepper) is worth every lira if you're in the mood to splurge. Fresh fish from the Adriatic is served daily. Order with care if you're on a budget—both meat and fish are priced according to weight and can run considerably higher than the prices mentioned above.

5 Near Ancient Rome

EXPENSIVE

Alvaro al Circo Massimo. Via dei Cerchi 53. ☎ **06/6786112.** Reservations required. Main courses 20,000L–60,000L ($12–$35). AE, CB, DC, DISC, MC, V. Tues–Sat 11am–3pm and 7–11pm, Sun 11am–3pm. Closed Aug. Metro: Circo Massimo. ITALIAN.

Alvaro al Circo Massimo, at the edge of the Circus Maximus, is the closest thing Rome has to a genuine provincial inn, right down to the corncobs hanging from the ceiling and the rolls of fat sausages. The antipasto and pasta dishes are fine, the meat courses are well prepared, and there's an array of fresh fish that's never overcooked. Other specialties are tagliolini with mushrooms and truffles and roasted turbot with potatoes. They're especially well stocked with exotic seasonal mushrooms, including black truffles rivaling those you'd find in Spoleto. A basket of fresh fruit rounds out the meal. The atmosphere is comfortable and mellow. Summer brings with it patio dining.

INEXPENSIVE

Abruzzi. Via del Vaccaro 1. ☎ **06/6793897.** Reservations recommended. Main courses 9,000L–22,000L ($5–$13). DC, MC, V. Sun–Fri 12:30–3pm and 7:30–10:30pm. Closed Aug. Bus: 46. ABRUZZESE/ROMANA.

Abruzzi, which takes its name from the region east of Rome, is at one side of Piazza SS. Apostoli, just a short walk from Piazza Venezia. The good food and reasonable prices make it a big draw for students. The chef offers a satisfying assortment of cold antipasto. With your starter, we suggest a liter of garnet-red wine; we once had one whose bouquet was suggestive of Abruzzi's wildflowers. If you'd like a soup as well, you'll find a good stracciatella (egg-and-Parmesan soup). A typical main dish is vitella tonnata con capperi (veal in tuna sauce with capers).

Hostaria Nerone. Via Terme di Tito 96. ☎ **06/4745207.** Reservations recommended. Main courses 14,000L–22,000L ($8–$13). AE, DC, MC, V. Mon–Sat noon–3pm and 7–11pm. Metro: Colosseo. ROMAN/ITALIAN.

Built atop the ruins of the palace that used to belong to Nero, this is a well managed trattoria run by the energetic De Santis family, who cook, serve, and handle the large crowds of hungry locals and visitors. Opened in 1929 at the edge of the Colle Oppio Park, it contains two compact dining rooms, plus a terrace lined with flowering shrubs that offers a view over the Colosseum and the majestic ruins of the Baths of Trajan. The copious antipasto buffet spans the bounty of Italy's fields and seas. The pastas include a savory version of spaghetti with clams and steaming bowlfuls of pasta fagiole (pasta with beans). There's also grilled crayfish and swordfish; Italian sausages garnished with polenta; veal and chicken dishes; and traditional rich desserts like zuppe inglese and panna cotta.

Dining Near the Spanish Steps & Ancient Rome

 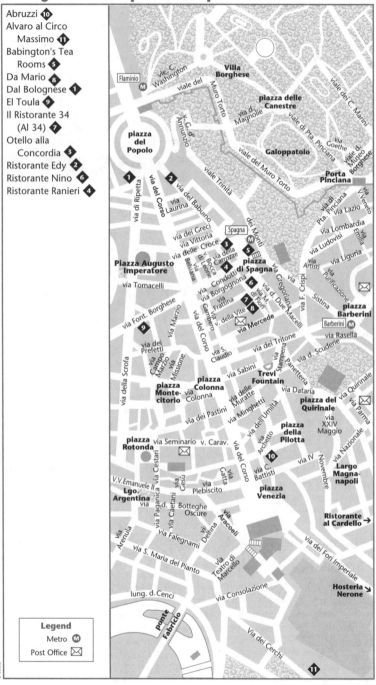

E-0352

Ristorante al Cardello. Via del Cardello 1 (at the corner of Via Cavour). ☎ **06/4745259.** Reservations recommended. Main courses 10,000L–14,000L ($6–$8). AE, DC, MC, V. Mon–Sat 12:30–3:30pm and 7:30–10:45pm. Closed Aug. Metro: Cavour. ROMAN/ABRUZZI.

Charming and conveniently close to the Colosseum, this restaurant has thrived since the 1920s, when it was opened in the semicellar (a room half above ground, half underground) of an 18th-century building. We always love the antipasto buffet, where the flavorful marinated vegetables represent the best of the Italian harvest—at 10,000L ($6) per person for a reasonable portion, it's a great deal. Then you might follow with bucatini (thick spaghetti) alla matriciana; roast lamb with potatoes, garlic, and mountain herbs; or a thick hearty stew.

6 Near Campo de' Fiori & the Jewish Ghetto

VERY EXPENSIVE

Il Drappo. Vicolo del Malpasso 9. ☎ **06/6877365.** Reservations required. Main courses 22,000L–28,000L ($13–$16); fixed-price menu (including Sardinian wine) 65,000L–70,000L ($38–$41). AE, CB, DC, V. Mon–Sat 8pm–midnight. Closed 2 weeks in Aug. Bus: 64. SARDINIAN.

Il Drappo, a favorite of the local artsy crowd, is on a narrow street near the Tiber and run by a woman known to her regulars only as "Valentina." You'll have your choice of two tastefully decorated dining rooms festooned with yards of patterned cotton draped from the ceiling. Flowers and candles are everywhere. Fixed-price dinners may include a wafer-thin appetizer called carte di musica (sheet-music paper), topped with tomatoes, green peppers, parsley, and olive oil, which is followed by fresh spring lamb in season, a fish stew made with tuna caviar, or a changing selection of strongly flavored regional specialties that are otherwise difficult to find in Rome. For dessert, try the seadas (cheese-stuffed fried cake in a special dark honey). The service is first-rate.

EXPENSIVE

✪ **Piperno.** Via Monte de' Cenci 9. ☎ **06/68806629.** Reservations recommended. Main courses 30,000L–40,000L ($17–$23). AE, DC, MC, V. Tues–Sat noon–2:30pm and 8–10:30pm, Sun noon–2:30pm. Bus: 23. ROMAN.

This longtime favorite, opened in 1856 and now run by the Mazzarella and Boni families, celebrates the Jerusalem artichoke by incorporating it into a number of tasty dishes to be devoured by guests. You'll be served by a uniformed crew of hard-working waiters whose suggestions are well worth taking. For example, they might advise you to start with fritto misto vegetariano, consisting of artichokes, cheese-and-rice croquettes, mozzarella, and stuffed squash blossoms, before moving on to a fish filet, veal, succulent beans, or a pasta creation. Many of the foods are fried or deep-fried and benefit from a technique that leaves them flaky and dry, not at all greasy. The deep-fried artichokes, when submerged in hot oil, open their leaves into a form akin to that of a lotus (and infinitely more delicious.)

MODERATE

✪ **Il Sanpietrino.** Piazza Costaguti 15. ☎ **06/68806471.** Reservations recommended. Main courses 22,000L–34,000L ($13–$20). AE, DC, MC, V. Mon–Sat 12:30–2:30pm and 8–11pm, Sat 8–11pm. Metro: Colosseo or Circo Massimo. ROMAN.

This Jewish Ghetto restaurant, with three formal dining rooms, is stylish but affordable, with a sophisticated selection of both traditional and modern dishes. Chef Marco Cardio uses market-fresh ingredients to prepare a seasonal cuisine that's varied and inventive year-round. His combinations are often a surprise but generally delightful—the pasta fagiole (bean soup) comes not only with the traditional ingredients but also with mussels and even octopus. The medley of fish antipasto is so tempting you might want to make a meal of it, enjoying items like fresh anchovies baked between layers of well-seasoned eggplant. Main courses (if you still have room after all that antipasto) include ravioli stuffed with sea bass or a bignolini, pastry baked with porcini mushrooms and a cheese fondue. We always go for the crème brulée for dessert, but if you want something lighter, the fresh tangerine sorbet is wonderful.

✪ **Ristorante da Pancrazio**. Piazza del Biscione 92. ☎ **06/6861246.** Reservations recommended. Main courses 18,000L–32,000L ($10–$19); fixed-price menu 45,000L ($26). AE, DC, MC, V. Thurs–Tues noon–3pm and 7:30–11:15pm. Closed 2 weeks in Aug (dates vary). Bus: 46, 62, or 64. ROMAN.

This place is popular as much for its archaeological interest as for its food. One of its two dining rooms is gracefully decorated in the style of an 18th-century tavern; the other occupies the premises of Pompey's ancient theater and is lined with marble columns, carved capitals, and bas-reliefs. In this historic setting you can enjoy traditional Roman dishes like risotto alla pescatora (with seafood), several kinds of scampi, saltimbocca, abbacchio al forno (roast lamb with potatoes), and ravioli stuffed with artichoke hearts. No one gets innovative around here—these dishes are prepared according to time-tested recipes.

✪ **Vecchia Roma**. Via della Tribuna di Campitelli 18. ☎ **06/6864604.** Reservations recommended. Main courses 23,000L–28,000L ($13–$16). AE. Thurs–Tues 1–3:30pm and 8–11pm. Closed Aug 10–25. Bus: 64, 90, 90b, 97, or 774. ROMAN/ITALIAN.

Vecchia Roma is a charming, moderately priced trattoria in the heart of the Ghetto. Movie stars have frequented the place, sitting at the crowded tables in one of the four small dining rooms (the back room is the most popular). The minestrone is made with fresh vegetables, and an interesting selection of antipasto, including salmon or vegetables, is always available. The owners are known for their selection of fresh seafood, and the "green" risotto with porcini mushrooms is reliably savory. The chef prepares excellent cuts of meat, including his specialties, lamb and la spigola (a type of white fish).

INEXPENSIVE

Da Giggetto. Via del Portico d'Ottavia 21–22. ☎ **06/6861105.** Reservations recommended. Main courses 16,000L–22,000L ($9–$13). AE, DC, MC, V. Tues–Sun 12:30–3pm and 7:30–11pm. Closed Aug 1–15. Bus: 23. ROMAN/JEWISH.

Da Giggetto is right next to the Theater of Marcellus; old Roman columns extend practically to its doorway. Romans flock to this bustling trattoria for its special traditional dishes. None is more typical than carciofi alla giudia, baby-tender fried artichokes—a true delicacy. The cheese concoction mozzarella in carrozza is another delight, as are the zucchini flowers stuffed with mozzarella and anchovies. You could also sample shrimp sautéed in garlic and olive oil, or saltimbocca.

✪ **Hostaria Grappolo d'Oro**. Piazza della Cancelleria 80–81. ☎ **06/6864118.** Reservations recommended Fri–Sat nights. Main courses 11,000L–16,000L ($6–$9). AE, MC, V. Mon–Sat noon–3pm and 7pm–1:30am. Closed 2 weeks in Aug. Bus: 9, 62, 64, or 116. ROMAN.

This early 18th-century building near Corso Vittorio Emanuele II and Campo de' Fiori welcomes a mainly local clientele, as it has for 150 years. The setting is pleasant, unpretentious, and polite despite the hysteria that sometime develops

In case you want to see the world.

At American Express, we're here to make your journey a smooth one. So we have over 1,700 travel service locations in over 120 countries ready to help. What else would you expect from the world's largest travel agency?

do more

Travel

In case you want to be welcomed there.

We're here to see that you're always welcomed at establishments everywhere. That's why millions of people carry the American Express® Card – for peace of mind, confidence, and security, around the world or just around the corner.

do more

Cards

In case you're running low.

We're here to help with more than 118,000 Express Cash

locations around the world. In order to enroll, just call

American Express before you start your vacation.

do more

And just in case.

We're here with American Express® Travelers Cheques and Cheques *for Two*® They're the safest way to carry money on your vacation and the surest way to get a refund, practically anywhere, anytime.

Another way we help you...

do more

Travelers Cheques

Dining Near Campo de' Fiori & Piazza Navona

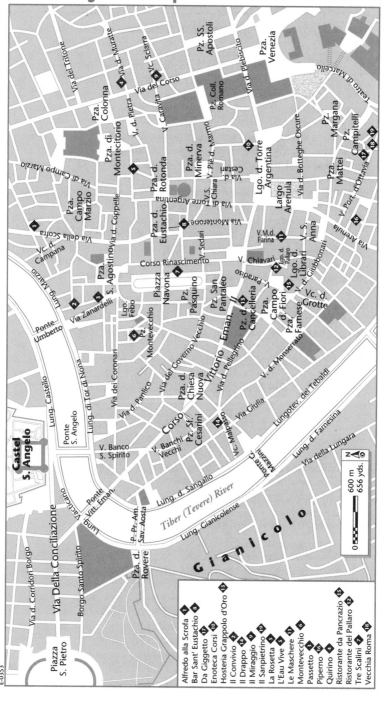

Alfredo alla Scrofa
Bar Sant' Eustachio **8**
Da Giggetto **17**
Enoteca Corsi
Hosteria Grappolo d'Oro **13**
Il Convivio
Il Drappo **2**
Il Miraggio **9**
Il Sanpietrino
La Rosetta **5**
L'Eau Vive **5**
Le Maschere **11**
Montevecchio **6**
Passetto
Piperno
Quirino **5**
Ristorante da Pancrazio **15**
Ristorante del Pallaro **12**
Tre Scalini **7**
Vecchia Roma

Castel
S. Angelo

E-0353

119

In Pursuit of Gelato

For devotees of gelato, that addictively tasty Italian ice cream, ☼ **Giolitti,** Via Uffici del Vicario (☎ **06/6991243**), is one of the city's most popular nighttime gathering spots and the oldest ice-cream shop in the city. To satisfy that craving, try a cup topped with whipped cream. Many people eat their gelato out on the streets; others enjoy it in the post-empire splendor of the salon inside. You can have your "cuppa" daily from 7am to 2am.

There are also many excellent smaller gelaterie throughout Rome; try those that advertise the cool delights as *produzione propria* (homemade). Other gela-teria include **Gelateria Tre Scalini,** Piazza Navona 28 (☎ **06/8801996**), which is celebrated for its tartufo, a mount of bittersweet chocolate chips bound together by a cone of chocolate ice cream and crowned by a dollop of freshly whipped cream. It is said you haven't really experienced Rome until you've eaten a tartufo at Tre Scalini. Another of our longtime favorites is **Palazzo del Freddo Giovanni Fassi,** Via Principe Eugenio 65–67 (☎ **06/4464740**), southeast of the rail station of Piazza Vittorio Emanuele. More than a hundred years old, this ice-cream outlet—part of a gelato factory—specializes in a rice ice cream, although you can also order more traditional flavors, including some made with fresh fruit. If your tastes gravitate to those frothy frulatti frappes for which Italy is famous, head at once to **Pascucci,** Via Torre Argentina (☎ **06/6864816**), off Corso Emanuele, lying east of Piazza Navona. Here blenders work all day grinding fresh fruit into concoctions guaranteed to tempt your tastebuds. If your tastes are more modern, sample the delight of **Yogufruit,** P.G. Travani Arquati 118 (☎ **06/ 587972**), lying near Piazza S. Sonnino, of Via della Lungaretta. This is especially popular with young Romans who line up to sample the tart frozen yogurt con-coctions blended with vine-ripened fruit from the Latium countryside.

when the place gets really busy. Menus read like a lexicon of traditional Roman cuisine, and individual items are prepared in generous, although not particularly innovative ways. Specialties include saltimbocca, penne a l'amatriciana, roast lamb with potatoes, Roman-style tripe, and a flavorful array of antipasto. It's the type of fresh and well-prepared food Romans love; chances are you will too.

Le Maschere. Via Monte della Farina 29 (near Largo Argentina). ☎ **06/6879444.** Reservations recommended. Main courses 12,000L–20,000L ($7–$12). AE, DC, MC, V. Tues–Sun 7:30pm–midnight. Closed Aug. Bus: 46, 62, or 64. CALABRESE.

Le Maschere specializes in the fragrant, often-fiery cookery of Calabria's Costa Viola—lots of fresh garlic and wake-up-your-mouth red peppers. In a 17th-century cellar decorated with regional artifacts of Calabria sit an enlarged kitchen and three dining rooms festooned with fantastic medieval- and Renaissance-inspired murals. Begin with a selection of antipasto calabresi. For your first course, you can try one of their many preparations of eggplant or a pasta—perhaps with broccoli or those devilish red peppers, garlic, bread crumbs, and more than a touch of anchovy. The chef also grills meats and fresh swordfish caught off the Calabrian coast. If you don't want a full meal, you can visit just for pizza and beer and listen to the music at the piano bar, beginning at 8pm. In summer, you can dine at a small table outside over-looking a tiny piazza.

☼ **Ristorante del Pallaro.** Largo del Pallaro 15. ☎ **06/68801488.** Reservations rec-ommended. Fixed-price menu 32,000L ($19). No credit cards. Tues–Sun 1–3pm and 7:30pm–1am. Bus: 46, 62, or 64. ROMAN.

The cheerful woman in white who emerges with clouds of steam from the bustling kitchen is owner Paola Fazi. She runs two simple dining rooms where value-conscious Romans go for good food at bargain prices. (She claims—though others dispute it—that Julius Caesar was assassinated on this very site.) No à la carte meals are served, but the fixed-price menu has made the place famous. As you sit down, your antipasto, the first of eight courses, appears. Then comes the pasta of the day, followed by roast veal, white meatballs or (Friday only) dried cod, along with potatoes and eggplant. For your final courses, you're served mozzarella, cake with custard, and fruit in season. The meal also includes bread, mineral water, and half a liter of the house wine. This is the type of hearty food you might be served if you were invited to the home of a prosperous Roman family.

7 Near Piazza Navona & the Pantheon

VERY EXPENSIVE

✪ **La Rosetta.** Via della Rosetta 8. ☎ **06/6861002.** Reservations recommended. Main courses 60,000L–100,000L ($35–$58). AE, DC, MC, V. Mon–Fri 1–3:30pm and 8–11:30pm, Sat 8–11:30pm. Closed the last 3 weeks of Aug. Bus: 70 to Largo Argentina. Metro: Spagna, then a long stroll. SEAFOOD.

You won't find any meat on the menu at this sophisticated (and ultra-expensive) choice near Piazza Navona, where members of the Riccioli family have been directing operations since the late 1960s. If money is no object, there's no better seafood in Rome. You'll likely be seated amid the arches and paneling of the soothingly decorated main dining room, although there's an alcove off to the side that's a bit more private. An excellent start to any meal, especially as the temperature begins to soar, is an insalata di frutti di mare, studded with squid, lobster, octopus, and shrimp. Menu items include just about every fish that's native to the Mediterranean, as well as a few from the Atlantic coast of France. There's even a sampling of lobster imported from Maine, which can be boiled with drawn butter or served Catalan style, with tomatoes, red onions, and wine sauce. Hake, monkfish, and sole can be grilled or roasted in rock salt and served with potatoes, and calamari is available deep-fried (breaded or unbreaded) or stewed. Everyone at our table agreed that the homemade spaghetti garnished with shrimp, squash blossoms, and pecorino cheese—with a drizzling of olive oil and herbs adding a savory zing—was tops among the pasta dishes.

EXPENSIVE

Il Convivio. Via dell'Orso 44. ☎ **06/6869432.** Reservations recommended. Main courses 42,000L–44,000L ($24–$26); fixed-price *menu degustazione* 100,000L ($58). AE, DC, MC, V. Mon 8–10:30pm, Tues–Sat 1–2:30pm and 8–10:30pm. Closed 1 week in Aug. Metro: Spagna, then a long stroll. ITALIAN/ROMAN.

The well-conceived pan-Italian menu here is definitely daring. The creativity is supplied by the Troiani brothers, who cook, welcome visitors, and compile the sophisticated wine list. We love to begin with ricotta romanda calda, warm ricotta dumplings stuffed with crunchy guanciale and bits of salt pork and served with sliced porcinis; zesty tomato sauce gives it an extra zing. The chef can sometimes be a little *too* bold, as with his roast rabbit, stuffed with mashed potatoes and porcini mushrooms—he intensifies the act by adding a sauce made with fresh anchovies, which unfortunately overpowers the delicate truffles topping the creation. But the seafood salad is a happy blend of squid, mussels, clams, white fish, and a large prawn, placed on a bed of al dente carrots and zucchini and topped with lemony sauce. The desserts are equally inventive.

Passetto. Via Zanardelli 14. ☎ **06/68806569.** Reservations recommended. Main courses 22,000L–50,000L ($13–$29). AE, DC, MC, V. Daily noon–4pm and 7pm–midnight. Bus: 70, 87, or 90. ROMAN/ITALIAN.

Passetto, dramatically positioned at the north end of Piazza Navona, has drawn patrons with its 145-year reputation for excellent Italian food. The stylish interior consists of a trio of high-ceilinged dining rooms, each outfitted with antique furniture and elaborate chandeliers and conveying a tasteful sense of the bourgeois Italy of a century ago. In summer, however, you'll want to sit outside looking out on Piazza Sant'Apollinare. The pastas are exceptional, including penne alla Norma (pasta with fresh herbs, garlic, tomatoes, and eggplant. One recommended main dish is orata al cartoccio (sea bass baked in a paper bag, with tomatoes, mushrooms, capers, and white wine—the paper bag keeps in the juices and the aroma and no, it doesn't catch fire). Another house specialty is rombo passetto (a fish similar to sole) cooked in cognac and pine nuts. An eternal Roman favorite is lamb in the style of Abruzzi (oven roasted with potatoes). Fresh fish is often priced by its weight, so tabs can soar quickly. Fresh vegetables are abundant in summer, and a favorite dessert is seasonal berries with fresh thick cream.

MODERATE

Alfredo alla Scrofa. Via della Scrofa 104. ☎ **06/68806163.** Reservations recommended. Main courses 20,000L–35,000L ($12–$20). Fixed-price menu 60,000L ($35). AE, DC, MC, V. Wed–Mon 12:30–3pm and 7:30–11:30pm. Metro: Spagna. ROMAN/INTERNATIONAL.

Menu items include tagliolini alla scoglia, concocted from Neapolitan tomatoes and shellfish; a platter containing two filet mignons, one with a sauce concocted from Barolo wine, the other with a Gorgonzola sauce; filetto di tacchino dorato (sautéed breast of turkey covered with thin slices of white truffles from Italy's Piedmont district); and filet mignon Casanova (prepared with wine sauce, pepper, and foie gras). Of course, you might want to skip all that in favor of the dish that was invented here in 1931—spaghetti alfredo. (Douglas Fairbanks and Mary Pickford liked it enough to present a golden spoon and fork to the owners when they parted with the recipe.)

Montevecchio. Piazza Montevecchio 22. ☎ **06/6861319.** Reservations required. Main courses 22,000L–32,000L ($13–$19). AE, MC, V. Tues–Sat 1–3pm and 8pm–midnight; Sun 8pm–midnight. Closed Aug 10–25 and Dec 26–Jan 9. Bus: 44, 46, 55, 60, 61, 62, 64, 65. Metro: Spagna, then a long stroll. ROMAN/ITALIAN.

To visit, you must negotiate the winding streets of one of Rome's most confusing neighborhoods, near Piazza Navona. The heavily curtained restaurant on this Renaissance piazza is where both Raphael and Bramante had studios and where Lucrezia Borgia spun many of her intrigues. The entrance opens onto a high-ceilinged room filled with rural mementos and bottles of wine. Your meal might begin with a strudel of porcini mushrooms followed by the invariably good pasta of the day, perhaps a bombolotti stuffed with prosciutto and spinach. Then you might choose roebuck with polenta, roast Sardinian goat, or veal with salmon mousse. Many of these traditional recipes are impossible to find on Roman menus anymore.

✪ **Tre Scalini.** Piazza Navona 30. ☎ **06/6879148.** Reservations recommended. Main courses 20,000L–38,000L ($12–$22). AE, DC, MC, V. Daily 12:15–3pm and 7–11pm. Closed Dec–Feb. Bus: 44, 46, 55, 60, 61, 62, 64, 65. Metro: Spagna, then a long stroll. ROMAN.

Opened in 1882, this is the most famous restaurant on Piazza Navona—a landmark for ice cream as well as more substantial fare. Yes, it's crawling with tourists, but its waiters are a lot friendlier and more helpful than those at the nearby Passetto, and the setting can't be beat. There's a cozy bar on the upper floor with a view over the piazza, but most visitors opt for the ground-floor cafe or restaurant. During warm weather, try to snag a table on the piazza, where the people watching is extraordinary.

House specialties are risotto with porcinis, spaghetti with clams, roast duck with prosciutto, a carpaccio of sea bass, saltimbocca, and roast lamb Roman style. No one will object if you order just a pasta and salad, unlike at other restaurants nearby. Their famous tartufo (ice cream coated with bittersweet chocolate, cherries, and whipped cream) and other ice creams cost 10,000L ($6) each.

INEXPENSIVE

Il Miraggio. Vicolo Sciarra 59. ☎ **06/6780226.** Reservations recommended. Main courses 12,000L–20,000L ($7–$12). AE, MC, V. Thurs–Tues 12:30–3:30pm and 7:30–11pm. Closed Feb 5–20. Bus: 56, 60, 62, 81, 85, 95, 160, 175, 492, 628. Metro: Barberini, then a long stroll. ROMAN/SARDINIAN/SEAFOOD.

You may want to want to escape the roar of traffic along Via del Corso by ducking into this informal spot on a crooked side street (about midway between Piazza Venezia and Piazza Colonna). It's a cozy neighborhood setting with good food. One of the most unusual pasta dishes in Rome is served here, spaghetti alla bottarga (pasta with a soft roe sauce). The spaghetti provides a perfect foil for the salty roe and the dish goes down velvety-smooth. Another special is spigola alla vernaccia (sea bass sautéed in butter and vernaccia wine from Tuscany). The meat dishes are well prepared, and there's an array of fresh fish. For dessert try the typical Sardinian seadas, thin-rolled pastry filled with fresh cheese, fried, and served with honey.

✪ **L'Eau Vive.** Via Monterone 85. ☎ **06/68801095.** Reservations recommended. Main courses 10,000L–30,000L ($6–$17); fixed-price menus 15,000L, 22,000L, and 30,000L ($9, $13, and $17). AE, MC, V. Mon–Sat 12:30–2:30pm and 8–10:30pm. Closed Aug 1–20. Bus: 70, 81, 87, or 115. Metro: Barberini, then a long stroll. FRENCH/INTERNATIONAL.

This offbeat spot is run by lay missionaries who wear the dress or costumes of their native countries. The restaurant occupies the cellar and ground floor of the 17th-century Palazzo Lantante della Rovere and is filled with monumental paintings under vaulted ceilings. In this formal atmosphere the waitresses sing religious hymns and "Ave Marias" every evening at 10. Pope John Paul II used to dine here when he was still archbishop of Krakow, and today some jet-setters have adopted it as their favorite spot. The tasteful place settings include fresh flowers and good glassware, and the cellar is well stocked with French wines. Main dishes range from beef filet flambéed with cognac to lighter selections such as couscous, perhaps with homemade pâté or a salad niçoise to begin. The chocolate mousse is a smooth finish. Your tip will be turned over for religious purposes.

Quirino. Via delle Muratte 84. ☎ **06/6794108.** Main courses 15,000L–30,000L ($9–$17); fish dishes 35,000L ($20). AE, MC, V. Mon–Sat 12:30–3:30pm and 7–11pm. Closed 3 weeks in Aug. Metro: Barberini. ROMAN/ITALIAN/SICILIAN.

Quirino is a good place to dine after you've tossed your coin into the Trevi Fountain. The atmosphere is typical Italian, with hanging chianti bottles, a beamed ceiling, and muraled walls. The food is strictly home cooking. We're fond of a mixed fry of tiny shrimp and squid rings that resemble onion rings. Specialties include vegetarian antipasto, homemade pasta with clams and porcini mushrooms, pasta alla Norma (a typical Sicilian plate made with fresh herbs, garlic, tomatoes, and eggplant), and a variety of fresh tasty fish. For dessert there's chestnut ice cream with hot chocolate sauce, or homemade cannoli.

8 Near Piazza di Spagna & Piazza del Popolo

EXPENSIVE

✪ **El Toulà.** Via della Lupa 29B. ☎ **06/6873498.** Reservations required for dinner. Main courses 40,000L–55,000L ($23–$32); fixed-price menus 100,000L–120,000L ($58–$70). AE, DC, MC, V. Tues–Sat 1–3pm; Mon–Sat 8–11pm. Closed Aug. Bus: 81, 115, 492, 590, or 628. Metro: Spagna, then walk west on Via Font. Borghese. ROMAN/VENETIAN.

El Toulà, offering sophisticated haute cuisine, is the glamorous flagship of an upscale chain that's gone international. The setting is elegant, with vaulted ceilings, large archways, and a charming bar. In honor of the restaurant's origins, the impressive ever-changing menu devotes a section to Venetian specialties. Items include fegato (liver) alla veneziana, vegetable-stuffed calamari, baccala (codfish mousse with polenta), and broetto, a fish soup made with monkfish and clams. Save room for the seasonal selection of sorbets and sherbets (the cantaloupe and fresh strawberry are celestial)—you can request a mixed plate if you'd like to sample several. El Toulà usually isn't crowded at lunchtime.

Ristorante Nino. Via Borgognona 11. ☎ **06/6795676.** Reservations recommended. Main courses 20,000L–50,000L ($12–$29). AE, DC, MC, V. Mon–Sat 12:30–3pm and 7:30–11pm. Closed Aug. Metro: Spagna. TUSCAN.

Ristorante Nino, off Via Condotti and a short walk from the Spanish Steps, is a tavern mecca for writers, artists, and the occasional model. If you had a Tuscan mamma mia, she might have cooked like the chefs here—hearty, robustly flavored Tuscan homestyle dishes that change with the season and have made Nino's famous. Beef, shipped in from Florence and charcoal-broiled, is pricier than the rest of the menu, but neither as succulent nor as tender as that served at the better-known (and more expensive) Girarrosto Toscano. A plate of cannelloni Nino (the house version of the popular dish, consisting of meat-stuffed pasta) is one of the chef's specialties. Other good dishes include grilled veal liver, fagiole cotti al fiasco (beans boiled in white wine, salt, ground black pepper, and herbs), codfish alla livornese (codfish cooked with tomatoes and onions), and zucchini pie. The reasonably-priced wine list is mainly Tuscan, with some especially good choices among the Chiantis.

MODERATE

Babington's Tea Rooms. Piazza di Spagna 23. ☎ **06/6786027.** Main courses 20,000L–38,000L ($12–$22); brunch 45,000L ($26). AE, MC, DC, V. Daily 9am–8:30pm. Metro: Spagna. ENGLISH/MEDITERRANEAN.

When Victoria was on the throne in 1893, an Englishwoman named Anne Mary Babington arrived in Rome and couldn't find a place for "a good cuppa." With stubborn determination, she opened her own tearooms near the foot of the Spanish Steps, and the rooms are still going strong, although prices are terribly inflated because of the fabulous location. You can order everything from Scottish scones and Ceylon tea to a club sandwich and American coffee. Brunch is served at all hours. Pastries cost 4,000L to 13,000L ($2.30 to $8); a pot of tea (dozens of varieties available) goes for 12,000L ($7).

✪ **Dal Bolognese.** Piazza del Popolo 1–2. ☎ **06/3611426.** Reservations required. Main courses 22,000L–28,000L ($13–$16); fixed-price menu 65,000L ($38). AE, MC, V. Tues–Sun 12:30–3pm and 8:15pm–1am. Closed 2 weeks in Aug. Metro: Flaminio. BOLOGNESE.

This is one of those rare, hip dining spots where the food is truly noteworthy and not merely secondary to the scene. Young actors, shapely models, artists from nearby Via Margutta, and even corporate types on expense accounts show up, trying to land one of the few sidewalk tables. To begin, we suggest a misto de pasta—four pastas, each with a different sauce, arranged on the same plate. A worthy substitute would be thin, savory slices of Parma ham or perhaps the prosciutto and melon (try a little freshly ground pepper on the latter). For your main course, specialties include lasagne verde, tagliatelle alla bolognese, and a recommendable cotolette alla bolognese (veal cutlet topped with cheese). They're not inventive, but they're simply superb.

You may want to cap your evening by calling on the **Rosati** cafe next door (or its competitor, the **Canova,** across the street), to enjoy one of the tempting pastries—that is, if the renovation on the piazza is ever finished, making this a lovely spot again.

Il Ristorante 34 (Al 34). Via Mario de' Fiori 34. ☎ **06/6795091.** Reservations required. Main courses 17,000L–28,000L ($10–$16); fixed-price menu 55,000L ($32). AE, DC, MC, V. Tues–Sun 12:30–3pm and 7:30–10:30pm. Closed 1 week at Easter and 3 weeks in Aug. Metro: Spagna. ROMAN.

Il Ristorante 34, very good and increasingly popular, is close to Rome's most famous shopping district. Its long, narrow interior is sheathed in scarlet wallpaper, ringed with modern paintings, and capped by a vaulted ceiling. In the rear, stop to admire a display of *dolce* proudly exhibited near the entrance to the bustling kitchen. The kitchen is highly reliable; the chef might whip caviar and salmon into the noodles to enliven a dish, or add generous chunks of lobster to the risotto. He also believes in rib-sticking fare like pasta-lentil soup or meatballs in a sauce with "fat" mushrooms. One of his most interesting pastas comes with a pumpkin-flavored cream sauce, and his spaghetti with clams is among the best in Rome.

Ristorante Ranieri. Via Mario de' Fiori 26 (off Via Condotti). ☎ **06/6786505.** Reservations required. Main courses 22,000L–32,000L ($13–$19). AE, DC, MC, V. Mon–Sat 12:30–3pm and 7:30–11pm. Metro: Spagna. INTERNATIONAL/ITALIAN.

The Ranieri is well into its second century (it opened in 1843). Neapolitan-born Giuseppe Ranieri was the chef to Queen Victoria, and his namesake restaurant still maintains its Victorian trappings. Start with prosciutto and melon or that classic Roman soup, stracciatella (made with eggs and cheese). Another starter might be crêpes alla Ranieri, with eight types of cheese; we've enjoyed it for years. Beefsteak from Florence is meltingly tender, as is the veal liver. You might also try the osso bucco Lombardy style.

INEXPENSIVE

✪ **Da Mario.** Via della Vite 55–56. ☎ **06/6783818.** Reservations recommended. Main courses 16,000L–25,000L ($9–$15); fixed-price menu 45,000L ($26). AE, DC, MC, V. Mon–Sat 12:30–3pm and 7:30–11pm. Closed Aug. Metro: Spagna. ROMAN/ FLORENTINE.

Da Mario is noted for its flavorful game specialties and excellent Florentine-style dishes (meats marinated in olive oil with fresh herbs and garlic and lightly grilled). The rich bounty of meats available during hunting season makes this a memorable choice, but even if you aren't feeling game (or like eating it) you'll find this a convivial and quintessentially Roman trattoria. A good beginning is the wide-noodle pappardelle, best when served with a game sauce (*caccia*) or with chunks of rabbit (*lepre*), available only in winter. *Capretto* (kid), beefsteaks, and roast quail with polenta are other good choices. The cellar is well stocked with sturdy reds, the ideal acccompaniments for the meat dishes. For dessert we heartily recommend the gelato misto, a selection of mixed ice cream. You can dine in air-conditioned comfort at street level or descend to the cellars.

Enoteca Corsi. 89 Via del Gesú. ☎ **06/6790821.** Reservations not necessary. Main courses 10,000L ($6) each; vegetable side dishes 4,000L ($2.30). AE, DC, MC, V. Mon–Sat noon–2:30pm. Closed Aug. Metro: Spagna. ROMAN.

This is a breath of unpretentious fresh air in a pricey neighborhood—an informal wine tavern open for lunch only. Both dining rooms are usually packed and full of festive din, as they've always been since 1943. The wine list includes affordable choices from around Italy, and the platters of straightforward cuisine will go perfectly with your selection. It's nothing fancy, just hearty fare like spaghetti matriciana, gnocchi, Roman tripe, and roasted codfish with garlic and potatoes.

Otello alla Concordia. Via della Croce 81. ☎ **06/6791178.** Main courses 12,000L–25,000L ($7–$15); fixed-price menu 36,000L ($21). AE, DC, MC, V. Mon–Sat 12:30–3pm and 7:30–11pm. Closed 2 weeks in Feb. Metro: Spagna. ROMAN.

On a side street amid the glamorous boutiques near the northern edge of the Spanish Steps, this is one of Rome's most popular and consistently reliable restaurants. A stone corridor from the street leads into the dignified Palazzo Povero. Choose a table in the arbor-covered courtyard or the cramped but convivial dining rooms. Displays of Italian bounty decorate the interior, where you're likely to rub elbows with many of the shopkeepers from the surrounding fashion district. The spaghetti alle vongole veraci (with clams) is excellent, as are Roman-style saltimbocca, abbacchio arrosto (roasted baby lamb), eggplant parmigiana, a selection of grilled or sautéed fish dishes, and several preparations of veal.

Ristorante Edy. Vicolo del Babuino 4. ☎ **06/36001738.** Reservations recommended. Main courses 15,000L–27,000L ($9–$16). AE, DC, MC, V. Mon–Sat noon–3pm and 7pm–midnight. Closed 1 week in Aug. Metro: Spagna or Flaminio. ROMAN/ABRUZZESE.

Named after the nickname (Edy) of Abruzzi-born owner Edmondo Campricotti, this likable and unpretentious family-run restaurant is midway between the Spanish Steps and Piazza del Popolo. You'll feel very Roman here, since the place is usually packed with an animated crowd of locals. Though in the heart of Rome, the restaurant enjoys a tranquil setting with a few tables on the street. Tried-and-true menu items include spaghetti with artichokes, fettuccine with mushrooms and ricotta, and a mixed seafood grill with calamari, shrimp, and (if available) turbot. But we can never resist the grilled roast lamb surrounded with roast potatoes in the Abruzzese style.

9 Near Vatican City

EXPENSIVE

✪ **Les Etoiles.** In the Hotel Atlante Star, Via Vitelleschi 34. ☎ **06/6893434.** Reservations required. Main courses 36,000L–58,000L ($21–$34). AE, DC, MC, V. Daily 12:30–2:30pm and 7:30–11pm. Metro: Ottaviano, then a long stroll. MEDITERRANEAN/INTERNATIONAL.

Les Etoiles ("The Stars") deserves all the stars it receives. At this garden in the sky you'll have an open window over Rome's rooftops—a 360° view of landmarks, including the floodlit dome of St. Peter's. A flower terrace contains a trio of little towers named Michelangelo, Campidoglio, and Ottavo Colle. In summer everyone wants a table outside, but in winter almost the same view is available near the picture windows. Along with the view, you can savor the textures and aromas of sophisticated Mediterranean cuisine with perfectly balanced flavors—perhaps a casserole of quail with mushrooms and herbs, artichokes stuffed with ricotta and pecorino cheese, Venetian-style risotto with squid ink, or roast suckling lamb with mint. The creative chef is justifiably proud of his many regional dishes, and the service is refined, with an exciting French and Italian wine list.

Dining in the Vatican Area

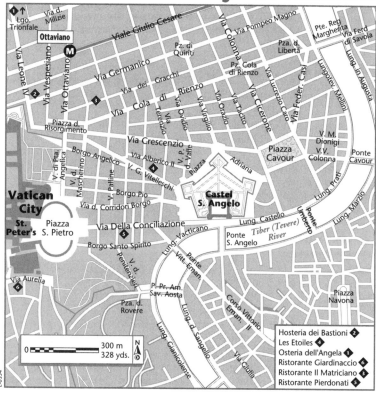

Hosteria dei Bastioni ❷
Les Etoiles ❹
Osteria dell'Angela ❶
Ristorante Giardinaccio ❻
Ristorante Il Matriciano ❸
Ristorante Pierdonati ❺

MODERATE

✪ **Ristorante Il Matriciano.** Via dei Gracchi 55. ☎ **06/3212327.** Reservations required. Main courses 20,000L–30,000L ($12–$17). AE, DC, MC, V. May–Oct, Sun–Fri 12:30–3pm and 8–11:30pm; Nov–Apr, Thurs–Tues 12:30–3pm and 8–11:30pm. Closed Aug 5–25. Metro: Ottaviano. ROMAN.

Il Matriciano is a family restaurant with a devoted following and a convenient location near St. Peter's. The food is good, but it's mostly country fare. Appropriately, the decor is kept to a minimum. In summer, try to get one of the sidewalk tables behind a green hedge and under a shady canopy. For openers you might enjoy zuppa di verdura (vegetable soup) or ravioli di ricotta. From many dishes, we recommend scaloppa alla valdostana or abbacchio (suckling lamb) al forno. The specialty, bucatini matriciana, is a variation on amatriciana, the favorite sauce in the Roman repertoire, richly flavored with bacon, tomatoes, and basil. Dining at the homelike convivial tables, you're likely to see an array of Romans, including prelates and cardinals ducking out of the nearby Vatican for a meal.

Ristorante Pierdonati. Via della Conciliazione 39. ☎ **06/68803557.** Reservations not necessary. Main courses 12,000L–40,000L ($7–$23); fixed-price menu 25,000L ($15). AE, MC, V. Fri–Wed noon–3:30pm and 7–10:30pm. Closed Aug. Bus: 62. ROMAN.

Ristorante Pierdonati has been serving wayfarers to the Vatican since 1868. In the same building as the Hotel Columbus, this restaurant was the former home of Cardinal della Rovere. Today it's the headquarters of the Knights of the Holy Sepulchre of Jerusalem and is the best choice for a sit-down lunch after touring St. Peter's.

Try such robust and filling fare as the calves' liver Venetian style, stewed veal with tomato sauce, or ravioli bolognese. Given this location, expect a crowd. Tuesday and Friday are fresh fish days.

INEXPENSIVE

Hostaria dei Bastioni. Via Leone IV 29. ☎ **06/39723034.** Reservations recommended Fri–Sat. Main courses 12,000L–20,000L ($7–$12). AE, DC, MC, V. Mon–Sat noon–3pm and 7–11:30pm. Closed July 15–Aug 1. Metro: Ottaviano. Bus: 23 or 49. ROMAN.

This simple but well-managed restaurant is about a minute's walk from the entrance to the Vatican Museums, and has catered to the appetites of everyone in the neighborhood since the 1960s. Although a warm-weather terrace doubles the establishment's size during the summer, many diners prefer the inside room as an escape from the roaring traffic outside. In a dining room suitable for only 50 people, you can order from the staples of Rome's culinary repertoire, including such dishes as a fisher's risotto (a broth-simmered rice dish studded with fresh fish, usually shellfish), a vegetarian fettuccine alla bastione with orange-flavored creamy tomato sauce (a succulent house special), an array of grilled fresh fish, and saltimbocca.

Osteria dell'Angelo. Via Giovanni Bettolo 24. ☎ **06/3729470.** Reservations recommended. Main courses at lunch 9,000L ($5) each; fixed-price dinner 35,000L ($20). No credit cards. Mon–Sat 12:30–3:30pm and 8pm–1:30am. Metro: Ottaviano. Bus 32, 62, or 64. ROMAN.

In an angular modern building erected in the Fascist style in 1922 (even its owners cheerfully refer to the architecture as a good example of "Mussoliniana"), this unpretentious trattoria has flourished almost since the building was inaugurated. Inside you'll find two dining rooms serving robust Roman cuisine with strong, well-conceived flavors. Menu items include saltimbocca, roast lamb with potatoes, fettuccine à la matriciana and à l'arrabbiatta, Roman-style tripe, and a medley of veal dishes. The chefs are especially proud of their square-shaped pasta, tonnarelli, served with a mixture of pecorino cheese and fresh pepper. The setting is cheerfully old-fashioned, with a casual, workaday atmosphere.

Ristorante Giardinaccio. Via Aurelia 53. ☎ **06/631367.** Reservations recommended, especially on weekends. Main courses 10,000L–16,000L ($6–$9). AE, DC, MC, V. Wed–Mon 12:15–3:30pm and 7:15–11pm. Bus: 46. ITALIAN/MOLISIAN/INTERNATIONAL.

This popular restaurant, operated by Nicolino Mancini, is only a stone's throw from St. Peter's. Unusual for Rome, it offers Molisian specialties from southeastern Italy. It's rustically decorated in the country-tavern style with dark wood and exposed stone. Flaming grills provide succulent versions of perfectly done quail, goat, and other dishes, but the mutton goulash is perhaps more adventurous. You can order many versions of pasta, including taconelle, a homemade pasta with lamb sauce. Vegetarians will like the large self-service selection of antipasto. This is robust "peasant" fare, a perfect introduction to the cuisine of an area rarely visited by Americans.

10 In Trastevere

VERY EXPENSIVE

✪ **Sabatini.** Piazza Santa Maria in Trastevere 13. ☎ **06/5812026.** Reservations recommended. Main courses 40,000L–80,000L ($23–$46). AE, DC, MC, V. Daily noon–3pm and 8pm–midnight. Closed 2 weeks in Aug (dates vary). Bus: 45, 75, 170, 181, or 280. ROMAN/SEAFOOD.

Dining in Trastevere

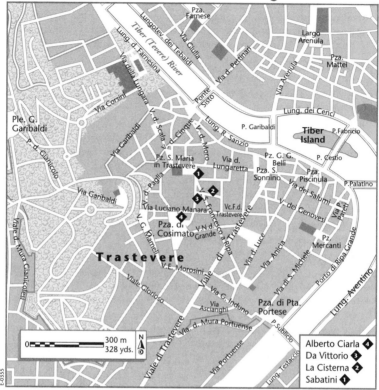

This is one of the most popular dining spots in Rome, a real neighborhood spot in a lively location. (You may have to wait for a table even if you have a reservation.) In summer, tables are placed out on the charming piazza and you can look across at the floodlit golden frescoes of the church. Inside, the dining room sports beamed ceilings, stenciled walls, lots of paneling, and framed oil paintings. The spaghetti with seafood is excellent, and fresh fish and shellfish, especially grilled scampi, may tempt you as well. For a savory treat, try pollo con pepperoni, chicken cooked with red and green peppers. (Order carefully, though; your bill can skyrocket if you choose grilled fish or the Florentine steaks.) Accompany it all with a frascati or a chianti classico in a hand-painted pitcher.

EXPENSIVE

✪ **Alberto Ciarla.** Piazza San Cosimato 40. ☎ **06/5818668.** Reservations required. Main courses 26,000L–46,000L ($15–$27); fixed-price menus 80,000L–90,000L ($46–$52). AE, DC, MC, V. Mon–Sat 8:30pm–12:30am. Bus: 44, 75, or 710. SEAFOOD.

Alberto Ciarla is the best restaurant in Trastevere, and one of the most expensive. In an 1890 building, set into an obscure corner of an enormous square, it serves truly elegant fish dishes. You'll be greeted with a cordial reception and a lavish display of seafood on ice. A dramatically modern decor plays shades of brilliant light against patches of shadow for a Renaissance chiaroscuro effect. Specialties include a handful of ancient recipes subtly improved by Signor Ciarla (an example is the soup of pasta and beans with seafood). Original dishes include a delectable fish in orange sauce, spaghetti with clams, and a full array of shellfish. The filet of sea bass is prepared in at least three ways, including an award-winning version with almonds.

MODERATE

La Cisterna. Via della Cisterna 13. ☎ **06/5812543.** Reservations recommended. Main courses 20,000L–35,000L ($12–$20). AE, DC, MC, V. Mon–Sat 7pm–midnight. Bus: 45, 75, 170, 181, or 280. ROMAN.

If you like traditional home cooking based on the best regional ingredients, head here. La Cisterna, named for an ancient well that was discovered in the cellar, lies deep in the heart of Trastevere. For more than 75 years it has been run by the Simmi family, who are genuinely interested in serving only the best as well as providing a good time for all. If it's rainy or cold you'll be in rooms decorated with murals. In summer you can dine at sidewalk tables, and inspect the antipasto right out on the street before going inside. Specialties include Roman-style suckling lamb (abbacchio), rigatoni a l'amatriciana, pappallini romana (wide noodles flavored with prosciutto, cheese, and eggs), shrimp, and fresh fish (try the sea bass baked with herbs).

INEXPENSIVE

✪ **Da Vittorio.** Via di San Cosimato 14A. ☎ **06/5800353.** Reservations not accepted. Pizzas 8,000L–10,000L ($4.80–$6); pastas 7,000L–8,000L ($4.05–$4.65). No credit cards. Mon–Sat 6:30pm–midnight. Take Metro to Largo Argentina, then bus 64. PIZZA/PASTA.

Although competition is fierce, we'll take a risk and say that Naples-born Vittorio Martino and his son, Enzo, consistently serve some of the best pizzas in Rome. They refer to their craft as "the real thing"—a pie that's soft and thick like those that pop out of the oven in Vittorio's southern hometown. When the weather's fair, diners—most often a young crowd—opt for a table outside, deep in the heart of Trastevere. Inside it's rather cramped, with a thrown-together decor of hanging utensils, shelves of wine bottles, and Neapolitan pin-ups on the walls. All the classics make an appearance: Napoletana (fresh tomatoes and anchovies), Margherita (tomato and mozzarella), and Capricciosa (ham, eggs, artichokes, and olives). Vittorio names one of the tastiest—fresh basil, fresh tomato, freshly grated parmesan, and lots of mozzarella—after himself. Other than a limited selection of antipasto and salads, the choice here is almost exclusively pizzas and pastas.

11 In Testaccio

MODERATE

✪ **Checchino dal 1887.** Via di Monte Testaccio 30. ☎ **06/5743816.** Reservations recommended. Main courses 13,000L–35,000L ($8–$20). AE, DC, MC, V. Tues–Sat 12:30–3pm and 8–11pm. Closed Aug and 1 week around Christmas. Bus: 713. ROMAN.

During the 1800s, a local wine shop flourished here, selling drinks to the butchers who worked in the nearby slaughterhouses. In 1887, the ancestors of the present owners began serving food, too, giving birth to the restaurant you'll find today. Slaughterhouse workers in those days were paid part of their meager salaries with the *quinto quarto* (fifth quarter) of each day's slaughter (the tail, feet, intestines, and other parts not for the squeamish). Following centuries of Roman tradition, Ferminia, the wine shop's cook, transformed these products into the tripe and oxtail dishes that form an integral part of the menu. Many Italian diners come here to relish these dishes, which might not be for you unless you're truly adventurous. They include rigatone con pajata (pasta with small intestines), coda alla vaccinara (oxtail stew), fagiole e cotiche (beans with intestinal fat), and other examples of *la cocina povera* (food of the poor). Safer, and possibly more appetizing, is the array of well-prepared salads, soups, pastas, steaks, cutlets, grills, and ice creams. The English-speaking staff is helpful and kind, tactfully proposing alternatives if you're not ready for Roman soul food.

12 On the Appian Way

INEXPENSIVE

✪ **Hostaria l'Archeologia.** Via Appia Antica 139. ☎ **06/7880494.** Reservations recommended, especially on weekends. Main courses 15,000L–30,000L ($9–$17); fixed-price menu from 26,000L ($15). AE, DC, MC, V. Fri–Wed 12:30–3:30pm and 8–10:40pm. Bus: 218 from San Giovanni or 660 from Colli Albani. ROMAN/ITALIAN.

Hostaria l'Archeologia is only a short walk from the catacombs of St. Sebastian. This family-run restaurant resembles an 18th-century village tavern—lots of atmosphere, strings of garlic and corn, oddments of copper hanging from the ceiling, earth-brown beams, and sienna-washed walls. In summer, you can dine in the garden out back under the wisteria. The Roman fare is first-rate; you can glimpse the kitchen from behind a partition in the exterior garden parking lot. Many Roman families visit on the weekend, sometimes in giant groups. Of special interest is the wine cellar, in an ancient Roman tomb, with bottles dating to 1800. (You go through an iron gate, down some stairs, and into the underground cavern. Along the way, you can still see the holes once occupied by funeral urns.)

13 Near Piazza Venezia

EXPENSIVE

✪ **Agata e Romeo.** Via Carlo Alberto 45. ☎ **06/4466115.** Reservations recommended. Main courses 40,000L ($23) each; fixed-price menus 85,000L–100,000L ($49–$58) without wine, 150,000L ($87) with wine. AE, DC, MC, V. Mon–Sat 12:30–3pm and 7:30–11:15pm. Closed Aug. Metro: Vittorio Emanuele. NEW ROMAN.

One of the most charming places near the Vittorio Emanuele monument is this striking duplex restaurant in turn-of-the-century Liberty style. You'll enjoy the creative cuisine of Romeo Caraccio (who manages the dining room) and his wife, Agata Parisella, who prepares her own version of sophisticated Roman food. Look for pasta garnished with broccoli and cauliflower and served in skate broth, as well as a crisp version of sformato loaded with eggplant, parmagiana, mozzarella, and Italian herbs. Fish might be served thin-sliced as roulade and loaded with capers and olives; beans will probably be studded with mussels, clams, and pasta. Carnivores, fish lovers, and vegetarians will all find something on the menu. If you're feeling flush and are interested in sampling a wide array of dishes, go all the way by ordering the 150,000L ($87) fixed-price menu, which includes at least four courses and a glass of wine to accompany each. For dessert, consider Agata's succulent version of millefoglie, a puff pastry stuffed with almonds and sweetened cream.

14 In Parioli

VERY EXPENSIVE

✪ **Relais Le Jardin.** In the Hotel Lord Byron, Via G. de Notaris 5. ☎ **06/3613041.** Reservations required. Main courses 45,000L–55,000L ($26–$32). AE, DC, MC, V. Mon–Sat 1–3pm and 8–10:30pm. Closed Aug. Bus: 26 or 52. ITALIAN/TRADITIONAL.

Relais Le Jardin is one of the best places to go for both traditional and creative cuisine, and a chichi crowd with demanding palates patronizes it nightly. There are places in Rome with better views, but not with this elegant setting, inside one of the capital's most exclusive small hotels. The lighthearted decor combines white lattice with bold colors and flowers. The service is impeccable.

The pastas and soups are among the finest in town. We were particularly taken by the tonnarelli pasta with asparagus and smoked ham served with concassé tomatoes. The chef can take a dish that in ancient times was eaten only by the plebes, bean soup with clams, for example, and make of it something elegant. For your main course you can choose from roast loin of lamb with artichokes romana or grilled beef sirloin with hot chicory and sautéed potatoes. The chef also creates a fabulous risotto with pheasant sauce, asparagus, black truffle flakes, and a hint of fresh thyme—it gets our vote as the best risotto around.

MODERATE

✪ **Al Ceppo.** Via Panama 2. ☎ **06/8419696.** Reservations recommended. Main courses 18,000L–28,000L ($10–$16). AE, DC, MC, V. Tues–Sun 12:30–3pm and 8–11pm. Closed the last 3 weeks of Aug. Bus: 53, 168. ROMAN.

Because the place is somewhat hidden (although it's only 2 blocks from the Villa Borghese, near Piazza Ungheria), you're likely to rub elbows with more Romans than tourists here. This is a longtime favorite, and the cuisine is as good as ever. "The Log" features an open wood-stoked fireplace on which the chef roasts lamb chops, liver, and bacon to charcoal perfection. The beefsteak, which hails from Tuscany, is also delicious. Other dishes are linguine monteconero (with clams and fresh tomatoes); a savory spaghetti with peppers, fresh basil, and pecorino cheese; a swordfish filet filled with grapefruit, parmagiana, pine nuts, and dry grapes; and a fish carpaccio (raw sea bass) with a green salad, onions, and green pepper. Save room for dessert, especially the apple cobbler, pear-and-almond tart, or chocolate meringue hazelnut cake.

Exploring Rome 6

Where else but in Rome could you admire a 17th-century colonnade designed by Bernini, while resting against an Egyptian obelisk carried off from Heliopolis while Christ was still alive? Or stand amid the splendor of Renaissance frescoes in a papal palace built on top of the tomb of a Roman emperor? Where else, for that matter, are vestal virgins buried adjacent to the Ministry of Finance?

Tourists have been sightseeing in Rome for 2,000 years. There is, in fact, almost too much to see, at least for visitors on a typical timetable. Would that we could travel as our 19th-century forebears did, in a coach with tons of luggage, stopping a month here and a month there. Instead, we swoop down from the sky, or roar up at the train station, and try to see everything in a few days. Travelers who approach a visit to Rome this way will find that they have met their match. An absolute minimum of time to see the city is 5 days, and that's pretty heavy-duty sightseeing. Seven days would be better. A lifetime, perhaps, adequate.

In addition to the top attractions in the city itself, there are several places in the environs of Rome worth visiting before leaving this part of the country. It would be a shame to strike out for Venice or Florence without having at least visited Hadrian's Villa and the Villa d'Este, not to mention Palestrina and Ostia Antica (see chapter 10).

SUGGESTED ITINERARIES

These itineraries obviously are designed for the first-time visitor; the more seasoned traveler will want to seek out other treasures. However, such sights as the Vatican Museum can be visited over and over, because each time something new and artistically different will be waiting.

If You Have 1 Day

Far too brief—after all, Rome wasn't built in a day nor can you see it in one—but you can make the most of your limited time. You'll basically have to choose between the legacy of Imperial Rome (mainly the Roman Forum, the Imperial Forum, and the Colosseum) or St. Peter's and the Vatican. Walk along the Spanish Steps at sunset. At night go to Piazza del Campidoglio for a fantastic view of the Forum below. Have a nightcap on Via Veneto which, although past its prime, is still a lure for the first-time visitor. Toss a coin in the Trevi Fountain and promise a return visit to Rome.

Major & Outlying Attractions

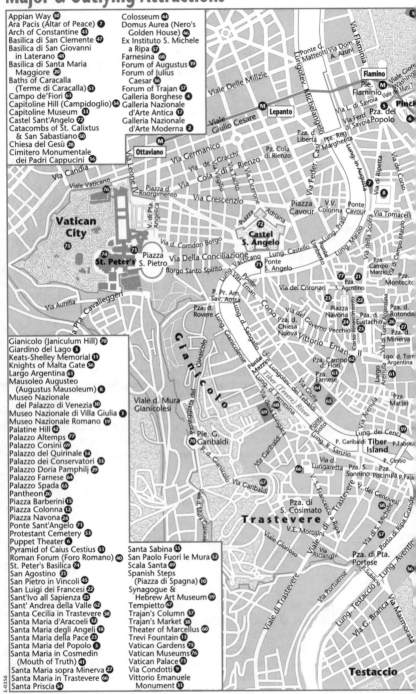

Appian Way 50
Ara Pacis (Altar of Peace) 7
Arch of Constantine 43
Basilica di San Clemente 47
Basilica di San Giovanni
  in Laterano 48
Basilica di Santa Maria
  Maggiore 20
Baths of Caracalla
  (Terme di Caracalla) 51
Campo de'Fiori 63
Capitoline Hill (Campidoglio) 64
Capitoline Museum 33
Castel Sant'Angelo 72
Catacombs of St. Calixtus
  & San Sabastiano 50
Chiesa del Gesù 28
Cimitero Monumentale
  dei Padri Cappucini 16

Colosseum 44
Domus Aurea (Nero's
  Golden House) 46
Ex Instituto S. Michele
  a Ripa 68
Farnesina 67
Forum of Augustus 39
Forum of Julius
  Caesar 36
Forum of Trajan 37
Galleria Borghese 4
Galleria Nazionale
  d'Arte Antica 17
Galleria Nazionale
  d'Arte Moderna 2

Gianicolo (Janiculum Hill) 70
Giardino del Lago 3
Keats-Shelley Memorial 11
Knights of Malta Gate 56
Largo Argentina 61
Mausoleo Augusteo
  (Augustus Mausoleum) 8
Museo Nazionale
  del Palazzo di Venezia 30
Museo Nazionale di Villa Giulia 1
Museo Nazionale Romano 19
Palatine Hill 42
Palazzo Altemps 77
Palazzo Corsini 69
Palazzo dei Quirinale 14
Palazzo dei Conservatori 35
Palazzo Doria Pamphilj 29
Palazzo Farnese 64
Palazzo Spada 65
Pantheon 26
Piazza Barberini 15
Piazza Colonna 12
Piazza Navona 24
Ponte Sant'Angelo 71
Protestant Cemetery 53
Puppet Theater 6
Pyramid of Caius Cestius 53
Roman Forum (Foro Romano) 40
St. Peter's Basilica 74
San Agostino 21
San Pietro in Vincoli 45
San Luigi dei Francesi 22
Sant'Ivo all Sapienza 25
Sant' Andrea della Valle 62
Santa Cecilia in Trastevere 58
Santa Maria d'Aracoeli 34
Santa Maria degli Angeli 18
Santa Maria della Pace 23
Santa Maria del Popolo 5
Santa Maria in Cosmedin
  (Mouth of Truth) 41
Santa Maria sopra Minerva 27
Santa Maria in Trastevere 66
Santa Priscia 54

Santa Sabina 55
San Paolo Fuori le Mura 52
Scala Santa 49
Spanish Steps
  (Piazza di Spagna) 10
Synagogue &
  Hebrew Art Museum 59
Tempietto 67
Trajan's Column 37
Trajan's Market 38
Theater of Marcellus 60
Trevi Fountain 13
Vatican Gardens 75
Vatican Museums 76
Vatican Palace 73
Via Condotti 9
Vittorio Emanuele
  Monument 31

E-0356

134

In the Vatican Museums you'll find many overstuffed galleries and few labels on the works. Buy the detailed guide available at the Vatican Tourist Office so you can make more sense of the incredible riches you'll be seeing.

If You Have 2 Days

If you elected to see the Roman Forum and the Colosseum on your first day, then spend Day 2 exploring St. Peter's and the Vatican Museum (or vice versa). Have dinner that night in a restaurant in Trastevere.

If You Have 3 Days

Spend your first 2 days as above. Go in the morning of Day 3 to the Pantheon in the heart of Old Rome, then try to explore two museums after lunch: the Castel Sant'Angelo and the Etruscan Museum. Have dinner at a restaurant on Piazza Navona.

If You Have 4 or 5 Days

Spend your first 3 days as above. On Day 4 head for the environs, either to Tivoli, where you can see the Villa d'Este and Hadrian's Villa, or to Ostia to explore the ruins of Ostia Antica; return to Rome for lunch, and visit the Capitoline Museum and Basilica di San Giovanni in Laterano in the afternoon. On Day 5, do the day trip above that you skipped on Day 4, then spend the rest of your time exploring and enjoying Rome.

1 The Vatican & St. Peter's

On the left side of the Piazza San Pietro is the **Vatican Tourist Office** (☎ 06/69884466), open Monday to Saturday from 8:30am to 7pm. It sells maps and guides, accepts reservations for tours of the Vatican Gardens, points you in the right direction for papal-audience tickets, and tries to answer any questions you might have. While here, it's wise to pick up a detailed floor plan of St. Peter's Basilica itself so you can identify the various sculptures, tombs, whatever—otherwise you'll feel a bit lost. A shuttle bus to the entrance to the Vatican Museum leaves daily from in front of this office, every 30 minutes from 8:45am to 1:45pm in summer and from 8:45am to 12:45pm in winter; the fare is 2,000L ($1.15). Take it. The walk to the museum entrance is long and generally uninteresting; from the bus route you'll pass through some of the Vatican's lovely gardens. The post office and rest rooms are adjacent to the Vatican tourist office.

✪ **St. Peter's Basilica (Basilica di San Pietro).** Piazza San Pietro. ☎ 06/69884466; 06/69885518 for reservations for excavation sites). Admission: Basilica (including the treasury and grottoes), free; guided tour of the excavations around St. Peter's tomb, 10,000L ($6); dome, 5,000L ($2.90) adults, 2,000L ($1.15) students, or 6,000L ($3.50) to take the elevator (reservations required). Basilica (including the sacristy and treasury), Mar–Sept, daily 7am–7pm; Oct–Feb, daily 7am–6pm. Grottoes daily 8am–5pm. Dome, Mar–Sept, daily 8am–5:45pm; Oct–Feb, daily 8am–4:45pm. Bus: 46.

As you stand in Bernini's **Piazza San Pietro** (St. Peter's Square), you'll be in the arms of an ellipse. Like a loving parent, the Doric-pillared colonnade reaches out to embrace the faithful. Holding 300,000 is no problem for this square.

In the center of the square is an **Egyptian obelisk,** brought from the ancient city of Heliopolis on the Nile delta, and used to adorn the nearby Nero's Circus.

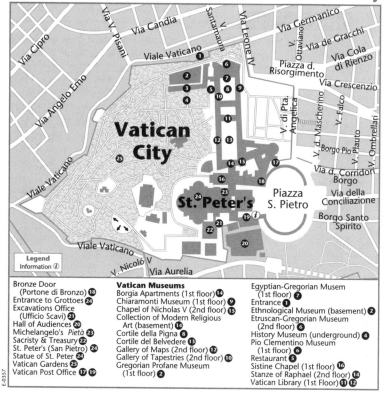

Vatican Museums

Bronze Door
(Portone di Bronzo) 18
Entrance to Grottoes 24
Excavations Office
(Ufficio Scavi) 21
Hall of Audiences 20
Michelangelo's *Pietà* 23
Sacristy & Treasury 22
St. Peter's (San Pietro) 24
Statue of St. Peter 24
Vatican Gardens 25
Vatican Post Office 17 19

Borgia Apartments (1st floor) 14
Chiaramonti Museum (1st floor) 9
Chapel of Nicholas V (2nd floor) 15
Collection of Modern Religious
Art (basement) 14
Cortile della Pigna 8
Cortile del Belvedere 13
Gallery of Maps (2nd floor) 12
Gallery of Tapestries (2nd floor) 10
Gregorian Profane Museum
(1st floor) 2

Egyptian-Gregorian Musem
(1st floor) 7
Entrance 1
Ethnological Museum (basement) 2
Etruscan-Gregorian Museum
(2nd floor) 6
History Museum (underground) 4
Pio Clementino Museum
(1st floor) 6
Restaurant 5
Sistine Chapel (1st floor) 16
Stanze of Raphael (2nd floor) 14
Vatican Library (1st Floor) 11 12

E-0357

Flanking the obelisk are two **17th-century fountains.** The one on the right (facing the basilica) by Carlo Maderno, who designed the facade of St. Peter's, was placed there by Bernini himself; the other is by Carlo Fontana.

Inside, the size of this famous church is awe-inspiring—although its dimensions (about the length of two football fields) are not immediately apparent. St. Peter's is said to have been built over the tomb of the crucified saint. Originally it was erected on the order of Constantine, but the present structure is essentially High Renaissance and baroque; it showcases the talents of some of Italy's greatest artists: Bramante, Raphael, Michelangelo, and Maderno.

Subtle is not the way to describe a church of such grandeur; almost overwhelming are its details of gilt, marble, and mosaic. The basilica is rich in art. In the nave on the right (the first chapel) is the best-known sculpture, the **Pietà,** sculpted by Michelangelo in his early 20s. In one of the worst acts of vandalism on record, a madman screaming "I am Jesus Christ" attacked the *Pietà* in the 1970s, battering the Madonna's stone arm, the folded veil, her left eyelid, and her nose. Now restored, the *Pietà* is protected by a wall of reinforced glass.

Impressions

As a whole St. Peter's is fit for nothing but a ballroom, and it is a little too gaudy even for that.

—John Ruskin, letter to the Rev. Thomas Dale, December 1840

Immediately beyond the *Pietà* is the **Chapel of the Crucifix,** a monument to Queen Christina of Sweden, who was simultaneously orphaned and made queen at the age of six. Educated as a prince, she even studied philosophy under Descartes. Abdicating the throne to become a Roman Catholic, she died in Rome in 1689. Moving up the nave you will encounter a bronze statue of a seated **St. Peter,** origin unknown. Some scholars have attributed it to Arnolfo DI Cambio, the 13th-century sculptor; others have suggested it might be a thousand years old. Note how the right foot has worn down. In 1857 Pope Pius IX granted an indulgence to anyone who kissed this foot.

At the papal altar, which you'll see in the center, stands Bernini's ***Baldacchino,*** sometimes referred to as the Tomb of St. Peter. (Actually, the body of the saint was never recovered after the barbarian invasions.) Nevertheless, this 1633 canopy enshrines the place where the devout believe the first pope was entombed. Commissioned by Pope Urban VIII, the Baldacchino stands as tall as a five-story building. The four columns are almost 100 feet high. Allegedly they once covered the crossbeams in the portico of the Pantheon, although analysis of the bronze seems to prove otherwise.

Directly ahead, beyond the apse, is **St. Peter's Throne,** a 1655 bronze altar encasing an ancient wooden chair. Legend has it that St. Peter sat in this chair while preaching to the Romans.

Immediately to the right is the **Tomb of Urban VIII,** which the pope commissioned Bernini to design for him. Unveiled in 1647, it was hailed as a masterpiece. A notable feature is a bronze skeleton registering the death of the pontiff in the Book of the Dead.

Facing the papal altar and the so-called tomb of St. Peter, the entrance to the sacristy, St. Peter's treasury, and the Museo Storico (historical museum) is signposted to the left, as is a separate entrance to the Vatican grottoes (see below).

The **treasury** is filled with jewel-studded chalices, reliquaries, and copes; one robe once worn by Pope Pius XII strikes a simple note in these halls of elegance. There is much to see in these nine small rooms, especially gifts to the popes from kings, emperors, and others down through the centuries. Heads of state who have presented gifts include Lyndon B. Johnson, who on one occasion showed up with a bust of himself. Most objects are of a religious nature, often in silver and gold and encrusted with jewels. This treasury was once far greater than it is today, however; over the years it has been plundered by everyone from the Vandals in 455 to Napoléon's troops in 1798.

The Museo Storico displays various treasures as well, including the large 15th-century bronze tomb of Pope Sixtus V by Antonio Pollaiuolo, plus numerous antique chalices.

An underground visit to the **Vatican grottoes** reveals both ancient and modern tombs. (Pope John XXIII gets the most adulation.) Along with pillars of an earlier church that stood on this spot, you can view the tombs of such pontiffs as Pius II, Pius XII, Paul VI, John Paul I, and even the only British pope, Nicholas Breakspear, who ruled under the name of Hadrian IV in 1154. An extraordinary gem is here: an **angel,** which is all that remains from Giotto's original mosaic from the first church.

To visit the area around St. Peter's tomb, you must apply several days beforehand to the excavations office. Applications are accepted Monday to Saturday from 9am to noon and 2 to 5pm under the arch to the left of the facade of St. Peter's. The guided tour costs 10,000L ($6) and goes to the tombs that were excavated in the 1940s, 23 feet beneath the floor of the church. In 1939, while digging for a tomb for Pius XI, workers discovered the ruins of the first basilica and part of the wall of Nero's circus, with an ancient necropolis beside it. Some of the tombs were of early Christians, but others were of patrician Romans in the second and third centuries. Graffiti, found approximately where St. Peter's grave is thought to have been, proclaimed, "Peter is here."

The grandest sight is yet to come: the climb to **Michelangelo's dome,** which towers about 375 feet high. *Warning:* Although you can walk up the steps, the climb isn't recommended if you're not in good shape or are claustrophobic; and there's no turning back once you've started. We recommend taking the elevator as far as it goes—it'll save you 171 steps, still leaving you with 320. At the top, your reward is a panoramic view of Rome's rooftops and the Vatican Gardens and papal apartments.

✪ **Vatican Museums & the Sistine Chapel.** Vatican City, Viale Vaticano. ☎ **06/69883333.** Admission 18,000L ($11) adults, 12,000L ($7) children, free for everyone the last Sun of each month (be ready for a crowd). Mid-Mar to late Oct, Mon–Fri and final Sun of the month 8:45am–4:45pm, Sat 8:45am–1:45pm. Off-season: Mon–Sat 8:45am–1:45pm. Closed Jan 6, Feb 11, Easter Mon, Thurs before the 7th Sun after Easter, May 1, Corpus Christi (9th Sun after Easter), June 29, Aug 15–16, Nov 1, and Dec 8, 25–26. Last admission 1 hour before closing. Closed religious holidays. Metro: Ottaviano.

In 1929 the Lateran Treaty between Pope Pius XI and the Italian government created the Vatican, the world's smallest independent state, located within Rome. Though small, this state contains a gigantic repository of treasures from antiquity and the Renaissance housed in labyrinthine galleries. The Vatican's art collection reaches its apex in the Sistine Chapel.

The Vatican museums comprise a series of lavishly adorned palaces and galleries built over the centuries. You can choose your route through the museum from four color-coded itineraries—A, B, C, or D—according to the time you have at your disposal (from 1½ to 5 hours) and your interests. You determine your choice by consulting large-size panels placed at the entrance, and following the letter/color of your choice.

Obviously, 1, 2, or even 20 trips will not be enough to see the wealth of the Vatican, much less digest it. With that in mind, we've previewed only a representative sampling of masterpieces (in alphabetical order). Numbers in parentheses refer to the "Vatican Museums Plan" map.

Borgia Apartments (#7): These apartments, frescoed with biblical scenes by Pinturicchio of Umbria and his assistants, were designed for Pope Alexander VI (the infamous Borgia pope). The rooms, although badly lit, boast great splendor and style. At the end of the Raphael Rooms is the Chapel of Nicholas V, an intimate room frescoed by the Dominican monk Fra Angelico, perhaps the most saintly of all Italian painters.

Chiaramonti Museum (#2): You'll find a dazzling array of Roman sculpture and copies of Greek originals in these galleries. In the Braccio Nuovo, you can admire *The Nile,* a magnificent reproduction of a long-lost Hellenistic original, and one of the most remarkable pieces of sculpture from antiquity. The imposing statue of Augustus of Prima Porta portrays him as a regal commander.

Collection of Modern Religious Art (#7): This museum, opened in 1973, represents American artists' first invasion of the Vatican. (Previously, the church had limited itself to European art created before the 18th century, but Pope Paul VI's hobby changed all that.) Of the 55 rooms in the new museum, at least 12 are devoted to American artists. All the works chosen for the museum were judged on the basis of their "spiritual and religious values." Among the American works is Leonard Baskin's 5-foot bronze sculpture of *Isaac.* Modern Italian artists such as de Chirico and Manzù are also displayed, and there's a special room for the paintings of the French artist Georges Rouault.

Egyptian-Gregorian Museum (#1): Experience the grandeur of the Pharaohs by studying sarcophagi, mummies, statues of goddesses, vases, jewelry, sculptured pink-granite statues, and hieroglyphics.

Etruscan-Gregorian Museum (#3): With sarcophagi, a chariot, bronzes, urns, jewelry, and terra-cotta vases, this gallery offers remarkable insights into an ancient civilization. One of the most acclaimed exhibits is the Regolini-Galassi tomb, unearthed at Cerveteri (see chapter 10) in the 19th century. It shares top honors with the *Mars of Todi,* a bronze sculpture that probably dates from the 5th century B.C.

Ethnological Museum (#12): This is an assemblage of works of art and objects of cultural significance from all over the world. The principal route is a half-mile walk through 25 geographical sections that display thousands of objects covering 3,000 years of world history. The section devoted to China is of particular interest.

History Museum (#13): This museum, founded by Pope Paul VI, recounts the history of the Vatican. Some of the exhibits of arms, uniforms, and armor date back to the early days of the Renaissance. The carriages on display are those used by the popes and cardinals in religious processions. Among the showcases of dress uniforms are the colorful outfits worn by the Pontifical Army Corps, which was discontinued by Pope Paul VI.

Pinacoteca (Picture Gallery) (#10): This gallery houses paintings and tapestries from the 11th to the 19th centuries. As you pass through room 1, note the oldest picture at the Vatican, a keyhole-shaped wood panel of the *Last Judgment* from the 11th century. In room 2 is one of the finest pieces of artwork in the gallery—the *Stefaneschi Triptych* (six panels) by Giotto and his assistants. Bernardo Daddi's masterpiece of early Italian Renaissance art, *Madonna del Magnificat,* is also displayed; and you'll see the works of Fra Angelico, the 15th-century Dominican monk who distinguished himself as a miniaturist (his *Virgin with Child* is justly praised—check the Madonna's microscopic eyes).

In the **Raphael salon** (room 8) you can view three paintings by this Renaissance giant—the *Coronation of the Virgin,* the *Virgin of Foligno,* and the massive *Transfiguration* (completed by Raphael shortly before his death). There are also eight tapestries made by Flemish weavers from cartoons by Raphael. In room 9, seek out Leonardo da Vinci's uncompleted masterpiece, *St. Jerome with the Lion,* Giovanni Bellini's *Pietà,* and one of Titian's greatest works, the *Virgin of Frari.*

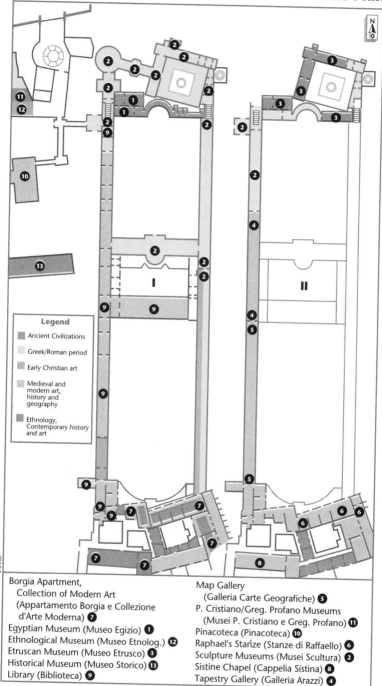

The Vatican Museums Plan

Legend
- Ancient Civilizations
- Greek/Roman period
- Early Christian art
- Medieval and modern art, history and geography
- Ethnology, Contemporary history and art

Borgia Apartment,
   Collection of Modern Art
   (Appartamento Borgia e Collezione
   d'Arte Moderna) ❼
Egyptian Museum (Museo Egizio) ❶
Ethnological Museum (Museo Etnolog.) ⓬
Etruscan Museum (Museo Etrusco) ❸
Historical Museum (Museo Storico) ⓭
Library (Biblioteca) ❾

Map Gallery
   (Galleria Carte Geografiche) ❺
P. Cristiano/Greg. Profano Museums
   (Musei P. Cristiano e Greg. Profano) ⓫
Pinacoteca (Pinacoteca) ❿
Raphael's Stanze (Stanze di Raffaello) ❻
Sculpture Museums (Musei Scultura) ❷
Sistine Chapel (Cappelia Sistina) ❽
Tapestry Gallery (Galleria Arazzi) ❹

E-0358

Finally, in room 10 feast your eyes on one of the masterpieces of the baroque period, Caravaggio's *Deposition from the Cross*.

Pio Clementino Museum (#2): Here you'll find Greek and Roman sculptures, many of which are instantly recognizable. The rippling muscles of the *Belvedere Torso*, a partially preserved Greek statue (1st century B.C.) much admired by the artists of the Renaissance, especially Michelangelo, reveals an intricate knowledge of the human body. In the rotunda is a large gilded bronze of Hercules that dates from the late 2nd century A.D. Other major works of sculpture are under porticoes that open onto the Belvedere courtyard. From the 1st century B.C., one sculpture shows Laocoön and his two sons locked in an eternal struggle with the serpents. The incomparable *Apollo of Belvedere* (a late Roman reproduction of a Greek work from the 4th century B.C.) has become a symbol of classic male beauty.

Stanze di Raphael (Raphael Rooms) (#6): While still a young man, Raphael was given one of the greatest assignments of his short life: the decoration of a series of rooms in the apartments of Pope Julius II. The decoration was carried out by Raphael and his workshop between 1508 and 1524. In these works, Raphael achieves the Renaissance aim of blending classic beauty with realism. In the first chamber, the Stanza dell'Incendio, you'll see much of the work of Raphael's pupils but little of the master's—except in the fresco across from the window. The figure of the partially draped Aeneas rescuing his father (to the left of the fresco) is sometimes attributed to Raphael, as is the surprised woman with a jug balanced on her head to the right.

Raphael reigns supreme in the next and most important salon, the Stanza della Segnatura, the first room decorated by the artist, where you'll find the majestic *School of Athens,* one of the artist's best-known works, which depicts such philosophers as Aristotle, Plato, and Socrates. Many of these figures are actually portraits of some of the greatest artists of the Renaissance, including Bramante (on the right as Euclid, bent over and balding as he draws on a chalkboard), Leonardo da Vinci (as Plato, the bearded man in the center pointing heavenward), even Raphael himself (looking out at you from the lower right corner). While he was painting this masterpiece, Raphael stopped work to walk down the hall for the unveiling of Michelangelo's newly finished Sistine Chapel ceiling. He was so impressed that he returned to his *School of Athens* and added to his design a sulking Michelangelo sitting on the steps. Another well-known masterpiece in this room is the *Disputà del Sacramento.*

The Stanza d'Eliodoro, also by the master, manages to flatter Raphael's papal patrons (Julius II and Leo X) without compromising his art (although one rather fanciful fresco depicts the pope driving Attila from Rome). Finally, there's the Sala di Constantino, which was completed by his students after Raphael's death. And the loggia, frescoed with more than 50 scenes from the Bible, was designed by Raphael, although the actual work was done by his loyal students.

✪ **Sistine Chapel (#8):** Michelangelo considered himself a sculptor, not a painter. While in his 30s, he was commanded by Julius II to stop work on the pope's own tomb and to devote his considerable talents to painting ceiling frescoes—an art form of which the Florentine master was contemptuous.

Michelangelo labored for 4 years (1508–12) on this epic project, which was so physically taxing that it permanently damaged his eyesight. Throughout the project he had to contend with the pope's incessant urgings to hurry up; at one point Julius even threatened to topple Michelangelo from the scaffolding—or so Vasari relates.

Seeing the Ceiling

To get the best view of the Sistine Chapel's ceiling, bring along binoculars.

It's ironic that this project, undertaken against the artist's wishes, would form his most enduring legend. Glorifying the human body as only a sculptor could, Michelangelo painted nine panels inspired by Genesis, and surrounded them with prophets and sibyls. The most notable panels detail the expulsion of Adam and Eve from the Garden of Eden, and the creation of man—where God's outstretched hand imbues Adam with spirit.

The Florentine master was in his 60s when he began to paint the masterly *Last Judgment* on the altar wall. Again working against his wishes, Michelangelo presents a more jaundiced view of people and their fate; God sits in judgment, and sinners are plunged into the mouth of hell.

A master of ceremonies under Paul III, Monsignor Biagio da Cesena, protested to the pope against the "shameless nudes" painted by Michelangelo. Michelangelo showed he wasn't above petty revenge by painting the prude, with the ears of a jackass, in hell. When Biagio complained to the pope, Paul III maintained that he had no jurisdiction in hell. However, Daniele de Volterra was summoned to drape clothing over some of the bare figures—thus earning for himself a dubious distinction as a haberdasher.

On the side walls are frescoes by other Renaissance masters such as Botticelli, Perugino, Luca Signorelli, Pinturicchio, Cosimo Roselli, and Ghirlandaio. We'd guess that if these paintings had been displayed by themselves in other chapels, they would be the object of special pilgrimages. But since they have to compete unfairly with the artistry of Michelangelo, they're virtually ignored by most visitors.

The restoration of the Sistine Chapel in the 1990s touched off a worldwide debate among art historians. The chapel was on the verge of collapse, from both its age and the weather, and the restoration took years, as restorers employed advanced computer analyses in their painstaking and controversial work. They reattached the fresco and repaired the ceiling, ridding the frescoes of their dark and shadowy look. Critics claim that in addition to removing centuries of dirt and grime—and several of the added "modesty" drapes—a vital second layer of paint was removed as well. They argue that many of the restored figures seem flat compared to the shadows and detail of the originals. Others have hailed the project as having saved Michelangelo's masterpiece for future generations to appreciate.

Vatican Library (#9): The Library is richly decorated and frescoed, representing the work of a team of mannerist painters commissioned by Sixtus V.

THE VATICAN GARDENS

Separating the Vatican from the secular world on the north and west are 58 acres of lush, carefully tended gardens filled with winding paths, brilliantly colored flowers, groves of massive oaks, and ancient fountains and pools. In the midst of this pastoral setting is a small summer house, the Villa Pia, built for Pope Pius IV in 1560 by Pirro Ligorio. You can visit the gardens only by guided tour, which must be arranged in advance and is limited to 33 people, so reserve as early as possible during the busy summer period. (*Note:* you cannot get tickets by phone.) Tours run Monday, Tuesday, and Thursday to Saturday at 10am. Tickets are 18,000L ($11) per person, and are available at the Vatican Tourist Office (see above).

Beneath It All: Touring Subterranean Rome

Talk about the "underground" and a growing number of Romans will excitedly take up the story, offering tidbits about where to go, who to talk to, what's been seen, and what's allegedly awaiting discovery, just around the next bend in the sewer. The sewer? That's right. **Subterranean Rome (Roma Sotteranea)** is neither subway nor trendy arts movement but rather the vast historic ruins of a city that has been occupied for nearly 3,000 years. The remains of Rome's first two millennia are now largely buried by natural sediment and manmade landfills; archaeologists estimate that these processes have left the streets of Ancient Rome as much as 20 yards beneath the surface.

A little too deep for you? Consider this: Each year, an inch of dust in the form of pollen, leaves, pollution, sand, and silt from disintegrating ruins settles over Rome. Archaeologists estimate that the ruins of a one-story Roman house will produce debris six feet deep over its entire floor plan. When you multiply that by more than 40,000 apartment buildings, 1,800 palaces, and numerous giant public buildings, a very real picture of the burial of the ancient city presents itself. Another contributing factor? The centuries-old Roman tradition of burying old buildings in landfills, which can raise the level of the earth several yards at one time. In fact, past builders have often filled up massive stone ruins with dirt or dug down through previous landfills to the columns and vaults of underlying structures, then laid a foundation for a new layer of Roman architecture.

As a result, many of the buildings on the streets today actually provide direct access to Rome's inner world. Secret doorways lead down to hidden crypts and shrines—the existence of which are closely guarded secrets. Nondescript locked doors in churches and other public buildings often open upon whole blocks of the ancient city, streets still intact. Take for instance **San Clemente,** the 12th-century basilica east of the Colosseum, where a staircase in the sacristy leads down to the original 4th-century church. Not only that, but a staircase near the apse of the church goes down to an earlier Roman apartment building and temple, which in turn leads down to a giant public building dating back to the Great Fire of A.D. 64. Another interesting doorway to the past is the one in the south exterior wall of **St. Peter's,** which leads down to an intact necropolis. That crumbling brick entry, located in the gardens on the east side of Esquiline Hill, carries you into the vast **Golden House (Domus Aurea),** Nero's residence, built upon the ruins left by the Great Fire.

PAPAL AUDIENCES

The pope gives public audiences each Wednesday morning except when he is absent from Rome. The audience begins at 10:30am, but sometimes at 10am in the hot summer. It takes place in the Paul VI Hall of Audiences, although the Basilica di San Pietro and Piazza San Pietro are sometimes used to accommodate very large attendances. Anyone is welcome, but you must obtain a free ticket first from the office of the Prefecture of the Papal Household, accessible from St. Peter's Square by the bronze door where the right-hand colonnade (as you face the basilica) begins. The office is open Monday to Saturday from 9am to 1pm. On Monday and Tuesday, tickets are readily available, but sometimes you won't be able to get into the office on Wednesday morning. Occasionally, if there's enough room, you can attend without a ticket.

Don't expect a coherent, step-by-step roadmap of this hidden world, as the nuggets you'll find will be interspersed with views of buildings set on the city's surface. Likewise, there's no cohesive labyrinth leading from one point to another.

A guided tour can be useful, especially one that focuses on Roman excavations and church crypts. Several tour companies now offer selected views of subterranean Rome. One of the most appealing is **Genti e Paesi** (☎ **06/83501755**), which, on demand, offers a 90-minute tour of the many crypts beneath the above-mentioned Church of San Clemente for 12,000L ($7) per person. Other tours last between 90 and 120 minutes and cost between 12,000L and 18,000L ($7 to $11) per person. One that gives a vivid sense of the layers of artifact-laden debris beneath Rome involves tours through the Castello Sant'Angelo. Two competitors of Genti e Paesi, with roughly equivalent offerings, are **Itinera** (☎ **06/2757323**) and **LUPA** (☎ **06/71356027**), both run by trained archaeologists with impressive amounts of experience in studying the structures and layout of the underlying city. **Città Nascosta** (☎ **06/3216059**) offers offbeat tours to less-visited churches and monuments. Each of the above-mentioned companies has either a receptionist or a recorded message to announce whatever tours they currently offer.

For those who want additional insights, but from the safety of their armchairs, the Italian monthly magazine *Forma Urbis* sometimes features the photographs of Carlo Pavia, who, armed with lights, camera, hip boots, and oxygen mask, slogs through ancient sewage and hordes of jumping spiders, giant rats, and albino insect populations to record parts of the ancient city that haven't been seen in centuries. Pavia's most bizarre discovery was a series of chlorophyll-starved plants from North Africa and the Arab world growing in rooms beneath the Colosseum. The theory is they grew from seeds that fell from the coats of exotic animals sent into the arena to battle gladiators.

Much of the underground will probably remain inaccessible to the general public. However, influential citizens such as Emanuele Gattis, a retired government archaeologist who oversaw more than 30 years worth of construction projects in Rome, are urging government leaders to seize the opportunity and direct part of the billions of lire being spent to beautify Rome for Jubilee 2000 into opening up more of the city's buried past.

You can also write ahead of time to the **Prefecture of the Papal Household,** 00120 Città del Vaticano (☎ **06/69883017**), indicating your language, the dates of your visit, the number of people in your party, and, if possible, the hotel in Rome to which the cards should be sent the afternoon before the audience. American Catholics, armed with a letter of introduction from their parish priest, should apply to the **North American College,** Via dell'Umiltà 30, 00187 Rome (☎ **06/690011**).

At noon on Sunday the pope speaks briefly from his study window and gives his blessing to the visitors and pilgrims gathered in St. Peter's Square. From about mid-July to mid-September the Angelus and blessing take place at the summer residence at Castelgandolfo, some 16 miles out of Rome and accessible by Metro and bus.

- Along with miles of headless statues and acres of paintings, Rome has 913 churches.
- Some Mongol khans and Turkish chieftains pushed westward to conquer the Roman Empire after it had ceased to exist.
- At the time of Julius Caesar and Augustus, Rome's population reached one million—the largest city in the Western world. Some historians claim that by the year A.D. 500 only 10,000 inhabitants were left.
- Pope Leo III sneaked up on Charlemagne and set an imperial crown on his head, a surprise coronation that launched a precedent of Holy Roman Emperors being crowned by popes in Rome.
- More than 90% of Romans live in private apartments, some of which rise 10 floors and have no elevators.
- The bronze of Marcus Aurelius in the Capitoline Museums, one of the world's greatest equestrian statues, escaped being melted down because the early Christians thought it was of Constantine.
- The Theater of Marcellus incorporated a gory realism in some of its stage plays: Condemned prisoners were often butchered before audiences as part of the plot.
- Christians may not have been fed to the lions at the Colosseum, but in one day 5,000 animals were slaughtered (about one every 10 seconds). North Africa's native lions and elephants were rendered extinct.

2 The Forum, the Colosseum & the Heart of Ancient Rome

✪ **Roman Forum (Foro Romano).** Via dei Fori Imperiali. ☎ **06/6990110.** Admission 12,000L ($8) adults, free for children 17 and under and for seniors 60 and over. Sun 9am–1pm; Apr–Sept, Mon–Sat 9am–6pm; Oct–Mar, Mon–Sat 9am–sunset. Last admission 1 hour before closing. Metro: Colosseo.

When it came to cremating Caesar, raping Sabine women, purchasing a harlot for the night, or sacrificing a naked victim, the **Roman Forum** was where the action was. Traversed by Via Sacra (the Sacred Way), it was built in the marshy land between the Palatine and the Capitoline hills. It flourished as the center of Roman life in the days of the Republic, before it gradually lost prestige to the Imperial Forums.

Be warned: Expect only fragmented monuments, an arch or two, and lots of over-turned boulders. That any semblance of the Forum remains today is miraculous, as it was used for years, like the Colosseum, as a quarry. Eventually it reverted to what the Italians call *campo vaccino* (cow pasture). But excavations in the 19th century began to bring to light one of the world's most historic spots.

By day, the columns of now-vanished temples and the stones from which long-forgotten orators spoke are mere shells. Bits of grass and weed grow where a triumphant Caesar was once lionized. But at night, when the Forum is silent in the moonlight, it isn't difficult to imagine that Vestal Virgins still guard the sacred temple fire.

You can spend at least a morning wandering alone through the ruins of the Forum. If you're content with just looking at the ruins, you can do so at your leisure. But if you want the stones to have some meaning, you'll have to purchase a

Ancient Rome & Attractions Nearby

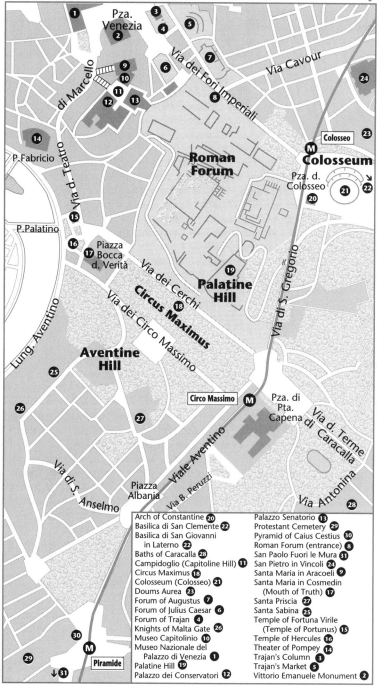

Pza. Venezia

Via dei Fori Imperiali

Via Cavour

di Marcello

Via d. Teatro

P. Fabricio

P. Palatino

Roman Forum

M Colosseo
Colosseum

Pza. d. Colosseo

Via dei Cerchi

Piazza Bocca d. Verità

Circus Maximus

Via dei Circo Massimo

Palatine Hill

Via di S. Gregorio

Aventine Hill

Lung. Aventino

Circo Massimo M

Pza. di Pta. Capena

Via d. Terme di Caracalla

Via di S. Anselmo

Viale Aventino

Via B. Peruzzi

Piazza Albania

Via Antonina

M Piramide

E-0359

Arch of Constantine ⓴
Basilica di San Clemente ㉒
Basilica di San Giovanni
  in Laterno ㉒
Baths of Caracalla ㉘
Campidoglio (Capitoline Hill) ⑪
Circus Maximus ⑱
Colosseum (Colosseo) ㉑
Doums Aurea ㉓
Forum of Augustus ⑦
Forum of Julius Caesar ⑥
Forum of Trajan ④
Knights of Malta Gate ㉖
Museo Capitolinio ⑩
Museo Nazionale del
  Palazzo di Venezia ①
Palatine Hill ⑲
Palazzo dei Conservatori ⑫

Palazzo Senatorio ⑬
Protestant Cemetery ㉙
Pyramid of Caius Cestius ㉚
Roman Forum (entrance) ⑧
San Paolo Fuori le Mura ㉛
San Pietro in Vincoli ㉔
Santa Maria in Aracoeli ⑨
Santa Maria in Cosmedin
  (Mouth of Truth) ⑰
Santa Priscia ㉗
Santa Sabina ㉕
Temple of Fortuna Virile
  (Temple of Portunus) ⑮
Temple of Hercules ⑯
Theater of Pompey ⑭
Trajan's Column ③
Trajan's Market ⑤
Vittorio Emanuele Monument ②

147

Historical Footnote

The function of the Vestal Virgins was to keep the temple's sacred fire burning—but to keep their own flames under control. Failure to do the latter sent them to an early grave. . . alive!

---

detailed map at the gate, as the temples are difficult to locate otherwise. The first half of our Walking Tour 1, "Rome of the Caesars," in chapter 7 will take you around what remains of the ancient buildings and temples, as well as up the Palatine Hill.

A long walk up from the Roman Forum leads to the **Palatine Hill** (you can visit on the same ticket, and at the same hours, as the Forum), one of the seven hills of Rome. The Palatine, tradition tells us, was the spot on which the first settlers built their huts, under the direction of Romulus. In later years the hill became a patrician residential district that attracted such citizens as Cicero. In time, however, the area was gobbled up by imperial palaces, and it attracted such famous and infamous tenants as Caligula (who was murdered here), Nero, Tiberius, and Domitian.

Only the ruins of its former grandeur remain today, and you really need to be an archaeologist to make sense of them, as they're more difficult to understand than the ruins in the Forum. But even if you're not interested in the past, it's worth the climb for the panoramic, sweeping view of both the Roman and Imperial forums, as well as the Capitoline Hill and the Colosseum. To explore, again, see our Walking Tour 1, "Rome of the Caesars," in chapter 7.

✪ **Colosseum (Colosseo).** Piazzale del Colosseo, Via dei Fori Imperiali. ☎ **06/7004261.** Admission: Street level, free; upper levels, 8,000L ($4.65). Free for children under 18 and for seniors over 60. Apr–Sept, Mon–Tues and Thurs–Sat 9am–7pm, Wed and Sun 9am–1pm. Oct–Mar Mon–Tues and Thurs–Sat 9am–3pm, Wed and Sun 9am–1pm. Metro: Colosseo.

In spite of the fact that it's a mere shell, the Colosseum remains the greatest architectural inheritance from ancient Rome. Vespasian ordered the construction of the elliptically shaped bowl, called the Amphitheatrum Flavium, in A.D. 72; it was inaugurated by Titus in A.D. 80 with a many-weeks-long bloody combat between gladiators and wild beasts. At its peak, under the cruel Domitian, the Colosseum could seat 50,000 spectators. The Vestal Virgins from the temple screamed for blood, as more and more exotic animals were shipped in from the far corners of the empire to satisfy jaded tastes (lion vs. bear, two humans vs. hippopotamus). Not-so-mock naval battles were staged (the canopied Colosseum could be flooded), in which the defeated combatants might have their lives spared if they put up a good fight. Many historians now believe that one of the most enduring legends linked to the Colosseum—that Christians were fed to the lions here—is unfounded.

Long after it ceased to be an arena to amuse sadistic Romans, the Colosseum was struck by an earthquake. Centuries later it was used as a quarry, its rich marble facing stripped away to build palaces and churches.

On one side, part of the original four tiers remains; the first three levels were constructed in Doric, Ionic, and Corinthian styles to lend it variety.

Arch of Constantine. Next to the Colosseum, Piazzale del Colosseo. Metro: Colosseo.

A highly photogenic memorial, the Arch of Constantine was erected in honor of Constantine's defeat of the pagan Maxentius (A.D. 306). It's a landmark in every way. Physically, it's beautiful, perhaps marred by the aggravating traffic that zooms around it at all hours, but so intricately carved and well preserved that you almost forget the racket of the cars and buses. Many of the reliefs have nothing whatsoever to do with Constantine or his works, but tell of the victories of earlier Antonine rulers—they were apparently lifted from other, long-forgotten memorials.

Historically, the arch marks a period of great change in the history of Rome and therefore the history of the world. Converted to Christianity by a vision on the battlefield, Constantine officially ended the centuries-long persecution of the Christians during which many devout followers of the new religion had been put to death in a most gruesome manner. Although Constantine did not ban paganism (which survived officially until the closing of the temples more than half a century later), he espoused Christianity himself and began the inevitable development that culminated in the conquest of Rome by the Christian religion. The arch is a tribute to the emperor erected by the Senate in A.D. 315.

Domus Aurea. Via Labicana, on the Esquiline Hill. Metro: Colosseo.

After visiting the Colosseum, it's also convenient to look at the site of the Domus Aurea, (Golden House of Nero); it faces the Colosseum and is adjacent to the Forum. The Domus Aurea was one of the most sumptuous palaces of all time, constructed by Nero after the disastrous fire that swept over Rome in A.D. 64. Not much remains of its former glory, but once the floors were made of mother-of-pearl and the furniture of gold. The area that is the Colosseum today was an ornamental lake, which reflected the grandeur and glitter of the Golden House. The hollow ruins—long ago stripped of their lavish decorations—lie near the entrance of the Oppius Park.

During the Renaissance, painters such as Raphael chopped holes in the long-buried ceilings of the Domus Aurea to gain admittance. Once there, they were inspired by the frescoes and the small "grotesques" of cornucopia and cherubs. The word *grotto* came from this palace, as it was believed to have been built underground. Remnants of these original, almost-2,000-year-old frescoes and fragments of mosaics remain. All interiors have been closed for years.

3 Near Ancient Rome

The Campidoglio (Capitoline Hill). Bus: 716.

Of the Seven Hills of Rome, the Campidoglio, Piazza del Campidoglio, is the most sacred—its origins stretch way back into antiquity (an Etruscan temple to Jupiter once stood on this spot). The approach to the Capitoline Hill is dramatic as you climb the long, sloping steps designed by Michelangelo. At the top is a perfectly proportioned square, Piazza del Campidoglio, also laid out by the Florentine artist. Michelangelo also positioned the ancient bronze equestrian statue of Marcus Aurelius in the center, but it was moved inside to protect it from pollution. You'll find a replacement copy out on the pedestal.

One side of the piazza is open; the others are bounded by the **Senatorium** (Town Council), the statuary-filled **Palazza dei Conservatori,** and the **Capitoline Museum** (Museo Capitolino; see below). The Campidoglio is dramatic at night (walk around to the back for a regal view of the floodlit Roman Forum). On your return, head down the small steps on your right. The other steps adjoining Michelangelo's approach will take you to the **Church of Santa Maria d'Aracoeli** (see below).

✪ **Capitoline Museum (Museo Capitolino) and Palazzo dei Conservatori.** Piazza del Campidoglio. ☎ **06/67102071.** Admission 10,000L ($6) for both; 5,000L ($2.90) for children under 18. Free last Sun of each month. Tues–Sun 9am–7pm. Bus: 44, 85, 87, 170, 175, 181, 628, 640, or 810.

913 Churches, One Synagogue—
Jews in the Capital of Christendom

Nestled midway between the Isola Tiberina and the monument to Vittorio Emanuele II, Rome's Jewish ghetto was designated during the administration of Pope Paul IV between 1555 and 1559. At the time it enclosed several thousand people into a cramped, 2½ -acre tract of walled-in, overcrowded real estate that did much to contribute to the oppression of the Jews during the Italian Renaissance.

Jews had played an important part in the life of Rome prior to that time. They migrated to the political center of the known world during the 1st century B.C., and within 200 years their community had grown to a highly noticeable minority. Most of it was based in Trastevere, a neighborhood that for many years was referred to as Contrada Iudaeorum (Jewish Quarter). By 1309 ordinances were passed that forced Jews to illustrate their religious and cultural backgrounds with special garments, and their ability to worship as they wished depended on the indulgence of the pope.

In 1363 additional ordinances were passed that limited Jewish cemeteries to an area adjacent to the Tiber, near the present-day Church of San Francesco a Ripa. During the 1400s the Jewish population regrouped onto the opposite side of the Tiber, in an area around the square that's known today as Piazza Mattei.

In 1492 Queen Isabella and King Ferdinand of Spain killed, tortured, forcibly converted, or forced the emigration of thousands of Jews from Spain. Many came to Rome, swelling the ranks of the city. Pope Alexander VI (1492–1503), whose political sympathies lay firmly with the Spanish monarchs, grudgingly admitted the refugees into his city, on condition that each pay a hefty fee in gold. His papal bull, *Cum nimis absurdium,* defined the borders of the Jewish ghetto within the boundaries of the Sant'Angelo district, and later enlarged them to include the muddy, frequently flooded banks of the Tiber. Water levels often reached the third floors of the houses of the poorest families, who were forced, by law and by economics, to settle here. Piling humiliation upon humiliation, the

These museums house some of the greatest pieces of classical sculpture in the world. **The Capitoline Museum** was built in the 17th century, based on an architectural sketch by Michelangelo. In the first room is *The Dying Gaul,* a work of majestic skill. It's a copy of a Greek original that dates from the 3rd century B.C. In a special gallery all her own *The Capitoline Venus* demurely covers herself. This statue (also a Roman copy of a 3rd century B.C. Greek original) has been considered a symbol of feminine beauty and charm down through the centuries. *Amore* (Cupid) and *Psyche* are up to their old tricks near the window.

The famous equestrian statue of Marcus Aurelius was restored recently. This is the only bronze equestrian statue to have survived from ancient Rome, mainly because for centuries it was thought to be a statue of Constantine the Great and Papal Rome respected the memory of the first Christian emperor. It's a beautiful statue even though the perspective is rather odd—it was designed to sit on top of a tall column, hence the foreshortened effect. The statue is housed in a glass-enclosed room on the street level; called the Cortile di Marforio, it's a kind of Renaissance greenhouse, surrounded by windows.

The Palace of the Conservatori, across the way, was also based on an architectural plan by Michelangelo, and is rich in classical sculpture and paintings. One of residents of the nearly uninhabitable riverbanks were forced to pay for the construction of the embankments that prevented the neighborhood from flooding. For centuries no one could enter or leave the ghetto between sundown and sunrise.

In 1848 the walls that had defined and confined the ghetto were demolished under the auspices of the relatively lenient Pope Leo XII. In 1883, during the surge of nationalism that preceded the unification of Italy, the ghetto was abolished altogether.

Tragically, on October 16, 1943, the segregation of Rome's Jews was reestablished when German Nazi soldiers rounded up most of the Jews from throughout Rome into a re-creation of the medieval ghetto and imposed a flabbergastingly high ransom on them. Amazingly, this fee—more than 100 pounds of gold per resident—was eventually collected. Despite having made the payment, the Jews were rounded up and deported to the death camps anyway, as part of one of the most horrible episodes of Italy's participation in the war years.

Today the neighborhood, centered around Piazza Mattei and its elegant Renaissance fountain, lacks any coherent architectural unity. However, this colorful hodgepodge of narrow, twisting streets and sometimes derelict buildings is the site of some of the most evocative memories in Rome. One of the most unusual streets is Via del Portico d'Ottavia, where medieval houses and pavements adjoin kosher food stores and simple trattorie that almost invariably feature carciofi alla Giudeai—deep-fried artichokes.

Although it bears the scars and honors of centuries of occupation by Jews, today this is a Jewish neighborhood mostly in name only. Its centerpiece is the Synagogue on Via Catalana. Built of travertine marble in 1904 in the Assyrian-Babylonian style, it's capped with a silvery dome crafted entirely of aluminum. Tours of the district are conducted on an as-needed basis from the **Service International de Documentation Judeo-Chrétienne (SIDIG),** Via Plebiscito 112 (☎ **06/6795307**).

the most notable bronzes—a work of incomparable beauty—is *Lo Spinario* (a little boy picking a thorn from his foot), a Greek classic that dates from the 1st century B.C. In addition, you'll find *Lupa Capitolina* (the Capitoline Wolf), a rare Etruscan bronze that may go back to the 5th century B.C. (Romulus and Remus, the legendary twins that the wolf suckled, were added at a later date). The palace also contains a "Pinacoteca"—mostly paintings from the 16th and 17th centuries. Notable canvases include Caravaggio's *Fortune-Teller* and his curious *John the Baptist, The Holy Family* by Dosso Dossi, *Romulus and Remus* by Rubens, and Titian's *Baptism of Christ.* The entrance courtyard is lined with the remains—head, hands, foot, and a kneecap—of an ancient colossal statue of Constantine the Great.

Santa Maria d'Aracoeli. Piazza d'Aracoeli. ☎ **06/6798155.** Free admission. Daily 7am–noon and 4–7pm. Bus: 44, 46, or 75.

Sharing a spot on Capitoline Hill, this landmark church was built for the Franciscans in the 13th century. According to legend, Augustus once ordered a temple erected on this spot, where a sibyl, with her gift of prophecy, forecast the coming of Christ. In the interior of the present building you'll find a coffered Renaissance ceiling and a mosaic of the Virgin over the altar in the Byzantine style. If you're sleuth enough, you'll also find a tombstone carved by the great Renaissance sculptor Donatello.

The church is known for its **Bufalini Chapel,** a masterpiece of Pinturicchio, who frescoed it with scenes illustrating the life and death of St. Bernardino of Siena. He also depicted St. Francis receiving the stigmata. These frescoes are a high point in early Renaissance Roman painting. You have to climb a long flight of steep steps to reach the church, unless you're already on the neighboring Piazza del Campidoglio, in which case you can cross the piazza and climb the steps on the far side of the Museo Capitolino.

Museo Nazionale del Palazzo di Venezia. Via del Plebiscito 118. ☎ **679-8865.** Admission 8,000L ($4.65) adults, free for children under 18. Tues–Sat 9am–2pm, Sun 9am–1pm. Bus: 57, 65, 70, or 75.

The Museum of the Palazzo Venezia, in the geographic heart of Rome, is the building that served until the end of World War I as the seat of the Embassy of Austria. During the Fascist regime (1928–43) it was the seat of the Italian government. The balcony from which Mussolini used to speak to the Italian people was built in the 15th century. You can now visit the rooms and halls containing oil paintings, porcelains, tapestries, ivories, and ceramics. No one particular exhibit stands out—it's the sum total that adds up to a major attraction. Currently the State Rooms are open only occasionally to host temporary exhibitions.

Standing outside the museum, you cannot help but notice the 20th-century monument to Victor Emmanuel II, king of Italy, built on part of the Capitoline Hill and overlooking the piazza, a lush work that has often been compared to a wedding cake. Here you'll find the Tomb of the Unknown Soldier, which was created in World War I.

Santa Maria in Cosmedin. Piazza della Bocca della Verità 18. ☎ **06/6781419.** Free admission. Daily 9am–1pm and 2:30–6pm. Bus: 81 or 175. Metro: Circo Massimo.

This little church was founded in the 6th century, but subsequently rebuilt—and a Romanesque campanile was added in the 12th century. The church is a popular destination, not for its great art treasures but for its **"Mouth of Truth,"** a large disk under the portico. As Gregory Peck demonstrated to Audrey Hepburn in *Roman Holiday,* the mouth is supposed to chomp down on the hand of liars who insert their paws. According to local legend, a former priest used to keep a scorpion in back to bite the fingers of anyone he felt was lying. On one of our visits to the church, a little woman, her head draped in black, sat begging a few feet from the medallion. A scene typical enough—except that this woman's right hand was covered with bandages.

Baths of Caracalla (Terme di Caracalla). Via delle Terme di Caracalla 52. ☎ **06/5758626.** Admission 8,000L ($4.65) adults, free for children 11 and under. Tues–Sat 9am–1pm. Bus: 628.

Named for the emperor Caracalla, the Terme di Caracalla were completed in the early part of the 3rd century. The richness of decoration has faded and the lushness can only be judged from the shell of brick ruins that remain. In their heyday, they sprawled across 27 acres and could handle 1,600 bathers at one time. A circular room, the ruined *caldarium* used for very hot baths, was the traditional setting for operatic performances in Rome, until it was discovered that the ancient structure was being severely damaged.

Saint Peter in Chains (San Pietro in Vincoli). Piazza di San Pietro in Vincoli 4A, off Via degli Annibaldi. ☎ **06/4882865.** Free admission. Spring–summer daily 7am–12:30pm and 3:30–7pm; autumn–winter daily 7am–12:30pm and 3–6pm. Metro: Via Cavour.

From the Colosseum, head up the "spoke" street Via degli Annibaldi to this church, founded in the 5th century A.D. to house the chains that bound St. Peter in Palestine—they're preserved under glass. But the drawing card is the tomb of Julius II, with one of the world's most famous pieces of sculpture, *Moses* by Michelangelo. As readers of Irving Stone's *The Agony and the Ecstasy* know, Michelangelo was to have carved 44 magnificent figures for Julius's tomb. That didn't happen, of course, but the pope was given one of the greatest consolation prizes—a figure intended to be "minor" that is now numbered among Michelangelo's masterpieces. In the *Lives of the Artists* Vasari wrote of the stern father symbol of Michelangelo's *Moses*, "No modern work will ever equal it in beauty, no, nor ancient either."

Basilica di San Clemente. Piazza di San Clemente, Via Labicana 95. ☎ **06/70451018.** Admission: Basilica, free; grottoes, 4,000L ($2.30). Mon–Sat 9am–12:30pm and 3–6pm, Sun 10am–noon and 3–6pm. Metro: Colosseo.

From the Colosseum, head up Via di San Giovanni in Laterano to the Basilica of Saint Clement. This isn't just another Roman church—far from it! In this church-upon-a-church, centuries of history peel away. In the 4th century a church was built over a secular house of the 1st century A.D., beside which stood a pagan temple dedicated to Mithras (god of the sun). Down in the eerie grottoes (which you can explore on your own—unlike the catacombs on the Appian Way), you'll discover well-preserved frescoes from the 9th through the 11th century A.D. After the Normans destroyed the lower church, a new one was built in the 12th century. Its chief attraction is the bronze-orange mosaic (from that period) that adorns the apse, as well as a chapel honoring St. Catherine of Alexandria with frescoes by Masolino.

Basilica di San Giovanni in Laterano. Piazza di San Giovanni in Laterano 4. ☎ **06/69886433.** Basilica, free; cloisters, 4,000L ($2.30). Summer daily 7am–6:45pm; off-season daily 7am–6pm. Metro: San Giovanni.

This basilica—not St. Peter's—is the cathedral of the diocese of Rome. Originally built in A.D. 314 by Constantine, the cathedral has suffered the vicissitudes of Rome, and was badly sacked and forced to rebuild many times. Only fragmented parts of the baptistery remain from the original structure.

The present building is characterized by its 18th-century facade by Alessandro Galilei; statues of Christ and the Apostles ring the top. (A terrorist bomb in 1993 caused severe damage, especially to the facade.) Borromini gets the credit (some say blame) for the interior, built for Innocent X. It's said that in the misguided attempt to redecorate, frescoes by Giotto were destroyed (remains believed to have been painted by Giotto were discovered in 1952 and are now on display against a column near the church entrance on the right inner pier). In addition, look for the unusual ceiling and the sumptuous transept, and explore the 13th-century cloisters with their twisted double columns.

The popes used to live next door at the **Lateran Palace** before the move to Avignon in the 14th century. Across the street is the **Santuario della Scala Santa** (Palace of the Holy Steps), Piazza San Giovanni in Laterano (☎ **06/70494619**). It's alleged that the 28 marble steps here (now covered with wood for preservation) were originally at Pontius Pilate's villa in Jerusalem and that Christ climbed them the day he was brought before Pilate. According to a medieval tradition, the steps were brought from Jerusalem to Rome by Constantine's mother, Helen, in 326, and they've been in this location since 1585. Today pilgrims from all over the world come here to climb the steps—on their knees in some cases. This is one of the holiest sites in Christendom, although some historians say the stairs may date only to the 4th century.

4 Around Campo de' Fiori & the Jewish Ghetto

Much of this area, along with the Piazza Navona & the Pantheon neighborhood, is covered on Walking Tour 3, "Renaissance Rome" (see chapter 7).

Campo de' Fiori. Bus: 64 from the Termini to Museo di Roma; then walk.

During the 1500s Campo de' Fiori was the geographic and cultural center of secular Rome, site of dozens of inns that would almost certainly have been reviewed by this guidebook had it existed at the time. From its center rises a statue of a severe-looking monk (Giordano Bruno), whose presence is a reminder of the occasional burnings at the stake in this piazza of religious heretics. Today, ringed by venerable and antique houses, the campo is the site of an **open-air food market** held Monday to Saturday from early in the morning until around noon, or whenever the food runs out.

An interesting remnant from the era of the Jewish ghetto is the **Church of San Gregorio,** Ponte Quattro Capi at the end of Via del Portico d'Ottavia. It has an inscription in both Hebrew and Latin asking Jews to convert to Catholicism.

Across the street from the church stands the **Sinagoga Ashkenazita** (☎ **06/6840061**), which is open only for services. Trying to avoid all resemblance to a Christian church, the building, constructed from 1874 to 1904, evokes Babylonian and Persian architectural details. The synagogue was attacked by terrorists in 1982 and since then has been heavily guarded by *carabinieri* armed with machine guns. It houses the **Jewish Museum** (☎ **06/6840061),** which is open Monday to Thursday from 9am to 4:30pm; Friday from 9am to 1:30pm, and Sunday 9:30am to noon. Admission is 8,000L ($4.65). Many rare and even priceless treasures are exhibited here, including a Moroccan prayer book from the early 14th century and ceremonial objects from the 17th-century Jewish Ghetto.

Palazzo Farnese. Piazza Farnese. Closed to the public. Bus: 116.

Built between 1514 and 1589, this palace was designed by Sangallo, Michelangelo, and others at an astronomical cost. Its famous residents have included a 16th-century member of the Farnese family, Pope Paul III, Cardinal Richelieu, and the former Queen Christina of Sweden, who moved to Rome after abdicating her throne. During the 1630s, when the building's heirs could no longer afford to maintain it, the palace became the site of the French embassy, a function it has performed ever since. It's presently closed to the public. The best view of the palazzo is from Piazza Farnese.

Palazzo Spada. Piazza Capo di Ferro 3. ☎ **06/6861158.** Admission 4,000L ($2.55) adults, free for children 17 and under and for seniors 60 and over. Tues–Sat 9am–7pm, Sun 9am–1pm. Bus: 19, 306, or 926.

Built around 1550 for Cardinal Gerolamo Capo di Ferro, and later inhabited by the descendants of several other cardinals, Palazzo Spada was sold to the Italian government in the 1920s. Its richly ornate facade, covered as it is in high-relief stucco decorations in the Mannerist style, is the finest of any building from 16th-century Rome. Although the State Rooms are closed to the public, the richly decorated courtyard and a handful of galleries of paintings are open.

Museo di Arte Ebraico della Comunità Israelitica de Roma. Lungotevere Cenci (Tempio). ☎ **06/6840061.** Admission 8,000L ($4.65) adults and children. June–Aug, Mon–Fri 9:30am–12:30pm; Sept–May, Mon–Thurs 9:30am–1pm and 3–5pm, Fri 9:30am–1:30pm. Bus: 23, 64, or 65.

This **museum of Hebraic art** houses a permanent exhibition of the Roman Jewish community. It contains Jewish ritual objects and scrolls from the 17th to the 19th century as well as copies of tombstones, paintings, prints, and documents that illustrate 2,000 years of Jewish history in Rome. The collection of silver ceremonial objects is important, as is a selection of ancient ceremonial textiles. The documents of Nazi persecution are of exceptional interest.

5 Near Piazza Navona & the Pantheon

Much of this area, along with the Campo de' Fiori neighborhood, is covered on Walking Tour 3, "Renaissance Rome" (see chapter 7).

Piazza Navona. Bus: 70, 81, 87, 115, 116, 186, 492, or 628.

Surely one of the most beautifully baroque sites in all of Rome is this ocher-colored gem, unspoiled by new buildings or even by traffic. The shape results from the ruins of the Stadium of Domitian, which lies underneath. Great chariot races were once held here, some rather unusual, such as the one in which the head of the winning horse was lopped off as it crossed the finish line and carried by runners to be offered as a sacrifice by the Vestal Virgins on top of the Capitoline Hill. In medieval times the popes used to flood the piazza to stage mock naval encounters. Today the most strenuous activities are performed by occasional fire-eaters, who go through their evening paces before an interested crowd of Romans and visitors.

Beside the twin-towered facade of the **Church of Saint Agnese** (17th century), the piazza boasts several other baroque masterpieces. The best known, in the center, is Bernini's **Fountain of the Four Rivers,** whose four stone personifications symbolize the world's greatest rivers—the Ganges, Danube, de la Plata, and Nile. It's fun to try to figure out which is which. (Hint: The figure with the shroud on its head is the Nile, so represented because the river's source was unknown at the time.) At the south end is the **Fountain of the Moor,** also by Bernini. The **Fountain of Neptune,** which balances that of the Moor, is a 19th-century addition. This fountain was restored after a demented 1997 attack by two men who broke off the tail of one of its sculptured sea creatures. During the summer there are outdoor art shows in the evening, but daylight visits are the best time to inspect the fragments of the original stadium, under a building on the north side of the piazza. If you're interested, walk out at the northern exit and turn left for a block. It's astonishing how much the level of the ground has risen since ancient times.

Sant'Ivo alla Sapienza. Corso del Rinascimento 40. No phone. Free admission. Sun 10am–noon. Closed mid-July to late Aug. Bus: 70, 81, 87, 115, 116, 186, 492, or 628.

One of Borromini's most distinctive churches, built between 1642 and 1660, St. Ivo's was crammed into the slightly claustrophobic courtyard of the Palazzo della Sapienza, a landmark that functioned as headquarters of the University of Rome between 1303 and 1935. Its steeple is capped with a bizarre and unique serpentine cone that twists its way upward to a cross-capped summit. Some of its aspects are best appreciated by professional architects, who are flabbergasted by combinations of convex and concave surfaces that couldn't be duplicated today. Their interactions create a high-energy symmetry that's based on an interlocking series of hexagons inspired by the wax hives built by a colony of bees. The building was commissioned by Urban VIII, a member of the Barberini family, whose family symbol was the bee. The only regularly scheduled visiting hours at this site are during Sunday mass. Otherwise, visiting hours vary according to the whim of the local prelates. Frankly, the exterior is much more fanciful than the relatively bare, white-sided interior, which is sometimes commandeered as a lecture hall.

Chiesa di San Luigi dei Francesi. Via Santa Giovanna d'Arco. ☎ **06/688271.** Free admission. Thurs 8am–12:30pm, Fri–Wed 8am–12:30pm and 3:30–7pm. Bus: 70, 81, or 87.

Founded in 1518, but not completed until 70 years later, this has been the national church of France in Rome since 1589. There's a stone salamander—the symbol of the Renaissance French monarch François I—subtly carved into its facade. Inside, in the last chapel on the left, are three critically acclaimed works from Caravaggio's early years in Rome: the celebrated *Calling of St. Matthew* on the left, *St. Matthew and the Angel* in the center, and *The Martyrdom of St. Matthew* on the right.

Chiesa di San Agostino. Piazza Sant'Agostino, Via della Scrofa 80. ☎ **06/68801962.** Free admission. Daily 7:45am–noon and 4:30–7:30pm. Bus: 70, 87, 115, 116, 186, or 913.

Originally commissioned by the archbishop of Rouen, France, and built between 1479 and 1483, this was one of the first churches erected during the Roman Renaissance. Its interior was altered and redecorated in the 1700s and 1800s. A painting by Caravaggio, *Madonna of the Pilgrims* (1605) hangs in the first altar on the left as you enter.

Chiesa di Santa Maria della Pace. Vicolo del Arco della Pace 5, off Piazza Navona. ☎ **06/6861156.** Free admission. Tues–Sat 10am–noon and 4–6pm, Sun 9–11am. Bus: 70, 81, or 87.

According to tradition, blood flowed from a statue of the Virgin above the altar after someone threw a pebble at it. This legend motivated Pope Sixtus IV to rebuild the church in the 1500s on the foundations of an even older sanctuary as a supplication to God to end some of the many armed conflicts engaging the Vatican at the time (hence its name, "Saint Mary of the Peace"). It was embellished in 1504 with the addition of a rather severe-looking cloister by Bramante, and again in 1656 with a lavish baroque facade. The interior contains Raphael's *Sibils,* painted in 1514, and Peruzzi's depiction of the *Madonna with Saints Bridget and Catherine.* Before you go, check to make sure it's open as there's no definite completion date for the ongoing renovations.

✪ **Pantheon.** Piazza della Rotonda. ☎ **06/68300230.** Free admission. Mon–Sat 9am–6pm, Sun 9am–1pm. Bus: 70, 81, 119, or 170.

Of all the great buildings of ancient Rome, only the Pantheon ("All the Gods") remains intact today. It was built in 27 B.C. by Marcus Agrippa, and later reconstructed by the emperor Hadrian in the first part of the 2nd century A.D. This remarkable building is among the architectural wonders of the world because of its dome and its concept of space.

The Pantheon was once ringed with white marble statues of Roman gods in its niches. Animals were sacrificed and burned in the center, and the smoke escaped through the only means of light, an opening at the top 27 feet in diameter. The Pantheon is 142 feet wide and 142 feet high. Michelangelo came here to study the dome before designing the cupola of St. Peter's (whose dome is 2 feet smaller than the Pantheon's).

Other statistics are equally impressive. The walls are 25 feet thick, and the bronze doors leading into the building weigh 20 tons each. The temple was converted into a church in the early 7th century, which helped save it from destruction.

About 125 years ago the tomb of Raphael was discovered in the Pantheon (fans still bring him flowers). Victor Emmanuel II, king of Italy, and his successor, Umberto I, are also interred here.

Attractions Near Campo de' Fiori & Piazza Navona

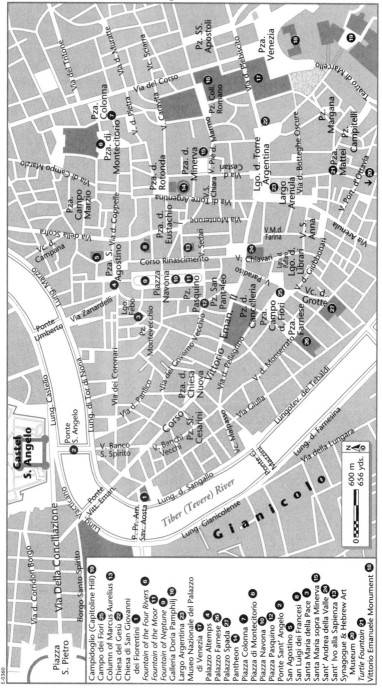

Campidoglio (Capitoline Hill) 19
Campo dei Fiori 26
Column of Marcus Aurelius 13
Chiesa del Gesù 22
Chiesa di San Giovanni
 dei Fiorentini 1
Fountain of the Four Rivers 11
Fountain of the Moor 9
Fountain of Neptune 10
Galleria Doria Pamphilj 16
Largo Argentina 23
Museo Nazionale del Palazzo
 di Venezia 17
Palazzo Altemps 4
Palazzo Farnese 25
Palazzo Spada 27
Pantheon 14
Piazza Colonna 7
Piazza di Montecitorio 6
Piazza Navona 12
Ponte Sant' Angelo 2
San Agostino 5
San Luigi dei Francesi 8
Santa Maria della Pace 3
Santa Maria sopra Minerva 15
Sant' Andrea della Valle 24
Sant' Ivo alla Sapienza 13
Synagogue & Hebrew Art
 Museum 20
Turtle Fountain 21
Vittorio Emanuele Monument 18

157

Chiesa di Santa Maria Sopra Minerva. Piazza della Minerva 42. ☎ **06/6793926.** Free admission. Daily 7am–noon and 4–7pm. Bus: 44, 46, or 116.

This is one of the most culturally diverse and eclectic churches in Rome, a building that gracefully bridges the gap between the worlds of ancient Rome, the Gothic period, and the Renaissance. In fact, it's the only Gothic church of any substance in all of Rome. Founded in the 700s, it was built in its present form during many stages between 1280 and 1453. It lies only a few steps from the Pantheon, on the foundations of what was originally a temple to the goddess Minerva (goddess of wisdom). The headquarters of Rome's Dominican order lie adjacent to this church, whose artistic and literary treasures include many icons of the high Renaissance, such as the body, the letters, and the religious writings of St. Catherine of Siena, and Michelangelo's statue of the Risen Christ (1521). The church's many tombs and graves include those of hundreds of ordinary Roman citizens, as well as the tomb of the Dominican monk and painter, Fra Angelico. Plaques on the building's facade record the height of the waters of the Tiber during some of its worst floods. The most disastrous of these occurred in 1598, when the level of the water rose 33 feet and drowned thousands. The whimsical baby elephant carrying a small obelisk in the piazza outside was designed by Bernini.

Piazza Colonna. Off Via del Corso. Bus: 119.

Its centerpiece is one of the most dramatic obelisks in town, the Column of Marcus Aurelius, a hollow bronze column rising 83 feet above the piazza. Built between A.D. 180 and 196, and restored (some say "defaced") in 1589 by a pope who replaced the statue of the Roman warrior on top with a statue of St. Paul, it's one of the ancient world's best examples of heroic bas-relief and one of Rome's most memorable sights. Beside the piazza's northern edge rises the Palazzo Chigi, official residence of the Italian prime minister.

Palazzo Altemps. Piazza S. Apollinare 8. ☎ **06/6833759.** Admission 8,000L ($4.65) Tues–Sat 9am–2pm and Sun 9am–1pm. Bus 70, 87, 119, or 186.

The third branch of the National Roman Museum (see below), this 15th-century palace—less archaeological museum than private gallery from the 16th and 17th centuries—was restored and opened to the public in December of 1997. It provides a home for a portion of the fabled **Ludovisi Collection** acquired by the Italian state in 1901. At the time this was the last great, privately owned gallery of Greek and Roman sculpture in Rome. Much of the collection now on display has been in storage for most of the 20th century.

The palace is filled with Venuses and nymphs, along with such homoerotic works as Pan and Daphnis. Many frescoes were uncovered in the palace, the earliest from the 12th century. A frescoed palace chapel is dedicated to St. Anicetus, the 2nd-century pope. The palazzo was purchased by Marco Sittico Altemps after he became a cardinal in 1561, but his once great collection of sculpture was dispersed by heirs, and key pieces now form part of national collections in Europe, including Paris.

Chiesa del Gesù. Piazza del Gesù. ☎ **06/697001.** Free admission. Apr–Sept, daily 6am–12:30pm and 4–7pm; Oct–Mar, daily 6am–12:30pm and 4:30–7:15pm. Bus: 44, 46, or 116.

Built between 1568 and 1584 by donations from a Farnese cardinal, the Chiesa del Gesù functioned for several centuries as the most potent and powerful church in the Jesuit order. Conceived as a bulwark against the perceived menace of the Protestant Reformation, it's sober, monumental, and very important to the history of the

Catholic Counter-Reformation. The sheathing of yellow marble that covers part of the interior was added during the 1800s.

Palazzo Doria Pamphili. Piazza Collegio Romano 2. ☎ **06/6797323**. Gallery, 13,000L ($8) per person adults, 10,000L ($6) students and seniors; apartments, 5,000L ($2.90). Fri–Wed 10am–5pm; private visits may be arranged. Bus: 56, 60, 62, 81, 85, 95, 117, 160, 175, 492, 628, or 850.

Located off Via del Corso, this museum offers visitors a look at what it was really like to live in an 18th-century palace. The palace has been restored to its former splendor and expanded to include four rooms long closed to the public. An architectural plan was discovered indicating the exact location of the art works as they were hung in the 18th century, and the palatial setting was readjusted to reflect the old arrangement. Like many Roman palaces of the period, the mansion is partly leased to tenants (on the upper levels), and there are even shops on the street level, but all this is easily overlooked after you enter the grand apartments of the historic princely Doria Pamphili family, which traces its lines to before the great 15th-century Genoese admiral Andrea Doria. The regal apartments surround the central court and gallery of the palace.

The 18th-century décor throughout the ballroom, drawing rooms, dining rooms, and even the family chapel is magnificent. Gilded furniture, crystal chandeliers, Renaissance tapestries, and portraits of family members are everywhere. The Green Room is especially rich in treasures, with a 15th-century Tournay tapestry, paintings by Memling and Filippo Lippi, and a seminude portrait of Andrea Doria by Sebastiano del Piombo. The Andrea Doria Room is dedicated to the admiral and to the ship of the same name. It contains a glass case with mementos of the great maritime disaster of the 1950s.

Skirting the central court is a picture gallery with a memorable collection of frescoes, paintings, and sculpture. Most important among a number of great works are the portrait of Innocent X by Velázquez, called one of the three or four best portraits ever painted; *Salome* by Titian; and works by Rubens and Caravaggio. Notable also are *The Bay of Naples* by Pieter Brueghel the Elder and a copy of Raphael's portrait of Principessa Giovanna d' Aragona de Colonna (who looks remarkably like Leonardo's *Mona Lisa*). Most of the sculpture came from the Doria country estates. It includes marble busts of Roman emperors, bucolic nymphs, and satyrs. Even without the paintings and sculpture, that gallery would be worth a visit just for its fresco-covered walls and ceilings.

6 Around Piazza di Spagna & Piazza del Popolo

Some of this area is covered on Walking Tour 2, "The Heart of Rome" (see chapter 7).

✪ **Spanish Steps (Piazza di Spagna).** Metro: Spagna.

The Spanish Steps were the last part of the outside world that Keats saw before he died in a house at the foot of the stairs (see the "Keats-Shelley Memorial," below). The steps—filled in the spring with flower vendors, jewelry dealers, and photographers snapping pictures of tourists—and the square take their names from the Spanish Embassy, which used to have its headquarters here. Designed by Italian architect Francesco de Sanctis between 1723 and 1725, they were funded almost entirely by the French as a preface to the French church, Trinità dei Monti, at the top.

At the foot of the steps is a boat-shaped fountain designed by Pietro Bernini (not to be confused with his son, Giovanni Lorenzo Bernini, a far greater sculptor).

About two centuries ago, when the foreign art colony was in its ascendancy, the 136 steps were covered with young men and women who wanted to pose for the painters—men with their shirts unbuttoned and women draped like Madonnas.

The steps and the piazza below are always packed: People stroll, read in the sun, browse the vendors' carts and check each other out. Near the steps you'll find an American Express office, public rest rooms (near the Metro stop) and the most sumptuous McDonald's we've ever seen.

Keats-Shelley Memorial. Piazza di Spagna 26. ☎ **06/6784235.** Admission 5,000L ($2.90). May–Sept, Mon–Fri 9am–1pm and 3–6pm; Oct–Apr, Mon–Fri 9am–1pm and 2:30–5:30pm. Metro: Spagna.

At the foot of the Spanish Steps is this 18th-century house where Keats died of consumption on February 23, 1821, at the age of 25. "It is like living in a violin," wrote Italian author Alberto Savinio. Since 1909, when the building was bought by English and American aficionados of English literature, it has been a working library to honor Keats, Shelley, and Byron. Shelley drowned off the coast of Viareggio with a copy of Keats's works in his pocket (both are buried in the Protestant Cemetery; see "Testaccio & South," later in this chapter). Mementos inside range from kitsch to the immortal, and are almost relentlessly laden with nostalgia. The apartment where Keats spent his last months, carefully tended by his close friend Joseph Severn, shelters a strange death mask of Keats as well as the "deadly sweat" drawing by Severn.

Via dei Condotti. From Piazza di Spagna to Via del Corso.

Both its edges are lined with the kinds of designer-name shops that make virtually anyone salivate. Even if you don't consider yourself particularly materialistic, this homage to the good life *a l'Italiana* might change your mind. The stores and shopping in general are covered fully in "Shopping A to Z" in chapter 8.

Augustus Mausoleum (Mausoleo Augusteo). Via di Ripetta and Piazza Augusteo Imperatore. Bus: 81, 115, or 590. Metro: Spagna.

This seemingly indestructible pile of bricks along Via di Ripetta has been here for 2,000 years and will probably remain for another 2,000. Like the larger tomb of Hadrian across the river, this was once a circular, marble-covered affair with tall cypress trees, symmetrical groupings of Egyptian obelisks, and some of the most spectacular ornamentation in Europe. Many of the emperors of the 1st century had their ashes deposited in golden urns inside this building, and it was probably because of the resultant crowding that Hadrian later decided to construct an entirely new tomb (today, the **Castel Sant'Angelo**) for himself in another part of Rome. After periods when it functioned as a Renaissance fortress, a bullfighting ring, and a private garden, the tomb was restored in the 1930s by Mussolini (perhaps he envisioned it as a burial place for himself). You cannot enter the mausoleum, but you should circumnavigate it along the four streets that encircle the exterior.

Altar of Peace (Ara Pacis). Via di Ripetta. ☎ **06/67103569.** Admission 10,000L ($6). Tues–Sat 9am–7pm, Sun 9am–6:45pm. Bus: 81.

In an airy glass-and-concrete building beside the eastern banks of the Tiber at Ponte Cavour rests a reconstructed treasure from the reign of Augustus. It was built by the Senate as a tribute to that emperor and the peace he had brought to the Roman world. You can see portraits of the imperial family—Augustus, Livia (his wife), Tiberius (Livia's son and the successor to the empire), even Julia (the unfortunate daughter of Augustus, exiled by her father for her sexual excesses)—on the

Attractions Near The Spanish Steps & Piazza del Popolo

Legend
Metro **Ⓜ**
Post Office ✉

E-0361

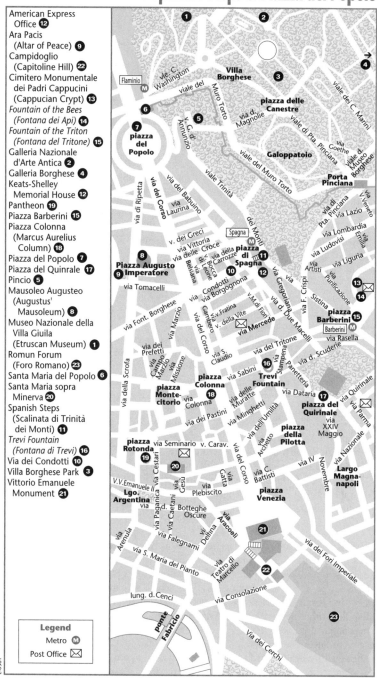

Fun Fact

On the southwestern corner of the Trevi Fountain's piazza, you'll see a somber, not particularly spectacular-looking church (Chiesa S.S. Vincenzo e Anastasio) with a strange claim to fame. Within this church are the hearts and intestines of several centuries of popes. According to legend, the church was built on the site of a spring that burst from the earth after the beheading of St. Paul, at one of three sites where his head is said to have bounced off the ground.

---

marble walls. The altar was reconstructed from literally hundreds of fragments scattered in museums for centuries. A major portion came from the foundations of a Renaissance palace on the Corso. The reconstruction—quite an archaeological adventure story in itself—was executed (and sometimes enhanced) by the Fascists during the 1930s.

✪ **Trevi Fountain (Fontana di Trevi).** Piazza di Trevi. Metro: Barberini.

As you elbow your way through the summertime crowds, you'll find it hard to believe that this little piazza was nearly always deserted before the film *Three Coins in the Fountain* brought the tour buses. Today it's a must on everybody's itinerary. To do it properly, hold your lira coin in the right hand, turn your back to the fountain, and toss the coin over your shoulder (being careful not to bean anyone behind you). Then the spirit of the fountain will see to it that you return to Rome some day—or that's the tradition, at least.

Actually, this is an evolution of an even older tradition of drinking from the fountain. Nathaniel Hawthorne (1804–64), in his novel *The Marble Faun,* wrote that anyone drinking this fountain's water "has not looked upon Rome for the last time." Because of pollution no one drank from it for years. Since the fountain was restored in 1994 and is running again, the water is supposedly pure, owing to an electronic device that keeps the pigeons at bay. We'd still suggest that you skip a "Trevi cocktail" and have a mineral water at a cafe instead.

Supplied by water from the Acqua Vergine aqueduct, and a triumph of the baroque style, the fountain was based on the design of Nicolo Salvi (who is said to have died of illness contracted while supervising the project) and completed in 1762. The design centers around the triumphant figure of Neptunus Rex, standing on a shell chariot drawn by winged steeds and led by a pair of tritons. Two allegorical figures in the side niches represent good health and fertility.

Piazza del Popolo. Metro: Flaminio. Bus: 95.

The "people's square" owes its present look to Napoléon's architect, Valadier, who added the elliptical arms and end fountains to enclose this piazza, which already contained the 3,200-year-old **obelisk** of Ramses II that Augustus had brought over from Egypt in the 1st century B.C. This square was the first sight most 19th-century Grand Tourists saw when they arrived in Rome through the **Porta del Popolo,** with a Bernini facade facing the piazza. If they rode in at Carnival time, they might also have witnessed gruesome public executions. Just to your left as you come through the city gate from the Metro stop at Piazzale Flaminio on the other side you'll find the **Church of Santa Maria del Popolo** (see below). Just beyond the church are the stairs that rise through the **Pincio gardens** to an overlook and the **Borghese Gardens** (see "Parks & Gardens," later in this chapter). The south end of the piazza is split by three major streets: Via di Ripetta on the right (to Augustus's Mausoleum), Via del Corso in the middle (to Piazza Venezia), and Via

Babuino on the left (to the Spanish Steps). Two almost identical Carlo Rainaldi–designed churches sit on the corners between these streets, and on either side of the trident lie two of Rome's more fashionable cafes, the Rosati and the Canova (see "The Cafe & Bar Scene" in chapter 9).

Santa Maria del Popolo. Piazza del Popolo 12. ☎ **06/3610836.** Free admission. Daily 7am–12:30pm and 4–7pm. Metro: Flaminio. Bus: 90, 90B, 95, 490, 495, or 926 (or tram no. 119 or 225) to Pzle. Flaminio; then walk through the city gate.

During the early days of the Christian church this site was believed to be haunted by the ghost of Nero, who, according to legend, had been secretly buried here by his nurse and mistress. In 1099 a simple chapel was built, supposedly to drive the demons away, and in the 1500s a majestic church was constructed by Pope Sixtus IV. Funds for its construction derived from the sale of church sinecures and the imposition of taxes on churches in Germany and other foreign lands. Inside, you'll find the oldest stained-glass windows in Rome (1509), an apse that was designed by Bramante, separate chapels designed by Raphael and Bernini, frescoes by Pinturicchio, and a pair of paintings (*The Crucifixion of St. Peter* and *The Conversion of St. Paul*) by Caravaggio that are known to students of art history around the world.

✪ **Galleria Borghese.** Piazzale del Museo Borghese, off Via Pinciano, in the Villa Borghese. ☎ **06/8548577** for reservations, 06/8417645 for information. Admission 10,000L ($6). Tues–Sun 9am–7pm; July 10–Sept 14, Tues–Sun 8:30–11:30pm. Bus: 910 from the Termini or 56 from Pz. Barberini.

In the spring of 1997, after a complete (and rather lengthy) restoration, this legendary art gallery reopened in all its fabulous glory.

The gallery's founder, Scipione Borghese, had by the time of his death in 1633 accumulated some of the greatest art of all time, including Bernini's early sculptures. Some paintings were spirited out of Vatican museums or confiscated when their rightful owners were hauled off to prison until they became "reasonable" about turning over their art. The great collection suffered at the hands of Napoléon's sister, Pauline, who married Camillo Borghese in 1807 and sold most of the ancient collection (many works are now on display in the Louvre). Ironically, one of the most-viewed sculptures in today's gallery is Canova's life-size sculpture of Pauline in the pose of Venus Victorious. When Pauline was asked whether she felt uncomfortable posing in the nude, she replied, "Why should I? The studio was heated."

Unfortunately, no more than 300 visitors are allowed on the ground floor at one time; no more than 90 on the upper floor. Prebooking is essential if you want to visit. You can call for a reservation, but the number invariably seems busy. For those who persevere, the chance to see such masterpieces as Bernini's *Apollo and Daphne, David,* and *The Rape of Persephone;* Titian's *Sacred and Profane Love;* Raphael's *Deposition,* and Caravaggio's *Jerome,* is well worth the effort. If you'll be in Rome for a few days, try stopping by on your first day to reserve in person tickets for a later day.

National Gallery of Modern Art (Galleria Nazionale d'Arte Moderna). Viale delle Belle Arti 131. ☎ **06/322981.** Admission 8,000L ($4.65) adults, free for children 17 and under. Tues–Sun 9am–10pm. Bus: 52, 53, 95, 490, 495, or 910.

The National Gallery of Modern Art is in the Villa Borghese Gardens, a short walk from the Etruscan Museum. With its neoclassical and romantic paintings and sculpture, it's a dramatic change from the glories of the Renaissance and Ancient Rome. Its 75 rooms also house Italy's largest collection of 19th- and 20th-century works by such artists as Balla, Boccioni, de Chirico, Morandi, Manzù, Marini, Burri, Capogrossi, and Fontana. Look for Modigliani's *La Signora dal Collaretto* and his large *Nudo.* There are also many works of Italian optical and pop art, and a good representation of foreign artists including Degas, Cézanne, Monet, and van Gogh. Surrealism and expressionism are well represented in works by Klee, Ernst, Braque, Miró, Kandinsky, Mondrian, and Pollock. You'll also find sculpture by Rodin and Canova. The collection of graphics, the storage rooms, and the department of restoration can be visited by appointment Tuesday to Friday.

✪ **National Etruscan Museum (Museo Nazionale di Villa Giulia).** Piazzale di Villa Giulia 9. ☎ **06/3226571.** Admission 8,000L ($4.65) adults, free for children 17 and under and for seniors 60 and over. Tues–Sat 9am–7pm, Sun 9am–2pm. Metro: Flaminio.

A 16th-century papal palace in the Villa Borghese Gardens shelters this priceless collection of art and artifacts by the mysterious Etruscans, who predated the Romans. Known for their sophisticated art and design, the Etruscans left a legacy of sarcophagi, bronze sculptures, terra-cotta vases, and jewelry, among other items. If you have time only for the masterpieces, head for room 7, which has a remarkable 6th century B.C. *Apollo* from Veio (clothed, for a change). The other two widely acclaimed pieces of statuary in this gallery are *Dea con Bambino* (a goddess with a baby) and a greatly mutilated, but still powerful, *Hercules* with a stag. In room 8 you'll see the lions' sarcophagus from the mid–6th century B.C., which was excavated at Cerveteri, north of Rome.

Finally, one of the world's most important Etruscan art treasures is the bride and bridegroom coffin from the 6th century B.C. (in room 9), also dug out of the tombs of Cerveteri. Near the end of your tour, another masterpiece of Etruscan art awaits you in room 33: the *Cista Ficoroni,* a bronze urn with paw feet, mounted by three figures, which dates from the 4th century B.C.

7 Around Via Veneto & Piazza Barberini

Via Veneto. Metro: Barberini.

Although this most famous of Roman streets may have passed its *la dolce vita* heyday in the golden 1950s, it remains a prime target for sightseers. The street cuts through the center of the gardens of what used to be one of the most princely villas in Rome, the 1662 Villa Ludovisi. In 1885 Prince Boncompagni Ludovisi built a glorious estate on Via Veneto, but was forced to sell it to pay the taxes. The buyer was Margherita, widow of King Umberto I. Today the palace, renamed the Villa Margherita, is the most famous building along the street and is the site of the heavily guarded American Embassy.

Major hotels and restaurants line the avenue, none more famous than the **Hotel Excelsior,** former haunt of movie stars such as Elizabeth Taylor in the 1950s era of "Hollywood on the Tiber" (see "Near Via Veneto & Piazza Barberini" in chapter 4). Sharing space with hotels, restaurants, and cafes like the Caffè de Paris (see "The Cafe & Bar Scene" in chapter 9) are the headquarters of banks, insurance companies, and publishers.

Today middle-age tourists revisiting Rome wonder what became of that *la dolce vita* atmosphere captured in Fellini's 1960 film. On weekends Roman officials close the street to traffic to make it more alluring, but as a nightlife center, Via Veneto's heyday has come and gone. One London critic reported: "What male visitors get today are bimbos on the doors of grotesquely expensive nightclubs, who entice them in to atrocious floorshows, terrible food, and sleazy company."

Monumental Cemetery of the Capuchin Brothers (Cimitero Monumentale dei Padri Cappucini). In the Church of the Immacolate Conception, Via Vittorio Veneto 27. ☎ **06/4871185.** Free admission (donation expected). Daily 9am–noon and 3–6pm. Metro: Barberini.

Qualifying as one of the most horrifying sights in all Christendom, this is a cemetery of skulls and crossbones woven into mosaic "works of art" just a short walk from Piazza Barberini. To make this allegorical dance of death, the bones of more than 4,000 Capuchin brothers were used. Some of the skeletons are intact, draped with Franciscan habits. The creator of this chamber of horrors? The tradition of the friars is that it was the work of a French Capuchin. Their literature suggests that the cemetery should be visited keeping in mind the historical moment of its origins, when Christians had a rich and creative cult for their dead and great spiritual masters mediated and preached with a skull in hand. Those who have lived through the days of crematoriums and other such massacres may view the graveyard differently, but to many who pause to think, this macabre sight of death has a message. It's not for the squeamish, however. The entrance is halfway up the first staircase on the right of the church.

Piazza Barberini. Metro: Pz. Barberini. Bus: 56, 60, 62, or 95.

The piazza lies at the foot of several Roman streets, among them Via Barberini, Via Sistina, and Via Vittorio Veneto. It would be a far more pleasant spot were it not for the heavy traffic swarming around its principal feature, Bernini's **Fountain of the Triton**. For more than three centuries the strange figure sitting in a vast open clam has been blowing water from his triton. Off to one side of the piazza is the clean, aristocratic side facade of the Palazzo Barberini, named for one of Rome's powerful families. The Renaissance Barberini reached their peak when a son was elected pope (Urban VIII). This Barberini pope encouraged Bernini and gave him great patronage.

As you go up Via Vittorio Veneto, look for the small fountain on the right-hand corner of Piazza Barberini, which is another of Bernini's works, the small **Fountain of the Bees.** At first they look more like flies, but they are the bees of the Barberini, the crest of that powerful family complete with the crossed keys of St. Peter above them (the keys were always added to a family crest when a son was elected pope).

National Gallery of Antique Art (Galleria Nazionale d'Arte Antica). Via delle Quattro Fontane 13. ☎ **06/4814430.** Admission 8,000L ($4.65) adults, free for children 17 and under. Mon–Fri 10am–2pm; Sat 9am–7pm; Sun and holidays 9am–1pm. Metro: Barberini.

Palazzo Barberini, right off Piazza Barberini, is one of the most magnificent baroque palaces in Rome. It was begun by Carlo Maderno in 1627 and completed in 1633 by Bernini, whose lavishly decorated rococo apartments within, called the **Gallery of Decorative Art,** are open to the public. The palace today houses the Galleria Nazionale. On the first floor of the palace, a splendid array of paintings includes works from the 13th to the 16th century, most notably a *Mother and Child* by Simone Martini, and works by Filippo Lippi, Andrea Solario, and Francesco Francia. Il Sodoma has some brilliant pictures here, including *The Rape of the Sabines* and *The Marriage of St. Catherine.* One of the best-known paintings is Raphael's beloved *La Fornarina,* the baker's daughter who was his mistress and who posed for his Madonna portraits. Titian is represented by *Venus and Adonis.* Other artists exhibited include Tintoretto, El Greco, and Holbein the Younger. Many visitors come here just to see the magnificent Caravaggios, including *Narcissus.*

The bedroom of Princess Cornelia Costanza Barberini and Prince Giulio Cesare Colonna di Sciarra still stands just as it did on their wedding night, and many household objects are displayed in the decorative art gallery. In the chambers, which have frescoes and hand-painted silk linings, you can see porcelain from Japan and Bavaria, canopied beds, and a wooden baby carriage.

Gore Vidal's Roma

Gore Vidal, the author of more than 22 novels, including an acclaimed multi-volume fictional chronicle of American history and the 1990s memoir *Palimpsest*, really began to discover Rome in 1948. He'd just published his first bestseller, *The City and the Pillar*, the first novel of any consequence about male homosexuality. He headed for Rome and the Excelsior Hotel, just as expatriates do today. The bar here along Via Veneto was, and still is, the center for rich foreigners. Later he moved to the Eden Hotel (now back in business, and better than ever following a major 1995 overhaul). He was joined by playwright Tennessee Williams, whom Vidal called "The Glorious Bird," and Rome and its "golden boys" of that era were ready to be plucked. Later the writers would compare notes from the night before over breakfast at the Doney on Via Veneto, while being observed by such visitors as Orson Welles.

Vidal viewed Rome after 1948 and throughout the 1960s and 1970s as a "sexual paradise." This was the pre-AIDS era when sex was "spontaneous and untroubled," according to Vidal. The orgies in his flat became famous throughout the Roman underground. Young men and women were eager to participate. Although Vidal later gave up his Roman flat of many years and moved to Ravello, he's still a frequent visitor to the city. However, Vidal finds the Rome of today "sullen, with mephitic air, and full of crime of every sort . . . prostitution is either very expensive or antiseptic, and, between AIDS and knives, too dangerous to be bothered with."

In the winter of 1962 Vidal, along with his longtime companion, Howard Auster, rented a ground-floor apartment on Rome's Via Giulia. Although they were to move elsewhere later, into an apartment overlooking the Tiber, "Gore & Howard" were always to live near Campo de' Fiori. They could often be seen shopping at this open-air market in their search for the freshest of ingredients (Vidal was particularly fond of fresh peas).

Later, Rome served Vidal as he gathered research notes and literary inspiration from the ruins of the Capitoline Hill and the stones of the city's ancient forums.

Le Quattro Fontane. At the corner of Via delle Quattro Fontane and Via del Quirinale. Metro: Barberini.

The unexpected presence of these fountains at the intersection of two narrow, traffic-clogged streets provides newcomers with the kind of aesthetic shock that's only possible in a truly great city. Composed of **four symmetrical fountains** built into the outside corners of four identical buildings, they were conceived as part of the Renaissance redevelopment of Rome ordained by Pope Sixtus IV between 1585 and 1590. The two female fountains represent either Juno and Diana or Strength and Fidelity (depending on your point of view); the two male fountains stand for the Tiber and the Nile. The site, incidentally, is close to the pinnacle of the Quirinale Hill, one of the seven summits on which ancient Rome was originally built.

Piazza del Quirinale. Metro: Barberini.

Until the end of World War II the palace on this piazza was the home of the king of Italy; before that it was the residence of the pope. Despite its renaissance, when virtually every important architect in Italy worked on some aspect of its sprawling premises, it's rich in associations to ancient emperors and deities. The **colossal statues** of the *dioscuri* Castor and Pollux, which now form part of the fountain in

The novel that emerged, *Julian,* was judged a critical success for its reinterpretation of the lives of the emperors during the Roman empire's final days. Urbane, knowledgeable, and uncommonly difficult to write, it examined Rome from the point of view of aristocratic, well-educated classicists who blamed the demise of their civilization squarely on the camp of the unwashed, uneducated rabble—that is, the Christians. Few other modern novels so evocatively portray the nostalgia of the ancient Romans' long-ago loss of empire, as well as breathe life so effectively into the value system of the pre-Christian era.

Eventually, Vidal came to emulate the travel patterns of the ancient emperors, retreating from the city's heat and midsummer smells to a windy and panoramic clifftop near Ravello, on the Amalfi Drive. There, he says, he can gaze over waters and coastlines whose geography is inextricably linked with the origin of many of the ancient Roman myths and fables.

When in Rome today, Vidal prefers to eat regularly at **Da Fortunato al Pantheon,** Pantheon 55 (☎ **06/6792788**), near Piazza della Rotonda. The place is overrun by politicians from the nearby Parliament buildings. Everyone flocks here for the "perfect" risotto, or, if it's Saturday, the "perfect" tripe. You might want to try their grilled sea bass, too.

Vidal was asked by Fellini to play himself in *Roma;* when questioned in the film as to why he chose to live in Rome, he responded: "Now the world has begun to dream of the world's end through nuclear war or overpopulation or pollution—take your pick—so what better place to watch the last act than in a city that calls itself Eternal?"

That, more or less, is what Vidal told movie audiences. But he later admitted that the "real reason" he enjoys Rome is because he enjoys human-scale village life. He felt that many Roman shops in the old neighborhoods were pretty much as they were 2,000 years ago. For his living room in Rome, he prefers the piazza in front of the Pantheon, following in the footsteps of George Eliot, Pietro Macagni, Stendhal, and Thomas Mann. He calls these former luminaries "our friendly ghosts—eternal presences—for the time being!"

the piazza, were found in the nearby great Baths of Constantine, and in 1793 Pius VI had the ancient **Egyptian obelisk** moved here from the Mausoleum of Augustus. The sweeping view of Rome from the piazza is itself worth the trip, and the palace, crowning the highest of the seven ancient hills of Rome, is open to the public on Sunday from 9am to 1pm. Admission is free, but a passport or similar ID is required to enter.

8 Near the Termini

Basilica di Santa Maria Maggiore (St. Mary Major). Piazza di Santa Maria Maggiore. ☎ **06/4881094.** Free admission. Daily 7am–7pm. Metro: Termini.

This great church, one of the four major basilicas of Rome, was originally founded by Pope Liberius in A.D. 358 and rebuilt by Pope Sixtus III from A.D. 432 to 440. Its **14th-century campanile** is the loftiest in the city. Much doctored in the 18th century, the church's facade is not an accurate reflection of the treasures inside. Restoration of the 1,600-year-old church has begun and is scheduled for completion in the year 2000. The basilica is especially noted for the **5th-century Roman mosaics** in its nave, as well as for its coffered ceiling, said to have been gilded with gold brought from the New World. In the 16th century Domenico Fontana built a now-restored "Sistine Chapel." In the following century Flaminio Ponzo designed the Pauline (Borghese) Chapel in the baroque style. The church contains the **tomb of Bernini,** Italy's most important sculptor and architect during the baroque era in the 17th century. Ironically, the man who changed the face of Rome with his elaborate fountains is buried in a tomb so simple it takes a sleuth to track it down (to the right near the altar).

Chiesa di Santa Maria degli Angeli. Piazza della Repubblica 12. ☎ **06/4880812.** Free admission. Daily 7:30am–12:30pm and 4–6:30pm. Metro: Repubblica.

On this site, which adjoins the National Roman Museum near the railway station, once stood the "tepidarium" of the 3rd-century Baths of Diocletian. But in the 16th century Michelangelo—nearing the end of his life—converted the grand hall into one of the most splendid churches in Rome. (but surely the artist wasn't responsible for those trompe-l'oeil columns in the midst of the genuine pillars.) The church is filled with tombs and paintings, but its crowning treasure is the genuine statue of *St. Bruno* by the great French sculptor Jean-Antoine Houdon. His sculpture is larger than life and "twice as natural."

✪ **National Roman Museum (Museo Nazionale Romano).** Via Enrico de Nicola 79. ☎ **06/4882298.** Admission 12,000L ($7). Tues–Sat 9am–2pm, Sun and holidays 9am–1pm. Metro: Repubblica.

Located near Piazza dei Cinquecento, which fronts the railway station, this museum occupies part of the 3rd-century A.D. Baths of Diocletian and a section of a convent that may have been designed by Michelangelo. It houses one of Europe's finest collections of Greek and Roman sculpture and early Christian sarcophagi.

The **Ludovisi Collection** is the apex of the museum, particularly the statue of the Gaul slaying himself after he has done in his wife (a brilliant copy of a Greek original from the 3rd century B.C.). Another prize is a one-armed Greek Apollo. A galaxy of other sculpted treasures includes *The Discus Thrower of Castel Porziano* (an exquisite copy), *Aphrodite of Cirene* (a Greek original), and the so-called *Hellenistic Ruler,* a Greek original of an athlete with a lance. A masterpiece of Greek sculpture, *The Birth of Venus,* is in the Ludovisi throne room. *The Sleeping Hermaphrodite* (Ermafrodito Dormiente) is an original Hellenistic statue. You can stroll through the cloister, filled with statuary and fragments of antiquity, including a fantastic mosaic.

On the same ticket, you can visit an extension of the collection at **Palazzo Massimo alle Terme,** largo di Villa Peretti (☎ **06/48903500**). This branch contains ancient treasures unearthed in excavations in and around Rome, and keeps the same hours as the parent museum above. The third and final branch of the museums is at the **Palazzo Altemps** which opened in 1997 (see above).

Santa Maria della Vittoria. Via XX Settembre 17. ☎ **06/4826190.** Daily 6:30am–noon and 4:30–6pm. Metro: Repubblica. Bus: 16, 36, 37, or 60.

Although far from being the largest baroque church in Rome, this is one of the most ostentatiously decorated, loaded with contrasting shades of marble, gilded stucco, and flickering candles. The Capella Cornaro (fourth opening on the left), contains one of the most frequently photographed baroque sculptures in the world, Bernini's controversial and highly theatrical *Ecstasy of St. Theresa,* where with a bit of imagination, you might doubt that the saint's ecstasy is entirely spiritual. Gazing down on her, with a smile that might be either sadistic or tender, is an angel about to pierce her with a golden arrow. Surrounding the emotionally charged setting, like

Attractions Near Via Veneto & Termini

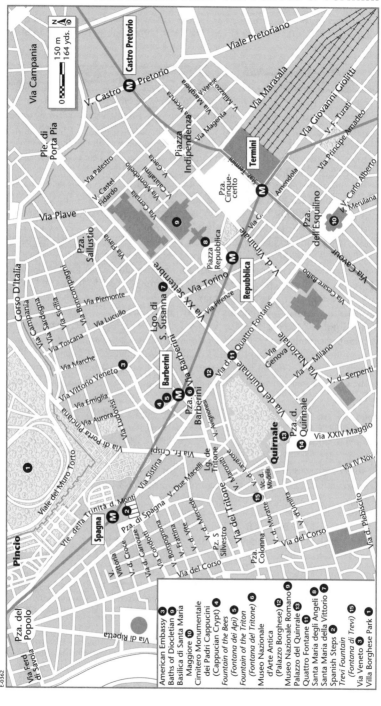

American Embassy 3
Baths of Diocletian 9
Basilica di Santa Maria Maggiore 10
Cimitero Monumentale dei Padri Cappucini (Cappucian Crypt) 4
Fountain of the Bees (Fontana dei Api) 5
Fountain of the Triton (Fontana del Tritone) 6
Museo Nazionale d'Arte Antica (Palazzo Borghese) 12
Museo Nazionale Romano 9
Palazzo del Quirinale 13
Quattro Fontane 11
Santa Maria degli Angeli 8
Santa Maria della Vittorio 7
Spanish Steps 2
Trevi Fountain (Fontana di Trevi) 15
Via Veneto 3
Villa Borghese Park 1

E-0362

169

members of the audience in a theater, are statues of the chapel's donor and eight members of his family. The church itself was built between 1608 and 1620, and restored in 1991.

9 The Catacombs of the Appian Way

Of all the roads that led to Rome, **Via Appia Antica** (Appian Way)—built in 312 B.C.—was the most famous. It eventually stretched all the way from Rome to the seaport of Brindisi, through which trade with the colonies in Greece and the East was funneled. According to Christian tradition, it was on the Appian Way that an escaping Peter encountered the vision of Christ, causing him to go back into the city to face subsequent martyrdom.

Along the Appian Way, patrician Romans built great monuments above the ground and Christians met in the catacombs beneath the earth—and you can visit the remains of both. In some dank, dark grottoes (never stray too far from either your party or one of the exposed lightbulbs), you can still discover the remains of early Christian art. The catacombs were dug from the middle of the 2nd century up until the middle of the 5th century as cemeteries and places of worship. Only someone wanting to write a sequel to *Quo Vadis?* would visit all these underground tunnels; of those open to the public, the **Catacombs of St. Callixtus** and those of **St. Sebastian** are the most important.

Of the Roman monuments on Via Appia Antica, the most impressive is the **Tomb of Cecilia Metella,** within walking distance of the catacombs. The cylindrical tomb honors the wife of one of Julius Caesar's military commanders from the Republican era. How did a minor historical figure like Cecilia Metella rate such an elaborate and enduring memorial? A trick of fate. When her tomb survived the decay that destroyed the others, she was unintentionally singled out for lasting fame.

Tomb of St. Sebastian (Catacombe di San Sebastiano). Via Appia Antica 136. ☎ **06/7887035.** Admission 8,000L ($4.65) adults, 4,000L ($2.30) children 6–15, free for children 5 and under. Wed–Mon 9am–noon and 2:30–5:30pm (to 5pm in winter). Bus: 218 from San Giovanni or 66 from Colli Albani.

Today the tomb of St. Sebastian is in the basilica, but his original tomb was in the catacombs under it. From the reign of the emperor Valerian to the reign of the emperor Constantine, the bodies of Saint Peter and Saint Paul were hidden in these catacombs dug from *tufo,* a soft volcanic rock. The big church was built here in the 4th century. The tunnels here, if stretched out, would reach a length of 7 miles. In the tunnels and mausoleums are mosaics and graffiti, along with many other pagan and Christian objects from centuries even before the time of Constantine.

Catacombs of St. Callixtus (Catacombe di San Callisto). Via Appia Antica 110. ☎ **06/5136725.** Admission 8,000L ($4.65) adults, 4,000L ($2.30) children 6–15, free for children 5 and under. Thurs–Tues 8:30am–noon and 2:30–5pm (to 5:30pm in summer). Bus: 218 from San Giovanni in Laterano to Fosse Ardeatine; ask driver to let you off at Catacombe di San Callisto.

"The most venerable and most renowned of Rome," said Pope John XXIII of these funerary tunnels. The founder of Christian archaeology, Giovanni Battista de Rossi (1822–94), called them "catacombs par excellence." They are the first cemetery of the Christian community of Rome, burial place of 16 popes in the 3rd century. They bear the name of St. Callixtus, the deacon whom Pope St. Zephyrinus put in charge of them and who was later elected pope (217–22) in his own right. The complex is made up of a network of galleries stretching for nearly 12 miles, structured in five different levels, and reaching a depth of about 20 meters. There are many sepulchral chambers and almost half a million tombs. Paintings, sculptures, and epigraphs (with such symbols as the fish, the anchor, and the dove) provide invaluable material for the study of the life and customs of the ancient Christians and the story of their persecutions.

Entering the catacombs, you see at once the most important crypt, that of the **nine popes.** Some of the original marble tablets of their tombs are still preserved. The next crypt is that of **St. Cecilia,** the patron of sacred music. This early Christian martyr received three ax strokes on her neck, the maximum allowed by Roman law, which failed to kill her outright. Farther on you'll find the famous **Cubicula of the Sacraments,** with its 3rd-century frescoes.

10 Testaccio & South

Only a city as ancient as Rome could boast an entire neighborhood built atop a rubbish heap where almost every pot shard is a valuable reminder of antiquity.

The area east of the Tiber and just west of Pyramide functioned as Rome's dockyards. In A.D. 55 Nero ordered that Rome's thousands of broken amphorae and terra-cotta roof tiles be stacked in a carefully designated pile. (Its name, Monte Testaccio, derived from *testae,* the ancient word for "pot shards.") Over the centuries the mound grew to a height of around 200 feet, then compacted to form the centerpiece for Testaccio, one of the city's most unusual neighborhoods. Eventually, houses were built on the terra-cotta mound, and caves were dug into its mass for the storage of wine and foodstuffs (thanks to the porosity of the terra-cotta, a constant temperature of 50°F is maintained throughout the year).

Because of this natural refrigeration, the neighborhood also began to attract dozens of simple, blood-soaked slaughterhouses. Laborers were paid part of their meager salaries with the *quinto quarto* (fifth quarter) of each day's slaughter (that is, the tail, the feet, the intestines, and the offal), which otherwise had no commercial value. With a history of transforming these organs into edible and flavorful food, the neighborhood cooks in Testaccio take much of the credit for developing the flavorful tripe and oxtail dishes that form an integral part of the Roman working-class diet to this day. One of the neighborhood's best and earthiest restaurants, Cecchino dal 1887, is recommended separately (see chapter 5).

Today the district is rustic, unglamorous, and working-class, but with a crude kind of charm that its aficionados compare to an unspoiled and relatively "undiscovered" version of Trastevere. A pivotal crossroads of the district lies at the intersection of Via Caio Cestio and Via Nicola Zabaglia.

Pyramid of Caius Cestius. Piazzale Ostiense. Metro: Piramide. Bus: 30.

Dating from the 1st century B.C., the Pyramid of Caius Cestius, about 120 feet high, looks as if it belongs to the Egyptian landscape. It was constructed during the "Cleopatra craze" in architecture that swept across Rome. The pyramid can't be entered, but it makes for a great photo op. And who was Caius Cestius? A rich magistrate in Imperial Rome whose tomb is more impressive than his achievements.

Protestant Cemetery. Via Caio Cestio 6. ☎ **06/5741141.** Admission free, but a 1,000L (60¢) offering is customary. Apr–Sept, Tues–Sun 9am–6pm; Oct–Mar, Tues–Sun 9am–5pm. Metro: Piramide. Bus: 23 and 27.

Near Porta San Paola, in a setting of cypress trees, lies the old cemetery where John Keats is buried. In a grave nearby, Joseph Severn, his "deathbed companion," was interred beside him six decades later. Dejected, and feeling his reputation as a poet diminished by the rising vehemence of his critics, Keats asked that the following epitaph be written on his tombstone: "Here lies one whose name was writ in water." A great romantic poet Keats certainly was, but a prophet, thankfully not.

Percy Bysshe Shelley, author of *Prometheus Unbound,* drowned off the Italian Riviera in 1822, before his 30th birthday. His ashes rest alongside those of Edward John Trelawny, fellow romantic and man of the sea. Trelawny maintained—but this was not proved—that Shelley may have been murdered, perhaps by petty pirates bent on robbery.

St. Paul Outside the Walls (Basilica di San Paolo Fuori le Mura). Via Ostiense. ☎ **06/5410341.** Free admission. Basilica, daily 7am–6:30pm; cloisters, daily 9am–1pm and 3–6pm. Metro: San Paolo Basilica.

The Basilica of St. Paul, whose origins go back to the time of Constantine, is the fourth great patriarchal church of Rome. It burned in 1823 and was subsequently rebuilt. This basilica is believed to have been erected over the tomb of St. Paul. From the inside its windows may appear to be stained glass, but they're actually translucent alabaster. With its forest of single-file columns and its mosaic medallions (portraits of the various popes), it's one of the most streamlined and elegantly decorated churches in Rome. Its single most important treasure is a 12th-century candelabrum designed by Vassalletto, who is also responsible for the remarkable cloisters containing twisted pairs of columns enclosing a rose garden. The Benedictine monks and students sell a fine collection of souvenirs, rosaries, and bottles of Benedictine water in the gift shop every day except Sunday and religious holidays.

11 In Trastevere

This most Roman of Roman neighborhoods is covered in detail on Walking Tour 4, "Trastevere" (see chapter 7), but here are the full descriptions of the major sights to get you started.

Chiesa di Santa Maria in Trastevere. Piazza di Santa Maria in Trastevere. ☎ **06/5814802.** Free admission. Daily 7am–7pm. Bus: 44, 75, 170, or 181.

This Romanesque church at the picturesque center of Trastevere was originally built around A.D. 350 and is one of the oldest in Rome. The body was added around 1100 and the portico in the early 1700s. The restored mosaics in the apse date from around 1140, and below them are the 1293 mosaic scenes from the life of Mary by Pietro Cavallini. The faded mosaics on the facade are 12th or 13th century, and the octagonal fountain in the piazza is an ancient Roman original restored and added to in the 17th century by Carlo Fontana.

Santa Cecilia in Trastevere. Piazza di Santa Cecilia. ☎ **06/5899289.** Church, free; Cavallini frescoes, free (but a donation is requested); excavations, 2,000L ($1.15). Main church, daily 10am–noon and 4–6pm; frescoes, Tues and Thurs 10–11:30am. Bus: 44, 75, 170, or 181.

A cloistered and still-functioning convent with a fine garden, Santa Cecilia contains a difficult-to-visit fresco by Cavallini in its inner sanctums, and a late 13th-century baldacchino by Arnolfo di Cambio over the altar. The church is built on the reputed site of Cecilia's long-ago palace, and for a fee you can descend under the church to inspect the ruins of some Roman houses as well as peer through a gate at the highly stuccoed grotto underneath the altar.

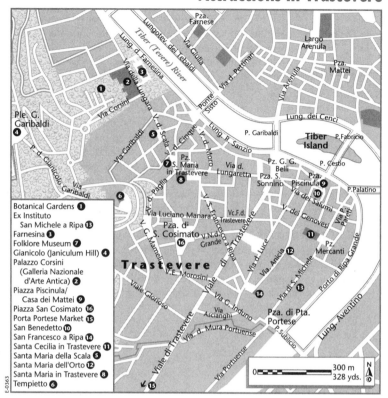

Botanical Gardens **1**
Ex Instituto
  San Michele a Ripa **13**
Farnesina **3**
Folklore Museum **7**
Gianicolo (Janiculum Hill) **4**
Palazzo Corsini
  (Galleria Nazionale
  d'Arte Antica) **2**
Piazza Piscinula/
  Casa dei Mattei **9**
Piazza San Cosimato **16**
Porta Portese Market **15**
San Benedetto **10**
San Francesco a Ripa **14**
Santa Cecilia in Trastevere **11**
Santa Maria della Scala **5**
Santa Maria dell'Orto **12**
Santa Maria in Trastevere **8**
Tempietto **6**

JANICULUM HILL (GIANICOLO)

From many vantage points in the Eternal City the views are panoramic. Those in search of the perfect panorama, however, have traditionally preferred the outlook from the Janiculum Hill (across the Tiber), not one of the "Seven Hills" but certainly one of the most visited (and a stopover on many bus tours). The view is at its best at sundown, or at dawn, when the skies are often fringed with mauve. The Janiculum was the site of a battle between Guiseppe Garibaldi and the forces of Pope Pius IX in 1870—an event commemorated today with statuary. To reach the Gianicolo, take bus no. 41 from Ponte Sant'Angelo.

12 Around Vatican City

In the middle of the Tiber's major bend on its way through the city is the site of one of the most famous executions of the Renaissance, **Piazza San Angelo.** Here, in 1599, Beatrice Cenci and several members of her family were beheaded on orders of Pope Clement VIII. Their crime? Plotting the murder of their very rich and very brutal father. Their tale later inspired a tragedy by Shelley and a novel by a 19th-century Italian politician named Francesco Guerrazzi.

Stretching across the river north of the piazza is the **Ponte Sant'Angelo.** The trio of arches in the river's center is basically unchanged since the bridge was built around A.D. 135; the arches that abut the river's embankments were added late in the 19th century as part of a flood-control program. On December 19, 1450, so many pilgrims gathered on this bridge (which at the time was lined with wooden buildings) that about 200 of them were crushed to death. Since the 1960s the bridge has been reserved exclusively for pedestrians who can stroll across and admire the statues designed by Bernini as they head toward the Castel Sant'Angelo at the bridge's northern end.

Castel Sant'Angelo. Lungotevere Castello 50. ☎ **06/6875036.** Admission 8,000L ($4.65), free for children 17 and under and for seniors 60 and over. Daily 9am–3pm. Closed last Tues of each month. Metro: Ottaviano. Bus: 23, 46, 49, 62, 87, 98, 280, or 910.

This overpowering structure, in a landmark position on the Tiber, was originally built in the 2nd century A.D. as a tomb for the emperor Hadrian; it remained an imperial mausoleum until the time of Caracalla. It resembles a fortress, and rightly so; that was its function in the Middle Ages when fleeing popes used the underground passageway linking it to the Vatican in order to escape from unwanted visitors (such as Charles V during his sack of the city in 1527.)

In the 14th century it became a papal residence, enjoying various connections with Boniface IX, Nicholas V, and even Julius II, patron of Michelangelo and Raphael. But its legend rests largely on its link with Pope Alexander VI, whose mistress bore him two children—Cesare and Lucrezia Borgia.

Today the highlight of the castle is a trip through the Renaissance apartments with their coffered ceilings and lush decoration. Their walls have witnessed plots and intrigues that make up some of the arch-treachery of the High Renaissance. Later you can go through the dank cells that once rang with the screams of Cesare's torture victims. The most famous figure imprisoned here was Benvenuto Cellini, the eminent sculptor and goldsmith, remembered chiefly for his classic, candid *Autobiography.* Now an art museum, the castle halls display the history of the Roman mausoleum, along with a wide-ranging selection of ancient arms and armor. You can climb to the top terrace for another one of those dazzling views of the Eternal City.

13 EUR—Mussolini's Marble Suburb

At the height of Mussolini's power, he launched a complex of modern buildings—many of them in cold marble—to dazzle Europe with a scheduled world's fair. But Il Duce got strung up, and **EUR** ("ay-your")—the area in question—got hung up. The new Italian government that followed inherited the uncompleted project and decided to turn it into a center of government and administration. It has also developed into a residential section of fairly deluxe apartment houses. Most of the cold edifices fail to escape the curse of *Il Duce moderno,* but the small "city of tomorrow" is softened considerably by a man-made lagoon, which you can row across in rented boats.

Italy's great modern architect, Milan-born Pier Luigi Nervi, designed the **Palazzo dello Sport** on the hill. One of the country's most impressive modern buildings, it was the chief site of the 1960 Olympics. Another important structure is the **Palazzo dei Congressi** in the center, an exhibition hall with changing displays of industrial shows that's well worth a stroll. You'll also spot architecture reminiscent of Frank Lloyd Wright, and a building that evokes the design of the United Nations in New York.

For still another look at Mussolini's architectural achievements, head across the river from EUR to the **Foro Italico.** Shades of 1932! This complex of sports stadiums blatantly honors Il Duce. At the entrance to the forum an obelisk bears the name MVSSOLINI so firmly engraved that to destroy the lettering would be to do away with the monument. It stands defiantly. Visitors on a sunny day walk across the mosaic courtyard with DVCE embedded repeatedly in the pavement. The big attraction of this freakish site is the **"Stadium of Marbles,"** encircled with 50 marble nude athletes—draped discreetly so as not to offend the eyes of the Golden Madonna on the hill beyond. Take bus no. 1 from Piazza della Repubblica.

Museo della Civiltà Romana. Piazza Giovanni Agnelli 10. ☎ **06/5926141.** Admission 5,000L ($2.90) adults, free for children under 18. Tues–Sat 9am–7pm, Sun 9am–1:30pm. Metro: Linea B to EUR Fermi.

This museum of Roman civilization houses Fiat-sponsored reproductions that recapture life in ancient Rome. Its major exhibition is a plastic representation in miniature of what ancient Rome looked like at the apex of its power. You'll see the Circus Maximus, the intact Colosseum, the Baths of Diocletian, and lots more—breathing life and a real feel of city layout to the few broken columns and sketchy foundations you see in the forums.

14 Parks & Gardens

The **Villa Borghese** park in the heart of Rome is 3½ miles in circumference. One of the most elegant parks in Europe, it was created by Cardinal Scipione Borghese in the 1600s. Umberto I, king of Italy, acquired it in 1902 and presented it to the city of Rome, renaming it Villa Umberto I. However, Romans preferred their old name, which has stuck. A park of landscape vistas and wide-open "green lungs," the greenbelt is crisscrossed by roads, but you can escape from the traffic and seek a shaded area—usually by pine or oak—to enjoy a picnic or simply relax. In the northeast of the park is a small zoo, and the park is home also to two of the top museums in Rome, the Galleria Borghese with its Renaissance and baroque masterpieces and the Villa Giulia Etruscan museum, as well as the fine national gallery of modern art (see "Around Piazza di Spagna & Piazza del Popolo," earlier in this chapter).

The **Villa Doria Pamphili,** behind the Vatican, acquired from Princess Orietta Doria Pamphili, was opened to the public in 1971. (The princess is descended from the world-famous naval commander Andrea Doria.) The park is about half as large as Central Park in New York, but it's more than twice the size of the Villa Borghese, filling a sad emptiness in the Roman capital by providing some much-needed green space. At one time the park belonged to Pope Innocent X, who planted it with exotic shrubbery, trees, and flowers. Take bus no. 23, 30, 32, 49, 51, or 64.

15 Especially for Kids

Children usually enjoy wandering around the Colosseum and the Roman Forum (see "The Forum, the Colosseum & the Heart of Ancient Rome," earlier in this chapter), as well as the climb to the top of the dome of St. Peter's Basilica. **The Fun Fair** (Luna Park), along Via delle Tre Fontane (☎ **06/5925933**), at EUR, is one of the largest in Europe. It's known for its "big wheel" at the entrance, and there are merry-go-rounds, miniature railways, and shooting galleries, among other attractions. Admission is free, but you pay for each ride. It's open November to May Monday to Friday from 3 to 8pm, Saturday from 3pm to 1am, Sunday and holidays from 10am to 10pm. April to October, it's open daily from 4pm to midnight. Metro: Magliana.

The **Teatro delle Marionette degli Accettella,** appearing at the Teatro Mongiovino, Via Giovanni Genocchi 16 (☎ **06/5139405**), has performances for children on Saturday and Sunday (except in July and August) at 4:30pm. Tickets are 12,000L ($7) for adults and children.

The **Puppet Theater on Pincio Square** (☎ **06/8601733**) in the Villa Borghese gardens has "Punch and Judy" performances nearly every day. While here, you might also like to take your children through the Villa Borghese park (it's closed to traffic). Children enjoy the fountain displays and the lake, and there are many wide spaces in which they can play. You can rent boats at the Giardino del Lago, and explore **the zoo** at Viale del Giardino Zoologico 20 (☎ **06/3216564**). It's open Monday to Friday from 8:30am to 5pm and on Saturday and Sunday from 8:30am to 6:30pm (it closes an hour earlier in winter). Admission is 10,000L ($6) for adults, free for children under 12. Take bus no. 52, 53, or 910; then walk.

At 4pm on any day, you can take your child to the **Quirinale Palace,** Piazza del Quirinale, the residence of the president of Italy. There's a military band and a parade at that time, as the guards change shifts.

16 Organized Tours

Because of the sheer volume of artistic riches in Rome, some visitors prefer to begin their stay with an organized tour. While few things can really be covered in any depth on these "overview tours," they're sometimes useful for getting the feel for the geography of a complicated city. One of the leading tour operators (among the zillions of possibilities) is **American Express,** Piazza di Spagna 38 (☎ **06/67641**). It's open Monday to Friday from 9am to 5:30pm and on Saturday from 9am to 12:30pm. Of the many tour operators functioning in Rome, American Express is the one whose tours are the most closely geared to the American language and American visitors.

One of the most popular tours is a 4-hour orientation tour of **Rome and the Vatican,** which departs most mornings at 9:30am. Another 4-hour tour focuses on **Rome of antiquity** and includes visits to the Colosseum, the Roman Forum, the ruins of the Imperial Palace, and the Church of San Pietro in Vincoli. Of the many excursions offered to sites outside the city limits of Rome, the most popular is a 5-hour bus tour to **Tivoli** to visit the Villa d'Este and its spectacular gardens and the ruins of the Villa Adriana. Each of the above-mentioned tours costs 70,000L ($41) per person.

If your time in Italy is rigidly limited, you might opt for 1-day excursions to points farther afield on tours that are marketed by (but not conducted by) American Express. Although rushed and far too short to expose the many-layered majesty of these destinations, a series of 1-day tours is offered to **Pompeii, Naples,** and **Sorrento** for 160,000L ($93) per person, to **Florence** for 190,000L ($110), and to **Capri** for 210,000L ($122). Lunch is included on these full-day trips, but you'll need a lot of stamina—each departs from Rome around 7am and returns sometime after 9 or 10pm.

Another option is **Scala Reale,** Via Varese 52 (☎ **888/467-1986,** in the U.S., or 06/44700898). Scala Reale is a cultural association founded by the American architect Tom Rankin. He offers small-group tours and excursions focusing on the architectural and artistic significance of Rome. Tours include visits to monuments, museums, and piazzas as well as to neighborhood trattorie. Custom-designed tours are also available. Tours begin at 60,000L ($35); children 12 and under are admitted free to walking tours. Tour discounts are available for groups of four or more.

17 Catching a Soccer Match & Other Outdoor Activities

SOCCER

Soccer (*calcio*) is one of the three or four all-consuming passions of thousands of Romans. Rome boasts two intensely competitive teams, Lazio and Roma, which play either against each other or against visiting teams from other parts of the world every Sunday afternoon. Matches are held at the **Stadio Olimpico,** Foro Italico dei Gladiatori (☎ **06/36851**), originally built by Mussolini as a nationalistic (Fascist) statement. Thousands of tickets are sold during the 2 or 3 hours before each game. Tickets must be purchased in person either at the stadium or at **Lazio Point,** Via Farini 24 (☎ **06/4826688**); prices vary from game to game, but an average ticket might go for about 40,000L ($24). The players usually take a break during June, July, and August, beginning the season with something approaching pandemonium in September.

OUTDOOR ACTIVITIES

BIKING The traffic is murderous and the pollution might make your head spin, but there are quiet times (early morning and Sunday) when a spin beside the Tiber or through the Borghese Gardens might prove highly appealing. You can find bike-rental stands on Viale della Pineto in the Villa Borghese and at the following Metro stops: Flaminio, Largo San Silvestro, Largo Argentina, and Piazza di Spagna.

BOWLING One of the city's largest bowling complexes, whose hordes of participants provide a spectacle almost more interesting than the game itself, is **Bowling Roma,** Viale Regina Margherita 181 (☎ **06/8551184**), off Via Nomentana.

GOLF Rome boasts several courses, which will usually welcome members of other golf clubs. Each, of course, will be under the greatest pressure on Saturday and Sunday, so as a nonmember it would be best to schedule your arrival for a weekday.

One of the capital's best courses, with its clubhouse in a villa built during the 1600s and fairways designed by Robert Trent Jones, is the **Country Club Castelgandolfo,** Via Santo Spirito 13, Castelgandolfo (☎ **06/9312301**). An older, more entrenched, and more prestigious course is the **Circolo del Golf Roma,** Via Appia Nuova 716/A (☎ **06/7803407**). About 8½ miles from the city center is the **Olgiata Golf Club,** Largo Olgiata 15, off Via Cassia (☎ **06/30889141**).

HORSEBACK RIDING The most convenient of Rome's several riding clubs is the **Associazione Sportiva Villa Borghese,** Via del Galoppatoio 25 (☎ **06/3200487**). Other stables are in the **Circolo Ippico Olgiata,** Largo Olgiata 15 (☎ **06/30888792**), off Via Cassia, and the **Società Ippica Romana,** Via del Monti della Farnesina 18 (☎ **06/3240591**). Tack and equipment are English style.

JOGGING Not only does jogging provide a moving view of the city's monuments, but it might improve your general health as well. Beware of the city's heat, however, and the speeding traffic. Several possible locations include the park of the Villa Borghese, where the series of roads and pathways provide a verdant oasis within the city's congestion. The best places to enter the park are at Piazza del Popolo or at the top of Via Veneto. **The Cavalieri Hilton,** Via Cadlolo 101, Monte Mario (☎ **06/35091**), has a jogging path (measuring a third of a mile) through the trees and flowering shrubs of its landscaping. The grounds that surround the Villa Pamphili contain three running tracks, although they might either be locked or in use by local teams. Certain stretches of the Lungotevere sidewalk along the river provide almost uninterrupted courses for runners. A final possibility, not recommended after dark, is the rounded premises of the Circus Maximus. Built by the ancient Romans, and now reduced to dust and grandiose rubble, the outward perimeter (ringed with roaring traffic) measures about a half mile.

SWIMMING   There are more than 90 swimming pools in Rome besides those found at hotels. Be warned that many require an annual membership fee even if you only plan to be in the city a short time. For more information on pools and their requirements or fees, contact the **Comitato Regionale Lazio Federazione Italiana Nuoto,** 8 Via Virgilio, 00193 Rome, Italy (☎ **06/3222818**). One of the busiest all-year pools is at the **Roman Sport Center,** Via del Galoppatoio 33 (☎ **06/3201667**), which lies adjacent to the parking lot on the grounds of the Villa Borghese. Open to the public, it contains two large swimming pools, squash courts, a gym, and saunas.

In another part of town, **Piscina della Rose,** Viale America (☎ **06/5926717**), is an Olympic-size pool open to the public (and crowded with teenagers and *bambini*) between June and September. More sedate, set in lushly landscaped gardens, and open to nonresidents, are two pools on the resort-inspired premises of the **Cavalieri Hilton,** Via Cadlolo 101 (☎ **06/35091**). Lap swimmers can exercise year-round at the **Villa Pamphili Sporting Club,** Via della Nocetta 107 (☎ **06/66158555**), adjacent to the Hotel Villa Pamphili.

TENNIS   The best tennis courts are at private clubs, usually in the suburbs. Players are highly conscious of proper tennis attire, so be prepared to don your most sparkling whites and your best manners. One of the best-known clubs is **Tennis Club Parioli,** Largo Uberto de Morpurgo 2, Via Salaria (☎ **06/86200882**), open daily from 8am to 6pm only. Because this is a private club, you must call in advance.

Strolling Through Rome

7

Visitors with very limited time might want to concentrate on Walking Tour 1, "Rome of the Caesars," and Walking Tour 2, "The Heart of Rome." Those with more time can explore "Renaissance Rome" and "Trastevere." Many of the major sights along these routes, especially on Walking Tours 2 to 4, are covered fully in chapter 6. These tours serve both to string the sights together—for those who have limited time or want more structure to their visit—and to cover some of the other, less well known sights along the way.

WALKING TOUR 1
Rome of the Caesars

Start: Via Sacra, in the Roman Forum.
Finish: Circus Maximus.
Time: 5½ hours.
Best Times: Any sunny day.
Worst Times: After dark, or when the place is overrun with tour groups.

This tour tries to incorporate the most central of the monuments that attest to the military and architectural grandeur of ancient Rome. As a whole, they comprise the most famous and evocative ruins in the world, despite such drawbacks as the roaring traffic that's the bane of the city's civic planners, and a general dustiness and heat that might test even the hardiest amateur archaeologists.

After the collapse of Rome and during the Dark Ages, the forums and many of the other sites on this tour were lost to history, buried beneath layers of debris, their marble mined by medieval builders, until Mussolini set out to restore the grandeur of Rome by reminding his compatriots of their glorious past.

THE ROMAN FORUM

The more westerly of the two entrances to the Roman Forum is at the corner of Via dei Fori Imperiali and Via Cavour, adjacent to Piazza Santa Maria Nova. The nearest Metro is the Colosseo stop. As you walk down into the Forum along a masonry ramp, you'll be heading for Via Sacra, the ancient Roman road that ran through the Forum connecting the Capitoline Hill, to your right, with the Arch of Titus (1st century A.D.), off to your left. The Roman Forum is the more dignified and more austere of the two forums you'll visit on this walking tour. Although it consists mostly of artfully evocative ruins scattered confusingly around a sun-baked terrain, it represents almost 1,000 years of Roman power during the severely disciplined period that preceded the legendary decadence of the later Roman emperors.

During the Middle Ages, when this was a cow pasture and all these stones were underground, there was a dual column of elm trees connecting the Arch of Titus with the Arch of Septimius Severus (A.D. 200), to your right.

Arriving at Via Sacra, turn right. The random columns on the right as you head toward the Arch of Septimius Severus belong to the:

1. **Basilica Aemilia**, formerly the site of great meeting halls and shops, all maintained for centuries by the noble Roman family who gave it its name. At the corner nearest the Forum entrance are some traces of melted bronze decoration that fused to the marble floor during a great fire set by invading Goths in A.D. 410.

The next important building is the:

2. **Curia**, or Senate house—it's the large brick building on the right that still has its roof. Romans had been meeting on this site for centuries before the first structure was erected, (and that was still centuries before Christ). The present building is the fifth (if one counts all the reconstructions and substantial rehabilitations) to stand on the site. Legend has it that the original building was constructed by an ancient king with the curious name of Tullus Hostilius. The tradition he began was a noble one indeed, and our present legislative system owes much to the Romans who met in this hall. Unfortunately, the high ideals and inviolate morals that characterized the early Republican senators gave way to the bootlicking of imperial times, when the Senate became little more than a rubber stamp. Caligula, who was only the third emperor, had his horse appointed to the Senate (it was a life appointment), which pretty much sums up the state of the Senate by the middle of the 1st century A.D.

The building was a church until 1937, when the Fascist government tore out the baroque interior and revealed what we see today. The original floor of Egyptian marble and the tiers that held the seats of the senators have miraculously survived. In addition, at the far end of the great chamber we can see the stone on which rested the fabled golden statue of Victory. Originally installed by Augustus, it was disposed of in the 4th century by a fiercely divided Senate, whose Christian members convinced the emperor that it was improper to have a pagan statue in such a revered place.

Outside, head down the Curia stairs to the:

3. **Lapis Niger,** the remains of black marble blocks that reputedly mark the tomb of Romulus. They bask today under a corrugated metal roof. Go downstairs for a look at the excavated tomb. There's a stone here with the oldest Latin inscription in existence, which unfortunately is nearly illegible. All that can be safely assumed is that it genuinely dates from the Rome of the kings, an era that ended in a revolution in 510 B.C.

Across from the Curia, the:

4. **Arch of Septimius Severus** was dedicated at the dawn of the troubled 3rd century to the last decent emperor who was to govern Rome for some time. The friezes on the arch depict victories over Arabs and Parthians by the cold but upright Severus and his two dissolute sons, Geta and Caracalla. Severus died on a campaign to subdue the unruly natives of Scotland, and at the end of the first decade of the 3rd century Rome unhappily fell into the hands of the young Caracalla, chiefly remembered today for the baths he had built.

Walking Tour—Rome of the Caesars

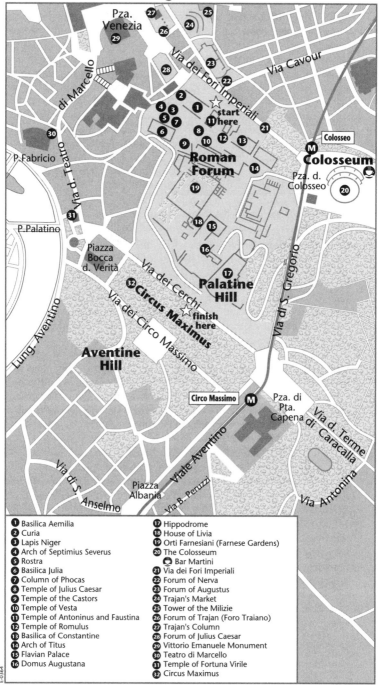

1. Basilica Aemilia
2. Curia
3. Lapis Niger
4. Arch of Septimius Severus
5. Rostra
6. Basilica Julia
7. Column of Phocas
8. Temple of Julius Caesar
9. Temple of the Castors
10. Temple of Vesta
11. Temple of Antoninus and Faustina
12. Temple of Romulus
13. Basilica of Constantine
14. Arch of Titus
15. Flavian Palace
16. Domus Augustana
17. Hippodrome
18. House of Livia
19. Orti Farnesiani (Farnese Gardens)
20. The Colosseum
    Bar Martini
21. Via dei Fori Imperiali
22. Forum of Nerva
23. Forum of Augustus
24. Trajan's Market
25. Tower of the Milizie
26. Forum of Trajan (Foro Traiano)
27. Trajan's Column
28. Forum of Julius Caesar
29. Vittorio Emanuele Monument
30. Teatro di Marcello
31. Temple of Fortuna Virile
32. Circus Maximus

E-0364

Walk around to the back of the Severus arch, face it, and look to your right. There amid the rubble can be discerned a semicircular stair that led to the famous:

5. **Rostra,** the podium from which dictators and caesars addressed the throngs of the Forum below. One can just imagine the emperor, shining in his white toga, surrounded by imperial guards and distinguished senators, gesticulating grandly like one of the statues on a Roman roofline. The motley crowd falls silent, the senators pause and listen, the merchants put down their measures, even the harlots and unruly soldiers lower their voices in such an august presence. Later emperors didn't have much cause to use the Rostra, making their policies known through edict and assassination instead.

Now, facing the colonnade of the Temple of Saturn, once the public treasury, and going to the left, you'll come to the ruins of the:

6. **Basilica Julia,** again little more than a foundation. The basilica gets its name from Julius Caesar, who dedicated the first structure in 46 B.C. Like many buildings in the Forum, the basilica was burned and rebuilt several times, and the last structure dated from those shaky days after the Gothic invasion of 410. Throughout its history it was used for the hearing of civil court cases, which were conducted in the pandemonium of the crowded Forum, open to anyone who happened to pass by. The building was also reputed to be particularly hot in the summer, and it was under these sweaty and unpromising circumstances that Roman justice, the standard of the world for a millennium, was meted out.

Walking back down the ruined stairs of the Basilica Julia and into the broad area whose far side is bounded by the Curia, you'll see the:

7. **Column of Phocas.** Probably lifted from an early structure in the near vicinity, this was the last monument to be erected in the Roman Forum, and it commemorates the Byzantine emperor Phoca's generous donation of the Pantheon to the pope of Rome, who almost immediately transformed it into a church.

Now make your way down the middle of the Forum nearly back to the ramp from which you entered. The pile of brick with the semicircular indentation that stands in the middle of things was the:

8. **Temple of Julius Caesar,** erected some time after the dictator was deified. Judging from the reconstruction, it was quite an elegant building. As you stand facing the ruins, with the entrance to the Forum on your left, you'll see on your right three columns originally belonging to the:

9. **Temple of the Castors.** This temple perpetuated the legend of Castor and Pollux, who appeared out of thin air in the Roman Forum and were observed watering their horses at the fountain of Juturna (still visible today), just as a major battle against the Etruscans turned in favor of Rome. Castor and Pollux, the heavenly twins—and the symbol of the astrological sign Gemini—are a favorite of Rome.

The next major monument is the circular:

10. **Temple of Vesta,** wherein dwelt the sacred flame of Rome, and the Atrium of the Vestal Virgins. A vestal virgin was usually a girl of good family who signed a contract for 30 years. During that time she lived in the ruin we're standing in right now. Of course, back then it was an unimaginably rich marble building with two floors. There were only six vestal virgins at a time during the imperial period, and even though they had the option of going back out into the world at the end of their 30 years, few did. The cult of Vesta came to an end in 394, when a Christian Rome secularized all its pagan temples. A man standing on this site before then would have been put to death immediately.

Stand in the atrium with your back to the Palatine and look beyond those fragmented statues of the former vestals to the:

11. Temple of Antoninus and Faustina. It's the building with the freestanding colonnade just to the right of the ramp where you first entered the Forum. Only the colonnade dates from imperial times; the building behind it is a much later church dedicated to San Lorenzo.

After you inspect the beautifully proportioned Antoninus and Faustina temple, head up Via Sacra away from the entrance ramp toward the Arch of Titus. Pretty soon, on your left, you'll see the twin bronze doors of the:

12. Temple of Romulus. It's the doors themselves that are really of note here—they're the original Roman doors, swinging on the same massive hinges they were mounted on in A.D. 306. In this case, the temple is not dedicated to the legendary cofounder of Rome, but to the son of its builder, the emperor Maxentius, who gave his son the name Romulus in a fit of antiquarian patriotism. Unfortunately for both father and son, they competed with a general who deprived them of their empire and lives. That man was Constantine, who, while camped outside Rome during preparations for one of his battles against Maxentius, saw the sign of the Cross in the heavens with the insignia *In hoc signo vinces* (in this sign shall you conquer). Raising the standard of Christianity above his legions, he defeated the emperor Maxentius and became the first Christian emperor.

At the time of Constantine's victory (A.D. 306), the great:

13. Basilica of Constantine (marked by those three gaping arches up ahead on your left) was only half finished, having been started by the unfortunate Maxentius. However, Constantine finished the job and affixed his name to this, the largest and most impressive building in the Forum. To our taste, the more delicate, Greek-influenced temples are more attractive, but you have to admire the scale and the engineering skill that erected this monument. The fact that portions of the original coffered ceiling are still intact is amazing. The basilica once held a statue of Constantine so large that his little toe was as wide as an average man's waist. You can see a few fragments from this colossus—the remnants were found in 1490—in the courtyard of the Conservatory Museum on the Capitoline Hill. As far as Roman emperors went, Christian or otherwise, ego knew no bounds.

From Constantine's basilica, follow the Roman paving stones of Via Sacra to the:

14. Arch of Titus, clearly visible on a low hill just ahead. Titus was the emperor who sacked the great Jewish temple in Jerusalem, and the bas-relief sculpture inside the arch shows the booty of the Jews being carried in triumph through the streets of Rome, while Titus is crowned by Victory, who comes down from heaven for the occasion. You'll notice in particular the candelabrum, for centuries one of the most famous pieces of the treasure of Rome. In all probability it lies at the bottom of the Busento River in the secret tomb of Alaric the Goth.

PALATINE HILL

When you've gathered your strength in the shimmering hot sun, head up the Clivus Palatinus, the road to the palaces of the Palatine Hill, or *Palatino*. With your back to the Arch of Titus, it's the road going up the hill to the left.

It was on the Palatine Hill that Rome first became a city. Legend tells us that the date was 753 B.C. The new city originally consisted of nothing more than the Palatine, which was soon enclosed by a surprisingly sophisticated wall, remains of which can still be seen on the Circus Maximus side of the hill. As time went on and Rome grew in power and wealth, the boundaries were extended and later enclosed by the Servian Wall. When the last of the ancient kings was overthrown (510 B.C.), Rome had already extended over several of the adjoining hills and valleys. As Republican times progressed, the Palatine became a fashionable residential district. So it remained until Tiberius—who, like his predecessor, Augustus, was a bit too modest to call himself "emperor" out loud—began the first of the monumental palaces that were to cover the entire hill.

It's difficult today to make sense out of the Palatine. The first-time viewer might be forgiven for suspecting it to be an entirely artificial structure built on brick arches. Those arches, which are visible on practically every flank of the hill, are actually supports that once held imperial structures. Having run out of building sites, the emperors, in their fever, simply enlarged the hill by building new sides on it.

The road goes on only a short way, through a small sort of valley filled with lush, untrimmed greenery. After about 5 minutes (for slow walkers), you'll see the ruins of a monumental stairway just to the right of the road. The Clivus Palatinus turns sharply to the left here, skirting the monastery of San Bonaventura, but we'll detour to the right and take a look at the remains of the:

15. **Flavian Palace.** As you walk off the road and into the ruins, you'll be able to discern that there were once three rooms here. But it's impossible for anyone but the most imaginative to comprehend quite how splendid these rooms were. The entire Flavian Palace was decorated in the most lavish of colored marbles and gold. Much of the decoration survived as late as the 18th century, when the greedy duke of Parma removed most of what was left. The room closest to the Clivus Palatinus was called the Lararium, and held statues of the divinities that protected the imperial family. The middle room was the grandest of the three. It was the imperial throne room, where sat the ruler of the world, the emperor of Rome. The far room was a basilica, and as such was used for miscellaneous court functions, among them audiences with the emperor. This part of the palace was used entirely for ceremonial functions. Adjoining these three rooms are the remains of a spectacularly luxurious peristyle. You'll recognize it by the hexagonal remains of a fountain in the middle. Try, if you can, to imagine this fountain surrounded by marble arcades planted with mazes and equipped with mica-covered walls. On the opposite side of the peristyle from the throne room are several other great reception and entertainment rooms. The banquet hall was here, and beyond it, looking over the Circus Maximus, are a few ruins of former libraries. Although practically nothing remains except the foundations, every now and again you'll catch sight of a fragment of colored marble floor in a subtle, sophisticated pattern.

The imperial family lived in the:

16. **Domus Augustana,** the remains of which lie toward the Circus Maximus, slightly to the left of the Flavian Palace. The new building that stands here—it looks old to us, but in Rome it qualifies as a new building—is a museum (usually closed). It stands in the absolute center of the Domus Augustana. In the field adjacent to the stadium well into the present century stood the Villa Mills, a gingerbread Gothic villa of the 19th century. It was quite a famous place, owned by a rich Englishman who came to Rome from the West Indies. The Villa Mills was the scene of many fashionable entertainments in Victorian times, and it's interesting to note, as H. V. Morton pointed out, that the last dinner parties that took place on the Palatine Hill were given by an Englishman. At any of several points along this south-facing belvedere of the Palatine Hill, you'll be able to see the faraway oval walls of the Circus Maximus. Continue with your exploration

of the Palatine Hill by heading across the field parallel to the Clivus Palatinus until you come to the north end of the:

17. Hippodrome, or Stadium of Domitian. The field was apparently occupied by parts of the Domus Augustana, which in turn adjoined the enormous stadium. The stadium itself is worth examination, although sometimes it's difficult to get down inside it. The perfectly proportioned area was usually used for private games, staged for the amusement of the imperial family. As you look down the stadium from the north end, you can see, on the left side, the semicircular remains of a structure identified as Domitian's private box. Some archaeologists claim that the "stadium" was actually an elaborate sunken garden.

The aqueduct that comes up the wooded hill used to supply water to the Baths of Septimius Severus, whose difficult-to-understand ruins lie in monumental poles of arched brick at the far end of the stadium.

Returning to the Flavian Palace, leave the peristyle on the opposite side from the Domus Augustana and follow the signs for the:

18. House of Livia. They take you down a dusty path to your left. Although legend says that this was the house of Augustus's consorts, it actually was Augustus's all along. The place is notable for some rather well-preserved murals showing mythological scenes. But more interesting is the aspect of the house itself—it's smallish, and there never were any great baths or impressive marble arcades. Augustus, even though he was the first emperor, lived simply compared to his successors. His wife, Livia, was a fiercely ambitious aristocrat who divorced her husband to marry the emperor (the ex-husband was made to attend the wedding, incidentally) and, according to some historians, the true power behind Roman policy between the death of Julius Caesar and the ascension of Tiberius. She even controlled Tiberius, her son, since she had engineered his rise to power through a long string of intrigues and poisonings.

After you've examined the frescoes in Livia's parlor, head up the steps that lead to the top of the embankment to the north. Once on top, you'll be in the:

19. Farnese Gardens (Orti Farnesiani), the 16th-century horticultural fantasy of a Farnese cardinal. They're constructed on top of the Palace of Tiberius, which, you'll remember, was the first of the great imperial palaces to be built on this hill. It's impossible to see any of it, but the gardens are cool and nicely laid out. You might stroll up to the promontory above the Forum and admire the view of the ancient temples and the Capitoline heights off to the left.

You've now seen the best of the Forum and the Palatine. To leave the archaeological area, you should now continue walking eastward along the winding road that meanders steeply down from the Palatine Hill to Via di San Gregorio. When you reach the roaring traffic of that busy thoroughfare, walk north toward the bulk of what some Romans consider the most potent symbol of their city:

20. The Colosseum. Its crumbling, oval bulk is the greatest monument of ancient Rome, and visitors are impressed with its size, its majesty, and its ability to conjure up the often cruel entertainments that were played out for the pleasure of the Roman masses. Either visit it now or return later.

TAKE A BREAK On a hill in back of the landmark Colosseum is the **Bar Martini,** Piazza del Colosseo 3A (☎ **06/7004431**). Have your coffee or cool drink outside at one of the tables and absorb one of the world's greatest architectural views: that of the Colosseum itself. A pasta dish costs 10,000L to 12,000L ($6 to $7); a sandwich, 3,000L to 5,000L ($1.75 to $2.90). Service is daily from 8:30am to midnight.

THE IMPERIAL FORUMS

Begun by Julius Caesar as an answer to the overcrowding of Rome's older forums during the days of the Empire, the imperial forums were at the time of their construction flashier, bolder, and more impressive than the old Roman Forum, and as such represented the unquestioned authority of the Roman emperors at the height of their absolute power. After the collapse of Rome and during the Dark Ages, they, like many other ancient monuments, were lost to history, buried beneath layers of debris until Mussolini, in an egomaniacal attempt to draw comparisons between his Fascist regime and the glory of ancient Rome, helped to restore the grandeur of Rome.

With your back to the Colosseum, walk westward along the:

21. **Via dei Fori Imperiali,** keeping to the right side of the street. It was Mussolini who issued the controversial orders to cut through centuries of debris and junky buildings to reveal many archaeological treasures and carve out this boulevard linking the Colosseum to the grand 19th-century monuments of Piazza Venezia. The vistas over the ruins of Rome's imperial forums from the northern side of the boulevard make for one of the most fascinating walks in Rome.

Some of the rather confusing ruins you'll see from the boulevard include the shattered remnants of the colonnade that once surrounded the Temple of Venus and Roma. Next to it, you'll see the back wall of the Basilica of Constantine. Shortly, on the street's north side, you'll come to a large outdoor restaurant, where Via Cavour joins the boulevard. Just beyond the small park across Via Cavour are the remains of the:

22. **Forum of Nerva,** best observed from the railing that skirts it on Via dei Fori Imperiali. It was built by the emperor whose 2-year reign (A.D. 96–98) followed that of the paranoid Domitian. You'll be struck by just how much the ground level has risen in 19 centuries. The only really recognizable remnant is a wall of the Temple of Minerva with two fine Corinthian columns. This forum was once flanked by that of Vespasian, which is now, however, completely gone. It's possible to enter the Forum of Nerva from the other side, but you can see it just as well from the railing.

The next forum you approach is the:

23. **Forum of Augustus,** built to commemorate the emperor's victory over the assassins Cassius and Brutus in the Battle of Philippi (42 B.C.). Fittingly, the temple that once dominated this forum—whose remains can still be seen—was that of Mars Ultor, or Mars the Avenger, in which stood a mammoth statue of Augustus that unfortunately has vanished completely. You can enter the Forum of Augustus from the other side (cut across the wee footbridge).

Continuing along the railing, you'll see next the vast semicircle of:

24. **Trajan's Market,** Via IV Novembre 95 (☎ **06/6790048**), whose teeming arcades stocked with merchandise from the far corners of the Roman world long ago collapsed, leaving only the ubiquitous cats to watch over things. The shops once covered a multitude of levels, and you can still wander around many of them. In front of the perfectly proportioned semicircular facade—designed by Apollodorus of Damascus at the beginning of the 2nd century—are the remains of a great library, and fragments of delicately colored marble floors still shine in the sunlight between stretches of rubble and tall grass.

While the view from the railing is interesting, Trajan's Market is worth the descent below street level. To get here, follow the service road you're on until you reach the monumental Trajan's Column on your left, where you turn right and go up the steep flight of stairs that leads to Via Nazionale. At the top of the stairs, about half a block farther on the right, you'll see the entrance to the market. It's open Tuesday to Sunday from 9am to 4:30pm. Admission is 3,750L ($2.15) for adults, 2,500L ($1.45) for students, and free for children 17 and under.

Before you head down through the labyrinthine passageways, you might like to climb the:

25. Tower of the Milizie, a 12th-century structure that was part of the medieval headquarters of the Knights of Rhodes. The view from the top (if it's open) is well worth the climb.

From the tower, you can wander where you will through the ruins of the market, and admire the sophistication of the layout and the sad beauty of the bits of decoration that still remain. When you've examined the brick and travertine corridors, head out in front of the semicircle to the site of the former library; from here, scan the retaining wall that supports the modern road and look for the entrance to the tunnel that leads to the:

26. Forum of Trajan (Foro Traiano), entered on Via IV Novembre near the steps of Via Magnanapoli. Once through the tunnel, you'll emerge in the newest and most beautiful of the imperial forums, designed by the same man who laid out the adjoining market. There are many statue fragments and pedestals that bear still-legible inscriptions, but more interesting is the great Basilica Ulpia, whose gray marble columns rise roofless into the sky. You wouldn't know it to judge from what's left, but the Forum of Trajan was once regarded as one of the architectural wonders of the world. Constructed between 107 and 113, it was designed by the Greek architect Apollodorus of Damascus.

Beyond the Basilica Ulpia is

27. Trajan's Column, which is in magnificent condition, with intricate bas-relief sculpture depicting Trajan's victorious campaign (although from your vantage point you'll only be able to see the earliest stages). The emperor's ashes were kept in a golden urn at the base of the column. If you're fortunate, someone on duty at the stairs next to the column will let you out there. Otherwise, you'll have to walk back the way you came.

The next stop is the:

28. Forum of Julius Caesar, the first of the imperial forums. It lies on the opposite side of Via dei Fori Imperiali, the last set of sunken ruins before the Victor Emmanuel monument. While it's possible to go right down into the ruins, you can see everything just as well from the railing. This was the site of the Roman stock exchange, as well as of the Temple of Venus, a few of whose restored columns stand cinematically in the middle of the excavations.

ON TO THE CIRCUS MAXIMUS

From here, retrace your last steps until you're in front of the white Brescian marble monument around the corner on Piazza Venezia, where the:

29. Vittorio Emanuele Monument dominates the piazza. The most flamboyant landmark in Italy, it was constructed in the late 1800s to honor the first king of Italy. An eternal flame burns at the Tomb of the Unknown Soldier. The interior of the monument has been closed to the public for many years.

Keep close to the monument and walk to your left, in the opposite direction from Via dei Fori Imperiali. You might like to pause at the fountain that flanks one of the monument's great white walls and splash some icy water on your face. Stay on the same side of the street, and just keep walking around the monument. You'll be on Via del Teatro Marcello, which takes you past the twin lions that guard the sloping stairs and on along the base of the Capitoline Hill.

Fun Fact

The Vittorio Emanuele Monument has been compared to everything from a frosty wedding cake to a Victorian typewriter.

Keep walking along this street until you come to the:

30. Teatro di Marcello, on your right. You'll recognize the two rows of gaping arches, which are said to be the models for the Colosseum. Julius Caesar is credited with starting the construction of this theater, but it was finished many years after his death (in 11 B.C.) by Augustus, who dedicated it to his favorite nephew, Marcellus. A small corner of the 2,000-year-old arcade has been restored to what presumably was the original condition. Here, as everywhere, there are numerous cats stalking around the broken marble.

The bowl of the theater and the stage were adapted many centuries ago as the foundation for the Renaissance palace of the Orsini family. The other ruins belong to old temples. To the right is the Porticus of Octavia, dating from the 2nd century B.C. Note how later cultures used part of the Roman structure without destroying its original character. There's another good example of this on the other side of the theater. Here you'll see a church with a wall that completely incorporates part of an ancient colonnade.

Keep walking along Via del Teatro Marcello away from Piazza Venezia for 2 more long blocks, until you come to Piazza della Bocca della Verità. The first item to notice in the attractive piazza is the rectangular:

31. Temple of Fortuna Virile. You'll see it on the right, a little off the road. Built a century before the birth of Christ, it's still in magnificent condition. Behind it is another temple, dedicated to Vesta. Like the one in the Roman Forum, it's round, symbolic of the prehistoric huts where continuity of the hearthfire was a matter of survival.

About a block to the south you'll pass the facade of the Church of Santa Maria in Cosmedin, set on Piazza della Bocca della Verità. Even more noteworthy, a short walk to the east, is the:

32. Circus Maximus, whose elongated oval proportions and ruined tiers of benches evoke the setting for *Ben Hur.* Today a formless ruin, the victim of countless raids on its stonework by medieval and Renaissance builders, the remains of the once-great arena lie directly behind the church. At one time 250,000 Romans could assemble on the marble seats, while the emperor observed the games from his box high on the Palatine Hill.

The circus lies in a valley formed by the Palatine Hill on the left and the Aventine Hill on the right. Next to the Colosseum, it was the most impressive structure in ancient Rome, located certainly in one of the most exclusive neighborhoods. Emperors lived on the Palatine, while the great palaces of patricians sprawled across the Aventine, which is still a rather nice neighborhood. For centuries the pomp and ceremony of imperial chariot races filled this valley with the cheers of thousands.

When the dark days of the 5th and 6th centuries fell on the city, the Circus Maximus seemed a symbol of the complete ruination of Rome. The last games were held in 549 on the orders of Totilla the Goth, who had seized Rome in 547 and established himself as emperor. He lived in the still-glittering ruins on the Palatine and apparently thought that the chariot races in the Circus Maximus would lend credence to his charade of empire. It must have been a pretty miserable show, since the decimated population numbered something like 500 when Totilla recaptured the city. The Romans of those times were caught between Belisarius, the imperial general from Constantinople, and Totilla the Goth, both of whom fought bloodily for control of Rome. After the travesty of 549, the Circus Maximus was never used again, and the demand for building materials reduced it, like so much of Rome, to a great dusty field.

To return to other parts of town, head for the bus stop adjacent to the Church of Santa Maria in Cosmedin, or walk the length of the Circus Maximus to its far end and pick up the Metro to Termini or anywhere else in the city that appeals to you.

WALKING TOUR 2
The Heart of Rome

Start: Palazzo del Quirinale.
Finish: Piazza Santi Apostoli.
Time: 3½ hours.
Best Times: Sunday mornings.
Worst Times: Morning and afternoon rush hours on weekdays.

This walking tour will lead you down narrow, sometimes traffic-clogged streets that have witnessed more commerce and religious fervor than any other neighborhood in Rome. Be prepared for glittering and very unusual shops that lie cheek by jowl with churches that date back to A.D. 500.

Begin in the monumental, pink-toned:

1. Piazza del Quirinale. Crowning the highest of the seven ancient hills of Rome, this is where Augustus's Temple of the Sun once stood (the steep marble steps that now lead to Santa Maria d'Aracoeli on the Capitoline Hill once serviced this spot), and part of the fountains in the piazza were built from the great Baths of Constantine, which also stood nearby. The palace, today home to the President of Italy, is open to the public only on Sunday mornings.

You can admire a view overlooking Rome from the piazza's terrace, then meander along the curiously lifeless streets that surround it before beginning your westward descent along Via della Dataria and your northerly descent along Via San Vincenzo to one of the most famous waterworks in the world, the:

2. Trevi Fountain. Supplied by water from the Acqua Vergine aqueduct, and a triumph of the baroque style, it was based on the design of Nicolo Salvi (who is said to have died of illness contracted during his supervision of the project) and completed in 1762. On the southwestern corner of the fountain's piazza you'll see a somber, not particularly spectacular-looking church (Chiesa S.S. Vincenzo e Anastasio) with a strange claim to fame. In it are contained the hearts and intestines of several centuries of popes. This was the parish church of the popes when they resided at the Quirinal Palace on the hill above, and for many years each pontiff willed those parts of his body to the church. According to legend, the church was built on the site of a spring that burst from the earth after the beheading of St. Paul, at one of three sites where his head is said to have bounced off the ground.

If you wish, throw a coin or two into the fountain to ensure your return to Rome, then walk around to the right of the fountain along streets whose names will include Via di Stamperia, Via del Tritone, and Via F. Crispi. These lead to a charming street, Via Gregoriana, whose relatively calm borders and quiet apartments flank a narrow street that inclines upward to one of the most spectacular public squares in Italy:

3. Piazza della Trinità dei Monti. Partly because of its position at the top of the Spanish Steps (which you'll descend in a moment), partly because of its soaring Egyptian obelisk and its lavish allegiance to perfect baroque symmetry, this is one of the most theatrical points of convergence in Italy. Flanking the piazza are buildings that have played a pivotal role in French politics for centuries, including the Church of Trinità dei Monti, begun by the French monarch Louis XII in 1502, and restored during Napoléon's occupation of Rome in the early 1800s. The eastern edge of the square, adjacent to Via Gregoriana, is the site of the 16th-century Palazzetto Zuccaro, built for the mannerist painter Federico Zuccaro with doorways and window openings fashioned into deliberately grotesque shapes inspired by the mouths of sea monsters. (It lies between Via Gregoriana, Via Sistina, and Piazza Trinità dei Monti.) In this building, at the dawn of the French Revolution, David painted the most politicized canvas in the history of France, *The Oath of the Horatii* (1784), which became a symbol of the Enlightenment then sweeping through the salons of Paris. Today the palazzetto is owned by the German Institute for Art History.

Begin your meandering descent of the most famous staircase in the world, the:

4. Spanish Steps (Scalinata della Trinità dei Monti), an azalea-flanked triumph of landscape design that takes its name (its English name, at least) from the Spanish Embassy, which was in a nearby palace during the 19th century. The Spanish, however, had nothing to do with the construction of the steps. Designed by Italian architect Francesco de Sanctis between 1723 and 1725, they were funded almost entirely by the French as a preface to the above-mentioned French church, Trinità dei Monti.

The Spanish Steps are at their best in spring, when they're filled with flowers that seem to cascade down into Piazza di Spagna, a piazza designed like two interconnected triangles. It's interesting to note that in the early–19th century the steps were famous for the sleek young men and women who lined the travertine steps, flexing muscles and exposing ankles in hopes of attracting an artist and being hired as a model.

The boat-shaped Barcaccia fountain, in the piazza at the foot of the steps, was designed by Bernini's father at the end of the 16th century.

There are two nearly identical houses at the foot of the steps on either side. One is the home of Babington's Tea Rooms (our "Take a Break," below); the other is the house where the English romantic poet John Keats lived—and died. That building contains the:

5. Keats-Shelley Memorial (Casina Rossa), at Piazza di Spagna 26. Keats died here on February 23, 1821, at the age of 25, during a trip he made to Rome to improve his failing health. Since 1909, when the building was bought by well-intentioned English and American aficionados of English literature, it has been a working library established in honor of Keats and Shelley, who drowned off the coast of Viareggio with a copy of Keats's work in his pocket. Mementos inside range from the kitschy to the immortal, and are almost relentlessly laden with literary nostalgia.

☕ **TAKE A BREAK**   Opened in 1893 by Miss Anna Maria Babington, **Babington's Tea Rooms,** Piazza di Spagna 23 (☎ **06/6786027**), has been serving homemade scones and muffins—along with a good cuppa—ever since, based on her original recipes. Celebrities and thousands of tourists have stopped off here to rest in premises inspired by England's Victorian age. Prices are high, however.

Walking Tour—The Heart of Rome

1. Piazza del Quirinale
2. Trevi Fountain
3. Piazza della Trinita dei Monti
4. Spanish Steps (Scalinata della Trinità dei Monti)
5. Keats-Shelley Memorial (Casina Rossa)
- Babington's Tea Rooms
6. Collegio di Propoganda Fide
7. Via Condotti
8. Augustus' Mausoleum (Mausoleo Augusteo)
9. Altar of Peace (Ara Pacis)
10. Borghese Palace (Palazzo Borghese)
11. Via del Corso
12. Palazzo Ruspoli
13. Chiesa di San Lorenzo in Lucina
14. Piazza Colonna
15. Piazza di Montecitorio
16. Chiesa San Marcello al Corso
17. Chiesa S.S. Apostoli

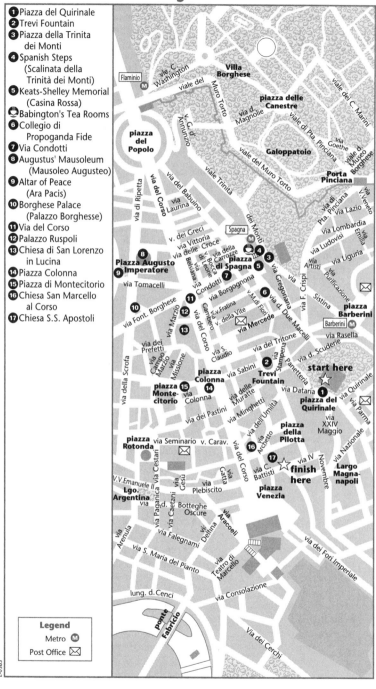

Legend
Metro Ⓜ
Post Office ✉

E-0365

191

In the past, the Piazza di Spagna area was a favorite of English lords, who rented palaces hereabouts and parked their coaches on the street. Americans predominate in the 20th century, especially since the main office of American Express is right on Piazza di Spagna and dispenses all those letters (and money) from home. Much to the dismay of many Romans, the piazza is also home to a McDonald's. To the extreme southern edge of the square—flanked by Via Due Macelli, Via Propaganda, and Piazza di Spagna—is an odd vestige of the Catholic church's sense of missionary zeal, the:

6. **Collegio di Propoganda Fide.** Established in 1627 as the headquarters of a religious organization devoted to the training of young missionaries, it later grew into one of the most important centers for missionary work in the world. Owned and administered by the Vatican, and therefore exempt from most of the laws and legalities of Italy, it contains design elements by two of the 17th century's bitterest artistic rivals, Bernini and Borromini.

The street that runs east-west as the logical continuation of the descent of the Spanish Steps is one of the most celebrated venues for style and materialism in Italy:

7. **Via Condotti,** lined with the bounty of the Italian fashion industry. Even the least materialistic will enjoy window shopping along this impressive line-up of the most famous names in international fashion. *Note:* Via Condotti is only the most visible of several upscale shopping streets in the neighborhood. For more of the same kind of temptation, detour onto a smaller but equally glamorous parallel street, Via della Croce, 2 blocks to the north, and wander at will amid the bounty. Make it a point, however, to eventually return to Via Condotti for the continuation of this walking tour.

Via Condotti ends at a shop-lined plaza, Largo Goldoni, where your path will fork slightly to the right onto Via Tomacelli. Staying on the right-hand (northern) edge of the street, turn right at the second intersection into Piazza Augusto, site of the:

8. **Augustus Mausoleum (Mausoleo Augusteo).** Once covered with marble and cypress trees, this tomb housed the ashes of many of the emperors of the 1st century all the way up to Hadrian (who built what is now Castel Sant'Angelo across the river for his own tomb). The imperial remains stayed intact within this building until the 5th century, when invading barbarians smashed the bronze gates and stole the golden urns, probably emptying the ashes onto the ground outside. The tomb was restored by Mussolini, and while you cannot enter the mausoleum itself, you can walk around it.

At the mausoleum's southwestern corner (Largo San Rocco), veer northwest until you reach the edge of the Tiber, stopping for a view of a bizarre, almost surreal compendium of ancient archaeological remnants restored, and in some cases enhanced, by Mussolini. It sits in an airy glass-and-concrete building beside the eastern banks of the Tiber at Ponte Cavour. Inside is one of the treasures of antiquity, the:

9. **Altar of Peace (Ara Pacis),** built by the Senate as a tribute to Augustus and the peace he had brought to the Roman world. Look closely at the marble walls for portraits of Augustus's imperial family. Mussolini collected the few fragments of this monument that were scattered in museums throughout the world and gave his archaeological engineers a deadline for digging out the bulk of the altar, which remained underground—below the water table and forming part of the foundation of a Renaissance palace on the Corso. Fearful of failing Il Duce, the engineers hit upon the idea of chemically freezing the water surrounding the altar and

simply chipping the relic out in huge chunks of ice, building new supports for the palace overhead as they went.

After a look at these fragments of another civilization's history, proceed southward along Via Ripetta, cross over Piazza di Porto di Ripetta, then fork left, walking southeast along Via Borghese for a block until you reach the austerely dignified entrance to the:

10. Borghese Palace (Palazzo Borghese). Although many of the art treasures that once graced its interior now form part of the Galleria Borghese collections (for details, see "Around Piazza di Spagna & Piazza del Popolo" in chapter 6), this huge and somewhat disjointed palazzo retains its status as the modern-day Borghese family's seat of power and prestige. Bought from another family in 1605 by the cardinal destined to become Pope Paul V, it was later occupied by Pauline Borghese, Napoléon's scandalous sister, a noted enemy of opera composer Rossini. Regrettably, the palace, carefully preserving its status as one of the most prestigious private homes in the world, is not open to the public.

From your vantage point, walk in a westerly direction along Via Fontanella Borghese back to a square you've already visited, Largo Goldoni, the western terminus of Via Condotti. The busy avenue on your right is one of the most richly stocked treasure troves of Italian merchandise in Rome:

11. Via del Corso. When compared to the many meandering streets with which it merges, the rigidly straight lines of Via del Corso are unusual. In the 18th century, residents of Rome commandeered the street to race everything from horses to street urchins, festooning the windows of buildings on either side of the narrow street with banners and flags. Although today its merchandise is not as chic (nor as expensive) as what you'll find along Via Condotti (see above), it's well worth more than a few glances to see what's up in the world of Italian fashion.

Walk south along Via del Corso's western edge, turning right (west) after 1 block into Piazza San Lorenzo in Lucina. The severely massive building on the piazza's northern edge is the:

12. Palazzo Ruspoli, a 16th-century testament to the wealth of a Florentine family, the Rucellai. Family members commissioned the same architect (Bartolommeo Ammannati) who designed parts of the Pitti Palace in Florence to build their Roman headquarters. Today the building belongs to a private foundation, although it's occasionally open for temporary, but infrequently scheduled exhibitions. The entrance is at Via del Corso 418A, although your best vantage point will be from Piazza San Lorenzo in Lucina. On the piazza's southern edge rises the:

13. Chiesa di San Lorenzo in Lucina. Most of what you'll see today was rebuilt around 1650, although if you look carefully, the portico and most of the bell tower have survived almost unchanged since the 1100s. According to tradition, this church was built on the site of the mansion of Lucina, a prosperous Roman matron who salvaged the corpses of Christian martyrs from prisons and amphitheaters for proper burials. The church was founded by Sixtus III, who reigned for 8 years beginning in A.D. 432. Inside, look for the tomb of the French painter Poussin (1594–1665), which was carved and consecrated on orders of the French statesman Chateaubriand in 1830.

After your visit, retrace your steps back to Via del Corso and walk southward until you reach the venerable perimeter of:

14. Piazza Colonna. Its centerpiece is one of the most dramatic obelisks in town, the Column of Marcus Aurelius, a hollow bronze column rising 83 feet above the piazza. Built between A.D. 180 and 196, and restored (some say "defaced") in

1589 by a pope who replaced the statue of the Roman warrior on top with a statue of St. Paul, it's one of the ancient world's best examples of heroic bas-relief and one of the most memorable sights of Rome. Beside the piazza's northern edge rises the Palazzo Chigi, official residence of the Italian prime minister.

Continue walking west from Piazza Colonna into another square a few steps to the east and you'll find yourself in a dramatic piazza designed by Bernini:

15. Piazza di Montecitorio. This was the site during ancient times of the cremations of the Roman emperors. In 1792 the massive obelisk of Psammetichus II, originally erected in Egypt in the 6th century B.C., was placed here as the piazza's centerpiece. Brought to Rome by barge from Heliopolis in 10 B.C., it was unearthed from a pile of rubble in 1748 at a site close to the Church of San Lorenzo in Lucina. The Palazzo di Montecitorio, which rises from the piazza's northern edge, is the modern-day site of the Italian legislature (the Chamber of Deputies) and is closed to the public.

Retrace your steps back to Via del Corso, then walk south, this time along its eastern edge. Within 6 blocks, just after crossing over Via dell'Umiltà, you'll see the solid stone walls of the namesake church of this famous shopping boulevard:

16. Chiesa San Marcello al Corso. Originally founded in the 4th century, and rebuilt in 1519 after a disastrous fire, it was ornamented in the late 1600s with a baroque facade by Carlo Fontana. A handful of ecclesiastical potentates from the 16th and 17th centuries, many resting in intricately carved sarcophagi, are contained inside.

After your visit, return to the piazza in front of the church, then continue walking for half a block south along Via del Corso. Turn left (eastward) onto Via S.S. Apostoli, then turn right onto Piazza S.S. Apostoli, and conclude this tour with a visit to a site that has witnessed the tears of the penitent since the collapse of the Roman Empire, the:

17. Chiesa S.S. Apostoli. Because of alterations to the site, especially a not-very-harmonious rebuilding that began in the early 1700s, there's very little to suggest the ancient origins of this church of the Holy Apostles. It was founded in the dim, early days of the Roman papacy, sometime between A.D. 556 and 561, by Pope Pelagius as a thanksgiving offering for the short-term defeat of the Goths at a battle near Rome. The most interesting parts of this ancient site are the fluted stone columns at the end of the south aisle, in the Cappella del Crocifisso; the building's front portico, added in the 1300s, which managed to incorporate a frieze from ancient Rome; and one of the first works executed by Canova, a painting near the high altar completed in 1787, shortly after his arrival in Rome. The church is open daily from 6:30am to noon and 4 to 7pm.

WALKING TOUR 3
Renaissance Rome

Start: Via della Conciliazione (Piazza Pia).

Finish: Galleria Doria Pamphili.

Time: 4 hours, not counting a tour of the Castel Sant'Angelo and visits to the Palazzo Spada and the Palazzo Pamphil.

Best Times: Early and mid-mornings.

Worst Times: After dark.

The threads that unify this tour are the grandiose tastes of Rome's Renaissance popes and the meandering Tiber river that has transported building supplies, armies, pilfered treasures from other parts of Europe, and such famous personages

Walking Tour—Renaissance Rome

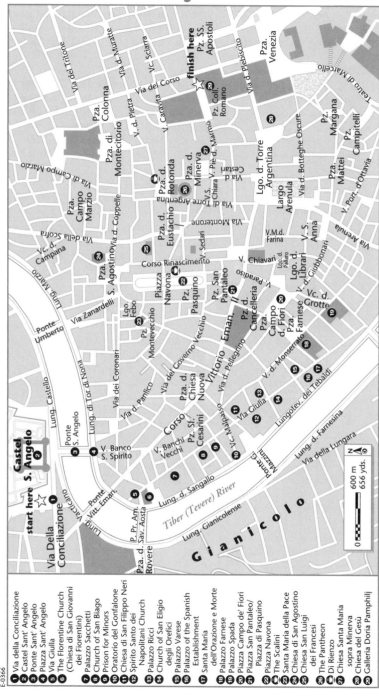

❶ Via della Conciliazione
❷ Castel Sant' Angelo
❸ Ponte Sant' Angelo
❹ Piazza Sant' Angelo
❺ Via Giulia
❻ The Florentine Church (Chiesa di San Giovanni dei Fiorentini)
❼ Palazzo Sacchetti
❽ Church of San Biago
❾ Prison for Minors
❿ Oratorio del Gonfalone
⓫ Chiesa di San Filippo Neri
⓬ Spirito Santo dei Napolitani Church
⓭ Palazzo Ricci
⓮ Church of San Eligio degli Orefici
⓯ Palazzo Varese
⓰ Palazzo of the Spanish Establishment
⓱ Santa Maria dell'Orazione e Morte
⓲ Palazzo Farnese
⓳ Palazzo Spada
⓴ Piazza Campo de' Fiori
㉑ Piazza San Pantaleo/ Piazza di Pasquino
㉒ Piazza Navona
㉓ The Scalini
㉓ Santa Maria della Pace
㉔ Chiesa di San Agostino
㉕ Chiesa San Luigi dei Francesi
㉖ The Pantheon
㉗ Di Rienzo
㉗ Chiesa Santa Maria sopra Minerva
㉘ Chiesa del Gesú
㉙ Galleria Doria Pamphilj

E-0366

195

as Cleopatra and Mussolini into Rome. Slower and less powerful than many of Italy's other rivers (such as the mighty Po, which irrigates the fertile plains of Lombardy and the north), the Tiber varies, depending on the season, from a sluggish ribbon of sediment-filled water only 4 feet deep to a 20-foot–deep torrent capable of flooding the banks that contain it.

The last severe flood to destroy Roman buildings occurred in 1870. Since then, civic planners have built mounded barricades high above its winding banks, a development that has diminished the river's visual appeal. The high embankments, as well as the roaring traffic arteries that parallel them, obscure views of the water along most of the river's trajectory through Rome. In any event, the waters of the Tiber are so polluted that many modern Romans consider their concealment something of a plus.

Begin your tour at Piazza Pia. (Don't confuse Piazza Pia with nearby Piazza Pio XII.) Piazza Pia is the easternmost end of Rome's most sterile and impersonal boulevard:

1. **Via della Conciliazione.** Conceived by Mussolini as a monumental preface to the faraway dome of St. Peter's Basilica, construction required the demolition of a series of medieval neighborhoods between 1936 and 1950, rendering it without challenge the most disliked avenue in Rome.

Walk east toward the massive and ancient walls of the:

2. **Castel Sant'Angelo.** Originally built by the emperor Hadrian in A.D. 135 as one of the most impressive mausoleums in the ancient world, it was adapted for use as a fortress, a treasure vault, and a pleasure palace for the Renaissance popes. Visit its interior, noting the presence near the entrance of architectural models showing the castle at various periods of its history. Note the building's plan (a circular tower set atop a square foundation), and the dry moats (used today for impromptu soccer games by neighborhood kids), which long ago were the despair of many an invading army.

After your visit, walk south across one of the most ancient bridges in Rome:

3. **Ponte Sant'Angelo.** The trio of arches in the river's center is basically unchanged since the bridge was built around A.D. 135; the arches that abut the river's embankments were added late in the 19th century as part of a flood-control program. On December 19, 1450, so many pilgrims gathered on this bridge (which at the time was lined with wooden buildings) that about 200 of them were crushed to death. Today the bridge is reserved exclusively for pedestrians, since vehicular traffic was banned in the 1960s. On the southern end of the bridge is the site of one of the most famous executions of the Renaissance:

4. **Piazza Sant'Angelo.** Here, in 1599, Beatrice Cenci and several members of her family were beheaded on orders of Pope Clement VIII. Their crime? Plotting the successful death of their very rich and very brutal father. Their tale later inspired a tragedy by Shelley and a novel by 19th-century Italian politician Francesco Guerrazzi.

From the square, cut southwest for 2 blocks along Via Paola (crossing the busy traffic of Corso Vittorio Emmanuele in the process) onto:

5. **Via Giulia.** Laid out during the reign of Pope Julius II (1503–13), Via Giulia's straight edges were one of Renaissance Rome's earliest examples of urban planning. Designed to facilitate access to the Vatican, it was the widest, straightest, and longest inner-city street in Rome at the time of its construction and was bordered by the 16th-century homes of such artists as Raphael, Cellini, and Borromini, and the architect Sangallo. Today the street is lined with some of the most spectacular antiques stores in Rome. At the terminus of Via Paola, the first building on Via Giulia you're likely to see is the soaring dome of the:

6. Florentine Church (Chiesa di San Giovanni dei Fiorentini), designated as the premier symbol of the city of Florence in papal Rome. Its design is the result of endless squabbling between such artistic rivals as Sansovino, Sangallo, and Maderno, each of whom added embellishments of his own. Michelangelo also submitted a design for the church, although his drawing did not prevail during the initial competition. Although most of the building was completed during the 1620s, Lorenzo Corsini added the facade during the 1700s.

Now walk in a southeasterly direction along Via Giulia, making special note of houses at **no. 82** (built in the 1400s, it was offered by Pope Julius II to the Florentine community), **no. 85** (the land it sits on was once owned by Raphael), and **no. 79** (built in 1536 by the architect Sangallo as his private home, it was later snapped up by a relative of Cosimo de' Medici).

In less than 3 short blocks, on the northwest corner of Vicolo del Cefalo, rises the symmetrical bulk of the:

7. Palazzo Sacchetti. Completed by Vasari in the mid-1500s, it was built for the Sacchetti family, a Florence-based family of bankers and merchants who moved to Rome after they lost an epic power struggle with the Medicis.

Continue walking south along Via Giulia. On your right rises the baroque facade of the unpretentious:

8. Church of San Biagio. Although its front was added in the early 1700s, it's one of the oldest churches in Rome, rebuilt from an even earlier model around 1070. The property of an Armenian Christian sect based in Venice, the church is named after an early Christian martyr (St. Biagio), a portion of whose throat is included among the sacred objects inside.

Walk another short block south along Via Giulia. Between Via del Gonfalone and Vicolo della Scimia are the barred windows of what was originally built early in the 19th century as a:

9. Prison for Minors. This, along with another nearby building (at Via Giulia 52, a few blocks to the south, which was built during the mid-1600s) incarcerated juvenile delinquents, political prisoners, debtors, common rogues, and innocent victims of circumstance for almost a hundred years. During its Industrial Revolution heyday, armed guards supervised all comings and goings along this section of Via Giulia.

Turn right onto Vicolo della Scimia and descend toward the Tiber. On your left, at no. 18, is a building used since the early 1500s as a guildhall for the flag-bearers of Rome, the:

10. Oratorio del Gonfalone. The guild of flag-bearers had, by the time this building was constructed, evolved into a charitable organization of concerned citizens and a rather posh social and religious fraternity. The frescoes inside were painted in 1573 by Zuccari. Restored during the early 1980s, they today form a backdrop for concerts held inside. The building is usually open Monday to Saturday from 9:30am to noon.

Walk to the very end of Vicolo della Scimia and make a hard left onto Vicolo Prigioni, which will eventually lead back to Via Giulia.

At this point, as you continue to walk south along Via Giulia, you'll notice a swath of trees and a curious absence of buildings flanking the corner of Via Moretta. In 1940 Mussolini ordered the demolition of most of the buildings along Via Moretta for the construction of a triumphal boulevard running from east to west. His intention—which was never fulfilled—was to link together the nearby Ponte Mazzini with Corso Vittorio Emanuele. One building that suffered was the:

11. **Chiesa di San Filippo Neri,** whose baroque facade sits near the corner. Originally funded during the early 1600s by a wealthy but ailing benefactor in hopes of curing his gout, the church retains only its facade—the rest of the building was demolished. Where choirs once sang and candles burned during masses, there is now a market for fruits and vegetables.

About another block to the south, on your right, rises the bulk of the:

12. **Spirito Santo del Napolitani Church.** Once one of the headquarters of the Neapolitan community in Rome, the version you see today is a product of a rebuilding during the 1700s, although parts of the foundation were originally constructed during the 1300s.

Slightly farther to the south, at Via Giulia 146, rises the:

13. **Palazzo Ricci,** one of the many aristocratic villas that once flanked this historic street. For a better view of its exterior frescoes, turn left from Via Giulia into Piazza Ricci to admire this building from the rear.

Returning to Via Giulia, walk south for a block, then turn right onto Via Barchetta. At the corner of Via di San Eligio, notice the:

14. **Church of San Eligio degli Orefici,** which was designed, according to popular belief, by Raphael in 1516. Completed about 60 years later, it was dedicated to (and funded by) the city's gold- and silversmiths.

Return to Via Giulia and notice, near its terminus, the:

15. **Palazzo Varese,** Via Giulia 16, built as an aristocratic residence in the Tuscan style; and, at Via Giulia 151, the:

16. **Palazzo of the Spanish Establishment.** Constructed in anticipation of the 1862 visit of Elizabeth, queen of Spain, for the occasion of her charitable visit to Rome, it was designed by Antonio Sarti.

Continue walking south along Via Giulia, past the faded grandeur of at least another half-dozen palazzi. These will include the **Palazzo Cisterno** (from about 1560), at no. 163; **Palazzo Baldoca/Muccioli/Rodd** (about 1700), at no. 167; and **Palazzo Falconieri** (about 1510), at no. 1.

Opposite the corner of Via dei Farnesi rise the walls of one of the most macabre buildings in Rome, the church of:

17. **Santa Maria dell'Orazione e Morte.** Built around 1575, and reconstructed about 160 years later, it was the property of an order of monks whose job it was to collect and bury the unclaimed bodies of the indigent. Notice the depictions of skulls decorating the church's facade. During the Renaissance, underground chambers lined with bodies led from the church to the Tiber, where barges carried the corpses away. Although these vaults are not open to the public, the church's interior decoration carries multiple reminders of the omnipresence of death.

After exiting the church, notice the covered passageway arching over Via Giulia. Built in 1603, and designed by Michelangelo, it connected the:

18. **Palazzo Farnese,** whose rear side rises to your left, with the Tiber and a series of then-opulent gardens and villas that no longer exist. The Palazzo Farnese was designed by Sangallo and Michelangelo, among others, and has housed dignitaries ranging from Pope Paul III to Queen Christina of Sweden. Today the French Embassy, it's closed to the public. For the best view of the building, cut west from Via Giulia along any of the narrow streets (Via Mascherone or Via dei Farnesi will do nicely) to reach Piazza Farnese.

To the southwest is a satellite square, Piazza Quercia, at the southern corner of which rises the even more spectacular exterior of the:

19. **Palazzo Spada,** Capo di Ferro 3. Built around 1550 for Cardinal Gerolamo Capo di Ferro, its ornate facade is stuccoed in high-relief in the mannerist style.

Although the State Rooms are closed to the public, the courtyard and several galleries are open.

From here, walk 2 blocks north along either Vicolo del Grotte or Via Balestrari till you reach one of the most famous squares of Renaissance Rome:

20. Piazza Campo de' Fiori. During the 1500s this square was the geographic and cultural center of secular Rome, with inns and the occasional burning at the stake of religious heretics. Today the campo hosts a morning open-air food market every day except Sunday.

After your visit, continue to walk northward for 3 meandering blocks along the narrow confines of Via Baullari to:

21. Piazza San Pantaleo/Piazza di Pasquino, whose interconnected edges are the site of both the Palazzo Massimo (to the east) and the Palazzo Braschi (Museo di Roma) to the north. The Palazzo Massimo (currently home to, among other things, the Rome campus of Cornell University) was begun as a private home in 1532 and designed with an unusual curved facade that corresponded to the narrow confines of the street. Regrettably, because it's open to the public only 1 day a year (March 17), it's viewed as a rather odd curiosity from the Renaissance by most passersby. More accessible is the **Palazzo Braschi,** built during the late 1700s by Pope Pius IV Braschi for his nephews. Severe and somewhat drab, it was the last palace ever constructed in Rome by a pope. Since 1952 it has contained the exhibits of the Museo di Roma, a poorly funded entity whose visiting hours and future are uncertain.

Continue walking north for 2 blocks until you reach the southernmost entrance of the most thrilling square in Italy:

22. Piazza Navona. Originally laid out in A.D. 86 as a stadium by the emperor Domitian, stripped of its marble in the 4th century by Constantine, and then embellished during the Renaissance into the lavish baroque form you'll see today, it has witnessed as much pageantry and heraldic splendor as any other site in Rome. The fact that it's reserved exclusively for pedestrians adds enormously to its charm, but makes parking in the neighborhood around it almost impossible. Wander around the confines of this baroque beauty, stopping to:

TAKE A BREAK   Established in 1882, **Tre Scalini,** Piazza Navona 30 (☎ **06/6879148**), is the most famous rendezvous point on the square. Literally hundreds of people go here every day to sample its tartufo (ice cream disguised with a coating of bittersweet chocolate, cherries, and whipped cream). There are simpler versions of gelato as well.

After your refreshment, head for the piazza's northwestern corner, adjacent to the startling group of heroic fountains at the square's northern edge, and exit onto Via di Lorenesi. Walk westward for 2 crooked blocks, forking to the left onto Via Parione until you reach the edge of one of the district's most charming churches:

23. Santa Maria della Pace. According to legend, blood flowed from a statue of the Virgin above the altar after someone threw a pebble at it. This legend motivated Pope Sixtus IV to rebuild the church in the 1500s on the foundations of an even older sanctuary. For generations after that, its curved porticos, cupola atop an octagonal base, and frescoes by Raphael helped make it one of the most fashionable churches for aristocrats residing in the surrounding palazzos.

After admiring the subtle, counterbalancing curves of the church, retrace your steps to the welcoming confines of Piazza Navona, then exit from it at its northernmost (narrow) end. Walk across the broad expanse of Via Zanardelli to its northern edge, then head east for 2 blocks to Piazza San Agostino, on whose northern flank rises the:

24. Chiesa di San Agostino. Built between 1479 and 1483, originally commissioned by the archbishop of Rouen, France, it was one of the first churches erected in Rome during the Renaissance. Its interior was altered and redecorated in the 1700s and 1800s. A painting by Caravaggio, *Madonna of the Pilgrims* (1605), hangs over the first altar on the left, as you enter.

After your visit, continue walking east along Via Zanardelli, turning south in about a block onto Via della Scrofe. Be alert to the fact that this street will change its name, in rapid order, to Largo Toniolo and Via Dogana, but regardless of how it's marked, walk for about 2 blocks south until, on the right, you'll see a particularly charming church, the:

25. Chiesa di San Luigi dei Francesi, which has functioned as the national church of France in Rome since 1589. Subtly carved into its facade is a stone salamander, the symbol of the Renaissance French monarch François I. Inside are a noteworthy series of frescoes by Caravaggio depicting *The Martyrdom of St. Matthew.*

Continue walking south for less than a block along Via Dogana, then turn left for a 2-block stroll along the Salita dei Crescenzi. Suddenly, at Piazza della Rotonda, there will emerge a sweeping view of one of our favorite buildings in all of Europe:

26. The Pantheon. Rebuilt by Hadrian around A.D. 125, it's the best-preserved ancient monument in Rome, a remarkable testimony to the skill of ancient masons, whose (partial) use of granite helped ensure the building's longevity. Originally dedicated to all the gods, it was transformed into a church (Santa Maria ad Martyres) by Pope Boniface IV in A.D. 609. Many archaeologists find the building's massive, slightly battered dignity thrilling. Its flattened dome is the widest in the world, exceeding the width of the dome atop St. Peter's by about 3 feet.

TAKE A BREAK   For contemplating the glory of the Pantheon, **Di Rienzo,** Piazza della Rotunda 8–9 (☎ **06/6869097**), is the most ideal cafe in Rome. Here you can sit at a table enjoying a pick-me-up while you view not only one of the world's premier ancient monuments, but also the lively crowd of people who come and go on this square, one of the most interesting in Rome.

After your coffee, walk southward along the eastern flank (Via Minerva) of the ancient building. That will eventually lead you to Piazza di Minerva. On the square's eastern edge rises the massive and severe bulk of a site that's been holy for more than 3,000 years:

27. Chiesa di Santa Maria Sopra Minerva. Beginning in 1280, early Christian leaders ordained that the foundation of an already ancient temple dedicated to Minerva (goddess of wisdom), be reused as the base for Rome's only Gothic church. Unfortunately, architectural changes and redecorations during the 1500s and the 1900s stripped this building of some of its original allure. Despite that, the roster of ornaments inside—including an awe-inspiring collection of medieval and Renaissance tombs—creates an atmosphere that's something akin to a religious museum.

After your visit, exit Piazza di Minerva from the square's easternmost edge, following Via del Gesù in a path that proceeds eastward, then meanders to the south. Continue walking southward until you eventually cross over the roaring traffic of Corso Vittorio Emanuele II/Via del Plebiscito. On the southern side of that busy avenue, you'll see a church that for about a century after the Protestant Reformation was one of the most influential in Europe, the:

28. Chiesa del Gesù. Built between 1568 and 1584 with donations from a Farnese cardinal, this was the most potent and powerful church in the Jesuit order for several centuries. Conceived as a bulwark against the perceived menace of the Protestant Reformation, it's sober, monumental, and historically very important to the history of the Catholic Counter-Reformation. The sheathing of yellow marble that covers part of the interior was added during the 1800s.

After your visit, cross back over the roaring traffic of Via del Plebiscito, walk eastward for 2 blocks, and turn left (north) onto Via de Gatta. Pass through the first piazza (Piazza Grazioli), then continue northward to Piazza del Collegi Romano, site of the entrance to one of Rome's best-stocked museums, the:

29. Galleria Doria Pamphili, Piazza del Collegio Romano 1. It's described fully under "Palazzo Doria Pamphili" in "Near Piazza Navona & the Pantheon" in chapter 6.

WALKING TOUR 4
Trastevere

Start: Isola Tiberina.
Finish: Palazzo Corsini.
Time: 3 hours, not counting museum visits.
Best Times: Daylight hours during weekday mornings, when the outdoor food markets are open, or early on a Sunday, when there's very little traffic.
Worst Times: After dark.

Not until the advent of the Fellini films (whose grotesqueries seemed to reflect many of the scenes you're likely to see in this neighborhood) did Trastevere emerge as a world-famous district of Rome. Set on the western bank of the Tiber, away from the bulk of Rome's most-visited monuments, Trastevere (whose name translates as "across the Tiber") seems a world apart from the ethics, mores, and architecture of the rest of Rome. Its residents have traditionally been considered less extroverted and more suspicious than the Romans across the river.

Because only a fraction of Trastevere has been excavated, it remains one of Rome's most consistently unchanged medieval neighborhoods, despite a trend toward gentrification. Amply stocked with dimly lit and very ancient churches, crumbling buildings angled above streets barely wide enough for a Fiat, and highly articulate inhabitants who have stressed their independence from Rome for many centuries, the district is the most consistently colorful of the Italian capital.

Be warned that street crime, pickpockets, and purse snatchers seem more plentiful here than in Rome's more frequently visited neighborhoods, so leave your valuables behind and be alert to what's going on around you.

Your tour begins on the tiny but historic:

1. Tiber Island (Isola Tiburtina). Despite its location in the heart of Rome, this calm and sun-flooded island has always been a refuge for the sick. The oldest bridge in Rome, the Ponte Fabricio, constructed in 62 B.C., connects the island to the Tiber's eastern bank. The church at the island's eastern end, **San Bartolomeo,** was built during the 900s by the Holy Roman Emperor Otto III, although dozens of subsequent renovations have removed virtually everything of the original structure. The complex of structures at the island's western end contain the hospital of Fatebenefratelli, whose foundations and traditions date back to the ancient world (the island was associated with the healing powers of the god Aesculapius, son of Apollo).

Walk south along the bridge (Ponte Cestio) that connects the island to the western bank of the Tiber. After crossing the raging traffic, which runs parallel to the riverbanks, continue south for a few steps. Soon, you'll reach:

2. **Piazza Piscinula.** Named after the Roman baths (*piscina*) that once stood here, the square contains the tiny but ancient Church of San Benedetto, whose facade was rebuilt in a simplified baroque style during the 1600s. It's classified as the smallest Romanesque church in Rome and supposedly is constructed on the site where St. Benedict, founder of the Benedictine order, lived as a boy. Directly opposite the church rises the intricate stonework of the Casa dei Mattei. Occupied during the Renaissance by one of the city's most powerful and arrogant families (the Mattei), it was abandoned as unlucky after several family members were murdered during a brawl at a wedding held inside. In reaction, the family moved to more elegant quarters across the Tiber.

Exit the piazza at the northwest corner, walking west along either the narrow Via Gensola or the somewhat wider Via della Lungaretta. In about 2 jagged blocks you'll reach the first of a pair of connected squares:

3. **Piazza Sidney Sonnino** (named after the Italian minister of foreign affairs during World War I); a few hundred feet to the north, facing the Tiber, is Piazza G. G. Belli, with a statue commemorating Giuseppe Gioacchino Belli (1791–1863), whose more than 2,000 satirical sonnets (written in Roman dialect) on Roman life have made him a particular favorite of the Trasteverans. From one edge of the piazza rise the 13th-century walls of the Torre degli Anguillara and the not-very-famous church of St. Agatha, and on the southern edge, across the street, stand the walls of the Church of San Crisogono. Founded in the 500s and rebuilt in the 1100s (when its bell tower was added), it contains stonework and mosaics that merit a visit.

Now, from a point near the southernmost expanses of these connected squares, cross the traffic-clogged Viale di Trastevere and head southeast into a maze of narrow alleyways. We propose at this point that you ask a passerby for Via dei Genovesi, as street signs in this maze of piazzas might be hard to find. Walking along Via dei Genovesi, traverse Via della Luce, then turn right onto Via Anicia (which was named after the family that produced the medieval leader Pope Gregory the Great). Then, at Via Anicia 12, on the west side of the street, you'll see the simple but dignified walls of the:

4. **Church of San Giovanni dei Genovesi.** Built during the 1400s for the community of Genoa-born sailors who labored at the nearby port, it has a tranquil garden on the opposite side of the street, which you may or may not be able to visit according to the whim of the gatekeeper.

After your visit, look across Via Anicia to the forbidding rear walls and ancient masonry of:

5. **Santa Cecilia in Trastevere.** (To reach its entrance, continue walking another block southeast along Via dei Genovesi, then turn right onto Via Santa Cecilia, which soon funnels into Piazza dei Mercanti.) A cloistered and still-functioning convent with a fine garden, Santa Cecilia contains in its inner sanctum hard-to-visit frescoes by Cavallini. (If you wish to visit the frescoes, call ☎ **06/5899289** to make an appointment. Viewing hours are Tuesday or

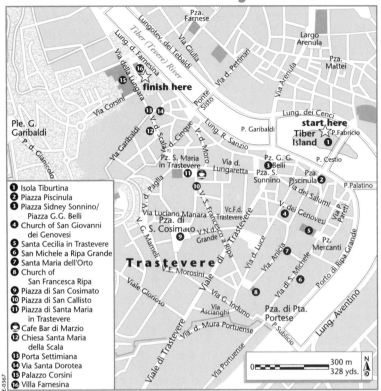

finish here

start here

1 Isola Tiburtina
2 Piazza Piscinula
3 Piazza Sidney Sonnino/
Piazza G.G. Belli
4 Church of San Giovanni
dei Genovesi
5 Santa Cecilia in Trastevere
6 San Michele a Ripa Grande
7 Santa Maria dell'Orto
8 Church of
San Francesca Ripa
9 Piazza di San Cosimato
10 Piazza di San Callisto
11 Piazza di Santa Maria
in Trastevere
Cafe Bar di Marzio
12 Chiesa Santa Maria
della Scala
13 Porta Settimiana
14 Via Santa Dorotea
15 Palazzo Corsini
16 Villa Farnesina

Friday from 10 to 11am.) The church is more easily visited and contains a white marble statue of the saint herself. The church is built on the reputed site of Saint Cecilia's long-ago palace and contains sections dating from the 12th to the 19th century.

St. Cecilia, who proved of enormous importance in the history of European art as a symbol of the struggle of the early church, was a wealthy Roman aristocrat condemned for her faith by a Roman prefect around A.D. 300. According to legend, her earthly body proved extraordinarily difficult for Roman soldiers to slay, affording the saint ample opportunity to convert bystanders to the Christian cause as she bled slowly to death over a period of 3 days.

TAKE A BREAK   About half a dozen cafes lie near this famous church. Any of them will serve frothy cups of cappuccino, tasty sandwiches, ice cream, and drinks.

After your refreshment, take the opportunity to wander randomly down three or four of the narrow streets outward from Piazza dei Mercanti. Of particular interest might be Via del Porto, which stretches south to the Tiber. A port—the largest in Rome—once flourished at this street's terminus (Porto di Ripa Grande). During the 1870s redesign of the riverfront, when the embankments were added, the port was demolished.

Retrace your steps northward along Via del Porto, turning left onto Via di San Michele. At no. 22, inside a stucco-covered, peach-colored building that never manages to loose its bureaucratic anonymity despite its age, you'll see:

6. San Michele a Ripa Grande. For many years this was the temporary home of the paintings of the Borghese Gallery until that gallery was restored and reopened. For more details, see the "Galleria Borghese" under "Around Piazza di Spagna & Piazza del Popolo" in chapter 6.

After your visit, turn north onto Via Madonna dell'Orto, a narrow street that intersects Via di San Michele. One block later, at the corner of Via Anicia, you'll see the baroque:

7. Santa Maria dell'Orto, which was originally founded by the vegetable gardeners of Trastevere during the early 1400s, when the district provided most of the green vegetables for the tables of Rome. Famous for the obelisks that decorate its cornices (added in the 1760s) and for the baroque gilding inside, it's one of the district's most traditional churches.

Now walk southwest along Via Anicia. In 2 blocks the street funnels into Piazza di San Francesco d'Assisi. On your left, notice the ornate walls of the:

8. Church of San Francesco a Ripa. Built in the baroque style, and attached to a medieval Franciscan monastery, the church contains a mannerist statue by Bernini depicting Ludovica Albertoni. It's Bernini's last known sculpture, and supposedly one of his most mystically transcendental.

Exit from Piazza di San Francesco d'Assisi and walk north along Via San Francesco a Ripa. After traversing the feverish traffic of Viale di Trastevere, take the first left onto a tiny street with a long name, Via Natale del Grande Cardinale Merry di Val. (Its name is sometimes shortened to simply "Via Natale," if it's marked at all on your map.) This funnels into:

9. Piazza di San Cosimato, known for its busy food market, which operates every weekday from early morning until around noon. On the north side of the square lies the awkwardly charming church of San Cosimato, sections of which were built around A.D. 900; it's closed to the public.

Exit from the piazza's north side, heading up Via San Cosimato (its name might not be marked). This will lead into:

10. Piazza di San Callisto. Much of the real estate surrounding this square, including the 17th-century Palazzo San Callisto, belongs to the Vatican. The edges of this piazza will almost imperceptibly flow into one of the most famous squares of Rome:

11. Piazza di Santa Maria in Trastevere. The Romanesque church that lends the piazza its name (Santa Maria in Trastevere) is the most famous building in the entire district. Originally built around A.D. 350 and thought to be one of the oldest churches in Rome, it sports a central core that was rebuilt around 1100 and an entrance and portico that were added in the 1840s. The much-restored mosaics on both the facade and in the interior, however, date from around 1200. Its sense of timelessness is enhanced by the much-photographed octagonal fountain in front (and the hundreds of pigeons).

TAKE A BREAK Try one of the many cafes that line this famous square. Although any would be suitable, a good choice might be the **Café Bar di Marzio,** Piazza di Santa Maria in Trastevere 14B, where rows of tables, both inside and out, offer an engaging view of the ongoing carnival of Trastevere.

After your refreshment, walk to the church's north side, toward its rear. Stretching from a point beginning at its northwestern edge is an ancient square, Piazza di San Egidio, with its own drab and rather nondescript 16th-century church (Chiesa di San Egidio) set on its western edge. Use it as a point of reference for the left-hand street that funnels from its base in a northeasterly direction, Via della Scalla.

The next church you'll see on your left, just after Via della Scalla, is:

12. Santa Maria della Scala, a 17th-century baroque monument that belongs to the Discalced Carmelite order of nuns. The interior contains works by Caravaggio and his pupils. There's also a pharmacological oddity in the annexes associated with the building: They include a modern pharmacy as well as a room devoted to arcane jars and herbal remedies that haven't changed very much since the 18th century.

In about 5 evocative blocks you'll reach a triumphal archway that marks the site of one of the ancient Roman portals to the city, the:

13. Porta Settimiana. Although during the 3rd century it was a vital link in the Roman defenses of the city, its partially ruined masonry provides little more than poetic inspiration today. Much of its appearance dates from the age of the Renaissance popes, who retained it as a site marking the edge of the ancient Aurelian wall. The narrow medieval-looking street leading off to the right is:

14. Via Santa Dorotea. Site of a rather drab church (Chiesa San Dorotea, a few steps from the intersection with Via della Scala), the street also marks a neighborhood that, according to legend, was the home of La Forinara, the baker's daughter. She was the mistress of Raphael, and he painted her as the Madonna, causing a scandal in his day.

Return to Via della Scala (which at this point has changed its name to Via della Lungara) and continue walking north. After Via Corsini, the massive palace on your left is the:

15. Palazzo Corsini, Via della Lungara 10. Built in the 1400s for a nephew of the pope, it was acquired by Queen Christina of Sweden, the fanatically religious monarch who abdicated the Protestant throne of Sweden for a life of devotion to Catholic causes. Today it houses some of the collection of the **National Gallery of Ancient Art,** plus European paintings of the 17th and 18th centuries. It's open Tuesday to Sunday from 9am to 2pm.

After your visit, cross Via della Lungara, heading east toward the Tiber, for a look at what was once the most fashionable villa in Italy, the:

16. Villa Farnesina. It was built between 1508 and 1511 by a Sienese banker, Agostino Chigi (Il Magnifico), who was believed to be the richest man in Europe at the time. After his death in 1520, the villa's frescoes and carvings were partially sacked by German armies in 1527. After years of neglect, the building was bought by the Farnese family, after whom it is named today, and in the 18th century, by the Bourbons of Naples. Graced with sculpture and frescoes (some by Raphael and his studio), it now belongs to the Italian government, and is the home of the National Print Cabinet (Gabinetto Nazionale delle Stampe), whose collections are open for view only by appointment. The public rooms, however, are open Monday to Saturday from 9am to 1pm, and also on Tuesday afternoon from 3 to 5:30pm.

8

Shopping

Rome offers shoppers temptations of every kind. This section will try to give you focus so that when you feel the urge—which is likely to overcome even the most stalwart of visitors—you'll be ready. You may well find charming shops and stores offering excellent value as you venture off the beaten track; what follows here is a description of certain streets known throughout Italy for their elegant shops. Be forewarned: The rents on these famous streets are very high, and those costs are passed on to the consumer. Nonetheless, a stroll down some of these streets usually presents a cross section of the most sought-after wares in Rome.

Cramped urban spaces and a sophisticated sense of taste have encouraged most Italian stores to elevate the boutique philosophy to its highest levels. Lack of space usually restricts an establishment's goods to one particular style, degree of formality, or mood. So browse at will, and let the allure of the shop window (particularly when shopping for fashions) communicate the mood and style of what you're likely to find inside.

Caveat: We won't pretend that Rome is Italy's finest shopping center (Florence, Venice, and Milan are), nor that its shops are unusually inexpensive—most of them aren't. But even on the most elegant of Rome's thoroughfares, there are values mixed in with the costliest boutiques. Shopping hours are generally Monday from 3:30 to 7:30pm, and Tuesday to Saturday from 9:30 or 10am to 1pm and from 3:30 to 7 or 7:30pm. Some shops are open on Monday mornings, however, and some shops don't close for the afternoon break.

1 The Shopping Scene

SHIPPING   Shipping can be a problem, but—for a price—any object can be packed, shipped, and insured. For major purchases, you should buy an all-risks insurance policy to cover damage or loss in transit. Since these policies can be expensive, check into whether using a credit or charge card to make your purchase will provide automatic free insurance.

TAX REBATES ON PURCHASES IN ITALY   Visitors to Italy are sometimes appalled at the high taxes and add-ons that seem to influence so many of the bottom-line costs of going to Italy. Those taxes, totaling as much as 19% to 35% for certain goods, apply to big-ticket purchases of more than 300,000L ($174) but can be

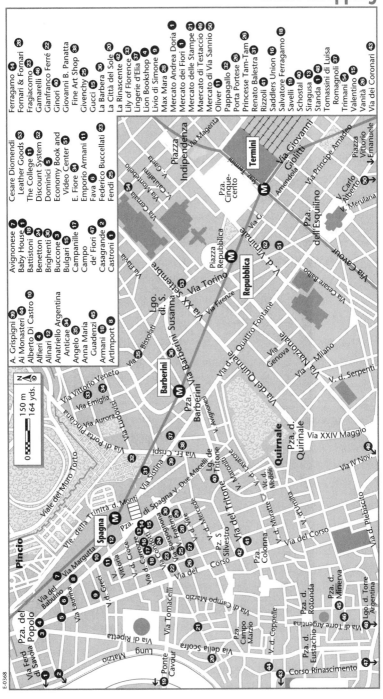

Ferragamo ⑭
Fornari & Fornari ㉒
Fragiacomo ㉓
Gamarelli ㉒
Gianfranco Ferré ㉒
Ginori ㊵
Giovanni B. Panatta
  Fine Art Shop ㊳
Givenchy ㉕
Gucci ⑳
La Barbera ㉒
La Città del Sole ⑳
La Rinascente ㊷
Lily of Florence ㊲
Lingerie d'Elia ㉒
Lion Bookshop ④
Livio di Simone ⑨
Max Mara

Mercato Andrea Doria ❶
Mercato dei Fiori ㉑
Mercato delle Stampe ㊿
Maercato di Testaccio ㉖
Mercato di Via Sannio ㊿
Oliver ⑪
Pappagallo ㉒
Porta Portese ㉖
Princesse Tam-Tam ㉖
Renato Balestra ㉛
Rizzoli ⑯
Saddlers Union ⑯
Salvatore Ferragamo ⑱
Savelli ⑲
Schostal ㉕
Siragusa ⑬
Standa ❶
Tomassini di Luisa
  Romagnoli ㊲
Trimani ㊿
Valentino ⑮
Vanità ④
Via dei Coronari ㊸

Cesare Diomendi
  Leather Goods ㊾
The College ⑪
Discount System ㉒
Dominici ⑤
Economy Book and
  Video Center ㊿
E. Fiore ㉞
Emporio Armani ⑪
Fava ⑥
Federico Buccellati ㉓
Fendi ㉖

Avignonese ⑦
Baby House ❶
Battistoni ⑱
Benetton ㉞
Brighenti ㊱
Buccone ③
Bulgari ⑮
Campanille ⑰
Campo
  de' Fiori ㊼
Casagrande ②
Castroni ❶

A. Grispigni ㊴
Ai Monasteri ㊸
Alberto Di Castro ⑩
Alfieri ④
Alinari ⑫
Anatriello Argentina
  Anticae ㉞
Angelo ④
Anna Maria
  Guadenzi ㊺
Armani ⑱
ArtImport ⑧

N

0   150 m
0   164 yds.

E-0368

207

refunded if you plan ahead and perform a bit of sometimes tiresome paperwork. When you make your purchase, be sure to get a receipt from the vendor. When you leave Italy, find an Italian Customs agent at the point of your exit from the country. The agent will want to see the item you've bought, confirm that it's physically leaving Italy, and stamp the vendor's receipt.

You should then mail the stamped receipt (keeping a photocopy for your records) back to the original vendor. The vendor will, sooner or later, send you a check representing a refund of the tax you paid at the time of your original purchase. Reputable stores view this as a matter of ordinary paperwork and are very businesslike about it. Less honorable stores might lose your receipts. It pays to deal with established vendors on purchases of this size.

MAJOR SHOPPING STREETS

Via Borgognona   It begins near Piazza di Spagna, and both the rents and the merchandise are chic and very, very expensive. Like its neighbor, Via Condotti, Via Borgognona is a Mecca for wealthy, well-dressed shoppers from around the world. Its architecture and its storefronts have retained their baroque or neoclassical facades.

Via Cola di Rienzo   Bordering the Vatican, this long, straight street runs from the Tiber to Piazza Risorgimento. Since the street is wide and traffic clogged, it is better to walk down one side and then back up the other rather than dash back and forth as the mood strikes. The street is known as a venue for stores selling a wide variety of merchandise—everything from jewelry to fashionable clothing—at reasonable prices. In particular, check out some of the inexpensive shoe outlets we've noted below.

Via Condotti   Easy to find because it begins at the base of the Spanish Steps, Via Condotti is the poshest upper-end shopping street in Rome, and the best example in Europe of a certain kind of avidly elegant consumerism. Even the invasion in recent years of a sampling of less classy stores hasn't diminished the allure of this street as a consumer's playground for the rich and the very, very rich.

Via del Corso   Not attempting the stratospheric image (or prices) of Via Condotti or Via Borgognona, Via del Corso's styles target younger consumers. There are, however, some gems scattered amid the shops selling jeans and sporting equipment. The most interesting shops are on the section nearest the fashionable cafes of Piazza del Popolo (at press time, however, Piazza del Popolo was a mess of scaffolding).

Via Francesco Crispi   Most shoppers reach this street by following Via Sistina (see below) one long block from the top of the Spanish Steps. Within a block of the intersection of these two streets are several shops that offer up unusual and not very expensive gifts.

Via Frattina   Running parallel to Via Condotti, it also begins at Piazza di Spagna. Part of its length is closed to traffic. The concentration of shops is denser, although some claim that its image is slightly less chic and that prices are lower than on Via Condotti. Via Frattina is usually thronged with shoppers who appreciate the lack of motor traffic.

Via Nazionale   Although its layout recalls 19th-century grandeur and ostentatious beauty, its traffic is horrendous and crossing over involves a good sense of timing and a strong understanding of Italian driving patterns. It begins at Piazza della Repubblica and runs down almost to Piazza Venezia. You'll find an abundance of leather stores—more reasonably priced than in many other parts of Rome—and a welcome handful of stylish boutiques.

Via Sistina   Beginning at the top of the Spanish Steps and running from Trinità dei Monti into Piazza Barberini, Via Sistina's shops are small, stylish, and reflect their owners' tastes. Pedestrian traffic is not as dense as it is on the other streets on this list.

Via Vittorio Veneto & Via Barberini   Evocative of *La Dolce Vita* fame and (now-diminished) fortunes, Via Veneto is filled these days with luxury hotels and cafes and an array of relatively expensive stores selling shoes, gloves, and leather goods. Although it's a desirable address by day, this street can be rough at night (muggings), and motor traffic is always dense and noisy.

BEST BUYS

The Italian aesthetic has exerted more power on the definition of beauty for Westerners than that of any other culture, and because of the Italians' consummate skill as manufacturers and designers, it's no surprise that consumers from all over the world flock to Italy's shops, trade fairs, and design studios to see what's new, hot, and salable back home.

Most obvious is **fashion,** which since World War II has played a major part in the economy of Milan, whose entrepreneurs view Rome as a principal distribution center. There are literally hundreds of famous designers for both men and women, most of whom make eminently stylish garments. Materials include silks, leathers, cottons, synthetics, and wool, often of the finest quality.

Italian design influences everything from typewriter keyboards to kitchen appliances to furniture. The Italian studios of Memphis-Milan and Studio Alchimia are two of the leaders in this field, and many of their products (and many rip-offs) are now highly visible in machines and furnishings throughout the world. You can preview many of Italy's new products and designs by reading a copy of *Domus,* a monthly photographic magazine that reports on many different aspects of the country's design scene.

Food and wine never go out of style, and many gourmets bring home to North America the gastronomic products that somehow always taste better in Italy. Many Roman shops sell chocolates, pastries, liqueurs, wines, and limited-edition olive oils. Be alert to restrictions against importing certain food products into North America, including anything fresh, such as fruit, and also prosciutto. Italian wines include many excellent vintages, and bottles of liqueurs (which are sometimes distilled from herbs and flowers) make unusual gifts. You can bring home only 1 liter of wine or spirits duty free—if, of course, you're 21 or over.

The **glassware** of Italy (and especially of Venice) is famous throughout the world and sold all over Rome. It's fragile enough that you should look into shipping it directly home with insurance.

Italy's **porcelain** may be elegant and sought after, but personally we prefer the hand-painted rustic plates and bowls of thick-edged **stoneware** known as Laveggio. Done in strong and clear glazes, and influenced by their rural origins, the bowls and plates are often used at the most formal dinners for their originality and style. The **tiles** and **mosaics** of Italy are virtually without equal in the world, whether used individually as drink coasters or decorative ornaments, or in groups set into masonry walls.

Lace was, for many years, made in convents by nuns. Venice became the country's headquarters. Handmade Italian lace is exquisite and justifiably expensive, crafted into a wide array of tablecloths, napkins, clothing, and bridal veils. Beware of machine-made imitations, although with a bit of practice you'll soon be able to recognize the shoddy copies.

Paper goods, stationery, elegantly bound books, prints, and engravings are specialties of Italy. The engravings you find amid stacks of dozens of others will invariably look stately when framed and hanging on a wall back home.

Fabrics, especially silk, are made near Lake Como, in the foothills of the Italian Alps. Known for their supple beauty and their ability to hold color for years (the thicker the silk, the more desirable), these silks are rivaled only by the finest of India, Thailand, and China. Their history in Italy goes back to the era of Marco Polo, and possibly much earlier.

Finally, Rome is the home to a **religious objects** industry. Centered around the streets near the Church of Santa Maria Sopra Minerva are dozens of shops selling pictures, statues, and reliefs of most of the important saints, the Madonna, Jesus, and John the Baptist.

2 Shopping A to Z

ANTIQUES

Some visitors to Italy come for its treasure trove of salable antiques alone. But long gone are the postwar days when you could find priceless treasures for pocket change. The prices of almost all antiques have risen to alarming levels as wealthy Europeans have increasingly outbid one another in frenzies of acquisitive lust. You might remember that any dealer who risks the high rents of central Rome to open an antiques store is acutely aware of the value of everything ever made, and will recognize anything of value long before his or her clients. Beware of fakes, insure anything you buy and have shipped, and for larger purchases, keep your paperwork in order for your eventual tax refund.

If you love antiques, one street you should frequent is **Via dei Coronari.** Buried in an ancient section of Campo Marzio (near Piazza Navona), Via dei Coronari is an antiquer's dream: There are more than 40 antiques stores within 4 blocks, literally lined with inlaid secretaries, gilded consoles, vases, urns, chandeliers, breakfronts, marble pedestals, chaises, refectory tables, candelabra—you name it. The entrance to the street is just north of Piazza Navona. Turn left outside the piazza, past the excavated ruins of Domitian's Stadium, and the street will be just ahead of you.

Via del Babuino is another major street for antiques in Rome, with some of the most prestigious stores found here, including Alberto di Castro (our favorite store for prints—see "Art," below), but many others as well, including **Cesare Lampronti,** Via del Babuino 67 (☎ **06/6795800**).

Ad Antiqua Domus. Via Paola 25–27. ☎ **06/6861530.**

As much a museum of Italian furniture design through the ages as it is a shop, you'll find Italian furniture from the days of Caesar through the 19th century for sale here. There's a second location at Via dei Coronari 227 (☎ **06/6861186**).

ArtImport. Via del Babuino 150. ☎ **06/3221330.**

An antique shopper's dream, this bazaar always has something for sale that's intriguing and tasteful—that is, if you can agree on a price. The store's motto is, "In the service of the table." As such, there is an emphasis on silver, although the objects run the gamut. The goblets, elegant bowls, candlesticks, and candelabra sold here are almost without equal in Rome.

ART

✪ **Alberto di Castro.** Via del Babuino 71. ☎ **06/3613752.**

Alberto di Castro is one of the largest dealers in antique prints and engravings in Rome. You'll find rack after rack of depictions of everything from the Colosseum to

Shopping Tips

Remember to bring your pocket calculator with you and keep in mind that stores are often closed between 1 and 4pm. Most important? Save your receipts! See the "Tax Rebates on Purchases in Italy" section in this chapter for important money-saving information.

---

the Pantheon, each evocative of the best architecture in the Mediterranean world, priced between $25 and $1,000, depending on the age and rarity of the engraving.

Giovanni B. Panatta Fine Art Shop. Via Francesco Crispi 117. ☎ **06/6795948.**

In business since 1890, this store is up the hill toward the Villa Borghese. Here you'll find excellent prints in color and black-and-white, covering a variety of subjects from 18th-century Roman street scenes to astrological charts. There's a good selection of attractive and reasonably priced reproductions of medieval and Renaissance art as well.

BOOKSTORES

Economy Book and Video Center. Via Torino 136. ☎ **06/4746877.**

Catering to the expatriate English-speaking communities of Rome, this bookstore sells only English-language books (both new and used, paperback and hardcover), greeting cards, and videos. Staffed by native English speakers, it lies about a block from the Piazza della Repubblica Metro station, and bus lines no. 64, 70, and 170.

The Lion Bookshop. Via del Greci 33. ☎ **06/32654007.**

The Lion Bookshop is the oldest English-language bookshop in town, specializing in both American and English literature. It also sells children's books and photographic volumes on both Rome and Italy. A vast choice of English-language videos is for sale or rent. Closed in August.

Rizzoli. Largo Chigi 15. ☎ **06/6796641.**

Rizzoli has one of the largest collections of Italian-language books in Rome. If your native language happens to be French, English, German, or Spanish, the endless shelves of this large bookstore will have a section to amuse, enlighten, and entertain you.

CHINA, PORCELAIN, & GLASSWARE

✪ **Richard Ginori.** Via de Tritone 177. ☎ **06/6793836.**

One of the city's most prestigious retail outlets for porcelain, both artworks and plates, contains a glittering, intensely fashionable roster of the impeccably crafted porcelain of Richard Ginori. Founded in 1735, it offers porcelain, china, and glassware that's almost sure to spark the acquisitive interest of the grand bourgeois and their wannabes. Anything you buy here can be shipped, or—if you prefer to acquire your porcelain at Ginori's outlets in North America (which include Tiffany's in New York)—you can at least check out the dozens of patterns produced by Italy's most glamorous manufacturer. The outlet on Via de Tritone was established in 1912.

DEPARTMENT STORES

La Rinascente. Piazza Colonna, Via del Corso 189. ☎ **06/6797691.**

This upscale department store offers clothing, hosiery, perfume, cosmetics, and other goods. It also has its own line of clothing (Ellerre) for men, women, and children. This is the largest of the Italian department-store chains, and its name is seen frequently on billboards and newspaper ads throughout the country.

Standa. Corso Francia 124. ☎ **06/3338719.**

Standa could not be considered stylish by any stretch of the imagination, but some visitors find it enlightening to wander—just once—through the racks of department-store staples to see what an average Italian household might accumulate. Other branches are at Corso Trieste 200, Via Cola di Rienzo 173, Viale Regina Margherita 17, and Viale Trastevere 60.

DISCOUNT SHOPPING

Certain stores that can't move their merchandise at any price often consign their unwanted goods to discounters. In Italy, the original labels are usually still inside the garment (and you'll find some very chic labels strewn in with mounds of garments bearing less enviable names). Know in advance, however, that these garments couldn't be sold at higher prices in more glamorous shops, and some garments are either the wrong size, the wrong "look," or have a stylistic mistake.

Discount System. Via del Viminale 35. ☎ **06/4823917.**

Discount System sells men's and women's wear by many of the big names (Armani, Valentino, Nino Cerruti, Fendi, and Krizia). Even if an item isn't from a famous designer, it often comes from a factory that produces some of the best quality Italian fashion. But don't give up hope: If you find something you like, it will be priced at around 50% of its original price tag in its original boutique, and it just might be a cut-rate gem well worth your effort.

FASHION

See also "Department Stores," "Discount Shopping," "Leather," "Lingerie," and "Shoes."

FOR MEN

Angelo. Via Bissolati 34. ☎ **06/4741796.**

Angelo is a custom tailor for discerning men and has been featured in such publications as *Esquire* and *GQ.* He employs the best cutters and craftspeople, and his taste in style and design is impeccable. Custom shirts, suits, dinner jackets, even casual wear, can be made on short notice. A suit, for instance, takes about 8 days. If you haven't time to wait, Angelo will ship anywhere in the world.

✪ **Emporio Armani.** Via del Babuino 119. ☎ **06/36002197.**

This store stocks relatively inexpensive menswear crafted by the couturier who has dressed perhaps more stage and screen stars than any other designer in Italy. The designer's more expensive line—sold at sometimes staggering prices that are nonetheless up to 30% less than what you'd pay in the United States—is a short walk away at **Giorgio Armani,** Via Condotti 77 (☎ **06/6991460**).

Schostal. Via del Corso. ☎ **06/6791240.**

Dating to 1870, this is the clothing store for men who like their garments conservative and well crafted. Featuring everything from underwear to cashmere overcoats, the prices are more reasonable than you might think, and a devoted staff is both courteous and attentive.

Valentino. Via Condotti 13. ☎ **06/6783656.**

This is a swank emporium for the men's clothing of the acclaimed designer. Here, if you can afford the high prices, you can become the most fashionable man in town. Valentino's women's haute couture is sold around the corner in an even bigger showroom at Via Bocca di Leone 15 (☎ **06/6795862**).

FOR WOMEN

Benetton. Via Condotti 18. ☎ **06/6797982.**

Despite the gracefully arched ceiling and its prized location, this branch of the worldwide sportswear distributor charges about the same prices as branches at less glamorous addresses. Famous for woolen sweaters, tennis wear, blazers, controversial advertisements, and the kind of outfits you'd want to wear on a private yacht, this company has suffered (like every other clothier) from inexpensive copies of its designs. The original, however, is still best for guaranteed quality. Their men's line is also worth a look.

Gianfranco Ferré. Via Borgognona 42B. ☎ **06/6797445.**

Here you'll find the women's line by this famous designer whose clothes have been called "adventurous."

Givenchy. Via Borgognona 21. ☎ **06/6784058.**

This is the Roman headquarters of one of the great designer names of France, a company known since World War I for its couture. In its Roman branch, the company emphasizes stylish read-to-wear garments for women, appropriate for the warm Italian weather. Tasteful shirts and pullovers for men are featured also.

Max Mara. Via Frattina 48 (at Largo Goldoni). ☎ **06/6793638.**

Max Mara is one of the best outlets in Rome for women's clothing. The fabrics are appealing and the alterations are free.

✪ **Renato Balestra.** Via Sistina 67. ☎ **06/6795424.**

Rapidly approaching the stratospheric upper levels of Italian fashion is Renato Balestra, whose women's clothing exudes a lighthearted elegance. This branch carries a complete line of the latest Balestra ready-to-wear. The company's administrative headquarters and the center of its couture department is nearby, at Via Ludovici 35 (☎ **06/4821723**), although advance appointments are recommended. Stop in at the Via Sistina branch for an idea of the designer's style before launching yourself into a dialogue with Balestra's couture department, if only to save time.

FOR CHILDREN

Baby House. Via Cola di Rienzo 117. ☎ **06/3214291.**

Baby House offers what might be the most label-conscious collection of children's and young people's clothing in all of Italy. With an inventory of clothes suitable for children and adolescents to age 15, they sell clothing by Valentino, Bussardi, and Laura Biagiotti, whose threads are usually reserved for adult, rather than juvenile, playtime.

Benetton. Via Condotti 19. ☎ **06/6797982.**

Benetton isn't as expensive as you might expect. This store is the famous sportswear manufacturer's outlet for children's clothes (from infants to age 12). You can find rugby shirts, corduroys and jeans, and accessories in a wide selection of colors and styles.

The College. Via Vittoria 52. ☎ **06/6784036.**

The College has everything you'll need to make adorable children more adorable. Part of the inventory is reserved for adult men and women, but most is intended for their infant and early adolescent offspring. A vast women's line is also featured.

SPORTSWEAR
Oliver. Via del Babuino 61. ☎ **06/36001906.**

Specializing exclusively in sportswear for men and women, this is the least expensive line of clothing offered by normally wallet-denting designer Valentino. His easy-to-wear, stylish clothing has warm climates in mind. In summer, there's more emphasis on women's clothes (especially sportswear) than men's, but the rest of the year, the inventories are about equally divided between men's and women's clothing.

FOOD
✪ **Castroni.** Via Cola di Rienzo 196. ☎ **06/6874383.**

This place carries a bountiful array of unusual foodstuffs from throughout the Mediterranean. If you want herbs from Apulia, peperoncino oil, cheese from Val d'Aosta, or that strange brand of balsamic vinegar whose name you can never remember, Castroni will probably have it. Large, old-fashioned, and filled to the rafters with the abundance of agrarian Italy, it also carries certain foods considered exotic in Italy but commonplace in North America, such as taco shells and corn curls. Remember, there are restrictions against importing certain food products into North America, including prosciutto and fresh produce.

GIFTS
Anatriello Argenteria Anticae e Moderna Roma. Via Frattina 123. ☎ **06/6789601.**

This store is known for stocking an inventory of new and antique silver, some of it among the most unusual in Italy. All the new items are made by Italian silversmiths, in designs ranging from the whimsical to the severely formal and dignified. Also on display are antique pieces of silver from England, Germany, and Switzerland.

A. Grispigni. Via Francesco Crispi 59 (at Via Sistina). ☎ **06/6790290.**

Here you'll find a constantly changing array of gifts including a large assortment of leather-covered boxes, women's purses, compacts, desk sets, and cigarette cases.

HOME ACCESSORIES
Avignonese. Via Margutta 16. ☎ **06/3614004.**

This specialty shop can be counted on to come up with unusual and tasteful objects for the home. Each object, from lamps to terra-cotta boxes, is unique.

JEWELRY
Since the days when the ancient Romans imported amethysts and pearls from the distant borders of their empire, and when the great trading ships of Venice and Genoa carried rubies and sapphires from Asia, the Italians have collected jewelry. Styles range from the most classically conservative to neo-punk–rock frivolous, and part of the fun is shopping for something you might never before have considered wearing.

✪ **Bulgari.** Via Condotti 10. ☎ **06/6793876.**

Bulgari is the capital's most prestigious jeweler and has been since the 1890s. The shop window, on a conspicuously affluent stretch of Via Condotti, is a bit of a visual attraction in its own right. Bulgari designs combine classical Greek aesthetics with Italian taste. Over the years Bulgari has managed to follow changes in style as well as cling to tradition. Prices range from affordable to insane.

E. Fiore. Via Ludovisi 31. ☎ **06/4819296.**

This store near Via Veneto is as multifaceted as its jewels. You can select a stone and have it set according to your specifications; choose from a rich assortment of charms, bracelets, necklaces, rings, brooches, corals, pearls, cameos, watches, silverware, and goldware; or have Fiore expertly repair your own jewelry and watches. Closed in August.

✪ **Federico Buccellati.** Via Condotti 31. ☎ **06/6790329.**

At this, one of the best gold- and silversmiths in Italy, neo-Renaissance creations will change your thinking about gold and silver designs. You'll discover the Italian tradition and beauty of handmade jewelry and hollowware whose principles sometimes hark back to the designs of Renaissance gold master Benvenuto Cellini.

LEATHER

Italian leather is among the very best in the world, and at its best can attain buttersoft textures more pliable than cloth. You'll find hundreds of leather stores in Rome, many of them excellent.

Alfieri. Via del Corso 2. ☎ **06/3611976.**

With the exception of blatant erotica, you'll find virtually any leather garment imaginable in this richly stocked store. Established in the 1960s, with a somewhat more funky and counterculture slant than Casagrande or Campanile, Alfieri prides itself on leather jackets, boots, bags, belts, shirts, hats, and pants for men and women; shorts reminiscent of German lederhosen, and skirts that come in at least 10 different—sometimes neon-inspired—colors. Although everything sold is made in Italy, be aware that the virtue of this place involves reasonable prices rather than ultrahigh quality in every case. So although you'll definitely find whimsy, an amazingly wide selection, and affordable prices, check the stitching and operability of zippers, or whatever, before you invest.

Campanile. Via Condotti 58. ☎ **06/6783041.**

Belying the postmodern sleekness of its premises, this outfit has a pedigree going back to the 1870s, and an impressive inventory of well-crafted leather jackets, belts, shoes, bags, and suitcases for both men and women. Quality is relentlessly high (as are prices), and as such, the store might function as the focal point of your window-shopping energies along either side of Rome's most glamorous shopping street.

Cesare Diomedi Leather Goods. Via Vittorio Emanuele Orlando 96–97. ☎ **06/4884822.**

Located in front of the Grand Hotel, this store offers one of the most outstanding collections of leather goods in Rome. And leather isn't all you'll find in this small, two-story shop; many other distinctive items, such as small gold cigarette cases and jeweled umbrellas, make this a good stopping-off point for that last gift. Up the spiral staircase is a wide assortment of elegant leather luggage and accessories.

Fendi. Via Borgognona 36A–39. ☎ **06/6797641.**

The House of Fendi is mainly known for its leather goods, but it also has furs, stylish purses, ready-to-wear clothing, and a new men's line of clothing and accessories. Gift items, home furnishings, and sports accessories are also sold here, all emblazoned with an "F." Closed Saturday afternoon from July to September.

Gucci. Via Condotti 8. ☎ **06/6790405.**

Gucci, of course, is a legend. An established firm since 1900, it sells high-class leather goods, such as suitcases, handbags, wallets, shoes, and desk accessories. It also has departments complete with elegant men's and women's wear, including tailored shirts, blouses, and dresses, as well as ties and scarves of numerous designs. *La bella figura* is alive and well at Gucci, and prices have never been higher. Among the many temptations is Gucci's own perfume.

Pappagallo. Via Francesco Crispi 115. ☎ **06/6783011.**

This is a suede and leather factory; the staff at the "parrot" makes their own goods, including bags, wallets, and suede coats. The quality is fine, and the prices reasonable.

Saddlers Union. Via Condotti 26. ☎ **06/6798050.**

This is a great place to look for well-crafted leather accessories such as bags, belts, wallets, shoes, briefcases, and more.

LINGERIE
Brighenti. Via Frattina 7–8. ☎ **06/6791484.**

Brighenti sells strictly lingerie *di lusso,* or perhaps better phrased, *haute corseterie.* The shop is amid several famous neighbors on Via Frattina; you may run across a "seductive fantasy." Closed two weeks in August.

Princesse Tam-Tam. Via Frattina 72. ☎ **06/6792524.**

This is the exclusive distributor in Rome for a line of French women's undergarments that, considering their quality and style, and the store's location on one of the most spectacularly desirable shopping streets of Rome, are less expensive than you might think. Established by two style-conscious sisters from Madagascar, and known for the quality and comfort of the all-cotton undergarments that have contributed to more than two dozen outlets in France alone, the organization's inventory includes swimsuits, dressing gowns, brassieres, panties, slips and half-slips, and some of the most appealing women's pajamas in Italy. Some have touches of lace. Don't expect a blatant appeal to eroticism here—the venue is "relatively calm," in the words of one of the managers.

Tomassini di Luisa Romagnoli. Via Sistina 119. ☎ **06/4881909.**

Tomassini di Luisa Romagnoli offers delicately beautiful lingerie and negligees, all original designs of Luisa Romagnoli. Most of the merchandise sold here is of shimmery Italian silk; other items, to a lesser degree, are of fluffy cotton or frothy nylon. Highly revealing garments are sold either ready-to-wear or are custom-made.

Vanità. Via Frattina 70. ☎ **06/6791743.**

The lingerie selection here spans the spectrum. Yes, you can get black or white, but take the time to browse and you'll find underthings from over, under, and all around the rainbow, including hues you've never dreamed of.

MARKETS
Piles of fresh vegetables arranged above ancient pavements in the streaming Italian sunshine is a sight few foreign visitors can resist. Here's a rundown on the Roman markets known for the freshest produce, the most uninhibited merchants, and the longest-running traditions.

Campo de' Fiori. Piazza Campo de' Fiori. Bus: 46, 62, 64, or 116.

During the Renaissance this neighborhood contained most of the inns that pilgrims and merchants from other parts of Europe used for lodgings. Today its battered and slightly shabby perimeter surrounds about a hundred merchants who arrange their produce every day into artful tapestries of Italian bounty.

Mercato Andrea Doria. Via Andrea Doria. Metro: Ottaviano.

After a visit to this open-air festival, you'll never look at the frozen vegetable section in your local supermarket the same way. Set near the Vatican, on a large, sun-baked stretch of pavement between Via Tunisi and Via Santamaura, the merchandise includes meats, poultry, eggs, dairy products, wines, an endless assortment of *frutta e verdura* (fruits and vegetables), and even some scruffy-looking racks of second-hand clothing.

Mercato dei Fiori. Via Trionfale. Metro: Ottaviano.

Most of the week this vast covered market sells flowers only to retail florists, who resell them to consumers. Every Tuesday, however, the industrial-looking premises open to the public, who crowd in for access to exotic, Mediterranean flowers at bargain-basement prices. Open to the public Tuesday from 10:30am to 1pm.

Mercato delle Stampe. Largo della Fontanella di Borghese. Bus: 70, 87, 116, or 186.

Virtually everything that's displayed in the dozens of battered kiosks here is dog-eared and evocatively ragtag. You'll find copies of engravings, books, magazines from the 1960s (or before), and prints and engravings that are either worthless or worthwhile, depending on their provenance. If your passion is the printed word, this is your place, and bargaining for value is part of the experience.

Mercato di Testaccio. Piazza Testaccio. Metro: Piramide.

Because their stalls are covered from the wind, rain, and dust of the rest of Rome, the vendors here are able to retain an air of permanence about their set-ups that most outdoor markets simply can't provide. Inside you'll find fishmongers, butchers, cheese sellers, a wide array of dairy products, and the inevitable fruits and vegetables of the Italian harvest.

Mercato di Via Sannio. Via Sannio. Metro: San Giovanni in Laterano.

If you like street fairs loaded with items that verge on the junky, but which contain occasional nuggets of value or eccentric charm, this is the market for you. Regrettably, rare or unusual items are getting harder to find here, as every antiques dealer in Italy seems to have combed through the inventories long before your arrival. Despite that, you'll find some ragtag values in the endless racks of clothing that await cost-conscious buyers.

Piazza Vittorio Emanuele. South of Stazione Termini. Metro: Termini.

Near Santa Maria Maggiore, the largest open-air food market in Rome takes place Monday through Saturday at Piazza Vittorio Emanuele. For browsing Roman style, head here any time between 7am and noon. Most of the vendors at this gigantic square sell fresh fruit, vegetables, and other foodstuffs, although many stalls are devoted to such items as cutlery, clothing, and other merchandise. The place has little to tempt the serious shopper, but is recommended for the insights into Roman life it provides.

Porta Portese. Via Portuense and Via Ippolito Nievo. Bus: 170, 181, 280, 717, 719, 774, or 780.

This is the largest and most famous *mercato delle pulci* (flea market) in Rome, a Sunday-morning staple (since the end of World War II) that many Romans consider much, much more interesting and colorful than attending church. Vendors sell merchandise ranging from secondhand paintings of Madonnas (the Italian market is glutted with these) to termite-eaten wooden Il Duce medallions. There are also pseudo-Etruscan hairpins, bushels of rosaries, television sets that haven't transmitted an image since 1965, books printed early in the 19th century, and rack after rack of secondhand (or never-sold) clothing. Serious shoppers can often ferret out a good buy. By 10:30am the place is full of people, (vendors sometimes arrive before dawn to get a desirable place to set up shop). As you would at any street market, beware of pickpockets. It's open only on Sunday, from 7am to 1pm.

MOSAICS

✪ **Savelli**. Via Paolo VI 27. ☎ **06/68307017.**

This company specializes in the manufacture and sale of mosaics, an art form as old as the Roman Empire itself. Many of the objects in the company's gallery were inspired by ancient originals discovered in thousands of excavations throughout the Italian peninsula, including those at Pompeii and Ostia. Others, especially the floral designs, rely on the whim and creativity of the artists. Objects include tabletops, boxes, and vases. The cheapest mosaic objects begin at around $125, and are unsigned products crafted by students at a school for artists that is partially funded by the Vatican. Objects made in the Savelli workshops that are signed by the individual artists (and also tend to be larger and more elaborate) range from $500 to as much as $25,000. The outlet also contains a collection of small souvenir items such as keychains and carved statues.

RELIGIOUS ART & FASHION

Anna Maria Guadenzi. Piazza della Minerva 69A. ☎ **06/6790431.**

Set in a neighborhood loaded with purveyors of religious art and icons, this shop claims to be the oldest of its type in Rome. If you collect depictions of Mary, paintings of the saints, exotic rosaries, chalices, small statues, or medals, you can feel secure knowing that thousands of pilgrims have spent their money here before you. Whether you view this type of merchandise as devotional aid or bizarre kitsch, this shop has it all. Closed in August.

Gamarelli. Via Santa Chiara 34. ☎ **06/68801314.**

Few laypeople ever really think about how or where a clergyman might clothe himself for mass, but in the Eternal City, the problem is almost universal. If you're looking for a gift for your parish priest, or a nephew who has decided to take the vows, head to this store that's known as the "Armani" of the priestly garment biz. Established 200 years ago, it employs a battalion of embroiderers, usually devout Catholics in their own right, who wield needles and either purple, scarlet, or gold threads like the legendary swords of the Counter-Reformation. The inventories are so complete that priests, bishops, and cardinals from around the world consider the this a worthwhile stopover during their pilgrimages to Rome. The store does not stock any garments for nuns.

Offbeat Shopping

- **Avignonese,** Via Margutta 16 (☎ **06/3614004**), can be counted on to come up with unusual and tasteful objects for the home. Each object, from lamps to terra-cotta boxes, is unique.
- **Alinari,** Via d'Albert 16A (☎ **06/6792923**), takes its name from the famed Florentine photographer of the 19th century. Original prints of Alinari are almost as prized as paintings in national galleries, and record the Rome of a century ago.
- **Fava,** Via del Babuino 180 (☎ **06/3610807**), recaptures the era when Neapolitans sold 17th- and 18th-century pictures of the eruptions of Vesuvius, once highly sought by collectors. Many of these "volcanic paintings" of yesterday—so eagerly purchased by Brits in particular—can still cause a conflagration today.
- **Livio di Simone,** Via San Giacomo 23 (☎ **06/36001732**), carries unusual suitcases (in many shapes and sizes) into which hand-painted canvas has been sewn. Every one is chic and lovely.
- **Battistoni,** Via Condotti 61A (☎ **06/6786241**), sells the finest men's shirts in the world. Having said that, as Marlene Dietrich once noted, you don't need to sell the shop anymore. In addition, they hawk a men's cologne, called Marte (Mars), for the "man who likes to conquer."
- **Siragusa,** Via delle Carrozze 64 (☎ **06/6797085**), is more like a museum than a shop, specializing in unusual jewelry, based on ancient carved stones or archaeological pieces. Handmade chains, for example, often hold coins and beads discovered in Asia Minor that date from the 3rd to the 4th century B.C.

SHOES

Dominici. Via del Corso 14. ☎ **06/3610591.**

An understated facade a few steps from Piazza del Popolo shelters an amusing and lighthearted collection of men's and women's shoes in a rainbow variety of vivid colors. The style is aggressively young-at-heart, and the children's shoes are adorable.

Ferragamo. Via Condotti 73–74. ☎ **06/6798402.**

Ferragamo sells elegant and fabled footwear, plus ties, women's clothing, and accessories in an atmosphere full of Italian style. The name became famous in America when such silent-screen vamps as Pola Negri and Greta Garbo began appearing in Ferragamo shoes. There are always many customers waiting to enter the shop; management allows them to enter in small groups. (Wear comfortable shoes for what may well be a 30-minute wait.)

Fragiacomo. Via Condotti 35. ☎ **06/6798780.**

Here you can buy shoes for both men and women in a champagne-colored showroom with gilt-touched chairs and big display cases.

Lily of Florence. Via Lombardia 38 (off Via Vittorio Veneto). ☎ **06/4740262.**

This famous Florentine shoemaker now has a shop in Rome, with the same merchandise that made the outlet so well known in the Tuscan capital. Colors come in a wide range, the designs are stylish, and leather texture is of good quality. Shoes for both men and women are sold, and American sizes are a feature.

SILVER

Fornari & Fornari. Via Frattina 133. ☎ **06/6780105.**

In the mid-1990s one of Rome's most prestigious purveyors of silver and luxury goods was reconfigured after a family dispute forever altered the older and more distinguished format. This new manifestation lies a short walk from the old setting, in a two-story showroom filled with silver, lamps, porcelain, crystal, furniture, and upscale gift items from many different manufacturers throughout Italy and Europe. Virtually anything can be shipped to private homes or wedding receptions around the world. Closed in August.

SUITCASES

Livio di Simone. Via San Giacomo 23. ☎ **06/36001732.**

Unusual suitcases in many shapes and sizes, into which hand-painted canvas has been sewn, are sold here. This outlet has one of the most tasteful yet durable collections in Rome.

TOYS

La Città del Sole. Via della Scrofe 65. ☎ **06/6875404.**

Other than the branch in Milan, this is the largest and best stocked of any of the stores in its 40-member chain. It specializes in amusements for children and adults, with a wide range of toys and games that don't make beeping noises. Many of the games are configured in English, others in Italian, and include the raw materials for the kind of pastimes that a family or inmates of a college dorm could spend time pursuing. Examples include role-playing games, battlefield strategy games, family games, and children's games that will challenge a young person's gray matter and probably drive their parents crazy. Also for sale are such rainy-day distractions as miniature billiards tables and tabletop golf sets.

WINES & LIQUORS

Ai Monasteri. Piazza delle Cinque Lune 76. ☎ **06/68802783.**

Italy produces a staggering volume of wines, liqueurs, and after-dinner drinks, and here you'll find a treasure trove of selections—liquors (including liqueurs and wines), honey, and herbal teas made in monasteries and convents all over Italy. You can buy excellent chocolates and other candies here as well. The shop will ship some items home for you. In a quiet atmosphere, reminiscent of a monastery, you can choose your spirits as they move you. Just 2 blocks from Piazza Navona. Closed in August.

Buccone. Via Ripetta 19. ☎ **06/3612154.**

This is a historic wine shop, right near Piazza del Popolo. Its selection of wines and gastronomic specialties is among the finest in Rome.

Trimani. Via Goito 20. ☎ **06/4469661.**

Trimani, established in 1821, sells wines and spirits from Italy, among other offerings. Purchases can be shipped to your home. It collaborates with the Italian wine magazine *Gambero Rosso,* organizing some lectures about wine where devotees can improve their knowledge and educate their tastebuds.

Rome After Dark 9

When the sun goes down, lights across the city bathe palaces, ruins, fountains, and monuments in a theatrical white light. There are few evening activities as pleasurable as a stroll past the solemn pillars of old temples, or the cascading torrents of Renaissance fountains glowing under the blue-black sky.

Of these fountains, the **Naiads** (Piazza della Repubblica), the Tortoises (Piazza Mattei), and of course, the **Trevi** are particularly beautiful at night. The **Capitoline Hill** is magnificently lit after dark, with its measured Renaissance facades glowing like jewel boxes. Behind the **Senatorial Palace** is a fine view of the illuminated **Roman Forum.** If you're across the Tiber, **Piazza San Pietro** (in front of St. Peter's Basilica) is particularly impressive at night, when the tour buses and crowds have departed. And a combination of illuminated architecture, Renaissance fountains, sidewalk stage shows and art expos enliven **Piazza Navona.** If you're ambitious and have a good sense of direction, try exploring the streets west of Piazza Navona, which resemble a stage set when they're lit at night.

Even if you don't speak Italian, you can generally follow the listings of special events and evening entertainment featured in *La Repubblica,* one of the leading Italian newspapers. *TrovaRoma,* a special weekly entertainment supplement (good for the coming week) is published in this paper on Thursday. The mini-mags *Metropolitan* and *Wanted in Rome* have listings of jazz, rock, and such and give an interesting look at expat Rome. The daily *Il Messaggero* lists current cultural news, especially in its Thursday magazine supplement, *Metro.* And *Un Ospite a Roma,* available free from the concierge desks of top hotels, is full of details on what's happening.

1 The Performing Arts

MAJOR COMPANIES

Rome's premier cultural venue is the Teatro dell'Opera (see below), where standards may not be as high as at Milan's legendary La Scala, but where performances are stellar nevertheless. The outstanding local troupe is the **Rome Opera Ballet** (see below).

Rome doesn't have a major center for classical music concerts, although performances of the most important orchestra, the **RAI Symphony Orchestra,** most often take place at the RAI Auditorium as well as at the Academy of St. Cecilia (see below).

Rome is also a major stopover for international stars. Rock headliners often perform at **Stadio Flaminio, Foro Italico,** and at two different places in the EUR, the **Palazzo della Civiltà del Lavoro** and the **Palazzo dello Sport**. Most of the concerts are at the Palazzo dello Sport. Instead of trying to call these venues, contact a ticket agent, **Orbis,** Piazza Esquilino 37 (☎ **06/474-4776**), which will not only let you know what's happening in Rome at the time of your visit, but will also sell you a ticket to the performance. The Orbis box office is open Monday to Saturday from 9:30am to 1pm and 4 to 7:30pm.

CLASSICAL MUSIC

Academy of St. Cecilia. Via della Conciliazione 4. ☎ **06/68801044.** Tickets 25,000L–80,000L ($15–$46).

Concerts given by the orchestra of the Academy of St. Cecilia usually take place at Piazza di Villa Giulia, site of the Etruscan Museum, from the end of June to the end of July; in winter they're held in the academy's concert hall on Via della Conciliazione. Sometimes other addresses are selected for concerts, including a handful of historic churches. Performance nights are either Saturday, Sunday, Monday, or Tuesday. Friday nights feature chamber music.

Teatro Olimpico. Piazza Gentile da Fabriano. ☎ **06/3234890.** Tickets 20,000L–80,000L ($12–$46), depending on the event.

Large and well publicized, this echoing stage hosts a widely divergent collection of singers, both classical and pop, who perform according to a schedule that sometimes changes at the last minute. Occasionally the space is devoted to chamber orchestras or visits by foreign orchestras.

OPERA

Teatro dell'Opera. Piazza Beniamino Gigli 1. ☎ **06/481601.** Tickets 20,000L–260,000L ($12–$151).

If you're in the capital for the opera season—usually from the end of December until June—you may want to attend a performance at the historic Rome Opera House, located off Via Nazionale. Nothing is presented here in August; in summer, the venue usually switches elsewhere. Call ahead or ask your hotel concierge before you go.

BALLET & DANCE

Performances of the Rome Opera Ballet are given at the **Teatro dell'Opera** (see above). The regular repertoire of classical ballet is supplemented by performances of internationally acclaimed guest artists, and Rome is on the agenda for major troupes from around the world. Watch for announcements in the weekly entertainment guides to see what's happening at the time of your visit, and to check on other venues, including the Teatro Olimpico and open-air performances.

MUSICAL MENUS

Da Ciceruacchio. On Piazza dei Mercanti, at Via del Porto 1, in Trastevere. ☎ **06/5806046.** 40,000L–60,000L ($23–$35). Tues–Sun 8pm–midnight.

This restaurant was once a sunken jail—the ancient vine-covered walls date from the 18th century. Folkloric groups appear throughout the evening, especially singers of Neapolitan songs, accompanied by guitars and harmonicas—a rich repertoire of old-time favorites, some with bawdy lyrics. There are charcoal-broiled steaks and chops along with lots of local wine, and bean soup is a specialty. The grilled mushrooms are another harmonious opening, as is the spaghetti with clams.

Da Meo Patacca. Piazza dei Mercanti 30, in Trastevere. ☎ **06/58331086.** Daily 8–11:30pm.

Da Meo Patacca would have pleased Barnum and Bailey. On a gaslit piazza from the Middle Ages, it serves bountiful self-styled "Roman country" meals to flocks of tourists. The atmosphere is one of extravaganza—primitive, colorful, and theatrical in a carnival sense—good fun if you're in the mood. Downstairs is a vast cellar with strolling musicians and singers. Many offerings are as adventurous as the décor (wild boar, wild hare, and quail), but you'll also find corn on the cob, pork and beans, thick-cut sirloins, and chicken on a spit. For 70,000L ($41) and up, you'll get fun and entertainment—not refined cuisine. In summer, you can dine at outdoor tables.

Fantasie di Trastevere. Via di Santa Dorotea 6. ☎ **06/5881671.** Cover (including the first drink) 35,000L ($20), 75,000L–90,000L ($44–$52) including dinner. Meals daily from 8pm; piano bar music 8:30–9:30pm; show 9:30–10:30pm.

Roman rusticity is combined with theatrical flair at Fantasie di Trastevere, the people's theater where the famous actor Petrolini made his debut. In the 16th century, this restaurant was an old theater built for Queen Cristina of Sweden and her court. The cuisine is bountiful, though hardly subtle. Such dishes as the classic saltimbocca (ham with veal) are preceded by tasty pasta, and everything is helped along by Castelli Romani wines. Accompanying the main dishes is a big basket of warm, country-coarse herb bread. Some two dozen folk singers and musicians in regional attire make it a festive affair.

2 The Club & Music Scene

NIGHTCLUBS

Alien. Via Vellertri 13–19. ☎ **06/8412212.** Cover (including the first drink) 30,000L–35,000L ($17–$20). Mon–Sun 11pm–4am.

In a setting devoted to celebrating hi-tech by means of futuristic rows of exposed pipes and ventilation ducts, you'll find a deliberately bizarre space-age view of future shock, bathed in strobe lights and techno music. Dull moments in any evening are punctuated with a cabaret-esque master or mistress of ceremonies with brief interludes of cabaret or comedy.

Alpheus. Via del Commercio 36. ☎ **06/5747826.** Cover 15,000L ($9) Fri–Sat. Tues–Sun 10:30pm–4am.

One of Rome's largest and most energetic nightclubs, Alpheus contains three sprawling rooms, each with a different musical sound and an ample number of bars. You'll find areas devoted to Latin music, to rock, and to jazz. Live bands come and go, and there's enough cultural variety in the crowd to keep virtually anyone amused throughout the course of the evening.

✪ **Arciliuto.** Piazza Monte Vecchio 5. ☎ **06/6879419.** Cover (including the first drink) 35,000L ($20), drinks 10,000L ($6). Mon–Sat 10pm–2am. Closed July 20–Sept 3.

This place reputedly once housed Raphael's studio, but now it is home to one of the most romantic candlelit spots in Rome. Guests listen to both a guitarist and a lutenist in an intimate setting. The evening's presentation also includes Neapolitan love songs, old Italian madrigals, even current hits from New York's Broadway or London's West End. Highly recommended, it's hard to find, but is within walking distance of Piazza Navona. From the west side of Piazza Navona, take Via di S. Agnese in Agone, which leads to Via di Tor Milliana, then follow this street into Piazza Monte Vecchio.

Rome Nightlife Alert

In addition to high charges (all nightclubs in Rome are expensive), many otherwise legitimate clubs have add-on expenses in the form of hookers plying their trade.

Another important warning: During the peak of summer tourism, usually in August, all nightclub proprietors seem to lock their doors and head for the seashore, where they operate alternate clubs. Some of them close at different times each year, so it's hard to keep up-to-date. Always have your hotel check to see whether a club is operating before you trek out to it.

Black Out. Via Saturnia 18. ☎ **06/70496791.** Cover (including the first drink) 10,000L ($6). Fri–Sat 1am–4am.

Counterculture, blasé, and clinging to musical models of London's punk-rock and Indie scenes, Black Out occupies an industrial-looking site. Occasionally a live band plays Fridays, otherwise various flavors of canned music reign. Regardless of the type of music playing, there's always one room (with an independent sound system) that functions as a lounge. This is one of the best sites in town for a view of counterculture alienation and rage as interpreted by modern Italian youth.

Club Picasso. Via Monte di Testaccio 63. ☎ **06/5742975.** No cover Tues–Thurs; 15,000L ($9) Fri–Sat (including the first drink). Tues–Sat 10pm–4am.

This high-energy dance spot attracts everyone from teeny-boppers to 50-year-olds—who remember some of the music as original to their college years—and lots of high-energy people-watchers in between. A strict bouncer at the door bars any potential rabble rousers.

Folkstudio. Via Frangipane 42. ☎ **06/4871063.** Tickets 10,000L–20,000L ($6–$12), plus a one-time membership fee of 5,000L ($3). Tues–Sun 9:30–11pm. Closed early July–late Sept.

Very little about this place has changed since its 1962 founding. It prides itself on a battered and well-used venue that resembles "an old underground cantina" from the earliest days of the hippie era. The PA system and lighting aren't very sophisticated, but the ambience is refreshing and fun, and the musical acts manage to draw some surprisingly likable performers of old-fashioned soul music, gospel, funk, and folk, as well as traditional Irish music. No drinks are served inside, as the place considers itself a concert hall rather than a nightclub, but several bars and cafes in the neighborhood sell bottles of beer and whisky in plastic cups to go, and no one at Folkstudio will object if you carry them in with you.

Gilda. Via Mario de' Fiori 97. ☎ **06/6784838.** Cover (including the first drink) 40,000L ($23); meals from 45,000L ($26). Disco: Tues–Sun midnight–4am; Restaurant and pizzeria: from 9:30pm.

Gilda is an adventurous combination of nightclub, disco, and restaurant known for its glamorous acts (past performances include Diana Ross and splashy Paris-type revues). The artistic direction assures first-class shows, a well-run restaurant (featuring international cuisine), and disco music played between the live acts. The disco presents music of the 1960s as well as modern recordings. The attractive piano bar, Swing, features Italian and Latin music.

Jackie O. Via Boncompagni 11. ☎ **06/42885457.** Cover (including the first drink) 40,000L ($23). Meals 50,000L ($29) without wine. Tues–Sun 10:30pm–4am.

Set close to Rome's American Embassy and the Via Veneto, this club sometimes succeeds at capturing the glittery flashiness of La Dolce Vita, as if the 1960s had never ended. Clientele tends to be well-dressed, affluent, and over 30. If you opt to go dancing in this serene atmosphere you begin your evening with a drink at the piano bar, and perhaps end it with a meal at the establishment's restaurant.

Magic Fly. Via Bassanello 15, Cassia-Grottarossa. ☎ **06/33268956.** Cover (including the first drink) 25,000L–30,000L ($15–$17). Wed–Sat 11pm–dawn.

Small-scale, and somewhat cramped when it really begins to rock, this club is more elegant than the norm, and lies about 3 miles to the northeast, outside the ring road that encircles the center of Rome. Music changes nightly; depending on the schedule you might hear anything from Latin salsa and merengue to American-style rock or British new wave. There's a posh feel throughout (enhanced by the many men in neckties). You'll need to take a taxi to get here.

Radio Londra. Via Monte Testaccio. No phone. Cover (including the first drink)15,000L ($9). Club: Wed–Mon 11:30am–4am; pub-pizzeria: Sun–Mon and Wed–Fri 9pm–3am, Sat 9pm–4am.

Radio Londra revels in the counterculture ambience of punk rock, inspired, as its name implies, by the chartreuse-haired, nose-pierced devotees common in London. Everyone here tries to look and act as freaky as possible. Since Radio Londra is near the popular gay L'Alibi (see below), the downstairs club attracts many brethren, although the crowd is mixed. Upstairs is a pub-pizzeria where bands often appear; you can even order a veggie burger with a Bud.

JAZZ, SOUL, & FUNK

Alexanderplatz. Via Ostia 9. ☎ **06/39742171.** Club membership (valid for 3 months) 12,000L ($7). Mon–Sat 9pm–2am, live music from 10:15pm.

At this leading jazz club, you can listen to the music or enjoy the good kitchen which serves everything from pesto alla genovese to gnocchi alla romana to Japanese cuisine.

✪ **Big Mama.** Vicolo San Francesco a Ripa 18. ☎ **06/5812551.** Cover 20,000L–30,000L ($12–$17) for big acts (free for minor shows), plus 10,000L–20,000L ($6–$12) for a 30-day or 1-year membership. Mon–Sat 9pm–1:30am. Closed July–Sept.

Big Mama is a hangout for jazz and blues musicians where you're likely to meet the up-and-coming jazz stars of tomorrow, and sometimes even the big names.

Fonclea. Via Crescenzio 82A. ☎ **06/6896302.** No cover Sun–Thurs; 10,000L ($6) Fri–Sat. Sun–Thurs 7pm–2am; Fri–Sat 7pm–3:30am. Closed July–Aug.

Fonclea offers live music every night—jazz, Dixieland, rock, rhythm and blues, and funk. This is basically a cellar jazz establishment that attracts a wide spectrum of Roman life. There's also a restaurant that features grilled meats, salads, and crêpes. Meals start at 35,000L ($21); if you want dinner it's best to reserve a table. Music usually starts at 9:15pm and lasts till about 12:30am.

✪ **Music Inn.** Largo dei Fiorentini 3. ☎ **06/68802220.** Cover 15,000L ($9). Thurs–Sun 8pm–2am. Closed July–Aug.

The Music Inn is among the leading jazz clubs of Rome. Some of the biggest names in jazz, both European and American, have performed here.

Notorious. Via San Nicolà de Tolentino 22. ☎ **06/4746888.** Cover 40,000L ($23). Tues–Sat 11pm–4am

Notorious really isn't. It's one of the most popular discos in the city, and the music is always recorded. Some of the most beautiful people of Rome show up in these crowded confines, often in their best disco finery. But show up late—it's more fashionable.

Saint Louis Music City. Via del Cardello 13A. ☎ **06/4745076.** Cover (including club membership) 7,000L ($4.05). Tues–Sun 9pm–2am.

This is another leading jazz venue. In large, contemporary surroundings, Saint Louis Music City features young and sometimes very talented newcomers rather than the big, better established names in jazz. Many celebrities have been known to patronize the place. Soul and funk music are performed on occasion. You can also enjoy meals at a restaurant on the premises, which cost 35,000L ($20) and up.

GAY & LESBIAN CLUBS

Angelo Azzuro. Via Cardinal Merry del Val 13. ☎ **06/5800472.** Cover (including the first drink) 10,000L ($6) Fri and Sun; 20,000L ($12) Sat. Fri–Sun 11pm–4am.

Angelo Azzuro is a gay "hot spot," deep in the heart of Trastevere. No food is served, nor is there live music. Friday is for women only.

✪ **The Hangar.** Via in Selci 69. ☎ **06/4881397.** No cover. Wed–Mon 10:30pm–2:30am. Closed 3 weeks in August.

Established in 1984 by an expatriate, Louisiana-born American, John, and his Italian partner, Gianni, this is the premier gay bar in Rome. It's set on one of Rome's oldest streets, adjacent to the Roman Forum in the house on the site of the palace inhabited by the emperor Claudius's deranged wife, Messalina. (Her ghost is rumored to inhabit the premises.) Each of the establishment's two bars has its own independent sound system.

Women are welcome any night except Monday, when videos and entertainment for gay men are featured. The busiest nights are Saturday, Sunday, and Monday, when as many as 500 patrons cram inside.

Joli Coeur. Via Sirte 5. ☎ **06/86216240.** Cover (including the first drink) 20,000L ($12). Sat–Sun 10:30pm–2am.

This bar caters to lesbians; and Saturdays are reserved for women only. A fixture in the city's lesbian nighttime scene, it also attracts women from around Europe. Information about Joli Coeur ("Pretty Heart") can be had by contacting The Hangar (see above), as Joli Coeur can be difficult to reach directly.

L'Alibi. Via Monte Testaccio 44. ☎ **06/5743448.** Cover 20,000L ($12). Wed–Sun 11pm–5am.

L'Alibi, in the Testaccio sector, away from the heart of Rome, is a year-round venue on many a gay man's agenda. The crowd, however, tends to be mixed: Roman and international, straight and gay, male and female. One room is devoted to dancing.

3 The Cafe & Bar Scene

It seems there's nothing Romans like better than sitting and talking over their favorite beverage—usually wine or coffee. So it's not surprising that there are a variety of places in which you, too, can enjoy these pleasures.

CAFES
ON VIA VENETO

Back in the 1950s—a decade that *Time* magazine gave to Rome, in the way it conceded the 1960s to London—**Via Vittorio Veneto** rose in fame and influence as the choicest street in Rome, crowded with aspiring and actual movie stars, their directors, and a fast-rising group composed of card-carrying members of the so-called jet set. Today the *bella gente* (beautiful people), movie stars, and directors wouldn't be caught

Neighborhood Nightlife

Testaccio may be radical chic personified, but it's also a 'hood with an edge (you don't want to wander around here alone at night.) However, Testaccio is *the* place to find out what's hot in Rome—ask around.

---

dead on Via Veneto—the street has moved into the mainstream of world tourism. Nevertheless, you may want to spend some time there.

✪ **Caffè de Paris.** Via Vittorio Veneto 90. ☎ **06/4885284.** Thurs–Tues 8am–1am.

Caffè de Paris rises and falls in popularity, depending on the decade. In the 1950s it was a haven for the fashionable; it's now a popular restaurant in summer where you can occupy a counter seat along a bar or a table inside. However, if the weather's right, the tables spill right out onto the sidewalk and the passing crowd walks through the maze.

Harry's Bar. Via Vittorio Veneto 50. ☎ **06/484643.**

Harry's Bar is a perennial favorite. Every major Italian city seems to have one, and Rome is no exception. This haunt of the IBF—International Bar Flies—at the top of Via Veneto is elegant, chic, and sophisticated. In summer, sidewalk tables are placed outside. For those who wish to dine outdoors, but want to avoid the scorching Roman sun, a new air-conditioned sidewalk cafe is open from May to November. Meals inside cost about double what you'd pay outside. In back is a small dining room, which serves some of the finest food in central Rome; meals go for 90,000L to 100,000L ($52 to $58). The restaurant inside is open Monday to Saturday from 12:30 to 3pm and 7:30pm to 1am; outside, you can eat from noon to midnight. The bar is open from 11am to 2am; closed Sunday and from August 1 to 10. The Piano Bar is open nightly from 11pm.

ON PIAZZA DEL POPOLO

This piazza is haunted with memories. According to legend, the ashes of Nero were enshrined here, until 11th-century residents began complaining to the pope about his imperial ghost. The Egyptian obelisk seen here today dates from the 13th century B.C., removed from Heliopolis to Rome during the reign of Augustus (it originally stood at the Circus Maximus). The present piazza was designed in the early 19th century by Valadier, Napoléon's architect. Two almost-twin baroque churches stand on the square, overseeing the never-ending traffic.

✪ **Café Rosati.** Piazza del Popolo 5A. ☎ **06/3225859.** Daily noon–11pm.

Café Rosati, which has been around since 1923, attracts guys and dolls of all persuasions who drive up in Maseratis and Porsches. It's really a combination of sidewalk cafe, ice-cream parlor, candy store, confectionery, and ristorante that has been swept up in the fickle world of fashion. The later you go, the more interesting the action.

Canova Café. Piazza del Popolo 16. ☎ **06/3612231.** Meals 20,000L ($12). Restaurant: daily noon–3:30pm and 7–11pm; bar: daily 7am–midnight or 1am.

Although the management has filled the interior of this cafe with boutiques selling expensive gift items, including luggage and cigarette lighters, many Romans still consider this the place to be on Piazza del Popolo. The Canova has a sidewalk terrace for people-watching, plus a snack bar, a restaurant, and a wine shop inside. In summer you'll have access to a quiet courtyard whose walls are covered with ivy and where flowers grow in terra-cotta planters.

Night & Day. 50 Via Dell'Oca. ☎ **06/3202300.** No cover. Drinks 5,000L ($2.90) Daily 5pm–5am.

It sounds like an old Cole Porter song, but it's actually one of the most patronized Irish pubs in the vicinity of Piazza de Popolo—it doesn't really get hot until 2am, when many dance clubs close for the evening. American music is played as you down your Harps and Guinness. Amazingly, foreigners are issued drink cards, making all their drinks 5,000L ($2.90) instead of the 8,000L ($4.65) usually charged. A young man in his 20s, who introduces himself only as "Simone," is your host and often works behind the bar himself.

IN TRASTEVERE

Just as Piazza del Popolo lured the chic crowd from Via Vittorio Veneto, several cafes in Trastevere, across the Tiber, threaten to do the same to Popolo. Fans who saw Fellini's *Roma* know what Piazza di Santa Maria in Trastevere looks like. The square—filled with milling throngs in summer—is graced with an octagonal fountain and a church dating from the 12th century. On the piazza, despite a certain amount of traffic, children run and play, and there's occasional guitar playing when the weather's good.

Café-Bar di Marzio. Piazza di Santa Maria in Trastevere 15. ☎ **06/5816095.** Tues–Sat 7am–2am.

This warmly inviting place, which is strictly a cafe (not a restaurant), has both indoor and outdoor tables at the edge of the square with the best view of its famous fountain.

NEAR THE PANTHEON

Despite the allures of Trastevere, many visitors to the Eternal City now view Piazza della Rotonda, at the Pantheon, as the "living room" of Rome. It's much easier to get to, and unlike somewhat remote Trastevere, there always seem to be taxis available. The neighborhood around the Pantheon (which many visitors consider their favorite building anywhere in Europe) is especially popular on a summer night.

✪ **Caffè Sant'Eustachio.** Piazza Sant'Eustachio 82. ☎ **06/6861309.** Tues–Fri and Sun 8:30am–1am; Sat 8:30am–1:30am.

Strongly brewed coffee is one of the elixirs of Italy, and many Romans will go out of their way for what they consider a superior brew. One of the most talked-about espresso shops, Sant'Eustachio, is on a small square near the Pantheon, where the city water supply comes from a source outside Rome that the emperor Augustus funneled in with an aqueduct in 19 B.C. Rome's most experienced judges of espresso claim that the water plays an important part in the coffee's flavor, although steam forced through ground Brazilian coffee roasted on the premises has an effect as well. Purchase a ticket from the cashier for as many cups of coffee as you want, and leave a small tip of 200L (10¢) for the person behind the counter when your receipt is presented.

✪ **Di Rienzo.** Piazza della Rotonda 8–9. ☎ **06/6869097.** Daily 7am–1 or 2am.

This is the most desirable cafe on this piazza; in fair weather you can sit at one of the sidewalk tables (if you can find one free). In cooler weather, you can retreat inside, where the walls are inlaid with the type of marble found on the Pantheon's floor. Many types of pastas appear on the menu, as does risotto alla pescatora (fisherman's rice) and several meat courses. You can also order pizzas.

ON THE CORSO

Autogrill. Via del Corso 181. ☎ **06/6789135.** Daily 7am–10pm.

Autogrill is a monumental cafe that's often filled with busy shoppers. On the premises you'll find just about every kind of dining facility a hurried resident of Rome could want. There's a stand-up sandwich bar with dozens of selections, and a cafeteria, both self-serve, and a sit-down area. The decor includes high coffered ceilings, baroque wall stencils, globe lights, crystal chandeliers, and black stone floors.

NEAR THE SPANISH STEPS

✪ **Antico Caffè Greco.** Via Condotti 84. ☎ **06/679-1700.** Mon–Sat 8am–9pm, closed 10 days in Aug.

Since 1760 Antico Caffè Greco has been the poshest and most fashionable coffee bar in Rome—previous sippers have included Stendhal, Goethe, D'Annunzio, and Keats. Today, although you're more likely to see American tourists, there's still plenty of atmosphere. In the front is a wooden bar, and beyond that a series of small salons with marble-topped tables of Napoleonic design. The waiters' black tailcoats nicely complement the backdrops of gold or red damask, romantic paintings, and antique mirrors. The house-specialty drink, paradisi, is made with lemon and orange.

NEAR PIAZZA NAVONA

Bar della Pace. Via della Pace 3–5. ☎ **06/6861216.** Tues–Sun 11am–2:30am.

Bar della Pace, located near Piazza Navona, has elegant neighbors, such as Santa Maria della Pace, a church with sybils by Raphael and a cloister designed by Bramante. The bar dates from the beginning of this century, and is decorated with wood, marble, and mirrors.

WINE BARS

✪ **Enoteca Fratelli Roffi Isabelli.** Via della Croce 76B. ☎ **06/6790896.**

Wine has played a prominent role in Roman life since the word bacchanalian was first invented (and that was very early indeed). One of the best places to taste the wines of Italy is at the Enoteca Fratelli Roffi Isabelli. A stand-up drink in these darkly antique confines is the perfect ending to a visit to the nearby Spanish Steps. Set behind an discrete facade in a chic shopping district, this is the city's best repository for Italian wines, brandies, and grappa. You can opt for a postage-stamp–sized table in back, or stay at the bar with its impressive display of wines stacked on shelves in every available corner.

IRISH PUBS

The two most popular Irish pubs in Rome draw mostly English-speaking expatriates. You can always see a cluster of disoriented local teenagers here and there, but their Italian is drowned in the sea of English, Scottish, Irish, Canadian, Australian, and sometimes American accents. If you want to mingle with people who speak your language, try one of these places. Both near Piazza di Santa Maria Maggiore, they may be a little difficult to find, but once you've found one, someone will direct you, or even walk with you, to the other.

Druid's Den. Via San Martino ai Monti 28. ☎ **06/4880258.** Daily 5pm–12:30am.

At the popular Druid's Den you can enjoy a pint of beer for 7,500L ($4.35), while listening to Irish music. One night we saw a group of young Irishmen dancing an Irish jig, much to the delight of the Roman lookers-on. The "den" is near Piazza di Santa Maria Maggiore and the train station.

Fiddler's Elbow. Via dell'Olmata 43. ☎ **06/4872110.** Daily 4:30pm–12:30am.

Fiddler's Elbow, near Piazza di Santa Maria Maggiore and the railway station, is reputedly the oldest pub in the capital. Sometimes, however, the place is so packed you can't find room to drink.

4 Movies

Pasquino Cinema. Vicolo del Piede 19, just off Piazza di Santa Maria in Trastevere. ☎ **06/5803622.**

Just off the corner of Piazza Santa Maria in Trastevere, the little Pasquino draws a faithful coterie of English-speaking fans, including Italians and expatriates. The average film—usually of recent vintage or a classic—costs 12,000L ($7). Most are in their original language (usually English) with Italian subtitles. There are three theaters with screenings daily as well as a bookshop, a cafe, and a video bar. New ownership and renovations in 1998 have expanded the facility—they now offer a cafe and video bar featuring many independent titles.

Side Trips from Rome

Most European capitals are ringed with a number of worthwhile attractions, but for sheer variety Rome tops them all. Just a few miles away, you can go back to the dawn of Italian history and explore the dank tombs the Etruscans left as their legacy or drink the golden wine of the towns in the Alban Hills (Castelli Romani). You can wander the ruins of Hadrian's Villa, the "queen of villas of the ancient world," or be lulled by the music of the baroque fountains in the Villa d'Este. You can turn yourself bronze on the beaches of Ostia di Lido or explore the remarkable ruins of Ostia Antica, Rome's ancient seaport.

Unless you're rushed beyond reason, allow at least 3 days to take a look at the attractions in the environs. We've highlighted the best of the lot below.

1 Tivoli

20 miles E of Rome

An ancient town, Tivoli's origins predate those of Rome itself. At the height of the empire, "Tibur," as it was called, was a favorite retreat for the rich. Horace, Catullus, Sallust, Maecenas, and a few emperors (notably Hadrian) maintained lavish villas here near the woods and waterfalls. It was popular enough to warrant a Roman road, Via Tiburtina, whose modern descendant funnels trucks and tour buses into today's Tivoli. During the Middle Ages Tivoli achieved a form of independence, which was to last through its rise in fortunes during the Renaissance. This latter period saw real-estate investment by several of the wealthier princes of the church, especially Cardinal Ippolito d'Este. By the late 19th century Tivoli had been incorporated into the new kingdom of Italy, and its former privileges of independence passed into history.

ESSENTIALS

GETTING THERE   Take Metro Linea B to the end of the line, the Rebibbia station. After exiting the station, catch an Acotral bus the rest of the 30-minute ride to Tivoli. Generally buses depart about every 20 minutes and cost 10,000L ($6) each.

By Car   Expect about an hour's drive with traffic on Via Tiburtina.

VISITOR INFORMATION For tourist information, check with **Azienda Autonoma di Turismo,** Largo Garibaldi (☎ **0774/334522).** Open Monday to Saturday from 9am to 6pm and on Sunday from 9am to 2pm.

EXPLORING THE TOWN

✪ **Hadrian's Villa (Villa Adriana).** Via di Villa Adriana. ☎ **0774/530203.** Admission 8,000L ($4.65) adults, free for children 17 and under. Daily 9am–sunset (about 6:30pm Apr–Oct, 4pm Nov–Mar). Closed Christmas Day, New Year's Day, and May Day. Bus: 2 or 4 from Tivoli.

Less than 4 miles from Tivoli, Hadrian built one of the greatest estates ever erected in the world, seeking to re-create some of the architectural wonders that had impressed him most on his many travels.

A patron of the arts, a lover of beauty, and even something of an architect, Hadrian did not wish merely to replicate rooms or even palaces he'd seen: rather he reconstructed entire valleys complete with the temples that had made them famous. The result was a self-contained world, (including a representation of hell) replete with theaters, baths, temples, fountains, gardens, and statuary-bordered canals; and fit for a vast royal entourage and the hundreds of servants and guards necessary to feed, bathe, and entertain them.

For a glimpse of what the villa used to be, see the plastic reconstruction at the entrance, as well as those in the little museum near the visitor center. Then, following the arrows, look in particular for the **Marine Theater** (ruins of the round structure with Ionic pillars); the **Great Baths,** with some intact mosaics; and the **Canopus,** with a group of *caryatids* (fully-draped, sculpted female figures used for support in the place of a column or pilaster) whose images are reflected in the pond, as well as a statue of Mars. For a closer look at some of the items excavated, you can visit the 2nd museum on the premises.

✪ **Villa d'Este.** Piazza Trento, Viale delle Centro Fontane. ☎ **0774/312070.** Admission 8,000L ($4.65) adults when the water jets are set at full power, 5,000L ($2.90) adults at other times; free for children 17 and under and for seniors 60 and over.

Like Hadrian centuries before, Cardinal Ippolito d'Este of Ferrara believed in heaven on earth, and in the mid-16th century he ordered this villa built on a hillside. The dank Renaissance structure, with its second-rate paintings, is hardly worth the trek from Rome, but the gardens below—designed by Pirro Ligorio—dim the luster of Versailles.

While descending a cypress-studded slope, visitors are greeted with everything from lilies to gargoyles spouting water, torrential streams, and waterfalls. The loveliest fountain is the *Fontana del'Ovato* designed by Pirro Ligorio. But nearby is the most spectacular achievement—the **hydraulic organ fountain,** dazzling with its water jets in front of a baroque chapel, with four tipsy-looking maidens. The work represents the genius of Frenchman Claude Veanard.

The moss-covered **Fountain of Dragons,** also by Ligorio, and the so-called **Fountain of Glass** by Bernini, are the most intriguing. The best walk is along the promenade, which has 100 spraying fountains. The garden, filled with rhododendron, is worth hours of exploration, but you'll need frequent rest periods after those steep climbs.

Villa Gregoriana. Largo Sant'Angelo. No phone. Admission 2,500L ($1.45) adults, 1,000L (60¢) children 11 and under. Daily: May–Aug 10am–7:30pm; Sept 9:30am–6:30pm; Oct–Mar 9:30am–4:30pm; Apr 9:30am–6pm. The bus from Rome stops near the entrance.

Side Trips from Rome

Viterbo ❶ ❷ ↗   ↖ ❸
Vignanello

A1

S2
Vetralla
Lago di Vico
Caprarola

Blera
Ronciglione
Cívita Castellana
Poggio Mirteto

Monti Sabatin

S2
Campagnano di Roma

S493
Lago di Bracciano
Bracciano   Anquillara

S3

A1 dir.   Monterotondo
S4   Mentana

↖
❹
E80

❺
❻ **Cerveteri**

A1

G.R.A.

Tivoli ❾
S5   ❿ ⓫ ⓬

A24

Palestrina ⓭

Fregene
A12   **S1**

ROME

A1 dir.
❿ **Frascati**

Fiumicino

E80   **S7**
Ostia Antica   **Marino**   ⓯
❼   ⓰ **Rocca di Papa**   **A1**
❽   ⓱ **Castel Gandolfo**
Lido di Ostia   **148**   ⓲ **Nemi**

Pomezia

Velletri

S601
Ardea   Aprília

Cisterna di Latina

Tyrrhenian Sea

S207

Latina

Nettuno   **S156**
Anzio

Legend
Airport ✈

E-0369

ITALY
ROME ★

Bagnaia ❷
Bomarzo ❸
Castel Gandolfo ⓱
Cerveteri ❻
Frascati ⓮
Hadrian's Villa (Villa Adriana) ❿
Lido di Ostia ❽
Marino ⓯
Necropolis of Cerveteri ❺

Nemi ⓲
Ostia Antica ❼
Palestrina ⓭
Rocca di Papa ⓰
Tarquinia ❹
Tivoli ❾
Villa d'Este ⓫
Villa Gregoriana ⓬
Viterbo ❶

Villa d'Este dazzles with artificial glamour, but Villa Gregoriana relies more on nature. The gardens were built by Pope Gregory XVI in the 19th century. At one point on the circuitous walk carved along a slope, you can stand and look out onto the most panoramic waterfall (Aniene) at Tivoli. The trek to the bottom on the banks of the Anio is studded with grottoes and balconies that open onto the chasm. The only problem is that if you do make the full journey, you may need a helicopter to pull you up again (the climb back is fierce). From one of the belvederes there's a panoramic view of the Temple of Vesta on the hill.

WHERE TO DINE

Albergo Ristorante Adriano. Via di Villa Adriana 194. ☎ **0774/535028.** Main courses 14,000L–32,000L ($8–$19); fixed-price menu 75,000L ($44). AE, DC, MC, V. Mon–Sat 12:30–2:30pm and 8–10pm, Sun 12:30–2:30pm. Bus: 2 or 4 from Tivoli. ITALIAN.

In a stucco-sided villa a few steps from the ticket office sits an idyllic stop either before or after you visit Hadrian's Villa. It offers terrace dining under plane trees or indoor dining in a high-ceilinged room with terra-cotta walls, neoclassical moldings, and white Corinthian pilasters. The food is home-style cooking, and the menu includes roast lamb, saltimbocca (veal cooked with ham), a variety of veal dishes, deviled chicken, salads and cheeses, and simple desserts—everything homemade. They're especially proud of their homemade pastas.

Le Cinque Statue. Via Quintillio Varo 8. ☎ **0774/335366.** Reservations recommended. Main courses 12,000L–25,000L ($7–$15). AE, DC, MC, V. Sat–Thurs 12:30–3pm and 7:30–10pm. Closed Aug 15–30. The Acotral bus from Rome stops nearby. ROMAN.

This restaurant takes its name from the quintet of old carved statues (like Apollo Belvedere and gladiators) decorating the place. Today this comfortable restaurant is maintained by a hardworking Italian family who prepares an honest, unpretentious cuisine. Everything is accompanied by the wines of the hill towns of Rome. Begin with a pastiche of mushrooms or make a selection from the excellent antipasto. Try the rigatoni with fresh herbs, tripe fried Roman style, or mixed fry of brains and vegetables. All the pasta is freshly made. They also have a wide array of ice creams and fruits.

2 Palestrina

24 miles E of Rome

Like Tibur, ancient Preneste (as Palestrina was called) was a superb holiday spot. It was the favorite of Horace and Pliny, and even Hadrian, who maintained a villa here.

ESSENTIALS

GETTING THERE   Buses leave every 30 to 45 minutes during the day from Rome; departures are from Via Castro Pretorio (take the Metro to the stop at Castro Pretorio to catch the bus). It takes about an hour to reach Palestrina and costs about 2,500L ($1.50).

By Car   Take either Via Prenestina (much less trafficked than Via Tiburtina), or the autostrada (A2) and get off at Valmontana; the latter route is much quicker.

EXPLORING THE TOWN

If you go out of Rome through the Porta Maggiore and travel on Via Prenestina for about 24 miles, you'll eventually come to Palestrina, a medieval hillside town that overlooks a wide valley.

When U.S. airmen flew over in World War II and bombed part of the town, they never imagined their actions would launch Palestrina as an important tourist attraction. After the debris was cleared, a pagan temple (once one of the greatest in the world) emerged: the **Fortuna Primigenia,** rebuilt in the days of the empire but dating from centuries before.

Palestrina predates the founding of Rome by several hundred years. It resisted conquest by the early Romans, and later took the wrong side in the civil war between Marius and Sulla. When Sulla won, he razed every stone in the city except the Temple of Fortune and then built a military barracks on the site. Later, as a favorite vacation spot for the emperors and their entourages, it sheltered some of the most luxurious villas of the Roman Empire. Its most famous child was Pier Luigi da Palestrina, recognized as the father of polyphonic harmony.

The Colonna-Barberini Palace. Palazzo Barberini. ☎ **06/4814591.** Admission 8,000L ($4.65) adults, free for children 17. Tues–Sun 9am to 1 hour before sunset. Follow the signs from the center to the top of the town.

High on a hill overlooking the valley, today the palace houses Roman statuary found in the ruins, plus Etruscan artifacts such as urns the equal of those in Rome's Villa Giulia. But worth the trip itself is the **Nile Mosaic,** a well-preserved ancient Roman work, and the most remarkable ever uncovered. The mosaic details the flooding of the Nile, a shepherd's hunt, mummies, ibises, and Roman warriors, among other things.

In Palestrina you'll also find a **Duomo** dating from 1100, with a mostly intact bell tower. It rests on the foundation of a much earlier pagan temple.

WHERE TO STAY & DINE

Albergo Ristorante Stella (Restaurant Coccia). Piazza della Liberazione 3, Palestrina, 00036 Roma. ☎ **06/9538172.** Fax 06/957-3360. 29 units. A/C TV TEL. 100,000L ($58) double; 160,000L ($93) suite. AE, DC, V. Free parking.

A buff-colored contemporary hotel and restaurant, the Stella is in the commercial district of town on a cobblestone square filled with parked cars, trees, and a small fountain. Although it was renovated in 1995, the bedrooms remain rather basic, but comfortable. The simple lobby is filled with warm colors and contains curved leather couches and autographed photos of local sports heroes.

The sunny restaurant serves a zesty Roman cuisine. Meals start at 40,000L ($24). There's a small bar where you might have an aperitif. The bar and restaurant are open daily from noon to 3pm and 7 to 9pm.

3 The Castelli Romani & Their Wines

For the Roman emperor and the wealthy cardinal in the heyday of the Renaissance, the **Castelli Romani (Roman Castles)** exerted a powerful lure, and they still do. The Castelli aren't castles but hill towns—many of them with an ancient history. The wines from the Alban Hills will add a little *feu de joie* to your life.

The ideal way to explore the hill towns is by car. But you can get a limited review by taking one of the buses (costing 2,000L ($1.20) that leaves every 20 minutes from Rome's Subaugusta stop on Metro Linea A.

MARINO

Marino, the closest to Rome (only 15 miles away), is about 4½ miles off Via Appia Nuova, quite near Ciampino Airport. Much of Marino's original charm has fallen victim to modern builders, but the town is still the place to go each October during the grape harvest. Check with the Rome tourist office for the actual dates, as they vary from year to year. At that time the town's fountains are switched from water to wine and everyone drinks for free.

ROCCA DI PAPA

This, the most attractive of the hill towns, lies only some 6 miles from Marino. By car the best route is 217 to the junction with 218, where you make a left turn. Before the intersection, you'll be high on a ridge above Lake Albano—the views of the lake, the far woods, and the papal palace of Castel Gandolfo on the opposite mountain are superb. Just before Rocca di Papa is the entrance to the toll road to Monte Cavo. A temple of Jove once stood on top of this mountain, and before that, the tribes of the area met with King Tarquin (the Proud) before Rome was a republic. At the top of the mountain is one of the most dramatic panoramic views in the hill towns, giving you a wide survey of the Alban Hills and the Castelli Romani. Down below, Rocca di Papa is a tangle of old streets and churches. A legend of dubious origin claims that Hannibal once camped just below the town in a wooded hollow.

NEMI

The Romans flock to **Nemi** in droves, particularly from April to June, for the succulent **strawberries** of the district—acclaimed by some gourmets as Europe's finest. In May, there's a strawberry festival. Nemi was also known to the ancients. A temple to the huntress Diana was erected on **Lake Nemi,** which was said to be her "looking glass."

EXPLORING THE TOWN

Looking from any of the balconies in Nemi, you'll see what looks like an airplane hangar in the valley right by the lakeshore. This unprepossessing building has the important-sounding name of **Ship Museum (Museo delle Navi),** Via di Diana 15 (☎ 06/9398040), and until World War II it held the remains of two luxurious barges that floated in the lake during Caligula's reign. The boats, fitted out lavishly with bronze and marble, were sunk during Claudius's reign (he succeeded the insane Caligula) and were entirely forgotten until Mussolini drained the lake in the 1930s. Then the barges were found, set up in a lakeside museum, and remained as a wonder of ancient Rome until the Nazis burned them during their retreat. Today the museum houses models of the ships and some of the metal and mosaic bits that survived the fire. Admission is 4,000L ($2.30) for adults, free for children 17 and under. It's open April to September daily from 9am to 6:30pm; October to March daily 9am to 1:30pm. To reach the museum, unless you're driving, you have to walk from the center of Nemi toward the lake.

WHERE TO DINE

✪ **Ristorante Il Castagnone.** in the Diana Park Hotel, Via Nemorense 44. ☎ **06/9364041.** Reservations recommended. Main courses 16,000L–35,000L ($9–$20). AE, DC, MC, V. Daily noon–3pm and 8–10pm. ROMAN/SEAFOOD.

This well-managed dining room of the town's best hotel takes definite pride in a Roman-based cuisine featuring seafood above meat. Attentive formal service is usually delivered with a kind of gentle humor. Amid neoclassical accessories and marble, you can order delectable veal, chicken, beef, and fish dishes such as fried calamari, spaghetti with shellfish in garlicky tomato-based sauce, and roasted lamb with potatoes and Mediterranean herbs. As you dine, expect a sweeping view from the restaurant's windows of the lake.

EN ROUTE TO CASTEL GANDOLFO

The road to Gandolfo leads us through a few "worth a visit" towns on the way. **Genzano,** on the other side of Lake Nemi, has views of the countryside and a 17th-century palace that belonged to the Sforza-Cesarini.

Ariccia is an ancient town that sent representatives to meet with Tarquin the Proud on top of Monte Cavo 2,500 years ago. After many centuries of changing hands, especially between medieval and Renaissance families, it has taken on a suburban look. The palace in the middle of town is still private and belongs to the Chigi family.

Albano practically adjoins Castel Gandolfo. It has a long history—this is the reputed site of Alba Longa, the so-called mother city of Rome, but it's quite built up and modern today. Trains going to Albano leave from Stazione Termini in Rome.

CASTEL GANDOLFO

Now we come to the summer residence of the pope. The papal palace, a 17th-century edifice designed by Carlo Maderno, stands practically on the foundations of another equally regal summer residence, the villa of the emperor Domitian. Unfortunately, the palace, the gardens, and the adjoining Villa Barberini can't be visited. You'll have to content yourself with a visit to Piazza della Libertà, the piazza out front with its church, Chiesa di San Tomaso di Villanova, and fountain by Bernini.

If you're here for lunch, as many are, your best bet is **Antico Ristorante Pagnanelli,** via Gramsci 4 (☎ **06/9360004**), which serves both regional and Italian national dishes, with meals starting at 45,000L ($26), with a high of 80,000L ($47) for the fresh seafood dishes. The restaurant is closed Tuesday.

FRASCATI

Lying 13 miles southeast of Rome, on Via Tuscolana, this is the best known of the hill towns. Some 1,073 feet above sea level, Frascati is celebrated for its **white wines.** Golden vineyards cover the surrounding northern slopes of the outer crater ring of the Alban Hills. From its lofty perch you'll see a panoramic view of the countryside and the other small towns.

ESSENTIALS

GETTING THERE   You can take an Acotral bus from the Anagnina station at the end of Metro Linea A in Rome. From there, take the Blue Cotral bus to Frascati; it takes 45 minutes and costs 2,000L ($1.20) each way. Remember that the transportation system in Italy is in a constant state of flux, so check your route at the station.

By Car   From the ring road around Rome (its southeast section), motorists head southeast along Route 215.

VISITOR INFORMATION   Tourist information is available at **Azienda di Soggiorno e Turismo,** at Piazza Marconi 1 (☎ **06/9420331**). Open April to October, Monday to Friday from 8am to 2pm and 3:30 to 6:40pm and on Saturday from 8am to 2pm.

WHAT TO SEE & DO: WINE TASTING, RENAISSANCE GARDENS, & ANCIENT RUINS

Although bottles of Frascati wine are exported—and served in many of the restaurants and trattorie of Rome—tradition holds that the wine is best near the golden vineyards from which it comes. To test this theory, head for **Cantina Comandini,**

Via E. Filiberto 1 (☎ **06/9420915**), right off Piazza Roma. Here, the Comandini family welcomes you to the tavern in which they sell Frascati wine from their own vineyards. A liter costs 6,000L ($3.50), a glass 1,500L (85¢). This is not a restaurant, but you can buy a sandwich to eat with your wine. The tavern is open Monday to Saturday from 4 to 8pm. Reservations are recommended.

For a less inebriating experience, stand in the heart of Frascati, at Piazza Marconi, to see the most important of the estates: **Villa Aldobrandini,** Via Massala. The finishing touches to this 16th-century villa were added by Maderno, who designed the facade of St. Peter's in Rome, but you can visit only the gardens. Still, with its grottoes, yew hedges, statuary, and splashing fountains it makes for an exciting outing. The gardens are open daily 9am to 1pm and 3 to 5pm, but you must go to the **Azienda di Soggiorno e Turismo,** Piazza Marconi 1 (☎ **06/9420331**), to ask for a free pass. The office is open Monday to Friday 8am to 2pm and 3:30 to 6:40pm and Saturday 8am to 2pm.

If you have a car, you can continue past the Villa Aldobrandini to **Tuscolo,** about 3 miles beyond the villa. An ancient spot with the ruins of an amphitheater dating from about the 1st century B.C., Tuscolo offers what may be one of Italy's most panoramic views.

WHERE TO DINE

Cacciani Restaurant. Via Armando Diaz 13. ☎ **06/9420378.** Reservations required on weekends. Main courses 19,000L–32,000L ($11–$19). AE, DC, MC, V. Tues–Sun 12:30–3pm and 7:30–10:30pm. Closed Jan 7–19 and Aug 18–27. ROMAN.

Cacciani is the choicest restaurant in Frascati, where the competition has always been tough. A modern restaurant in the town center, it boasts a terrace commanding a view of the valley. The kitchen is exposed to the public, and it's fun just to watch the women wash the sand off the spinach (well, at least it's more fun than doing it yourself). To get you started, we recommend the pasta specialties, such as fettuccine or rigatoni alla vaccinara (oxtail in tomato sauce). For a main course, the baby lamb with a sauce of white wine and vinegar is always reliable. There is, of course, a large choice of wines, which are kept in a cave under the restaurant. If you call ahead, the Cacciani family will arrange a combined visit to several of Frascati's wine-producing villas along with a memorable meal at their restaurant.

4 Ostia

16 miles SW of Rome

Ostia was the port of ancient Rome and a city in its own right. The currents and uneven bottom of the Tiber prevented Mediterranean shipping from going farther upstream, so merchandise was transferred to barges for the remainder of the trip. Ostia's fate was tied closely to that of the empire. At the peak of Rome's power, the city had 100,000 inhabitants—hard to imagine looking at today's ruins. Ostia was important enough to have had a theater (still standing in reconstructed form), numerous temples and baths, great patrician houses, and a large business complex. Successive emperors, notably Claudius and Trajan, enlarged and improved the facilities, but by Constantine's time (4th century A.D.), the worm had turned. The barbarian sieges of Rome in the 5th century spelled the end of Ostia.

Without the empire to trade with and Rome to sell to, the port quickly withered, reverting in a few centuries to a malarial swamp without a trace of Roman civilization. The excavations, still only partial, were started by the papacy in the 19th century, but the really substantial work took place between 1938 and 1942 under the Mussolini government.

Today **Ostia Antica** is one of the area's major attractions, particularly of interest to those who can't make it to Pompeii.

ESSENTIALS

GETTING THERE   Take Metro Linea B from the Stazione Termini to the Magliana stop. Change there for the Lido train to Ostia Antica, about 16 miles from Rome. Departures are about every half hour, and the trip takes only 20 minutes. The Metro lets you off across the highway that connects Rome with the coast. From here it's just a short walk to the ruins.

By Car   Drive out Via Ostiense heading for Route 8 (signposted LIDO DI ROMA OSTIA).

EXPLORING THE RUINS & THE BEACH

If, having paid your respects to Ancient Rome, you're craving the 20th century, reboard the Metro to visit the beach, **Lido di Ostia.** Italy may be a strongly Catholic country, but the Romans don't allow religious conservatism to affect their bathing attire. This is the beach where the denizens of the capital frolic on the seashore and at times create a merry carnival atmosphere, with dance halls, cinemas, and pizzerias. The Lido is set off best at Castelfusano, against a backdrop of pine woods. This stretch of shoreline is referred to as the Roman Riviera.

✪   **Rome's Ancient Seaport (Ostia Antica).** Viale dei Romagnoli 717. ☎ **06/56358099.** Admission 8,000L ($4.65) adults, free for children 18 and under. Apr–Sept daily 9am–7pm; Oct–Mar daily 9am–sunset. Metro: Ostia Antica Line Roma-Ostia-Lido.

A thriving, prosperous city developed, full of temples, baths, theaters, and patrician homes. Ostia Antica flourished for about 8 centuries before it began to wither away. Gradually it became little more than a malaria bed, a buried ghost city that faded into history. Although a papal-sponsored commission launched a series of digs in the 19th century, the major work of unearthing was carried out under Mussolini's orders from 1938 to 1942 (the work had to stop because of the war). The city is only partially dug out today, but it's believed that all the chief monuments have been uncovered.

The principal monuments are clearly labeled. The most important spot in all the ruins is **Piazzale delle Corporazioni,** an early version of Wall Street. Near the theater, this square contained nearly 75 corporations, the nature of their businesses identified by the patterns of preserved mosaics.

Greek dramas were performed at the **ancient theater,** built sometime in the early days of the empire. The classics are still aired here in summer (check with the tourist office for specific listings), but the theater as it looks today is the result of much rebuilding. Every town the size of Ostia had a forum, and during the excavations a number of pillars of the ancient Ostia Forum were uncovered. At one end is a 2nd-century B.C. temple honoring a trio of gods—Minerva, Jupiter, and Juno (little more than the basic foundation remains). In addition, there's a well-lit museum in the enclave that displays Roman statuary along with some Pompeii-like frescoes. There are perfect picnic spots beside fallen columns or near old temple walls.

5 Fregene

24 miles N of Rome

The fame of this coastal city north of the Tiber dates back to the 1600s when the land belonged to the Rospigliosi, a powerful Roman family. Pope Clement IX, a member of that wealthy family, planted a forest of pine that extends along the shoreline for 2½ miles and stands half a mile deep to protect the land from the strong winds of the Mediterranean. Today the wall of pines makes a dramatic backdrop for the golden sands and luxurious villas of the resort. If you'd like to sample an Italian beach, head here instead of to the more polluted beaches along Ostia's Lido.

ESSENTIALS

GETTING THERE You can catch the Fregene bus, which leaves from the Lepanto Metro stop in Rome and carries passengers to the center of Fregene. A ticket costs 4,800L ($2.90) and travel time is 1 hour.

By Car Follow Autostrada 1 (also known as Via Aurelia Malagrotta) heading west, crossing over the bypass that encircles Rome. After Castello di Guido, 14 miles west of Central Rome, exit onto the secondary road marked MACCARESE-FREGENE Then continue southwest for another 10 miles, following the signs to Fregene. There is no tourist information office.

WHERE TO STAY & DINE

La Conchiglia. Lungomare di Ponente 4, Fregene, 00050 Roma. ☎ **06/6685385.** Fax 06/668-5385. 36 units. A/C MINIBAR TV TEL. 160,000L–180,000L ($93–$104) double. Rates include breakfast. AE, DC, MC, V.

La Conchiglia means "The Shellfish"—an appropriate name for this hotel and restaurant right on the beach with views of the water and the pines. Built in 1934, the hotel features a circular lounge with built-in curving wall banquettes facing a cylindrical fireplace with a raised hearth. A resort aura is created by the large green plants. The bar in the cocktail lounge, which faces the terrace, is also circular. The guest rooms are comfortable and well furnished.

It's also possible to stop by just for a meal, and the food is good. Try, for example, spaghetti with lobster and grilled fish or one of many excellent meat dishes. Meals start at 50,000L ($29). The restaurant is in the garden and open daily from 1 to 3pm and 8 to 10pm.

6 Cerveteri & Tarquinia

As Livy's Trojans landed in ancient Italy, so did the Etruscans. Who were they? We still don't know, and the many inscriptions they left behind—mostly on graves—are no help since the Etruscan language has not been completely deciphered. We deduce the date of their arrival on the west coast of Umbria at around 800 B.C.

Two former strongholds of the Etruscans can be visited today, Cerveteri and Tarquinia. (For Etruscan museums in Rome, see the Vatican's Etruscan Museum and the Etruscan Museum of the Villa Giulia, both in chapter 6.)

CERVETERI

28 miles NW of Rome

Cerveteri is older than Rome and stands on the site of a major Etruscan stronghold called Caere. If you drive here, you'll pass through the rolling hills of the Roman countryside, and eventually see the city's medieval walls up in the hills on your right. To the left are the modern towers of Ladispoli, a rapidly growing seaside town.

ESSENTIALS

GETTING THERE   The best way to reach Cerveteri is by car. Head out Via Aurelia, northwest of Rome, for a distance of 28 miles.

By Bus   Take Metro Linea A in Rome to the Lepanto stop. From Via Lepanto, you can catch an Acotral coach to Cerveteri (☎ **06/3244724**); the trip takes about an hour and costs 4,900L ($2.85). Once at Cerveteri, it's a 1¼-mile walk to the necropolis—just follow the signs.

EXPLORING THE TOWN

As you walk through the Etruscan Museum in Rome (Villa Giulia), you'll often see the word Caere written under a figure vase or a sarcophagus. This is a reference to the nearby town known today as Cerveteri, one of the great Etruscan cities of Italy, whose origins may go as far back as the 9th century B.C.

Of course, the Etruscan town has long since faded, but not the **Necropolis of Cerveteri** (☎ **06/9940001**). The effect is eerie; Cerveteri is often called a "city of the dead." When you go beneath some of the mounds, you'll discover the most striking feature of the necropolis—the tombs are like rooms in Etruscan homes. The main burial ground is called the **Necropolis of Banditacca.** Of the graves thus far uncovered, none is finer than the **Tomba Bella** (sometimes called the Reliefs' Tomb), the burial ground of the Matuna family. Articles such as utensils and even house pets were painted in stucco relief. Presumably these paintings were representations of items the dead family would need in the world beyond. The necropolis is open May to September, Tuesday to Sunday from 9am to 6pm; October to April, Tuesday to Sunday from 9am to 3:30pm. Admission is 8,000L ($4.65).

Relics from the necropolis are displayed at the **Museo Nazionale Cerite,** Piazza Santa Maria Maggiore (☎ **06/9941354**). The museum is housed within the ancient walls and crenellations of Ruspoldi Castle. It's open Tuesday to Sunday from 9am to 7pm. Admission is free.

TARQUINIA
60 miles NW of Rome

An even more striking museum is at Tarquinia, near Civitavecchia, which was the port of Rome in the days of Trajan. Tarquinia is commandingly situated atop a rocky cliff with a view of the sea. It's medieval in appearance, with its fortifications and nearly two dozen towers.

ESSENTIALS

GETTING THERE   As for public transportation, the train is the preferred choice; a *diretto* train from the Stazione Termini in Rome takes 50 minutes and costs 9,800L ($6).

By Bus   Eight buses a day leave from the Via Lepanto Metro stop in Rome for the 2-hour trip to the neighboring town, Barriera San Giusto, which is 1½ miles from Tarquinia. The cost is 4,900L ($2.95). Bus schedules are available by calling ☎ **0766/856384.**

By Car   Take Via Aurelia outside Rome and continue on the autostrada toward Civitavecchia. Bypass Civitavecchia and continue another 13 miles north until you see the exit signs for Tarquinia.

VISITOR INFORMATION Tourist information is available at the tourist office at Piazza Cavour (☎ **0766/856036**), 1½ miles from Tarquinia. It's open Monday to Friday from 8am to 2pm and 4 to 7pm.

EXPLORING THE TOWN

If you wish to see tombs even more striking and more recently excavated than those at Cerveteri, go to Tarquinia where the medieval turrets and fortifications seem to contradict the Etruscan name of Tarquinia. Actually, Tarquinia is the adopted name of the old medieval community of Corneto, in honor of the major Etruscan city that once stood nearby. The main attraction in the town is the ✪ **Tarquinia National Museum,** Piazza Cavour (☎ **0776/856036**), which is devoted to Etruscan exhibits and sarcophagi excavated from the necropolis a few miles away. The museum is housed in the Palazzo Vitelleschi, a Gothic palace that dates from the mid-15th century. Among the exhibits are gold jewelry, black vases with carved and painted bucolic scenes, and sarcophagi decorated with carvings of animals and relief figures of priests and military leaders. But the biggest attraction is in itself worth the ride from Rome—the almost life-size pair of winged horses from the pediment of a Tarquinian temple. The finish is worn here and there, and the terra-cotta color shows through, but the relief stands as one of the greatest Etruscan masterpieces ever discovered. The museum is open Tuesday to Sunday from 9am to 7pm, and admission is 8,000L ($4.65).

A 5,000L ($2.90) ticket admits you to the ✪ **Etruscan Necropolis** (☎ **0766/856308**), covering more than 2½ miles of rough terrain near where the ancient Etruscan city once stood. Thousands of tombs have been discovered, some of which haven't yet been explored. Others, of course, were discovered by looters, but many treasures remain. The paintings on the walls of the tombs have helped historians reconstruct the life of the Etruscans. Many of the paintings—in vivid colors mixed from iron oxide, lapis lazuli dust, and charcoal—depict feasting couples and convey an earthy, vigorous, sex-oriented life among the wealthy Etruscans. The tombs are generally open Tuesday to Sunday from 9am to an hour before sunset (to 2pm November to March). You can reach the grave sites by taking a bus from the Barriera San Giusto to the Cimitero stop. Or try the 20-minute walk from the museum. Inquire at the museum for directions.

7 Viterbo

61 miles N of Rome

The 2,000 years that have gone into the creation of the city of Viterbo make it one of the most interesting day trips from Rome. While it traces its history back to the Etruscans, the bulk of its historical architecture dates from the Middle Ages and the Renaissance, when the city was a residence—and hideout—for the popes. The old section of the city is still surrounded by the thick stone walls that once protected the inhabitants from papal (or antipapal, depending on the situation at the time) attacks.

ESSENTIALS

GETTING THERE From Rome take Metro Linea A to Flaminio. At the Flaminio station, follow the signs pointing to Roma Nord station. Once there, purchase a combined rail and bus ticket to Viterbo, costing 7,000L ($4.05) one-way. The train takes you to Saxa Rubra in just 15 minutes. At Saxa Rubra, take an Acotral bus for the 1½-hour trip to Viterbo. Especially if you're trying to see Viterbo on a day trip, it might be worth the extra money to take a taxi from Saxa Rubra the remainder of the way. Call ☎ **0761/3328333** for transportation information.

By Car   Take Autostrada 2 north to the Orte exit.

VISITOR INFORMATION   Tourist information is at Piazzale dei Caduti 16 (☎ **0761/304795**). Open Monday to Saturday from 8am to 2pm.

WHAT TO SEE & DO

The only way to see Viterbo properly is to wander through the narrow cobblestone streets of the medieval town, pausing in front of the antiquity-rich structures. **Piazza del Plebiscito,** dominated by the 15th-century town hall, impresses with the fine state of preservation of Viterbo's old buildings. The courtyard and fountain in front of the town hall and the 13th-century governor's palace are favorite meeting places for townsfolk and visitors alike.

Just down Via San Lorenzo is **Piazza San Lorenzo,** the site of Viterbo's cathedral, which sits atop the former Etruscan acropolis. The **Duomo,** dating from 1192, is a composite of architectures, from its pagan foundations to its Renaissance facade to its Gothic bell tower. Next door is the 13th-century **Palazzo Papale,** built as a residence for the pope, but also serving as a hideout when the pope was in exile. It was the site of three papal elections. The exterior staircase and the colonnaded loggia combine to make up one of the finest examples of civil Roman architecture from the Gothic period.

The finest example of medieval architecture in Viterbo is the **San Pellegrino Quarter,** reached from Piazza San Lorenzo by a short walk past Piazza della Morte. This quarter, inhabited by working-class Viterboans, is a maze of narrow streets, arched walkways, towers, steep stairways, and ornamental fountains.

Worth a special visit is the **Convent of Santa Maria della Verità,** dating from 1100. The church contains 15th-century frescoes by Lorenzo da Viterbo, student of Piero della Francesca.

Park of the Monsters (Parco dei Mostri). Villa delle Meraviglie, Bomarzo. ☎ **0761/924029.** Admission 15,000L ($9) adults, 13,000L ($8) children 6 and under. Daily 8am–dusk. Bus: 6 from Piazza Martiri d'Ungheria in Viterbo.

About 8 miles east of Bagnaia at Bomarzo lies the Park of the Monsters. Prince Vicino Orsini had it built in a deep valley that's overlooked by the Orsini Palace and the houses of the village. On the other side of the valley are stone cliffs. Prince Orsini's park, Bosco Sacro (Sacred Wood), is filled with grotesque figures carved from natural rock. Nature and art have created a surrealistic fantasy; the Mouth of Hell (an ogre's face so big that people can walk into its gaping mouth), a crude Hercules slaying an Amazon, nymphs with butterfly wings, a huge tortoise with a statue on its shell, a harpy, a mermaid, snarling dogs, lions, and much, much more.

✪ **Villa Lante.** Bagnaia. ☎ **0761/288008.** Admission (30-minute garden tour) 6,000L ($3.50). May–Aug, Tues–Sun 9am–7:30pm; Mar–Apr and Sept–Oct, Tues–Sun 9am–5:30pm; Nov–Feb, Tues–Sun 9am–4pm. Bus: 6 from Viterbo.

The English author Sacheverell Sitwell called Villa Lante, located in Bagnaia, a suburb of Viterbo, "the most beautiful garden in Italy." Water from Monte Cimino flows down to the fountains of the villa, running from terrace to terrace until it reaches the central pool of the regal garden, with statues, stone banisters, and shrubbery. Two symmetrical Renaissance palaces make up the villa. The estate is now partly a public park, which is open during the day. The gardens that adjoin the villa, however, can only be visited on a guided tour. (The gatekeeper at the guard house will show you through, usually with a group that has assembled.) The interiors of the twin mansions can't be visited.

Appendix

A Basic Vocabulary

English	Italian	Pronunciation
Thank you	Grazie	graht-tzee-yey
Please	Per favore	*pehr* fah-*vohr*-eh
Yes	Si	see
No	No	noh
Good morning *or* **Good day**	Buongiorno	bwohn-*djor*-or-noh
Good evening	Buona sera	*bwohn*-ah say-rah
Good night	Buona notte	*bwohn*-ah *noht*-tay
How are you?	Come sta?	*koh*-may *stah*
Very well	Molto bene	*mohl*-toh *behn*-ney
Goodbye	Arrivederci	ahr-ree-vah-*dehr*-chee
Excuse me (to get attention)	Scusi	*skoo*-zee
Excuse me (to get past someone on the bus)	Permesso	pehr-*mehs*-soh
Where is? . . .	Dov'è? . . .	doh-*vey*? . . .
the station	la stazione	lah stat-tzee-*oh*-neh
a hotel	un albergo	oon ahl-*behr*-goh
a restaurant	un ristorante	oon reest-ohr-*ahnt*-eh
the bathroom	il bagno	eel *bahn*-nyoh
To the right	A destra	ah *dehy*-stra
To the left	A sinistra	ah see-*nees*-tra
Straight ahead	Avanti (*or* sempre diritto)	ahv-vahn-tee (*sehm*-preh dee *reet*-toh)
How much is it?	Quanto costa?	*kwan*-toh *coh*-sta?

The check, please	Il conto,	eel kon-toh
	per favore	*pehr* fah-*vohr*-eh
When?	Quando?	*kwan*-doh
Yesterday	Ieri	ee-*yehr*-ree
Today	Oggi	*oh*-jee
Tomorrow	Domani	doh-*mah*-nee
Breakfast	Prima colazione	*pree*-mah coh-laht-tzee-*ohn*-ay
Lunch	Pranzo	*prahn*-zoh
Dinner	Cena	*chay*-nah
What time is it?	Che ore sono?	kay *or*-ay *soh*-noh
Monday	Lunedì	loo-nay-*dee*
Tuesday	Martedì	mart-ay-*dee*
Wednesday	Mercoledì	mehr-cohl-ay-*dee*
Thursday	Giovedì	joh-vay-*dee*
Friday	Venerdì	ven-nehr-*dee*
Saturday	Sabato	*sah*-bah-toh
Sunday	Domenica	doh-*mehn*-nee-kah

NUMBERS

1	**uno** (*oo*-noh)	22	**venti due** (*vehn*-tee *doo*-ay)
2	**due** (*doo*-ay)	30	**trenta** (*trayn*-tah)
3	**tre** (tray)	40	**quaranta** (kwah-*rahn*-tah)
4	**quattro** (*kwah*-troh)	50	**cinquanta** (cheen-*kwan*-tah)
5	**cinque** (*cheen*-kway)	60	**sessanta** (sehs-*sahn*-tah)
6	**sei** (say)	70	**settanta** (seht-*tahn*-tah)
7	**sette** (*set*-tay)	80	**ottanta** (oht-*tahn*-tah)
8	**otto** (*oh*-toh)	90	**novanta** (noh-*vahnt*-tah)
9	**nove** (*noh*-vay)	100	**cento** (*chen*-toh)
10	**dieci** (dee-*ay*-chee)	1,000	**mille** (*mee*-lay)
11	**undici** (*oon*-dee-chee)	5,000	**cinque milla** (*cheen*-kway
20	**venti** (*vehn*-tee)		*mee*-lah)
21	**ventuno** (vehn-*toon*-oh)	10,000	**dieci milla** (dee-*ay*-chee *mee*-lah)

B Italian Menu Savvy

Abbacchio   roast haunch or shoulder of lamb baked and served in a casserole and sometimes flavored with anchovies.

Agnolotti   a crescent-shaped pasta shell stuffed with a mixture of chopped meat, spices, vegetables, and cheese; when prepared in rectangular versions, the same combination of ingredients is identified as ravioli.

Amaretti   crunchy, very sweet, almond-flavored macaroons.

Anguilla alla veneziana   eel cooked in sauce made from tuna and lemon.

Antipasto   succulent tidbits served at the beginning of a meal (before the pasta), whose ingredients might include slices of cured meats, seafood (especially shellfish), and cooked and seasoned vegetables.

Aragosta   lobster.

Arrosto   roasted meat.

Baccalà   dried and salted codfish.

Bagna cauda   hot and well-seasoned sauce, heavily flavored with anchovies, designed for dipping raw vegetables; literally translated as "hot bath."

Bistecca alla fiorentina Florentine-style steaks, coated before grilling with olive oil, pepper, lemon juice, salt, and parsley.

Bocconcini veal layered with ham and cheese, and fried.

Bollito misto assorted boiled meats served on a single platter.

Braciola pork chop.

Bresaola air-dried spiced beef.

Bruschetta toasted bread, heavily slathered with olive oil and garlic and often topped with tomatoes.

Bucatini hollow, coarsely textured spaghetti.

Busecca alla milanese tripe (beef intestines) flavored with herbs and vegetables.

Cacciucco ali livornese seafood stew.

Calzone pizza dough rolled with the chef's choice of sausage, tomatoes, cheese, etc., then baked into a kind of savory turnover.

Cannelloni tubular dough stuffed with meat, cheese, or vegetables, then baked in a creamy white sauce.

Cappellacci alla ferrarese pasta stuffed with pumpkin.

Cappelletti small ravioli ("little hats") stuffed with meat or cheese.

Carciofi artichokes.

Carpaccio thin slices of raw cured beef, sometimes in a piquant sauce.

Cassatta alla siciliana a richly caloric dessert combining layers of sponge cake, sweetened ricotta cheese, and candied fruit, bound together with an icing of chocolate buttercream.

Cervello al burro nero brains in black-butter sauce.

Cima alla genovese baked filet of veal rolled into a tube-shaped package containing eggs, mushrooms, and sausage.

Coppa cured morsels of pork filet encased in sausage skins, served in slices.

Costoletta alla milanese veal cutlet dredged in breadcrumbs, fried, and sometimes flavored with cheese.

Cozze mussels.

Fagiole white beans.

Fave fava beans.

Fegato alla veneziana thinly sliced calves' liver fried with salt, pepper, and onions.

Focaccia ideally, concocted from potato-based dough left to rise slowly for several hours, then garnished with tomato sauce, garlic, basil, salt, and pepper drizzled with olive oil; similar to a high-pan, deep-dish pizza most popular in the deep south, especially Bari.

Fontina rich cows'-milk cheese.

Frittata Italian omelet.

fritto misto a deep-fried medley of whatever small fish, shellfish, and squid are available in the marketplace that day.

Frutti di mare seafood (literally, "fruits of the sea").

Fusilli spiral-shaped pasta.

Gelato (produzione propria) ice cream (homemade).

Gorgonzola one of the most famous blue-veined cheeses of Europe; strong, creamy, and aromatic.

Gnocchi dumplings usually made from potatoes (*gnocchi alla patate*) or from semolina (*gnocchi alla romana*), often stuffed with combinations of cheese, spinach, vegetables, or whatever combinations strike the chef's fancy.

Granita flavored ice, usually with lemon or coffee.

Insalata di frutti di mare seafood salad (usually including shrimp and squid) garnished with pickles, lemon, olives, and spices.

Involtini thinly sliced beef, veal, or pork, rolled, stuffed, and fried.

Minestrone a rich and savory vegetable soup usually sprinkled with grated parmesan cheese and studded with noodles.

Mortadella mild pork sausage, fashioned into large cylinders and served sliced; the original lunchmeat baloney (because its most famous center of production is Bologna).

Mozzarella a nonfermented cheese made from the fresh milk of a buffalo (or, if unavailable, from a cow), boiled and then kneaded into a rounded ball, served fresh.

Mozzarella con pomodori (*also* **caprese**) fresh tomatoes with fresh mozzarella, basil, pepper, and olive oil.

Nervetti a northern Italian antipasto concocted from chewy pieces of calves' foot or shin.

Osso buco beef or veal knuckle slowly braised until the cartilage is tender, and then served with a highly flavored sauce.

Pancetta herb-flavored pork belly, rolled into a cylinder and sliced—the Italian bacon.

Panettone sweet, yellow-colored bread baked in the form of a brioche.

Panna heavy cream.

Pansotti pasta stuffed with greens, herbs, and cheeses, usually served with a walnut sauce.

Pappardelle alle lepre pasta with rabbit sauce.

Parmigiano parmesan, a hard and salty yellow cheese usually grated over pastas and soups but also eaten alone; also known as *granna*.

Peperoni green, yellow, or red sweet peppers.

Pesci al cartoccio fish baked in a parchment envelope with onions, parsley, and herbs.

Pesto a flavorful green sauce concocted from basil leaves, cheese, garlic, marjoram, and (if available) pine kernels.

Piccata al marsala thin *escalope* of veal braised in a pungent sauce flavored with marsala wine.

Piselli al prosciutto peas with strips of ham.

Pizza specific varieties include: *capricciosa* (its ingredients depend on the whim of the chef and can vary widely depending on his or her culinary vision and the ingredients at hand), *margherita* (incorporates tomato sauce, cheese, fresh basil, and memories of the first queen of Italy, Marguerite di Savoia, in whose honor it was first concocted by a Neapolitan chef), *napoletana* (includes ham, capers, tomatoes, oregano, cheese, and the distinctive taste of anchovies), *quatro stagione* (translated as "four seasons" because of the array of fresh vegetables in it; it also contains ham and bacon), and *siciliana* (contains black olives, capers, and cheese).

Pizzaiola a process whereby something (usually a beefsteak) is covered in a tomato-and-oregano sauce.

Polenta thick porridge or mush made from cornmeal flour.

Polenta de uccelli assorted small birds roasted on a spit and served with polenta.

Polenta e coniglio rabbit stew served with polenta.

Polla alla cacciatore chicken with tomatoes and mushrooms cooked in wine.

Pollo all diavola highly spiced grilled chicken.

Ragù meat sauce.

Ricotta a soft and bland cheese made from cow's or sheep's milk.

Risotto   Italian rice.

Risotto alla milanese   rice with saffron and wine.

Salsa verde   "green sauce," made from capers, anchovies, lemon juice and/or vinegar, and parsley.

Saltimbocca   veal scallops layered with prosciutto and sage; the name literally translates as "jump in your mouth," a reference to its tart and savory flavor.

Salvia   sage.

Scaloppina alla Valdostana   *escalope* of veal stuffed with cheese and ham.

Scaloppine   thin slices of veal coated in flour and sautéed in butter.

Semifreddo   a frozen dessert; usually ice cream with sponge cake.

Seppia   cuttlefish (a kind of squid); its black ink is used for flavoring in certain sauces for pasta, and also in risotto dishes.

Sogliola   sole.

Spaghetti   a long, round, thin pasta, variously served: *alla bolognese* (with ground meat, mushrooms, peppers, etc.), *alla carbonara* (with bacon, black pepper, and eggs), *al pomodoro* (with tomato sauce), *al sugo/ragù* (with meat sauce), and *alle vongole* (with clam sauce).

Spiedini   pieces of meat grilled on a skewer over an open flame.

Stracciatella   broth containing egg and cheese.

Strangolaprete   small nuggets of pasta, usually served with sauce; the name is literally translated as "priest-choker."

Stufato   beef braised in white wine with vegetables.

Tagliatelle   flat egg noodles.

Tiramisù   richly caloric dessert containing layers of triple-crème cheeses and rum-soaked sponge cake.

Tonno   tuna.

Tortelli   pasta dumplings stuffed with ricotta and greens.

Tortellini   rings of dough stuffed with minced and seasoned meat and served either in soups or as a full-fledged pasta covered with sauce.

Trenette   thin noodles served with pesto sauce and potatoes.

Trippe alla fiorentina   beef tripe (intestines).

Vermicelli   very thin spaghetti.

Vitello tonnato   cold sliced veal covered with tuna-fish sauce.

Zabaglione/zabaione   egg yolks whipped into the consistency of a custard, flavored with marsala, and served warm as a dessert.

Zampone   pig's trotter stuffed with spicy seasoned pork, boiled and sliced.

Zuccotto   a liqueur-soaked sponge cake, molded into a dome and layered with chocolate, nuts, and whipped cream.

Zuppa inglese   sponge cake soaked in custard sauce and rum.

C Glossary of Architectural Terms

Ambone   a pulpit, either serpentine or simple in form, erected in an Italian church.

Apse   the half-rounded extension behind the main altar of a church; Christian tradition dictates that it be placed at the eastern end of the church, the side closest to Jerusalem.

Atrium   a courtyard, open to the sky, in an ancient Roman house; the term also applies to the courtyard nearest the entranceway of an early Christian church.

Baldacchino (*also* **ciborium**)   a columned stone canopy, usually placed above the altar of a church; spelled in English as baldachin or baldaquin.

Basilica   any rectangular public building, usually divided into three aisles by rows of columns; in ancient Rome, this architectural form was frequently used for places of public assembly and law courts; later, Roman Christians adapted the form for many of their early churches; in theological terms, a basilica is a Catholic church given special ceremonial privileges.

Caldarium   the steam room of a Roman bath.

Campanile   a bell tower, often detached, of a church.

Capital   the top of a column, often carved and usually categorized into one of three different orders: Doric, Ionic, or Corinthian.

Cavea   the curved row of seats in a classical theater; the most prevalent shape was that of a semicircle.

Cella   the sanctuary, or most sacred interior section, of a Roman temple.

Chancel   section of a church containing the altar.

Choir   the part of the church between the nave and the altar where the choir sits or where music or ceremonies are performed.

Cornice   the decorative flange that defines the uppermost part of a classical or neoclassical facade.

Cortile   courtyard or cloisters ringed with a gallery of arches or lintels set atop columns.

Crypt   a church's main burial place, usually located below the choir.

Cupola   a dome.

Duomo   cathedral (literally, "dome").

Forum   the main square, and principal gathering place, of any Roman town, usually adorned with the city's most important temples and civic buildings.

Grotesques   carved and painted faces, deliberately ugly, used by everyone from the Etruscans to the architects of the Renaissance; they're especially amusing when set into fountains.

Loggia   a roofed porch, balcony, or gallery.

Lozenge   an elongated four-sided figure which, along with stripes, was one of the distinctive signs of the architecture of Pisa.

Narthex   the anteroom, or enclosed porch, of a Christian church.

Nave   the largest and longest section of a church, usually devoted to sheltering and/or seating worshippers, and often divided by aisles.

Pietra dura   richly ornate assemblage of semiprecious stones mounted on a flat decorative surface, perfected during the 1600s in Florence.

Portico   a porch, usually crafted from wood or stone.

Putti   plaster cherubs whose chubby forms often decorate the interiors of baroque chapels and churches.

Stucco   colored plaster composed of sand, powdered marble, water, and lime, either molded into statuary or applied in a thin, concretelike layer to the exterior of a building.

Telamone   a structural column carved into a standing male form; the female version is called a *caryatid.*

Terme   Roman baths.

Transenna   stone (usually marble) screen separating the altar area from the rest of an early Christian church.

Travertine   known as the stone from which ancient and Renaissance Rome was built, it's known for its hardness, light coloring, and tendency to be pitted or flecked with black.

Tympanum   the half-rounded space above the portal of a church, whose semicircular space usually showcases a sculpture.

Index

See also separate Accomodations and Restaurant indexes, below.
Page numbers in italics refer to maps.

FROMMER'S® COMPLETE TRAVEL GUIDES

Alaska
Amsterdam
Arizona
Atlanta
Australia
Austria
Bahamas
Barcelona, Madrid & Seville
Belgium, Holland & Luxembourg
Bermuda
Boston
Budapest & the Best of Hungary
California
Canada
Cancún, Cozumel & the Yucatán
Cape Cod, Nantucket & Martha's Vineyard
Caribbean
Caribbean Cruises & Ports of Call
Caribbean Ports of Call
Carolinas & Georgia
Chicago
China
Colorado
Costa Rica
Denver, Boulder & Colorado Springs
England
Europe
Florida
France

Germany
Greece
Greek Islands
Hawaii
Hong Kong
Honolulu, Waikiki & Oahu
Ireland
Israel
Italy
Jamaica & Barbados
Japan
Las Vegas
London
Los Angeles
Maryland & Delaware
Maui
Mexico
Miami & the Keys
Montana & Wyoming
Montréal & Québec City
Munich & the Bavarian Alps
Nashville & Memphis
Nepal
New England
New Mexico
New Orleans
New York City
New Zealand
Nova Scotia, New Brunswick & Prince Edward Island
Oregon
Paris
Philadelphia & the Amish Country
Portugal

Prague & the Best of the Czech Republic
Provence & the Riviera
Puerto Rico
Rome
San Antonio & Austin
San Diego
San Francisco
Santa Fe, Taos & Albuquerque
Scandinavia
Scotland
Seattle & Portland
Singapore & Malaysia
South Pacific
Spain
Switzerland
Thailand
Tokyo
Toronto
Tuscany & Umbria
USA
Utah
Vancouver & Victoria
Vermont, New Hampshire & Maine
Vienna & the Danube Valley
Virgin Islands
Virginia
Walt Disney World & Orlando
Washington, D.C.
Washington State

FROMMER'S® DOLLAR-A-DAY GUIDES

Australia from $50 a Day
California from $60 a Day
Caribbean from $60 a Day
England from $60 a Day
Europe from $50 a Day
Florida from $60 a Day

Greece from $50 a Day
Hawaii from $60 a Day
Ireland from $50 a Day
Israel from $45 a Day
Italy from $50 a Day
London from $75 a Day

New York from $75 a Day
New Zealand from $50 a Day
Paris from $70 a Day
San Francisco from $60 a Day
Washington, D.C., from $60 a Day

FROMMER'S® PORTABLE GUIDES

Acapulco, Ixtapa & Zihuatanejo
Alaska Cruises & Ports of Call
Bahamas
California Wine Country
Charleston & Savannah
Chicago

Dublin
Las Vegas
London
Maine Coast
New Orleans
New York City
Paris

Puerto Vallarta, Manzanillo & Guadalajara
San Francisco
Sydney
Tampa & St. Petersburg
Venice
Washington, D.C.

FROMMER'S® NATIONAL PARK GUIDES

Family Vacations in the
  National Parks
Grand Canyon

National Parks of the
  American West
Yellowstone & Grand Teton

Yosemite & Sequoia/
  Kings Canyon
Zion & Bryce Canyon

FROMMER'S® MEMORABLE WALKS

Chicago
London

New York
Paris

San Francisco
Washington D.C.

FROMMER'S® IRREVERENT GUIDES

Amsterdam
Boston
Chicago

London
Manhattan

New Orleans
Paris

San Francisco
Walt Disney World
Washington, D.C.

FROMMER'S® DRIVING TOURS

America
Britain
California

Florida
France
Germany

Ireland
Italy
New England

Scotland
Spain
Western Europe

THE COMPLETE IDIOT'S TRAVEL GUIDES

Boston
Cruise Vacations
Planning Your Trip to Europe
Hawaii

Las Vegas
London
Mexico's Beach Resorts
New Orleans

New York City
San Francisco
Walt Disney World
Washington D.C.

THE UNOFFICIAL GUIDES®

Branson, Missouri
California with Kids
Chicago
Cruises
Disney Companion

Florida with Kids
The Great Smoky &
  Blue Ridge
  Mountains

Las Vegas
Miami & the Keys
Mini-Mickey
New Orleans

New York City
San Francisco
Skiing in the West
Walt Disney World
Washington, D.C.

SPECIAL-INTEREST TITLES

Frommer's Britain's Best Bike Rides
The Civil War Trust's Official Guide
  to the Civil War Discovery Trail
Frommer's Caribbean Hideaways
Frommer's Gay & Lesbian Europe
Israel Past & Present
Monks' Guide to California
Monks' Guide to New York City
New York City with Kids
New York Times Weekends
Outside Magazine's Adventure Guide
  to New England
Outside Magazine's Adventure Guide
  to Northern California

Outside Magazine's Adventure Guide
  to Southern California & Baja
Outside Magazine's Adventure Guide
  to the Pacific Northwest
Outside Magazine's Guide
  to Family Vacations
Places Rated Almanac
Retirement Places Rated
Washington, D.C., with Kids
Wonderful Weekends from Boston
Wonderful Weekends from New York City
Wonderful Weekends from San Francisco
Wonderful Weekends from Los Angeles

ODDLY ENOUGH, GETTING YOUR SCHEDULE STRAIGHT HELPS YOU KEEP YOUR PRIORITIES STRAIGHT.

Palm III
Connected Organizer

Address book Date book Memo pad To do list

It fits in your pocket. It's elegantly simple. The Palm III™ connected organizer keeps names, phone numbers, schedules, memos, and e-mail right at your fingertips. And HotSync® technology lets you exchange all that information back and forth with your PC. You can even personalize your organizer with thousands of available applications. Wherever your life takes you, your Palm III organizer can come along. Palm Computing® connected organizers start as low as $249.* To learn more visit www.palm.com or call 1-800-861-2529.

WHEREVER YOU TRAVEL, *H*ELP IS NEVER FAR AWAY.

From planning your trip to providing travel assistance along the way, American Express® Travel Service Offices are always there to help you do more.

Rome

American Express Travel Service
Piazza Di Spagna 38
(39) (06) 67641

http://www.americanexpress.com/travel

**American Express Travel Service Offices are
found in central locations throughout Rome.**